Controligarchs

Controligarchs

Exposing the Billionaire Class,

Their Secret Deals, and

the Globalist Plot

to Dominate Your Life

SEAMUS BRUNER

SENTINEL

SENTINEL
An imprint of Penguin Random House LLC
penguinrandomhouse.com

Copyright © 2023 by Seamus Bruner
Foreword copyright © 2023 by Peter Schweizer
Penguin Random House supports copyright. Copyright fuels creativity, encourages diverse voices, promotes free speech, and creates a vibrant culture. Thank you for buying an authorized edition of this book and for complying with copyright laws by not reproducing, scanning, or distributing any part of it in any form without permission. You are supporting writers and allowing Penguin Random House to continue to publish books for every reader.

SENTINEL and colophon are registered trademarks of Penguin Random House LLC.

Most Sentinel books are available at a discount when purchased in quantity for sales promotions or corporate use. Special editions, which include personalized covers, excerpts, and corporate imprints, can be created when purchased in large quantities. For more information, please call (212) 572-2232 or email specialmarkets@penguinrandomhouse.com. Your local bookstore can also assist with discounted bulk purchases using the Penguin Random House corporate Business-to-Business program. For assistance in locating a participating retailer, email B2B@penguinrandomhouse.com.

Library of Congress Cataloging-in-Publication Data

Names: Bruner, Seamus, author.
Title: Controligarchs / Seamus Bruner.
Description: New York : Sentinel, [2023] | Includes index.
Identifiers: LCCN 2023020541 (print) | LCCN 2023020542 (ebook) |
ISBN 9780593541593 (hardcover) | ISBN 9780593541609 (ebook)
Subjects: LCSH: Oligarchy—United States. | Elite (Social sciences)—United States. |
Rich people—United States. | Conspiracy theories—United States.
Classification: LCC JC419 .B78 2023 (print) | LCC JC419 (ebook) |
DDC 321/.5—dc23/eng/20230808
LC record available at https://lccn.loc.gov/2023020541
LC ebook record available at https://lccn.loc.gov/2023020542

Printed in the United States of America
1st Printing

BOOK DESIGN BY CHRIS WELCH

Contents

Foreword

by Peter Schweizer

Over the past ten years, I've watched Seamus Bruner unearth crucial connections between money and the ruling class in his work with me at the Government Accountability Institute (GAI). In his first book, *Compromised*, he documented the connections between officials in the Obama administration's Justice Department and within the senior ranks of the FBI, showing how public officials used the phony details of the so-called Steele Dossier as a pretext for spying on a presidential campaign. Seamus's second book, *Fallout*, showed his deep understanding of the international scene and his ability to uncover obscure facts and figures. In your hands right now is further proof of his unique skillset: exposing corruption and presenting his revelations in a compelling, readable exposé.

Controligarchs is his most ambitious project yet. Here he investigates the billionaire philanthropists, tech titans, plutocrat profiteers, and other self-anointed masters of the universe who plot and scheme with the political establishment to subvert the American people.

In this book, you will read about their ambitions to reshape the world. Exposing the arrogance of Bill Gates or the havoc unleashed on our criminal justice system by George Soros, Seamus's timely warnings hit hard and stick.

How so? In the near future, they say, the concept of private property will be a thing of the past. The masses will "own nothing and be happy." That is one of the proud predictions of the World Economic Forum, an invite-only annual assemblage of the world's richest people hosted by founder Klaus Schwab in Davos, Switzerland. The World Economic Forum is full of such pronouncements, as you will read.

Beyond their disdain for our country's most fundamental principles, Seamus shows how these powerful elites leverage the world's crises to usher in a global authoritarian regime. You can anticipate losing control over your home thermostat and having your every movement tracked and traced via electric vehicles and a "smart" power grid, while all your transactions and affiliations are linked to digital currencies and IDs.

Meanwhile, Gates and fellow plutocrats Mark Zuckerberg and Jeff Bezos are investors in companies creating "alternative proteins" for you to eat to reduce the world's reliance on cattle, whose various forms of "bovine flatulence" are supposedly to blame for the rise in global temperatures. In this book, Seamus shows how these tech oligarchs will push fake meats onto your dinner plate in the name of climate change, health concerns, and animal rights. I was horrified to learn about the lab-grown "hamburgers," fermented fungi patties, and even insect-based protein shakes that they are hoping the public will consume.

Finally, Seamus shows how every crisis is an opportunity for the elite political class. The worldwide COVID-19 pandemic—one of the most consequential crises in modern history—and the coordinated public-private response destroyed jobs, industries, and even whole economies. And the globalist response to the pandemic (with their nebulous proposals such as the "Great Reset" and "Build Back Better") was simply convenient packaging for a set of ideas that were already on their minds. The pandemic was the ultimate opportunity to begin a transition to a new system of control.

And while this new system means that our behaviors will have to change, theirs almost certainly won't. The billionaires who fly to Davos aboard gas-guzzling private jets want to end cheap and abundant fuels for the rest of us. They want us to transition to expensive electric cars while exempting their jets from emissions restrictions. Smartphone apps that track our movements are now championed as ways to "stop the spread" of illnesses. Meanwhile, our small businesses have been deemed "nonessential" while their large companies have used the pandemic opportunity to consolidate their market share.

Controligarchs is a window into *their* vision for *your* future: a world where they decide what we can own, how many children we can have, and what we are allowed to eat is decided for us. Our losses are their gains.

It is vital to read this book not as a fait accompli but as your wake-up call. As citizens of the United States, we have the right to oppose arrogant political overreaches and to protect our freedom of speech and privacy from Big Tech's creepy intrusions. It is our responsibility to ensure the survival of liberty for generations to come.

Just as Seamus has done in his two previous books, here he sounds the alarm on relevant issues and stays well ahead of the curve. His pinpoint research and uncanny ability to follow the money not only shows his readers the raw facts, but also the jaw-dropping figures that no one else has quantified.

I have watched Seamus spend more than two years investigating the characters in this book. He studied thousands of primary source documents and uncovered unsettling video evidence. He also spent incredible amounts of time poring over complex corporate filings, nonprofit disclosures, and other official records. To crunch the staggering numbers contained herein, Seamus created spreadsheets and mapped what he calls the "Controligarch cash trail" with unprecedented precision. Everything he gathered—all the facts and calculations—can be replicated. Seamus uses *zero anonymous sources.*

I am often asked whether I am discouraged by the widespread corruption in government that we at GAI unearth and expose to the public. My answer is an emphatic *no*. We believe in the power of the American people, and of free people everywhere, to resist the control schemes created by people with more money than empathy.

We arm ourselves with the facts and do battle with a cheerful, optimistic purpose.

Introduction

Using the most conservative estimates, the combined personal net worth of the characters in this book tops $1 trillion (that is with a *t*). But the awesome power and staggering influence at their fingertips is worth far more.

With a single phone call, they can bankrupt an entire nation and destroy its economy for generations. They can also create brand-new markets and launch them into the stratosphere. They can take mere mortals to the stars, literally. They are revered and reviled the world over because they own almost everything, including our elected officials.

After years of studying them, I decided that the best name for this group of powerful men and women is the "Controligarchs."

What is a Controligarch? Well, an oligarchy is a system run by the ultrawealthy few. It is an inherently antidemocratic system. But ours is not just a textbook oligarchy like, say, the Russian government. Unlike the Kremlin-friendly industrialists looking to preserve an old oppressive regime, the American oligarchs are a new breed of philanthropists, entrepreneurs, and tech titans seeking to impose an unprecedented system of control not only in the US, but around the world. While they would like us to believe they are innovating for the better, people such as Bill Gates, Jeff Bezos, Mark Zuckerberg, and Elon Musk are creating technology and making investments that will micromanage every aspect of your life.

The truth is they hoard unimaginable riches at our expense. The ten wealthiest men on the planet—including Gates, Bezos, Zuckerberg, and Musk—doubled their personal net worth over the course of the COVID-19 pandemic. Also, the entire billionaire class—fewer than three thousand individuals around the world, or 0.00004 percent of the global population—added more than $5 trillion to their combined personal net worth while the dwindling middle class suffered, and more than 160 million people were pushed into poverty. I have done the calculations myself and the numbers are mind-blowing:

In 2019, the assets of a shadowy group of billionaires concerned with overpopulation—which included Bill Gates, George Soros, Michael Bloomberg, and the Rockefeller Foundation—totaled $263,429,906,000. Postpandemic, they increased by 37.4 percent to $362,009,025,000.[1]

Bill Gates's personal net worth grew 33.7 percent from $96,500,000,000 in 2019 to $129,000,000,000 in 2022. His foundation's assets grew 6.2 percent from $51,852,234,000 in 2017 to $55,067,310,000 in 2021.

The personal net worth of George Soros increased by nearly $300,000,000 between 2019 and 2022.

Assets managed by the top financial Controligarchs—BlackRock, Vanguard, and State Street—grew by 34.6 percent between 2019 and 2022, from $16,529,633,000,000 to $22,250,000,000,000.

The top 25 largest World Economic Forum members have a combined post-COVID value of nearly $10,000,000,000,000—thanks in large part to Big Pharma's and Big Tech's gains—up from $8,000,000,000,000 prior to the pandemic.[2]

That's $10 *trillion* up from $8 *trillion*—larger than the gross domestic product (GDP) of most countries!

The Controligarchs share an ambition to reshape the world. Their wealth

gives them the influence to do it. They accomplish it through crony alliances, shady takeovers, sustained corporate welfare, and sometimes flat-out
corruption. Their influence is not limited to any particular industry. As I
will show you, it has permeated the media, technology, energy, education,
the economy, our food industry, and so much more.

In this book, I will reveal shocking new evidence that shows how the
Controligarchs' sinister agenda is well on its way to becoming reality. You
will learn about their investments into eugenics research that will allow
them to predetermine their children's traits, creating a new caste system in
which the ultrawealthy are able to hack their own biology to become superhuman. You will learn about the billions of dollars in taxpayer-funded crony
stimulus and other forms of inflation-inducing corporate welfare that has
allowed this tiny elite faction to add *trillions of dollars* to their collective
holdings—while we work harder to earn far less. You will see what they are
planning for "the next pandemic," which I can assure you means lockdowns,
new waves of small-business closures, and, ultimately, consolidating the
ownership of everything into fewer and fewer hands.

Living through daily disasters like bank collapses, disease outbreaks, and
food and energy crises, Americans know that the world is changing for the
worse. And most are tempted to point fingers at politicians. But who is *really*
organizing the broadside against the US Constitution? Who is behind censorship, cancel culture, and the propaganda that is being pushed in our schools
and media? Who is orchestrating the attacks on the nuclear family? Who is
buying off public officials at home and abroad by the thousands? Who trademarked the phrase Trust the Science™ and then weaponized it? Why do they
want to dictate virtually every aspect of our daily existence, from our energy
usage right down to what foods and medicines we put into our bodies?

Most importantly—how much worse will things get?

This book answers those questions and reveals so much more. These
grave stories about the widespread political corruption and corporatism
that plague our planet—and the ever-growing sense that democracy and
even free will may just be illusions—require an optimistic ending. This book

provides accountability through forced transparency and, further, delivers hopeful recommendations for how citizens can take back control.

The story of how these billionaires, bureaucrats, and other global elites are seizing control of every major industry (and will not be happy until you own nothing) is moving quickly.

Let us get started.

Controligarchs

1

The Good Club

Some even believe we are part of a secret [club] working against the best interests of the United States, characterizing my family and me as "internationalists" and of conspiring with others around the world to build a more integrated global political and economic structure—one world, if you will. If that's the charge, I stand guilty, and I am proud of it.[1]

—*David Rockefeller*, Memoirs, 2002

O n a cloudy spring day in 2009, Bill Gates arrived at one of the very last private, single-family, residential mansions on the crowded island of Manhattan in New York City.

Gates was joined that May afternoon by a dozen other billionaire philanthropists—David Rockefeller, George Soros, Ted Turner, Michael Bloomberg, Warren Buffett, and Oprah Winfrey, as well as the heads of Cisco, Blackstone Group, and Tiger Management, to name a few—who had gathered for a secret meeting at the Rockefeller University, on Manhattan's posh Upper East Side. They were there to save the world—or, at least, to set the agenda for the future of global health.[2]

It was a fitting setting. After all, it was there in 1901 that John D. Rockefeller Sr. established the Rockefeller Institute for Medical Research, which was the nation's first biomedical and research laboratory. Rockefeller modeled his facility after the prestigious Pasteur and Koch institutes in France and Germany. In doing so, he elevated the prestige of America's scientific and medicinal research to Europe's level.

Now, Rockefeller University was the hub of the Rockefellers' biomedical empire. Gates and a few of his closest billionaire buddies met in the President's House, which is nestled in the northeast corner of the university's relatively lush sixteen-acre campus. This private, brutalist-style building also offered a tightly secured fortress of climate-controlled personal breathing space in the otherwise overcrowded island that is Manhattan. These tycoons called their group the Good Club.

The May 2009 meeting of the Good Club was convened by three of the most consequential, wealthy, and powerful men in modern world history: Bill Gates, Warren Buffett, and David Rockefeller.[3] These men had invested heavily in Barack Obama and Joe Biden's 2008 campaign, and the timing of the meeting—fifteen weeks into the new administration—came at the right time for the Good Club to capitalize on their victory.

The global financial crisis had recently ravaged much of the American economy. As the middle and lower classes suffered more foreclosures and bankruptcies than at any point in recent memory, the billionaires no doubt knew that a peasant revolt may be on the horizon.

The gathering was thus a planning meeting for a public-relations stunt called the Giving Pledge, which kicked off a massive movement of cash from the billionaire class to charitable causes. When billionaires pledge to give away half their wealth, this can mean that they will be transferring billions from their pockets to the coffers of their family foundations—through a byzantine network of tax-exempt NGOs.[4]

Only a few scant details of the meeting were anonymously leaked to the press. *The Times* of London and a few other European outlets shared only a glimpse of the inside. The Good Club members spent fifteen minutes each outlining their proposals for an "umbrella" philanthropic cause they could collectively prioritize.[5]

The group had much in common, beyond its members' monumental wealth and shared interest in philanthropy. All the members were convinced globalists, who positioned themselves as being uniquely able to do good for humanity.

CNN founder Ted Turner tried to dominate the meeting. Oprah Winfrey mostly listened. Gates's presentation impressed the other club members greatly, and taking their cues from him, they agreed to prioritize the goal that Gates now urged upon them: overpopulation. Gates had said at a conference in Long Beach, California, the previous year that he believed that the world's population should be capped at 8.3 billion.[6]

Ironically, the Good Club's top priority in serving humanity was to make sure that there was less of it.

The timing was crucial because the Democrats controlled the White House and both houses of Congress. The next eight years could determine if the Controligarchs' agenda would succeed or fail.

The Good Club members—particularly the Rockefellers—had already done much to influence a major decrease in global population. Global birth rates peaked in the 1960s and have been in steep decline ever since the Rockefellers started plowing massive sums into the development of every birth control measure from contraceptive devices to "the pill" to abortion—years before the 1973 *Roe v. Wade* decision.[7]

Crucially, the Good Club members had, over the course of decades, persuaded the general population that reducing birth rates was in the planet's best collective interest because fewer people equals less pollution.[8]

Oprah had used her powerful platform to champion birth control and abortion for decades. Soros, Buffett, Rockefeller, Bloomberg, and Gates had poured more than $1.5 billion into increasing women's access to contraceptives and abortions—enough to fund the termination of approximately three million unborn babies.[9]

At the time that Gates brought them all together, the Good Club members had been acquainted, at least socially, for years or even decades, and their philanthropic interests often overlapped.

Gates and Buffett had been close friends since Gates's mother, Mary Maxwell Gates, introduced them in 1991.[10] Also, before Gates and Patricia Stonesifer combined several of Gates's smaller charitable endeavors into a single foundation in 1999, Gates had already begun partnering with the

Rockefellers, particularly on "population and health research," including the joint funding of vaccine-related initiatives.[11]

In the months and years following the Good Club meeting, Controligarchs such as Gates and the Rockefellers developed a global response to a hypothetical pandemic. They could not have known that barely a decade later the world would face the first global pandemic in nearly a century, and everyone would beg them for solutions. (Their answers involve seismic transfers of wealth from the lower classes to the billionaire class.)

But that is exactly the kind of power they dreamed of.

As it happened, by the time COVID-19 made worldwide headlines in early 2020, the Good Club and its partners had already been working for decades on medical and technological breakthroughs they hoped could cure every human ill, from poverty to infectious diseases. COVID-19 presented an "opportunity" to introduce these technocratic panaceas.

And Gates and the Rockefellers had key partners to urge their solutions upon heads of state the world over. Dr. Anthony Fauci, for example, had long been acquainted with Good Club members. The Rockefeller Foundation, which had worked intimately with Fauci's National Institute of Allergy and Infectious Diseases for decades, dramatically elevated his profile when it featured him in a December 2019 video about the HIV/AIDS pandemic. Notably, this video was released as COVID-19 cases began to emerge in Wuhan, China.[12]

Prior to the COVID-19 outbreak, Rockefeller and Gates had sponsored multiple training exercises for just such a coronavirus pandemic. The Rockefellers had nearly a century's head start on Gates in pandemic planning experience, having been the leading viral research entity beginning in 1901—well before the 1918 Spanish flu pandemic.

A 2010 Rockefeller training exercise titled "Lock Step" and Gates's more innocuously titled "Event 201" in October 2019—just two months before China recorded its first official case of COVID-19—were especially prescient.[13]

The training exercises produced a long list of recommendations that were eerily prophetic. Possible solutions included mandatory quarantines, face masks, temperature checks, and biometric identification for all citizens. Moreover, the exercises addressed lockdowns, enforced cooperation, and virus surveillance programs such as contact tracing.[14]

By 2017, Rockefeller and Gates had begun their digital identification ("digital ID") push with an initiative called ID2020. At the time, this initiative did not get much publicity in major outlets. But when COVID struck the United States in early 2020, the Rockefeller Foundation sprang into action and immediately began implementing a Lock Step–type game plan. The foundation rolled out an international contact-tracing surveillance operation to officially usher in a global digital ID regime.[15]

A digital ID—like a QR code in your phone's digital wallet scanned by a restaurant hostess—provides a point of entry for this unprecedented level of access to personal information. In August 2021, with funding from the Gates and Rockefeller foundations, the World Health Organization (WHO) published its vaccine passport guidelines, which were filled with requirements and mandates.[16]

The Rockefeller Foundation had previously committed $1 billion, not just toward ending the pandemic but also to use the pandemic as leverage to address climate change, social justice, and other "inequities made worse by this virus." Moreover, the foundation sought to "catalyze a more inclusive, green recovery from the COVID-19 pandemic." In the words of Rockefeller Foundation president Rajiv Shah in October 2020:

> There's no going back to the past, to before-Covid. We need to reimagine the future we want. To meet this moment, we must leverage all our resources and relationships to build an equitable, sustainable future, where everyone has the opportunity to realize their full potential and climate disaster is avoided. The time to act is right now to make sure vulnerable children and families are included in the pandemic response and recovery.[17]

Gates may have convened the 2009 meeting, but the Rockefellers had been working to curb overpopulation since before Gates was born in 1955, which made them the obvious hosting choice.[18]

The Rockefellers did not just pioneer the Controligarch model; they perfected it. While other dynastic billionaire families—such as the Fords, Vanderbilts, and Carnegies—amassed fortunes, none have been able to maintain their power and prominence across generations as have the Rockefellers, who are still one of the world's most powerful families in their seventh generation.[19]

The Rockefellers found that meeting the needs of consumers is not enough to perpetuate multigenerational wealth. For more than a century, they kept the money flowing, and, through their charitable foundations, shaped the beliefs, morals, and behavior of society. It gave them control.

The story of how the Rockefellers became the greatest influencers in global health policy, and the central planners of pandemic responses, is complex and spans over a century. It is sometimes a triumphant tale of victory over viruses such as smallpox and polio and, at other times, a sordid story marred by the Rockefellers' funding of racist selective breeding and eugenics programs, Nazi experiments, and forced sterilizations.

To say that the Rockefeller family helped build the modern world would be an understatement. From energy to finance to education to public health to computing, the Rockefellers had a hand in developing every major field and industry.

By examining these Controligarch prototypes in close detail, we can understand how their modern descendants—such as the Big Tech titans—push authoritarianism from every angle.

The Controligarch Prototype: "A National Menace"

John D. Rockefeller Sr., or "Senior" as he was known, may well go down in history as the greatest businessman the world has ever seen, and rightly so.

Nearly all his heirs—more than 250 of them and counting—look up to him with pride and gratitude, as they should.[20]

Senior is famous for creating one of the largest monopolies in American history: Standard Oil Company, or "The Standard." In less than two decades, The Standard achieved control of more than 95 percent of the US petroleum industry—from the first step in the production process, drilling for crude oil; to the next step, refining the crude; to the transportation of the finished product, refined oil. This was possible because Rockefeller owned everything: the oil wells, the refineries, and the complex oil tank system that traveled by railroad car.[21]

The Rockefeller patriarch believed that his ability to get rich was his divine purpose. "I believe the power to make money is a gift from God," Senior said, and "having been endowed with the gift I possess, I believe it is my duty to make money and still more money and to use the money I make for the good of my fellow-man according to the dictates of my conscience."[22]

Within thirty years of The Standard's founding, it had become the most powerful conglomerate in the country and was exerting influence abroad in ways that made even the US government jealous. For example, the Rockefellers were influencing China a full century before President Richard Nixon's famous visit in the early 1970s.

To achieve The Standard's monopoly, Senior's soldiers spied on and sabotaged his enemies, The Standard leveraged its massive buying power to squeeze out smaller operators, and Rockefeller attorneys used secret contracts and lawfare to effectively steal from The Standard's competitors. Senior's tactics paid off, and the value of The Standard grew exponentially. By 1910, as one reporter put it, "when a glass of beer cost a penny and a loaf of bread less than a nickel, when a three-room apartment went for five dollars a month and a good pair of shoes for a dollar, Rockefeller had assets of over $800 million" (which is nearly $25 billion today).[23]

But there was a problem—a problem that is rarely studied or acknowledged. The reputational costs of such success—and the ruthlessness of the methods that Rockefeller used to achieve it—were mounting. The Rockefellers had attained oligarch status, and as their wealth surged, the public's opinion of the family turned to skepticism and eventually to ire. More importantly, the US Congress took notice of The Standard's monopolistic practices.

By the early 1900s, the press routinely ran hit pieces on The Standard's shady business practices and raked Senior over the coals. More concerning, federal investigations began targeting The Standard for anticompetitive tactics, and the dreaded word *antitrust* was percolating up through the Justice Department.

Senior needed a trustworthy lieutenant to manage both the fabulous wealth and the negative press that came with it.

And he knew exactly the right man for the job. Senior met Baptist minister Frederick T. Gates (no direct relation to Bill) nearly twenty years prior at the University of Chicago. Gates had experience leading flour magnate George Pillsbury's philanthropic endeavors, which impressed Senior. Soon, the reverend was fielding all Rockefeller donation solicitations and handling many other aspects of the Rockefeller business.

But managing such a staggering amount of wealth was no small task. Gates famously told Senior that his fortune was "rolling up like an avalanche!" The eldest Rockefeller needed to dole out funds faster than he was accumulating them. "If you do not, it will crush you, and your children, and your children's children," Gates warned.[24]

Gates knew that wealthy families had historically passed down their enormous fortunes with "scandalous results to their descendants and powerful tendencies to social demoralization." Gates worried that his benefactor's good family name might be in jeopardy. "I trembled as I witnessed the unreasoning popular resentment at Mr. Rockefeller's riches," he wrote. To the public at the time, Rockefeller was a "national menace," and protestors would gather by the thousands to rally against the company and vandals sabotaged The Standard's oil tankers.[25]

Gates saw only one solution: John Sr. and John Jr. must "form a series of great corporate philanthropies for forwarding civilization in all its elements in this land and all lands; philanthropies, if possible, limitless in time and amount, broad in scope, and self-perpetuating."[26]

As Senior got older, Reverend Gates increasingly worked closely with Junior to realize his vision for the Rockefeller fortune. The two men operated as a tag team to steer capital toward mutually agreed upon initiatives. Gates was the "brilliant dreamer and creator," and Junior was the "salesman" who was able to pitch his father at the opportune moment.

The Rockefeller philanthropic strategy, unlike The Standard's strategy, was a family affair from day one, and each of Senior's heirs was taught, in the eldest Rockefeller's words, "the difficult art of giving."[27]

Senior's first frontier of charitable good: public health.

Viruses and Vaccines: A Business Model

Founded in 1901, the Rockefeller Institute for Medical Research (RIMR, which later became Rockefeller University) would become the headquarters for the Rockefellers' biomedical empire. Within a decade, RIMR became the leading incubator of infectious disease research and trained the world's top virologists.[28]

Before 1900, deadly diseases such as smallpox, tuberculosis, cholera, typhus, diphtheria, and yellow fever routinely ravaged populations around the globe. New York City was especially hazardous and before 1900 "had a higher mortality rate than London or Paris, Boston or Philadelphia, making it one of the most dangerous places in the western world."[29]

One in five babies died, and of those fortunate enough to survive childhood, 25 percent died before they reached their thirties. The only mitigation strategy for these diseases was to quarantine the infected. The concept of "eradication" seemed inconceivable at the time.[30]

Nearly two decades before the first global pandemic in modern history—the 1918 Spanish flu (which Rockefeller scientists were the first to isolate)—the Rockefellers began studying communicable diseases and seeking to treat them.[31]

Along the way, they learned that curing diseases was hard work, but even when they failed to eradicate a disease, they gained important experience that led to something even more important: control. With each successive disease they identified and sought to control, their influence and authority over the scientific and medical communities grew—both at home and abroad. The Rockefellers with their institutes and foundation effectively became the global authors of public health policy.

The Rockefeller research was truly revolutionary, and that was by design. The foundation had specifically decided to "confine itself to projects of an important character, too large to be undertaken, or otherwise unlikely to be undertaken, by other agencies" and to "go to the root of individual or social ill-being and misery."[32]

In 1905, a deadly outbreak of cerebrospinal meningitis struck New York City. RIMR's first director, Simon Flexner, had worked with that disease at Johns Hopkins (a critical Rockefeller partner in academia and medical research, particularly through the COVID pandemic) and immediately got to work taking blood samples from the morgue to inject cultures into lab monkeys and infect them with the disease. Flexner successfully developed a serum to inject into the base of the spine of human patients.

"Cure Is Found for Meningitis with John D's Aid," read a *New York Times* headline. The development put RIMR on the map. Shortly after, a different medical institution asked Senior's contemporary, Andrew Carnegie, for a donation, but he refused. "That is Mr. Rockefeller's specialty," Carnegie said. "Go see him."[33]

With a major win under its belt and ample funding, RIMR set out to find and tackle a bigger problem, and Frederick Gates sought to use "wholesale" rather than "retail" philanthropy to address "root causes." Hookworm—a debilitating parasite that afflicted mostly southern US communities—fit the bill.

The Rockefellers established their Sanitary Commission for the Eradication of Hookworm Disease in 1909 with a five-year, one-million-dollar pledge. The hookworm plan was simple (later becoming the blueprint for Bill Gates's infectious disease efforts): try to break transmission cycles by installing sanitary outhouses and privies to prevent soil and drinking water contamination.

The Rockefellers' hookworm blueprint pioneered another critical tactic: test all citizens and inspect their homes. It was the largest and most complex public health initiative in American history to date.

Studies showed that the Rockefeller hookworm initiative helped some but failed to eradicate the illness. Nonetheless, a century later the Rockefellers promoted their hookworm blueprint for COVID-19. And again, mass testing failed to prevent transmission. So why did they use the blueprint? Simply put, it was profitable and lent itself to controlling the population.[34]

The Rockefellers learned something very important to future global health efforts via the hookworm campaign: the next best thing to disease eradication (or possibly the best thing) is disease *control*.

The term "eradication" was quietly dropped from research proposals and other literature in favor of "control." Thus, instead of seeking to eliminate diseases from the entire population, the Rockefellers opted for the more loosely defined "disease control," which lowered expectations and allowed them to retain the prestige, profitability, and power that dictating public health policies provided. The Rockefellers' disease-control model soon spread to more than fifty countries on six continents.[35]

In the process of developing disease-control programs, the Rockefeller Institute's top researcher, Flexner, began waging a fifty-year war against the polio virus. Soon, the Rockefeller Institute built the world's foremost polio research center with Flexner at the helm.

The New York Times ran a glowing piece on the Rockefeller Institute's efforts in 1911.

"We have already discovered how to prevent infantile paralysis," the *Times* wrote. The piece suggested that polio would soon be eradicated like typhus, smallpox, and other conquered plagues. "The achievement of a cure,

I may conservatively say, is not now far distant," wrote the *Times*, using only Flexner as its source for the grand claim.[36] But it would be many years—with lethal mistakes made along the way—before the Rockefellers' polio efforts would pay off.

In the meantime, RIMR set its sights on conquering a different disease: yellow fever. In 1914, a Rockefeller Foundation report titled "Yellow Fever: Feasibility of Its Eradication" kicked off a forty-year attack against the disease and resulted in not one but two Rockefeller-funded vaccines.[37]

The first yellow fever vaccine was produced at RIMR and injected into nearly eight thousand people. A lead scientist declared success before the results were deemed inconclusive, and the Rockefellers "quietly discontinued its distribution" in 1926. A competing vaccine by the French Pasteur Institute led to "neurologic reactions" that negatively affected the injected individual's central nervous system.

A second Rockefeller-funded yellow fever vaccine, known as the 17D strain vaccine, took more than a decade to develop and, by 1937, was ready for human trials. Soon, more than one million people in Brazil were vaccinated with the Rockefeller vaccine, and it was subsequently deemed safe enough to give to US soldiers headed off to fight in World War II.[38]

In January 1941, the US War Department worried that the Japanese were going to unleash swarms of mosquitoes carrying yellow fever as a form of biological warfare. The president of the Rockefeller Foundation was called to Washington, DC, to meet with the surgeon general and the vice president.[39] The foundation agreed to generously donate enough doses to vaccinate "virtually all" American army recruits between January 1941 and April 1942—a staggering seven million shots.[40]

Unfortunately, the vaccines were tainted with hepatitis B and caused widespread illness among the troops. But it took more than forty years for a 1987 study by the Veterans Administration Medical Center to determine that the botched Rockefeller 17D vaccine had led to more than three hundred thousand hepatitis B infections in US troops (General Joseph

"Vinegar Joe" Stilwell among them)—the largest recorded outbreak of that kind to date.[41]

Tainted jabs notwithstanding, in 1951, the Rockefeller Foundation appointed its top yellow fever scientist who had developed the 17D vaccine, Dr. Max Theiler, as Director of Laboratories in New York. Later that year, Theiler won the Nobel Prize in Physiology or Medicine. The foundation boldly declared: "In all likelihood yellow fever will cease to be a public health menace."[42]

Throughout the process of developing the 17D vaccine, scientists discovered that yellow fever has a "sylvatic" (from the Latin *silva*, meaning forest) or "jungle" transmission cycle. A sylvatic virus can be transmitted between human and other animals via mosquitoes and other biting insects. The virus can then reside and replicate indefinitely throughout nonhuman animal populations, which makes eradication all but impossible.[43]

Notably, SARS-CoV-2, the coronavirus that causes COVID-19, appears to have a sylvatic transmission cycle, meaning that eradication, or "COVID zero," is a pipe dream.[44]

The yellow fever campaign was costly, and the Rockefellers sank considerable resources to eliminate not only the virus but also the primary transmission vector (the Aedes aegypti mosquito) that spreads the virus. In addition to the financial cost, there were human costs to working for Rockefeller research initiatives—including the deaths of at least six brilliant scientists killed by yellow fever.[45]

While some diseases, such as smallpox, have been almost entirely vanquished, yellow fever has not and likely never will be. Eventually, the Rockefeller Foundation abandoned its mission to accomplish this goal. Nonetheless, the Rockefeller efforts deserve credit for successfully decreasing the prevalence of yellow fever.

Today, the 17D vaccine is the only method for controlling yellow fever, though Rockefeller attempts to exterminate disease-carrying mosquitoes through genetic modification have ramped up dramatically. And the

Rockefellers' protégé, Bill Gates, has funneled at least $93 million into controversial efforts to engineer and release roughly two billion genetically modified mosquitoes—first in Florida and California—and then, he hopes, everywhere.[46]

The Rockefellers' international yellow fever efforts gave them authority. And more importantly, the more diseases the Rockefellers tried to control, the more power and influence they gained in the international health community. The more influence they gained over public health, the more they could influence people's behavior for their own benefit. And, since these activities were all done in the name of philanthropy, the better they looked in the eyes of the public.

The foundation dumped even more resources into studying more diseases. Many of the viruses that the foundation studied could not be totally eradicated because of their sylvatic cycles. If a disease can hide out in animal "reservoirs," then it cannot be cured—only controlled through treatments. And treatments are a cash cow, while cures are not.

Just as The Standard had used patents to its enormous benefit, so, too, would the Rockefeller institutes and foundations.[47] The Rockefeller Institute's 1901 founding charter declared that "all discoveries and inventions" made by Rockefeller personnel belonged to the Rockefeller Institute to "place at the service of humanity in accordance with the beneficent purposes of the founder." In other words, the Rockefeller Institute was founded with the explicit purpose to discover, invent, own, and ultimately control its research and findings. But unlike The Standard, the Rockefeller Foundation struggled with who should retain ultimate control over its discoveries.[48]

For roughly fifty years, the Rockefeller directors and staff were divided over the issue of patents. The doctors and scientists did not want to stockpile the patents to their biomedical inventions (some scientists wanted to share this intellectual property freely with the world), while the directors believed that it was necessary to maintain strict control over their patents, which were invariably linked with the production (and thus the purity) of the products.[49]

In 1950, the Rockefeller Foundation directors finally arrived at an official policy: "We have a policy of having no policy but to deal with each case as it arises," the directors boldly declared. This "flexible approach" meant that Rockefeller entities retained their profitable intellectual property (which was often developed with taxpayer assistance) as they saw fit.[50]

Over time, the infectious disease research of the Rockefellers' institute and foundation began to pay off. In addition to the virus control experience, intellectual property, and the positive reputational dividends, the Rockefellers had built powerful international relationships and formed global health alliances.[51] The Rockefeller disease initiatives effectively formed a joint venture with governments all over the world—particularly in the resource-rich regions of Africa, Asia, and South America.[52]

Waging war on diseases with the family's signature ruthless zeal—particularly in underdeveloped countries—elevated the Rockefellers and transformed their reputation from self-interested monopolists to socially conscious oligarchs. The expansion of their international footprint allowed them to be perceived as global saviors (which would later explain how cutthroat oil barons could change their stripes to become darlings of the environmental Left).[53]

And while Rockefeller drugs and treatments poured into these regions as "charity," energy resources flowed out. For one full century, the Rockefellers extracted energy resources from the very governments that had become reliant upon the foundation's health programs. The governments that granted the energy licenses also bought Rockefeller fuel and agricultural products. For the family and its partners, it was a mutually beneficial arrangement and one that future Controligarchs would replicate.[54]

By controlling entire industries, the Rockefellers influenced the lives of people on just about every continent.

However, just prior to the new millennium, the staff at the Rockefeller Foundation realized that the wealth distribution in the twenty-first century would effectively be determined by debates among intellectual-property owners. Indeed, hoarding intellectual property through patents would soon become the means for the Controligarchs to control everything from medi-cine to energy to computer technology and even food.[55]

The power that came with trying to heal sick people was only the begin-ning. Trying to control microscopic organisms and meddling with the genetics of plants and insects was very clever, but what if the Rockefellers could modify—and ultimately control—the genetics of *humans*? The Rocke-feller foray into medical research—particularly the areas of genetic and bio-medical engineering—kicked off a dark era in American history: the period of eugenics.

Cleansing Populations through Birth Control

By the time the American eugenics movement—a sweeping effort to breed "fit" populations and eliminate "unfit" ones—was really starting to take off, Senior had already turned over the keys to his financial kingdom to Junior, his only son.

Junior was by far the most outspoken Rockefeller proponent of eugenics and the largest funder of the earliest eugenics organizations. In the move-ment, he saw an opportunity to change not only the science of reproduction but also public sentiment about family, sex, and who deserved to live or die. If the right people came to accept birth control as normal or even desirable, the problem of overpopulation might just take care of itself.

Starting around 1910, Junior gave more than $6 million—at least $150 million in today's dollars—to eugenics organizations, such as the Eugenics Record Office, the Bureau of Social Hygiene, and the American Eugenics Society. By 1924, he saw potential in a pro-eugenics feminist who would transform the public view of eugenics from a social necessity to a charitable good: Margaret Sanger.[56]

Today, Sanger's legacy organization, Planned Parenthood, is easily the largest abortion provider in the United States and operates all over the world.[57] Sanger dedicated her life to controlling women's ability to give birth—especially among the mentally disabled and in the black community—because she viewed pregnancy as "biological slavery."[58]

Before *Roe v. Wade* legalized abortions nationwide in 1973, Planned Parenthood and its predecessor organizations focused mainly on preventing the "unfit" from breeding—which, according to Sanger, included black babies, babies born into poverty, and the disabled—by providing and promoting contraceptives and sterilization.[59]

One paper that Sanger published, titled "Birth Control and the Negro," stated that "negroes present the great problem of the South" and have "the greatest economic, health and social problems." The paper outlined a birth control strategy for African Americans, whom Sanger and her colleagues denigrated as the "largely illiterate" who "still breed carelessly and disastrously."[60]

Junior and the Rockefeller's Bureau of Social Hygiene steadily backed Sanger's American Birth Control League (one of Planned Parenthood's predecessors), as well as Sanger's Birth Control Clinical Research Bureau and the National Committee on Federal Legislation for Birth Control. The Rockefellers funded more organizations run by one of Sanger's eugenicist colleagues, including the American Gynecological Society and the Committee on Maternal Health.

Junior's top advisor, Raymond Fosdick, justified the massive amounts of largesse to Sanger's causes since "population [growth] constitutes one of the great perils of the future." By 1940, Junior, his sons "JDR" III and Nelson, and their wives were all, individually and collectively, major funders of birth control. When the Bureau of Social Hygiene permanently closed in 1934, the Rockefeller Foundation's "Medical Sciences Division" took its place as the top financier of the birth control effort.[61]

The eugenics movement was thriving in the United States, and soon the Rockefellers decided to take it global. Adolf Hitler and the Nazis were especially keen on exterminating so-called inferior populations while attempting to breed a superior race. Thanks to Rockefeller support, Nazi scientists learned directly from American eugenicists.[62]

In the 1930s, IG Farben—the manufacturer of Bayer aspirin—was among the largest funders of Hitler's campaign and the Nazi Party. While in partnership with the Rockefellers, IG Farben manufactured Zyklon B, the gas used in the genocidal concentration camps that made the pharmaceutical giant one of the sinister profiteers of the Nazi campaigns that exterminated millions of Jews and other minorities.[63]

According to a 1944 IG Farben memo, forming a partnership with Rockefeller's Standard Oil "was necessary for technical, commercial, and financial reasons."[64] IG Farben would later be linked to a Rockefeller-distributed abortifacient pill called RU-486, which is still distributed by Planned Parenthood to this day.[65]

The Rockefeller family's decades-long funding of research and organizations that advanced both *positive* eugenics (breeding the "fit") and *negative* eugenics (culling the "unfit") is undeniable. While the Rockefeller Foundation was searching for cures to infectious diseases in every corner of the world, it was also bankrolling research into human fitness and a variety of ways to control human reproduction.[66]

The Rockefellers underwrote all kinds of birth-reducing efforts. Less controversial methods included intrauterine devices (IUDs), such as Norplant (whose manufacturer faced a critical class-action lawsuit); the daily hormone-based birth control pill; and the "morning after" pill. Highly controversial methods included pregnancy terminators such as abortifacients (RU-486) and abortions at any stage of pregnancy, even right up until birth.[67]

Beyond the eugenic goals and outcomes, Rockefeller Inc. receives financial benefits by retaining the distribution rights to birth control products. They receive further financial benefits through investments in the pharmaceutical companies that advance birth control products. The Rockefeller Foundation has coined a term for this type of "philanthropic" profiteering: "impact investing." This means addressing "social and/or environmental problems while also turning a profit."[68]

As the Rockefellers were monetizing birth control (which their associates successfully rebranded as "family planning" or "maternal health," because of the negative connotations of the word *control*[69]), they pioneered a new field called sex research.[70]

As with curing humankind of infectious diseases, the Rockefellers believed that the illnesses plaguing the human mind might be cured—or at least controlled. Psychology and psychoanalysis—particularly surrounding the historically taboo study of sexual intercourse—were fields that Rockefeller scientists believed could be vastly improved, if not perfected, by following a program that the Rockefellers were uniquely able to prescribe.

Eliminating the consequences of sex (pregnancies) while destigmatizing promiscuity could serve both ideological and profit motives. As the Rockefellers increased the availability of population-reducing contraceptives, they could simultaneously benefit by increasing the demand for such products. A "sexual revolution" (for which the Rockefeller Foundation proudly claims credit) could create that demand.

In 1941, an entomologist named Alfred Kinsey got his first grant from the National Research Council (NRC)—a predominantly Rockefeller-funded organization. Just a few years later, the NRC allotted $40,000 per year for Kinsey's sex project. That funding—more than $600,000 annually, adjusted for inflation—came entirely from the Rockefeller Foundation.[71]

Between 1941 and 1954, Rockefeller-backed organizations promoted sex research, including the Kinsey Scale—which asserts that human sexuality is largely nonbinary—and the concept of gender fluidity. In the 1960s, the Rockefellers' Population Council in partnership with Planned Parenthood proposed advancing alternative sexual preferences to "reduce fertility." The resultant "transgenderism" has arguably become a social contagion. It has exploded into a $2.1 billion annual windfall for medical and pharmaceutical companies and is expected to more than double to $5 billion by 2030.[72]

Decades later, America is still grappling with the sexual revolution's deleterious effects, which include massive surges in unplanned pregnancies (and thus abortions), sexually transmitted diseases, spiking divorce rates, and single-parent households.

Today, the Rockefeller Foundation celebrates the Kinsey Reports, which "transformed American society by challenging American attitudes toward sexual normalcy."[73]

Your Body, Rockefeller's Choice

Anticipating a surge in sexual activity, as well as the prospect of a resultant baby boom, the Rockefellers focused on increasing access to contraceptives and abortions. Beginning in 1952, the Rockefeller Foundation began funding a project that endeavored to create the "Model Penal Code." This sweeping effort prescribed legal changes in areas that ranged from theft and obscenity to capital punishment, and, crucially, to sex offenses and abortion.[74]

Between 1962 (when the Rockefellers' Model Penal Code was published) and 1973 (when the *Roe v. Wade* decision took place), nineteen states "reformed" their abortion restrictions—and some states adopted the Model Penal Code's abortion justifications wholesale. With a new set of liberal laws ready to be implemented, the Rockefellers set out to reshape public opinion on the ethics of something called "reproductive rights."[75]

The Rockefellers not only sought to influence women's sexual and reproductive behavior—their ultimate goal was to rationalize even more radical objectives. In 1969, JDR III and the Rockefeller Foundation provided the primary funding for the first bioethics research institute, called the Hastings Center. This facility pioneered the field of bioethics to study such controversial topics as population control, behavioral control, euthanasia, and genetic engineering. Within two years, the center began publishing a journal that became the "early bible of secular bioethics."[76]

The Hastings Center and particularly its cofounder, Daniel Callahan, were instrumental in legalizing and normalizing abortion at a time when the procedure was still largely taboo. The Rockefellers' Population Council (along with the Ford Foundation) paid for Callahan to study methods of contraception around the world. A once-devout Catholic, Callahan eventually renounced his faith and made strong arguments in favor of both contraceptives and abortion.[77]

The Rockefeller efforts to bring reproductive issues into the mainstream had a profound effect on the political will to use taxpayer monies for population reduction. For decades, the funding for birth control–related research came mostly from private sources, such as the Rockefeller foundations and private drug companies.

Between 1973 and 1987, government funding for reproductive and contraceptive research increased substantially, while private funding decreased. During that time, the US government spent a staggering $572.6 million ($3.9 billion in today's dollars) on population control research. The Controligarchs (mainly the Rockefeller and Ford foundations) spent $72.2 million ($486.5 million in today's dollars) during the same time. All told, roughly $5 billion (adjusted) was spent on population control research in less than fifteen years.[78]

In 1988, while abortion was going mainstream, the Rockefeller Foundation announced that it was making strong progress on another population control front: the development of an "antifertility vaccine" that could block hCG, an essential hormone for fertilization. The foundation had completed early trials in New Delhi of three versions of an antifertility vaccine for women. The following year, the National Institutes of Health (NIH) published a paper titled "Anti-fertility Vaccines," which touted the Rockefellers' research in New Delhi and revealed that "vaccines are under development for the control of fertility in males and females."[79]

By 1991, international collaborative efforts to create an antifertility vaccine were finally paying off. After eighteen years of research, the Rockefellers and their partners at the World Bank, the UN Population Fund, and the WHO Task Force on Vaccines for Fertility Regulation had developed an injection that could prevent pregnancies. Much of that research had been backed by the Rockefellers, who spent roughly $25 million—$62.2 million adjusted—on health and population grants in one year alone (1988).[80]

"As a result of this international, collaborative effort," the WHO task force boasted, "a prototype anti-hCG vaccine is now undergoing clinical testing, raising the prospect that a totally new family planning method may be available before the end of the current decade."[81]

Thanks to the Rockefeller-funded sexual revolution, unprotected sex in America soared. By the mid-1990s, 57 percent of pregnancies (3.6 million) each year were "unplanned," according to a *Washington Post* analysis. Of those 3.6 million, unplanned teenage pregnancies accounted for roughly 20 percent. During his 1992 campaign, President Bill Clinton had declared that abortion should be "safe, legal, and rare," but before the end of his first term, one-third of all American pregnancies had ended in abortion—more than in any industrialized nation. The Rockefellers' efforts to control population growth were working.[82]

In 1970, the year after the Hastings Center was founded, New York governor Nelson Rockefeller (Junior's son and David's brother) signed a bill, narrowly passed by the legislature, legalizing abortion with limited restrictions. The law made New York one of the nation's first states to allow abortion and the only state without a residency requirement. Hundreds of thousands of women from other states flocked to New York to abort their unborn babies. By far the nation's most sweeping abortion-rights law, the New York legislation allowed abortions to be performed at a hospital or an abortion "clinic."[83]

In May 1972, when the New York State legislature passed legislation overturning the proabortion law, Governor Rockefeller vetoed it, and seemingly unaware of the obvious irony, he stated, "I do not believe it right for one group to impose its vision of morality on an entire society."[84]

The Hastings Center's 1987 report titled "Guidelines on the Termination of Life-Sustaining Treatment and the Care of the Dying" provided ethical and legal justifications for a new human right: the "right to die," meaning that a patient (or the patient's family, in the event of a patient's vegetative state) had the right to tell a doctor to turn off life support (affirmed by the US Supreme Court in 1990).[85]

That same year, the center produced a report titled "Imperiled Newborns," which discussed the ethics surrounding terminating the lives of newborn babies with genetic abnormalities such as Down syndrome.[86]

Several months later, in 1988, the Hastings Center published "The Ethics of Fetal Tissue Transplants," which found that, within limits, using aborted fetus body parts "will not erode important ethical values" and essentially opened the door for organizations to sell aborted fetal tissue for medical research.[87]

In 1992, Bill Clinton was elected and immediately became the most proabortion American president to date. Notably, Clinton's Rockefeller connections ran deep. In 1969, a young Bill Clinton was able to legally dodge (or "defer") the Vietnam War draft thanks to a connection to Arkansas governor Winthrop Rockefeller (Junior's son and David's brother). And when Clinton ran for president, the Rockefellers, so-called lifelong Republicans, supported his campaign.[88]

The Rockefellers and the Clintons had a politically powerful mutual friend in Planned Parenthood. The Rockefellers had been among the abortion provider's most prolific funders dating back to its founding by Margaret Sanger. And Planned Parenthood became one of Bill and Hillary Clinton's most ardent backers. The ties between the three ran deep.

It was on his second full day in office that Clinton sealed his fate as the most proabortion president. On January 22, 1993, Clinton issued a series of executive orders and memoranda broadening abortion access in ways that the United States had never seen.

With the sweep of a pen, Clinton overturned President Ronald Reagan's Title X regulations that banned abortion-clinic referrals by federal employees, repealed the "Mexico City Policy" that banned US funding to legalize or perform abortions in foreign countries, and overturned the ban on funding fetal tissue transplants. Clinton authorized hospitals run by the US military to perform abortions and tasked the Food and Drug Administration

(FDA) with reviewing the import ban on the abortion pill mifepristone, or RU-486.[89]

The distribution of RU-486 in the United States would likely not have been possible without Rockefeller efforts. Not only did the Rockefeller institutes develop the fetus-killing drug in 1983 (with FDA approval), but once the pill was developed and deemed safe for use, the developer granted the Rockefellers' Population Council the patent rights to market and sell the abortion pill in the United States.[90]

In 1997, the Population Council transferred those rights to a shadowy pharmaceutical start-up called Danco Laboratories. Danco had an unlisted phone number and its only known address was "somewhere in 'midtown Manhattan.'"[91]

Transferring the rights from the *nonprofit* Population Council to the *for-profit* Danco Labs allowed Danco's secret investors to cash in. It took several years to uncover the investors, but it just so happened that Good Club members George Soros and Warren Buffett were among the lucky Controligarchs to profit from RU-486.[92]

Clinton's actions led to a windfall for birth control and abortion companies. Danco was incorporated in 1995 in the Cayman Islands and refused to name its investors and the manufacturer. More evidence that Danco was linked to the Rockefellers came out when it was revealed that the Rockefeller Foundation helped a Chinese manufacturer obtain an FDA production license to manufacture RU-486 for Danco.[93]

The Hastings Center had provided research on all these topics, and while its reports often presented the case against the federal funding of abortion, abortifacients (i.e., RU-486), assisted suicide, and fetal tissue research, among others, Hastings' bioethicists also made strong ethical arguments in favor of these controversial issues. And usually, there was little doubt in which direction the center's advocacy pointed.[94]

In September 2018, the NIH provided a grant to the Hastings Center to study the ethical questions surrounding "human-animal chimera research," whereby scientists insert human cells into lab animals. "Many people hope that research with chimeras will yield enormous benefits, including more accurate models of human disease," the Hastings Center wrote.[95]

While chimera research may "yield enormous benefits," it also comes with a lot of risks. In 2021, the NIH revealed that "experiments it funded through a US-based nonprofit in 2018 and 2019 at the Wuhan Institute of Virology (WIV) in China had the 'unexpected result' of creating a coronavirus that was more infectious in mice." Critics of chimera research immediately jumped on the admission as proof that the NIH was funding risky "gain of function" research in Wuhan.[96]

The Hastings Center has also provided arguments for voluntary sterilization for women, a "plan to expand access to health care for the undocumented uninsured" in New York City, and "gene editing in the wild" (such as publicly releasing massive amounts of genetically modified mosquitoes—a practice the Rockefeller institutes pioneered and Bill Gates has advanced more recently with the Biden administration's permission). And when the Centers for Disease Control and Prevention (CDC) finally relented to parents' demands to reopen schools after COVID-19 closures had wreaked havoc on children's mental health, the Hastings Center president panned the move as "political and unethical."[97]

CRISPR-Cas9 is one of the latest innovations in genetics research. CRISPR, an acronym for "clustered regularly interspaced short palindromic repeats," has been described as "genetic scissors" because the technology allows for "an efficient, simple, and cheap technology to edit the genome of any organism." In 2018, a Chinese scientist announced that he had used the technology to genetically alter twin babies to be less susceptible to HIV.[98]

It should come as no surprise that Rockefeller scientists also pioneered CRISPR technology. Rockefeller University scientist Dr. Luciano Marraffini has been awarded more than a dozen prizes for his groundbreaking work on the CRISPR gene-editing technology (which began around 2008). Two of these were bestowed in 2017: the Albany Medical Center Prize (received jointly with two future Nobel Prize–winning CRISPR scientists) and the NIH Director's Pioneer Award.[99]

Rockefeller involvement with the CRISPR innovation led to a dispute with fellow Good Club members Eli and Edythe Broad, whose institute holds several CRISPR-related patents that Rockefeller University believed it deserved to own jointly. In early 2018, the parties reached an amicable settlement and agreed that the Broad patents "will remain unchanged."[100]

While the Rockefellers pioneered the research (and continue to fund it to this day), fellow Good Club members Bill Gates and the Broads are heavily involved in the CRISPR field, and Mark Zuckerberg's Facebook associate Sean Parker is on the cutting edge of gene-editing technology. CRISPR has successfully achieved the type of eugenics that Margaret Sanger could have only dreamed of.[101]

Today, there is a whole slew of organizations, initiatives, and public policies that have roots in eugenics-based population control. They hide behind euphemisms such as "family planning" and "reproductive health" (terms that were created specifically to avoid the negative connotations of "birth control") or simply "studying genetics." Also, the Rockefellers are among the most involved philanthropists who continue to fund research into embryonic stem cells, fetal tissue, and euthanasia.

"Stem cell" and "fetal tissue" research programs can more vividly be described as the exploitation of human embryos and the trafficking of unborn baby body parts, while "euthanasia" is the extermination of the elderly and the genocide of disabled individuals, such as those with Down syndrome.

The Club of Rome and the Vilification of Mankind

Over the past century, the Rockefellers and their fellow Controligarchs have spent incalculable sums seeking to reduce population growth and reshape opinions on traditions like the nuclear family. Their efforts have been wildly successful.

The human birth rate on planet Earth peaked in the 1960s. That was the decade when Planned Parenthood (directed by Bill Gates Sr. at the time) and the Rockefellers' Population Council sponsored a proposal that became known as the Jaffe Memo. This obscure document outlined highly controversial ways to halt population growth, including through such medical means as making contraceptives cheap and plentiful, encouraging mass sterilizations, and enacting "compulsory" abortion policies. The Jaffe Memo also recommended more bizarre methods to bring down birth rates, such as propaganda campaigns to "alter the ideal family size," to encourage "women to work," as well as to promote "increased homosexuality."[102]

Perhaps the most alarming method proposed in the memo was to dump "fertility control agents in the water supply." The memo also suggested "discouragement of private home ownership" and one proposal under the "Economic Deterrents/Incentives" section contained just two mysterious words: "Chronic Depression." The Controligarch-funded memo as well as the contemporaneous "Kissinger Report" (1974) and the World Bank's "Population Planning" report (1972) promoted similar methods.[103]

By 2021, the US population growth rate had nearly flatlined—the lowest rate since the nation's founding. The Controligarchs' efforts to curb population growth was so successful that the American birth rate was now dangerously below replacement levels.[104]

These efforts would not have been so successful without the assistance of yet another Rockefeller-linked group. One that, like the Good Club, has been among the most secretive but influential billionaire boys clubs ever: the Club of Rome.

Most people have never heard of this shadowy alliance, but its influence is no less profound. The Club of Rome (CoR) began as an "informal, non-political, multi-national group of scientists, intellectuals, educators, and business leaders deeply concerned with" solving global "issues that confront mankind."[105]

Today, CoR consists of roughly one hundred members, including many of the world's top thought leaders in various fields as well as heads of state, diplomats, leading scientists, and other technocrats. CoR produces prophetic reports that steer global foreign and domestic policies throughout the

Western world—typically through CoR's daughter organization: the World Economic Forum (WEF).

In 1968, the Club of Rome held its inaugural meeting at the Accademia dei Lincei on the outskirts of Rome. It was there that the club's founders reached a consensus on what they called "the problematique," or "the predicament of mankind."

Two years later, CoR produced its first report, a "proposal" titled "The Predicament of Mankind," which reads like a technocratic manifesto on how to achieve world domination by identifying terrifying existential problems, garnering reactions to those problems, and then offering the solutions CoR's members have identified and hyped. According to CoR members, the predicament of mankind is that humanity has become too advanced for its own good. Mankind has accumulated "extraordinary technological capital" but has failed to adopt a "global view" that would lead to "policies requisite to an inter-dependent world."[106]

In other words, overpopulation and pollution are too big for any one country to solve on its own and, therefore, humanity needs a global governance structure if it wants to survive.

Over the next few decades, CoR published a series of eerie reports strategizing how to unite world governments around various global ills. But in 1991, CoR published a book titled *The First Global Revolution* that laid its agenda bare:

> In searching for a common enemy against whom we can unite, *we came up with the idea* that pollution, the threat of global warming, water shortages, famine and the like, would fit the bill. . . . But in designating these dangers as the enemy, we fall into the trap, which we have already warned readers about, namely mistaking symptoms for causes. All these dangers are caused by human intervention in natural processes, and it is only through changed attitudes and behaviour that they can be overcome. *The real enemy then is humanity itself* (emphasis added).[107]

Indeed, the Rockefellers' actions over the past century appear, on the surface, to be rooted in altruism. What had begun as a way for John D. Rockefeller Sr. to build good relations with the public had, in just two generations, given his family an alarming amount of control over humanity. Senior's grandson, David Rockefeller Sr., proudly confessed that he was part of a cabal working to destroy the interests of the United States. But the Controligarchs are not just anti-American; they are antihuman, as their Club of Rome reports (and their transhumanist exploits, which we will explore in Chapter Nine) explicitly claim.

The real enemy is humanity itself.

The implications of CoR's prophetic reports (and its founding of the WEF) will be discussed in the next chapter, but suffice it to say, the Good Club's 2009 meeting on overpopulation had been decades of precedent.

And perhaps the Good Club could achieve what CoR had not yet achieved: enough billionaires committing their wealth toward solving the problematique. It was at the meeting of the Good Club that the so-called Giving Pledge—the promise to transfer one's fortunes to an ideologically aligned nonprofit organization—was devised.[108]

Of the dozen or so billionaires who attended the Good Club meeting, all have signed Gates's Giving Pledge except for Soros and the notoriously private Oprah Winfrey. When asked why, a representative for Soros said that the veteran philanthropist was "delighted by the pledge and to learn that others planned to join him in doing what he has done for decades, giving away half his income. He plans to donate his entire fortune."[109]

The current estimate of total Giving Pledge transfers is $600 billion—notably, there are only about 150 charities in the world that are capable of managing a hypothetical nine-figure donation, and if each of those major charities were to receive a $200 million donation, only about 5 percent of the total Giving Pledge total would be consumed. In other words, the Giving Pledge endowment is more than enough to dramatically change the world for the better, and if it fails to do so, one must wonder why.[110]

It appears that forty years of WEF attempts to control everything from population growth to climate change were not to the Rockefellers', Gates's, Buffett's, or Soros's liking, so they convened the Good Club in May 2009. And after that Good Club meeting, the WEF began to prepare for a "Great Reset" to usher in a new era of elitist authoritarian rule around the world.

All that the WEF needed was the right crisis to exploit.

2

The Gates of Hell

It's possible, you can never know, that the universe exists only for me. If so, it's sure going well for me, I must admit.[1]

—*Bill Gates, January 1997*

On February 7, 2020, Bill Gates laced up his white tennis shoes and took to the clay courts for the sixth annual "Match for Africa" charity tennis tournament in Cape Town, South Africa. Gates looked uncharacteristically fit, albeit with hints of more characteristic atrophy, in his sporty white-and-green tennis outfit. Beyond his physique, he appeared as he had for decades—nerdy, with his square-frame sports lenses and tousled, now grayish brown hair.

Gates had teamed up with Swiss tennis legend Roger Federer before to raise money for a good cause. "Four legends, one match," hailed the promotional materials.[2]

Gates and Federer handily beat their opponents—number two world-ranked tennis star Rafael Nadal and *Daily Show* comedian and South African native Trevor Noah—in the celebrity doubles tournament. Gates even won a few points (though, as expected, the exhibition match was mostly Federer versus Nadal), and his victorious grins masked any concerns he may have been wrestling with on the eve of the first global pandemic in over a century.[3]

The South Africa tennis match would be one of Gates's last public appearances as just another normal billionaire philanthropist. Soon, Gates would become one of the most polarizing figures on the planet. To some, he would be revered as the benevolent billionaire hero working tirelessly to help humanity. To others, he would be reviled as the world's foremost villain—the face of a "Plandemic."

Some believe that Gates planned COVID based on his prior pandemic predictions and his foundation's financial interests in viruses and vaccines. But where COVID came from, whether from a Chinese lab or nature, matters less than how it was handled. And the response caused more devastation than the disease. The truth is that the Controligarchs—led by Gates—planned *for* a pandemic, and they were well positioned to benefit from one.

Within a few weeks of the match, Gates was the private sector counterpart to the public sector's Dr. Anthony Fauci. The two men worked as a tag team to issue flawed pandemic guidance from their respective perches.

Once back in Seattle after the match, Gates convened his global health brain trust. Having committed up to a whopping $100 million to steer the coronavirus response efforts just two days prior, Gates was the first major private financier of the bourgeoning pandemic response. But the world would need more than money. More than anything, the world needed guidance and a unified strategy. Gates filled the gap.[4]

Gates seemed confident that some of the anticompetitive practices he had perfected over the years could be implemented to control—and profit from—this chaotic virus. Microsoft had a strategy for monopolizing the software industry called Embrace-Extend-Extinguish (or Exterminate).[5] This strategy got Gates's company in trouble with Clinton's Justice Department, but he has not yet received a similar slap on the wrist for applying it to the infectious disease industry—which he also bought his way into.

Gates set up his foundation in the 1990s amid Microsoft's antitrust controversy—much as the Rockefellers had under similar circumstances—and the Gates Foundation soon embraced the pandemic preparedness industry. Over the next two decades, he extended his influence over it by donating to an increasing number of pandemic-related NGOs, initiatives, and Big Pharma companies (like the WHO, the global vaccine alliance [Gavi], and Pfizer, respectively). Finally, during the coronavirus pandemic, his proposed remedies crushed the competition: nonpharmaceutical alternatives (generics, vitamins, exercise, and sunshine).[6]

Now, Gates needed his brain trust to get on board with his ideas.

"I turned to a favorite tactic that I've been relying on for years: the working dinner," Gates recalled in his 2022 book titled *How to Prevent the Next Pandemic*. Gates is the type of billionaire who solves the world's problems over a hot meal surrounded by his advisors. There is no agenda at a typical Gates working dinner. He simply wines and dines "a dozen or so smart people" and urges them to start brainstorming ideas.[7]

It is a tactic that Gates had used to great effect in the past. In fact, it was at one of these dinners in the late 1990s that Gates met Fauci. At the time, Gates was embroiled in a bitter antitrust battle with the Clinton Justice Department over Microsoft's monopolistic business practices while his father, Bill Sr., oversaw the emerging Gates Foundation.[8]

On a separate occasion, Gates had invited renowned disease experts such as Fauci to the house that Microsoft built: a palatial sixty-six-thousand-square-foot Seattle-area estate dubbed Xanadu 2.0 after the fictitious mansion in Orson Welles's *Citizen Kane*.[9]

Fauci fondly recalled being pulled aside from the rest of the dinner attendees for a secret conversation in the "amazingly beautiful" Gates library. The younger Bill was beginning to take a more active role in foundation affairs and wanted to discuss a mutually beneficial arrangement with the US government's foremost vaccine expert.

"Tony, you run the biggest infectious disease institute of the world," Gates said before he proposed the unofficial partnership: "I want to be sure the money I spent is well spent." John D. Rockefeller Sr. chose a man of faith—a Baptist minister—to guide the Rockefeller Foundation. Bill Gates chose *the* man of science.

This working dinner, where Gates first teamed up with Fauci, along with another in 1998 dubbed "the lamb chop dinner," when Gates pledged $750 million to develop childhood vaccinations for "killer diseases," marked the beginning of the end of Gates's first career as a software monopolist. It was the start of something much grander: his second career as a medicine monopolist.[10]

Fauci would be an essential, legitimizing force in Gates's reputational transition from a cutthroat computer tycoon to a new man, a decidedly good man—one who even his foes at the Justice Department could admire. Indeed, one aide from the Clinton era switched teams and founded a firm that worked closely with the expanding Gates Foundation.[11]

Twenty years later, Gates's transition was complete. He was the most prolific philanthropist in the world and the de facto head of global health policy. He scheduled the coronavirus working dinner for Friday, February 14, 2020, at the Gates Foundation headquarters in Seattle. Even as Gates was publicly telling the world to abolish meat in favor of more patentable proteins (which will be discussed in Chapter Five), his inner circle of health experts would be savoring beef short ribs that evening as they talked about the virus spreading beyond Wuhan, China.[12]

Though they may not have known it at the time, Gates and his brain trust were meeting directly at the epicenter of the American coronavirus outbreak. While they were enjoying their short-rib dinner, the first US coronavirus cases were incubating at a nursing home just sixteen miles away, in Kirkland, and soon dozens of its residents would be dead.[13]

Gates went into the working dinner all but certain that the coronavirus would require a major global response. That same day, he told a packed crowd of America's top scientists and bureaucrats—the ones who would be implementing the COVID response measures—exactly what they should do.[14]

"COVID-19 could be a once-in-a-century pandemic, but the good news is that there are steps we can take now to slow its impact and help us respond more effectively when the next epidemic arrives. #COVID19," Gates tweeted on February 28 (just twelve days before the WHO officially declared the pandemic). His proposals sounded like a subtle declaration of war—not just against the virus but, as it turned out, against American freedoms.[15]

Gates hardly needed the working dinner to craft his opening salvo to America's top scientists. He had been preaching dire pandemic predictions to anyone who would listen for years. "We've always known that the potential for either a naturally caused or intentionally caused pandemic is one of the few things that could disrupt health systems, economies, and cause more than ten million excess deaths," Gates told the packed audience on Valentine's Day. He spoke often about the significant resources his foundation had spent over the years to help the world prepare for something like this.[16]

Indeed, Gates had long feared that a global pandemic was coming, and his foundation—currently the largest private charity in the world—had been laser focused on pathogens since its founding decades prior, during the Clinton administration. Most notably, Gates gave a TED Talk in 2015 with alarming predictions—chief among them was that a global pandemic was guaranteed, and that the world was not ready for it.[17]

Over nearly two decades, starting in 2000, Gates funneled more than $10 billion into various vaccination and antivirus efforts—including the tens of millions that he had invested in messenger ribonucleic acid (mRNA) technology. He called this eleven-figure outlay the "best investment" he had ever made due to a clever accounting trick that estimated a staggering $200 billion return in ill-defined "social and economic benefits."[18]

From the start of the COVID crisis, Gates was ahead of the curve. In an early and widely circulated dispatch, Gates laid out the path forward: treatments, vaccines, testing, contact tracing, and "policies for opening up." In addition, his unofficial partnership with Fauci seemed stronger than ever, and along the way, he had cultivated relationships with other disease experts, including the lesser-known face of the US government's pandemic response, Dr. Deborah Birx.[19]

Both Gates and Fauci had repeatedly warned that a pandemic was an impending threat. In addition to becoming the largest individual funder of the

WHO, Gates had dumped at least $3.1 billion into various programs run by Drs. Fauci and Birx (much of which were HIV/AIDS related). Therefore, their pandemic response strategies had long since synced. Simply put, they all seemed to be using the same talking points—ones that government officials at every level regurgitated as if reading from the same script.[20]

In April 2020, the prestigious *New England Journal of Medicine* published Gates's coronavirus response blueprint. On the standard disclosure form that identifies whether the author has any conflicts of interest, Gates checked the box, "Yes." What were his conflicts of interest? "Numerous," he wrote.[21]

Conflicts notwithstanding, the National Institutes of Health (Fauci's ultimate employer) cited Gates and effectively gave his blueprint the NIH seal of approval.[22]

The mainstream media also amplified his status as the de facto leader of the global pandemic response. News outlets such as MSNBC (the *M* and *S* are for Microsoft, which cofounded the network) and *The Washington Post* (owned by Gates's friend and fellow billionaire Jeff Bezos) gushed over Gates's pandemic prescience, hailing him as "one of the world's most accomplished innovators" and granting him the odd laudatory title "The Billionaire Who Cried Pandemic." His "science-based solutions" might just save the world (or at least bring about a "return to normalcy").[23]

In early 2020, Gates's foundation poured nearly $80 million (which has ballooned to more than $165 million since 2016) into the Imperial College London, which published terrifying pandemic models projecting mass deaths. According to the models, millions would die in the United States within months without radical interventions.[24]

Lockdowns were essential, Gates implored. The extreme models that he had funded said so. The requirements for reprieve included face masks, social distancing, quarantines, temperature checks, and travel restrictions (among other unnatural things). Even more unsettling was the fact that the models were wildly inaccurate. The Imperial College London's death projections were later determined to be off by orders of magnitude. The modeler resigned after he was caught flouting lockdown protocols, ironically, but the interventions lived on.[25]

Far from being voluntary, these measures must be mandated, Gates urged. Without these controls, he threatened, "we cannot return to the business as usual or stop the virus."[26]

But when can we get back to normal? the world asked. "Normalcy only returns," Gates declared, "when we've largely vaccinated the entire global population." Luckily, Gates's own "normal" was never disrupted. Whenever he needed a break, he could scamper away to a remote island on one of his private jets. Everyone else would be a hostage to his guidance.[27]

Gates cheerfully suggested, Fauci and Birx dictated, and the world dutifully obeyed. Almost everyone in the West stayed home hoping that it would, as Gates assured, save lives (Grandma's not least among them). They struggled through ineffective remote schooling with their children—Gates had said it was necessary. They sacrificed their families' mental and economic health on Gates's altar of "nonpharmaceutical interventions." Most Americans believed the billionaire's promises of a return to normalcy, and they did their part—they wore the masks, they socially distanced, they submitted to endless COVID testing, and they allowed their contacts to be traced. And most obeyed Gates's favorite pharmaceutical intervention: they got the shots.

Vaccinate, vaccinate, vaccinate was Gates's mantra even before the WHO declared the coronavirus a global pandemic. The reason the world took Gates so seriously on this subject was simple: he had accurately predicted it. And the man famous for being the world's richest disease expert was exactly whom frightened citizens hoped they could trust amid new chaos and uncertainty.

But the public's faith soon turned into skepticism. Why was Gates completely dismissing (or ignoring) potential COVID treatments—especially widely available and inexpensive ones, such as zinc, vitamin C, and vitamin D—that had virtually no downside? Why wasn't Gates talking about the benefits of exercise and sunshine? And most curious of all, why was Gates pushing a vaccine that did not yet exist?

Gates of course profits from investing in vaccines. But there is another underexamined effect: vaccines give the vaccine provider major social con-trol. The Rockefellers, after all, had profited immensely from taking over entire countries' health-care systems for purposes of "disease control."

For Gates, vaccines play an important role in curbing population growth. Gates believes that more vaccines mean that more children survive to adult-hood, which in turn means that parents will decide to have fewer children. Drawing on decades of medical and social hygiene efforts (eugenics and popu-lation control), Rockefeller, Gates, and their fellow Good Club members had decided that overpopulation is the most important issue facing humanity.[28]

In a 2010 TED Talk, Gates succinctly explained his rationale for funding vaccines and birth control to curtail population growth on Earth. "The world today has 6.8 billion people. That's headed up to about 9 billion," Gates warned. "Now, if we do a really great job on new vaccines, health care, re-productive health services, we could lower that by, perhaps, ten or fifteen percent."[29]

Curing the Diseased of Their Overpopulation Ills

Crucial to Gates's population control effort was his wife, Melinda. Bill Jr. married Melinda French Gates in 1994. She became his partner in philan-thropy and life, and they had three children. Along with Bill Sr., the three of them had a shared love for population reduction and vaccines. He calls her a "truly equal partner," adding that they are a lot alike, but she has a better sense of humor, and "she's better with people than I am."[30]

Simply put, they were a power couple—arguably the most influential on the planet. Also, having a woman co-lead the Gates Foundation allowed them to relate to both genders and add more credibility to their women's health agenda—perhaps in ways that a male computer nerd never could.

Melinda was Bill Jr.'s employee at Microsoft when they went out on their first date in 1987. From the start, they were on equal intellectual footing. Before long, they were financial equals, and the money gave Melinda real standing in the world. She became intimately involved in the Gates Foundation and remained so even after their divorce in 2021—which she claims she initiated because of Bill's complicated friendship with convicted sex offender Jeffrey Epstein.[31]

Melinda had valid concerns. Her husband had reportedly spent time with Epstein on dozens of occasions, even after Epstein was found guilty of pedophilia-related crimes. Members of Gates's inner circle were close to Epstein, including Boris Nikolic and Melanie Walker. Epstein met Walker in 1992 and hired her as an advisor in 1998.[32]

The overlap between Gates's and Epstein's networks was significant. Both Gates and Epstein had a deep interest in scientific breakthroughs, and both funded gene-editing (eugenics) projects. Gates and Epstein's mutual contacts, which include Wuhan-linked virus hunter Nathan Wolfe, lead directly to Gates's pandemic efforts via an unlikely partnership with JPMorgan.[33]

In a now-famous photo of Gates and Epstein together, the two men are flanked by Nikolic and a JPMorgan executive with whom Gates later established an epidemic preparedness initiative. That initiative funded vaccine and mRNA technology before 2015. In addition to Gates and his advisors, Epstein was also close with other Good Club members, such as Michael Bloomberg, and Epstein even served on the board of the Rockefellers' university, where the Good Club met.[34]

Epstein, like Gates and other Good Club members, was concerned about overpopulation and funded genetic tinkering and disease-related projects. Epstein also wanted to "seed the human race" with his own DNA by impregnating scores of women. When it came to procreation, Epstein's mentality seemed to be "Rules for thee, but not for me!"[35]

According to *The New York Times*, Epstein worried that saving lives by curing diseases would not advance the population control agenda. But Bill and Melinda apparently do not see it that way. While Melinda acknowledges that saving lives to reduce the population may *seem* counterintuitive, she insists that it is not.[36]

"When more children live past the age of five," Melinda said in a 2018 interview, "and when mothers can decide if and when to have children, population sizes don't go up." Crucial to this formula are the population control efforts in which Bill and Melinda Gates pour billions of dollars: contraceptives, pills, and abortion.[37]

The simple formula for Gates's plan to save the world appears to be the following: vaccines plus birth control equals sustainability. It just so happens that Bill Gates profits from both sides of this equation.

The Product of a Corporate Attorney

When Bill Gates convened the meeting of the Good Club, he pledged to give away half his wealth. Thirteen years later, his net worth had more than doubled and sat at a staggering $118 billion. What makes this figure even more remarkable is that Bill and Melinda have transferred at least $39 billion to their foundation since 1994.[38]

Generally speaking, Bill Gates has amassed at least two dollars for every dollar that he has pledged to give away. Is it magic?

The truth about Bill Gates Jr. is far less mystical. Coming from a long line of rich and powerful men who perfected a strategy for complete control over generations, *Gates was born to take over the world.*

But it was not without struggle.

Gates rarely talks about his parents' role in his success. The story that he would much rather tell is the one starring a child prodigy who dropped out of Harvard to build the world's most successful software company by pulling all-nighters and outsmarting everyone. All from his parents' garage.

History tells a different, albeit less glamorous, story: Bill Gates's father was the true brains behind the operation. Gates Sr. was directly responsible not only for the rise of Microsoft but also for the rise of other Seattle-based megacorporations, such as Amazon and Starbucks.[39]

The Gates family was destined for greatness long before Bill Jr. was born. His maternal grandfather and great-grandfather were influential West Coast bankers (the former even became a high-ranking official at the Federal

Reserve bank in San Francisco). Bill Jr.'s paternal great-grandfather was a gold rush prospector, and his grandfather was a wealthy businessman. Bill Jr. is the last of four William Henry Gates's, a dynasty with a long lineage.[40]

Their pedigree set up the Gates family for prestige and power.

Bill Gates the youngest, William Henry Gates III (commonly known as Bill Jr.), was born on October 28, 1955, in Seattle, Washington. Bill Jr. wrote his first computer program at age thirteen. By 1986, he was a billionaire and by the mid-1990s, he was worth tens of billions and was arguably the world's richest man. Until the late 1990s, Bill Jr. was a mostly private individual and "preferred to stay out of the public eye, handling civic and philanthropic affairs indirectly through one of his foundations."[41]

Bill Jr.'s father, William Henry Gates II (commonly known as Bill Sr.), was a prominent corporate attorney in Seattle, and Bill Jr.'s mother, Mary Maxwell Gates, was an influential socialite serving on the boards of many local and national nonprofit organizations. Their social circle was impressive from the start. Bill Sr.'s scoutmaster went on to become the mayor of Seattle (and later a deputy cabinet secretary in the Nixon administration). Bill Sr. met Mary Maxwell thanks to a mutual friend who later became a cabinet secretary in the Carter administration.

Maxwell Gates was born to be a debutante and prominent socialite. Her high-level social connections certainly deserve a lion's share of the credit for her son's rise to global tech oligarch. More than a decade before Mary introduced the younger Bill to legendary billionaire investor Warren Buffett in 1991, she made an even more crucial introduction to her friend John Opel, the CEO and chairman of International Business Machines (IBM). Without IBM's licensing of Microsoft's operating system, it is possible that Microsoft would have never gotten off the ground.[42]

But Bill Sr. was perhaps even more instrumental to his son's long-term success than the boy's mother was.

Bill Sr. was well on his way to becoming one of the most influential attorneys in Seattle before Bill Jr. was born, and Bill Sr. became so by representing powerful corporate interests. Decades before there was a Big Tech in

Silicon Valley, his first clients were technology and biomedical companies. Through his efforts representing these interests, he became an expert in monopolizing intellectual property, cornering markets, and using his power to build political capital. In short, the younger Bill had the perfect mentor.

Bill Jr. was a difficult child—always at war with his mother, who wanted him to socialize, be punctual, and be tidy. They would get into explosive battles over trivial things. "He was nasty," recalled Bill's younger sister, Libby Armintrout (later Libby MacPhee).

One night at the dinner table, the younger Bill was being so vicious that his typically subdued father splashed a glass of water in his adolescent son's face. When the younger Bill's parents sent him to a therapist to sort out what his problem was, Bill recalls telling the therapist, "I'm at war with my parents over who is in control."[43]

Bill Sr. attributed the future success of his son (whom they called Trey) to, in part, his love for reading and competition. "Trey was so competitive he always wanted to win [the school's summer reading contest] and often did," the elder Gates wrote in his memoir. Young Trey's favorite board games were Monopoly and Risk, games that give players the twin thrills of cornering the market and dominating the world.[44]

When Trey was just a toddler in 1957, Bill Sr. landed a client called Physio-Control Corporation. Physio-Control was a Seattle-based innovator, a fledgling biotech company, and it pioneered electronic medical-device technology. The company struggled in its early years, but Bill Sr.'s counsel and contacts would change all that.

Physio-Control became the world's largest manufacturer of external defibrillators, generating massive sums from licensing fees and royalties. Years later, Microsoft would adopt this licensing model—along with several other Physio-Control management strategies, including pep rally–style corporate meetings, referring to employees as "team members" and implementing a four-day workweek in some locations.[45]

When Gates Sr. cofounded the law firm Shidler, McBroom, and Gates in 1964, he brought Physio-Control with him, and he remained involved both financially and legally with the defibrillator company through its initial public stock offering (IPO) several years later.[46]

In 1966, Gates Sr. persuaded a fellow University of Washington (UW) alum, W. Hunter Simpson, to leave his prestigious job as the head of IBM's Seattle division to serve as president of Physio-Control. The move surprised the IBM executive's friends and colleagues because Physio-Control was struggling at the time—with just three employees and on the verge of bankruptcy—while IBM was one of the world's largest corporations.[47]

Under Bill Sr.'s direction and Simpson's leadership, Physio-Control became one of the world's top manufacturers of defibrillators and other heart-monitoring technology. When Eli Lilly acquired the company for $149 million in 1980, Simpson remained at the helm.[48]

The elder Gates's role in securing Physio-Control's intellectual property, licensing its products, and pulling off its subsequent IPO put Gates Sr. and his firm on the map. He also became the president of the Seattle-King County Bar Association in 1969 and the president of the Washington State Bar Association in 1986. When Trey was in sixth grade, his father sent him to Physio-Control to learn from the client for a school-paper assignment.[49]

This valuable experience in the fledgling field of biotechnology—particularly the mastery of manufacturing technology derived from taxpayer-funded research, licensing that technology, monopolizing intellectual property, and leveraging IPOs for personal benefit—would serve the younger Gates *very* well. The elder Gates devised a system and taught the younger Gates how to work that system.[50]

By the time he got to high school, Bill Jr. put the self-confidence that his father had instilled in him to the test. He and several older classmates formed the Lakeside Programming Group that would eventually lead to the founding of Microsoft. Lakeside High—the most elite prep school in Seattle—was perhaps the only academy in the country with a computer terminal after Lakeside's "Mothers Club" purchased it with proceeds from a rummage sale in 1968.[51]

Bill Jr. and a classmate two years his senior named Paul Allen wanted to use the expensive machine so often that when they often exhausted their limits (it was costly to use the computer), Bill Jr. and Paul snuck into the UW computer department to use the machines after hours, and their programmer group was banned by a local computer company for exploiting bugs in the system to get free time.[52]

The Lakeside Programming Group was essentially a for-profit venture run by high school students. It benefited from contacts at the Gates's alma mater, UW, but got off to a rocky start. The elder programmers kicked young Bill Jr. out of the club because of a lack of clientele. His departure was short lived, however, and soon they asked him to come back—perhaps hoping to gain client referrals from Bill Jr.'s father.

"Look, if you want me to come back you have to let me be in charge," an uppity Gates told his buddies. "But this is a dangerous thing," he warned them, "because if you put me in charge this time, I'm going to want to be in charge forever after."[53]

Upon his return, Bill Jr. proved his value to the Lakeside programmers when he leveraged his father's connection. The young programmers got a big break when one of Bill Sr.'s law clients helped them build a device to analyze traffic patterns. It was June 1972, and Bill Jr. and Paul Allen were working on the primitive computer system that they called Traf-O-Data. A local computer company called Intermec, which was fortunate to have found Bill Sr. as one of its early investors, directors, and general counsel, basically did much of the heavy lifting for young Bill Jr. and Paul Allen.[54]

Gates met several of the other Traf-O-Data developers while borrowing time on a big mainframe computer near the UW physics building (now named Mary Gates Hall). While his résumé claims that he "designed and put together" the traffic analyzer, the younger Bill later admitted in an interview that he "got some guys at Intermec to build [the original Traf-O-Data tape reader]."[55]

The Intermec example is instructive. Time and again, Bill Gates has claimed that *he* invented something revolutionary and was credited thusly. But Physio-Control, Intermec, and finally Microsoft were almost entirely built by other developers that he or his father had hired, and the elder Bill played the primary role securing the younger Bill's early tech deals and steering his businesses toward success.[56]

Around the same time that Bill Jr. and Paul Allen were sealing their fate as lifelong business partners on the Traf-O-Data project, Bill Sr. was working with Physio-Control colleagues on a lucrative patent transfer scheme that would take government-subsidized intellectual property from universities and place that technology in the hands of private corporations.[57]

Bill Sr., Physio-Control's Hunter Simpson, and their fellow UW alum Tom Cable began working on the scheme in the mid-1970s, and the resultant Washington Research Foundation (WRF) was incorporated several years later. A tribute to Simpson after his 2006 passing describes the scheme candidly:

> In the mid-1970s, Physio-Control began manufacturing two products derived from research done at the UW. Although the university was known for the quality of its researchers, it had no mechanism in place to commercialize any technology arising from research. Hunter took the unusual step of paying voluntary royalties to the UW for the technologies that Physio-Control commercialized.
>
> Hunter also took one more step toward securing revenue for the UW from its technology. Hunter and a group of friends that included Tom Cable, Bill Gates Sr. and others with close ties to the UW decided to form WRF as an independent foundation to facilitate the transfer of technology to the private sector. The WRF was incorporated in 1981, and its patenting and licensing program has since generated hundreds of millions of dollars in revenues.[58]

The Washington Research Foundation immediately began filing patents to formalize ownership of UW research. It was a brilliant plan. On average, it took nearly twenty years for the first two patent applications to receive approval, but since the patents were "pending," Gates Sr. and his colleagues were able to "immediately establish licensing agreements with dozens of biotech and pharmaceutical companies."

Among the first UW discoveries that Gates Sr. and WRF capitalized on involved "diagnostic and therapeutic proteins" and the use of "yeast technology to create vaccines." Notably, this critical technology featuring vaccines and fermented yeast that helped launch Bill Sr.'s early patent transfer scheme was strikingly similar to innovations that Bill Jr. later spearheaded.[59]

Young Trey had resented his parents for not giving him control sooner, but by the time the younger Bill Gates, now a billionaire running the world's leading software conglomerate, had embarked on his journey to become the world's leading philanthropist, the elder Gates was clearly proud of him and let him be his own man, albeit on the path that Bill Sr. had laid out.

Like his father, Bill Jr. came to admire vaccines—they are a "miracle" in his words—and he has found them immensely profitable. In May 2022, Bill Jr. estimated that he has spent "tens of billions" on vaccination efforts.[60]

The Gates family—the elder Bill with his law firm and WRF and the younger Bill with Microsoft—almost singlehandedly turned Seattle into a leading biotech hub. This, in turn, increased their wealth and power, both locally and nationally (and eventually internationally).[61]

The cross-pollination between the elder and younger Bills' ventures was substantial, particularly via the revolving door and mutual funding arrangements between their respective ventures. Lawyers from Gates Sr.'s firm went on to work for Microsoft. Funding from Microsoft and the Gates Foundation flowed to the Gates law firm's clients. Scientists from Gates's corporate clients went on to work for both Microsoft and the Gates Foundation. This revolving door between Gates partners and affiliates created a "Microsoft effect."[62]

The Gates Control Strategy: Embrace-Extend-Exterminate

In 1981, Jr.'s mother helped secure for Microsoft one of the most consequential deals in its history. After many software companies had submitted their bids, IBM had officially chosen Microsoft to create its software.[63]

The deal was enormously beneficial for both IBM and Microsoft. *Time* magazine reported in 1983 that within three years of engaging Microsoft, "IBM has already captured 21% of the $7.5 billion US market for personal computers, a staggering feat in so short a time, and is virtually tied with pacesetter Apple Computer, which had a four-year head start." By 1984, Microsoft had become the most influential software company in the world.[64]

IBM's exclusive licensing of the Microsoft operating system meant that Gates's customers were growing by the millions without IBM's having produced (let alone marketed) a physical product. Bypassing consumers and selling his software directly to hardware manufacturers was a novel concept and basically eliminated the possibility of competition on an IBM computer. This was a business model that Gates could (and would) exploit.

There was one problem, however: IBM's machines were not the only machines, and Apple Computers made a better product. Something would need to be done about Apple.

Apple founder Steve Jobs knew that his company had the larger market share—and he intended to keep it. To do so, Jobs hired Pepsi-Cola's president, John Sculley, and Sculley's view toward the Microsoft-IBM partnership was less combative than Jobs's. Sculley did not view the budding rivalry as "a bruising fight for market share" but saw instead that there was room for both companies to be "major participants." Perhaps that is why Apple let the fox into the henhouse.[65]

Shortly after Gates got a sneak peek at his competitor's software, Microsoft announced its new Windows operating system, with multiple applications that appeared to be exact copies of Apple's software. Apple's CEO was enraged. Even the new Windows menu bar looked almost identical.[66]

In March 1988, Apple sued Microsoft for copyright infringement, alleging that at least 189 elements of Microsoft's new operating system were blatant copies of Apple's Macintosh operating system. If Gates's 1980 purchasing of the "quick and dirty" operating system, rebranding of it, and licensing of it to IBM was a coup, then the Macintosh imitation in 1985 was the coup de grâce.[67]

The legal battle between the biggest rivals in computing dragged on for several years. In July 1989, a judge ruled that most of the features that Microsoft had cribbed from Apple were covered by a previous licensing agreement between the two companies (apparently Apple's lawyers failed to realize that working with Gates's company meant that Microsoft could legally copy Apple's designs). Also, most of the features that were not covered under the licensing arrangement were free for Microsoft to imitate under something called the "merger doctrine," which holds that ideas cannot be copyrighted.[68]

In August 1993, Microsoft won the lawsuit, and the Supreme Court declined to hear Apple's final appeal in February 1995. Microsoft had legally appropriated Apple's innovative design. Gates later admitted that he had pilfered Microsoft designs from Xerox and accused Jobs of having done the same earlier.[69]

As Microsoft and Apple were battling in court, the Federal Trade Commission (FTC) had begun to take notice of Microsoft's possible anticompetitive collusion with IBM and opened an investigation in 1990. The commissioners were divided over whether to act against Microsoft's apparent monopolistic behavior and closed the investigation because of the stalemate.[70]

Frustrated by the FTC's failure to act, the Clinton Justice Department opened its own antitrust probe in 1993, which resulted in a 1994 consent decree—a settlement, basically—meaning that the Justice Department would not penalize Microsoft for past behavior if Microsoft promised not to use its dominant position to stifle competition moving forward.[71]

In 1997, the Justice Department had evidence that Microsoft was violating the 1994 consent decree and imposed a one-million-dollar-per-day fine on Microsoft for squelching competition, though a judge later threw out the fines. By 1998, twenty attorneys general from various states had joined with the Justice Department and filed suit against Microsoft for violating antitrust laws. These officials alleged hundreds of facts and numerous examples demonstrating how Microsoft had abused its market dominance to stifle competition in the computing industry.[72]

In the trial, it was revealed that Microsoft executives wanted to "extinguish" "smother," and "cut off [a competitor's] air supply." In fact, perhaps the most shocking revelation from the Microsoft antitrust trial was that the company actually had a name for its monopolization strategy—one that Gates continues to employ to this day: Embrace-Extend-Extinguish (or Exterminate).[73]

Gates's strategy worked in three phases. In the first phase, he enters an existing market—software in the case of Microsoft—and *embraces* the existing rules (or "standards"), creating a product with "cross-compatibility." Next, Gates *extends* his position and begins introducing new features that are not compatible with his competitors' products. Finally, when Gates's new features become a de facto standard, he closes the noose and *extinguishes* the competitors who are unable to support his new features.

Gates employed this strategy to crush competitors in multiple industries and even offered "secret side payments potentially amounting to hundreds of millions of dollars" to suffocate his competition. A Stanford professor of e-commerce, strategic management, and economics described the strategy simply: "We will embrace it, we will make it ours, we will apply it to our operating system, and we will kill it."[74]

Philanthropy as a PR Strategy

The Justice Department and the public—at home *and* abroad—were outraged. They both hammered Microsoft for its monopolistic practices, such as the Embrace-Extend-Extinguish strategy. Several notorious troublemakers threw multiple cream pies in Bill's face—a sneak attack—on a street in Brussels.[75]

Throughout the trial, Microsoft's defense was deemed laughable. In the videotaped depositions, Gates was evasive and nonresponsive and appeared, at times, robotic. He also came across as arrogant. Channeling his inner Bill Clinton, who famously stated that his guilt "depends on what the definition of the word *is*, is," Gates's defense depended on the definitions of the words *we*, *compete*, and *concerned*, among others.[76]

"I have no idea what you're talking about when you say 'ask,'" Gates said. *Bloomberg News* reported that Gates was so evasive and feigned amnesia (stating "I don't recall") so often "that even the presiding judge had to chuckle."[77]

The court ruled that Microsoft was a monopoly that uses its power to stifle competition at the expense of consumers, and on June 7, 2000, Microsoft was ordered to break up into two separate companies.[78]

"For the first time in my life, I actively sought distraction," Gates said.[79]

The Apple lawsuit, the FTC investigation, and the decade-long Justice Department antitrust saga took an undeniable toll on Gates's reputation. Gone was "Bill Gates: the business savvy computer whiz." That image was replaced by "Bill Gates: cutthroat monopolist who would do anything to get ahead." Much like the Rockefellers, Gates had brought the world into a new age with tactics that made him an enemy of the people he had claimed to help.

"There can be no doubt that the Microsoft monopoly forced consumers to overpay, denied access to new and better products, and stifled overall quality improvements," said the Consumer Federation of America, calling Microsoft's monopolistic practices "fundamentally abhorrent to the American consumer."[80]

Thanks to these tactics, Gates's wealth was accumulating so fast that, much like Rockefeller's avalanche, it threatened to crush him. The Gates Foundation eventually had such a large endowment that Internal Revenue Service (IRS) rules required Gates to give it away by the hundreds of millions (or even billions).[81]

So, taking a page from the Rockefeller playbook (and under his father's savvy counsel), Gates decided to clean up his reputation the old-fashioned way: he became a philanthropist and began buying good press (wholesale, in the case of MSNBC).

Prior to his legal troubles, Bill Jr. was not a prolific philanthropist. In fact, he did not care for philanthropy at all—at least not at first. When his mother advised before her death in 1994 that he give some of his time and enormous profits to charity, he resisted.[82]

The first charitable endeavor that bore Gates's name was the William H. Gates Foundation. Bill Sr. would run his son's foundation, established in 1994, and would use the latter's growing mountain of wealth to advance a cause they were both passionate about: reproductive health. The elder Gates believed that a woman's ability to prevent or terminate a pregnancy was an essential component of "empowering women."[83]

Bill Sr. set the course of his son's charitable efforts from the start, and the Gates Foundation has remained on that course. From the outset, the Gates Foundation's primary focus was "family planning," a euphemism that Rockefeller-funded propagandists developed for abortion and other forms of birth control.

In fact, Bill Sr. and each of the individuals he brought in to run the Gates Foundation's most critical programs had a long history of passing through a revolving door of Rockefeller-backed population control efforts, including the Rockefellers' Population Council, Planned Parenthood, and a Seattle-based birth control organization called Program for the Introduction and Adaptation of Contraceptive Technology, which later rebranded itself as the Program for Appropriate Technology in Health (PATH).[84]

Starting at the top, Bill Sr. had been a longtime director—both locally and nationally—for Planned Parenthood. The elder Gates made perhaps the most consequential hire for the nascent Gates charitable enterprise: a Canadian birth control expert and Planned Parenthood director named Gordon Perkin. Perkin began as a contraceptive salesman in the 1950s, when birth control was still taboo.

In the 1960s and 1970s, Perkin worked with the Rockefellers' Population Council on a joint population control project with the Ford Foundation. This was around the time when Bill Sr. was directing Planned Parenthood and when the Population Council and Planned Parenthood produced the Jaffe Memo, which argued for compulsory sterilizations, abortions, and chronic depression as means to reducing birth rates. In 1977, Perkin and several other birth control enthusiasts in Seattle founded PATH's predecessor, which worked closely with Jaffe Memo participants.[85]

In the 1980s, Perkin was hired by the UN Population Fund to give tours of Western contraceptive factories to Chinese pharmaceutical companies as China implemented its barbaric one-child policy. He and other research associates continued to work with Rockefeller and other Controligarch-backed birth control initiatives through the 1990s, when Perkin joined the Gates Foundation.[86]

The elder Gates's priorities—ultimately, the Rockefellers'—became young Bill Jr.'s priorities.

In addition to Perkin, Bill Sr. brought in Suzanne Cluett, another Planned Parenthood director who happened to be his neighbor and a close friend, to help him run his son's early charitable endeavor.[87]

Bill Sr. has been called "the conscience of the Gates family," and Bill Jr. credits his father with shaping the foundation and turning it into a philanthropic juggernaut. Perkin was the brains behind Gates's population control initiatives and the creation of the Global Alliance for Vaccines and Immunization (Gavi).[88]

The population control pipeline of Rockefeller alums to Gates Foundation leadership continues to the present day. The current president of Global Development at the Gates Foundation, Christopher Elias, worked for the Rockefellers' Population Council before succeeding Perkin as president of PATH. These decades-long relationships date back to when Bill Jr. was a child, which means that the Gates Foundation's priorities have always been driven by forces larger than the whims of a tech mogul.[89]

The William H. Gates Foundation began with an endowment of $106 million. In 1999, the foundation merged with the Gates Learning Foundation (a much smaller education-related initiative) to form the Bill & Melinda Gates Foundation. That year, Gates poured a staggering $15 billion into his new megafoundation, turning it into America's largest nonprofit almost overnight.[90]

Within a few years, Gates's and Buffett's tax-mitigating transfers would balloon the Gates Foundation's assets to over $60 billion. The more money Gates gave to his foundation, the less he paid in taxes and the more his investments apparently benefited. His net worth continued to climb, particularly when he added $26 billion to his *personal* holdings in the first year of the pandemic.[91]

And his public image soared. Once reviled in the mainstream press, Bill Gates was described as a hero soon after setting up the Bill & Melinda Gates Foundation, and by 2005, the couple were celebrated as *Time* magazine's "Persons of the Year."[92]

The Gates business model works like this: Bill Gates personally invests his money in some new venture. Then his foundation pours millions (or even billions) into ensuring that his venture takes off. Occasionally, he funnels his personal profits back into his foundation and calls it charity while taking sizable tax refunds. It is hardly a unique business model—the Rockefellers, George Soros, Warren Buffett, and other billionaires do the same thing. Gates's Giving Pledge is essentially one (legal) tax-avoidance scheme with the added benefit of buying good publicity.

A close friend of Bill Gates Jr. since 1978, Andrew Evans had worked with Microsoft before the company got its big break with IBM. Gates became the godfather of all three of Evans's children, and they remained close friends even after Evans and his wife were convicted of swindling a Seattle-based bank. Evans and his wife went to prison in the mid-1980s, and when they were released, Gates hired this convicted felon to manage his money.[93]

After his release from prison, Evans set up a company called Dominion Income Management and began trading stocks on Gates's behalf. Several years before the establishment of the Bill & Melinda Gates Foundation, Dominion invested in vaccine maker Novavax. Novavax has since received more than $100 million in grants from the Bill & Melinda Gates Foundation to develop vaccines, and its efforts to produce a COVID-19 vaccine were highlighted on Gates's personal blog.[94]

In May 2020, an entity called the Coalition for Epidemic Preparedness Innovations (CEPI) extended $384 million in grants and forgivable loans to Novavax to speed up the development of a COVID-19 vaccine. That financial package (partially funded by taxpayers) helped Novavax produce a vaccine and led to $476 million in revenue for 2020.[95]

Gates's funding of Novavax's research over the years via the Bill & Melinda Gates Foundation demonstrates Gates's long-term commitment to his vaccine business model. And the taxpayer-funded financial package that led to a nine-figure COVID windfall for Novavax showed vaccines can be a very good business model indeed.

As previously mentioned, Gates's foundation poured more than $10 billion into vaccination efforts, which he claimed netted the world a $200 billion return. Part of these efforts included funding collaborators on the controversial "gain of function" virus research at the Wuhan Institute of Virology lab (the Gates and Rockefeller foundations along with Dr. Fauci's agency also funded this research).[96]

Gates's Wuhan connection is the culmination of more than a decade of gain-of-function virus research. When a virus is genetically modified, as with gain of function, the new Frankenstein-esque virus becomes known as a chimera virus, named after the mythical snake-goat-lion hybrid beast.

Chimeric viruses have been under development for decades for use as bioweapons. The Soviets were working on weaponizing smallpox in the late 1980s, and evidence suggests that work continued even after the Soviet Union fell. The Gates Foundation has had chimeric viruses on its radar since at least 2005 and spent more than $6 million in one year alone (2016) to study these viruses.[97]

As it happens, scientists had been genetically modifying coronaviruses such as SARS-CoV-1 (2002) and SARS-CoV-2 (2019) and creating chimeric viruses for more than a decade before the COVID-19 pandemic. President Obama banned the risky research in 2014, which forced the NIH and others to outsource gain-of-function operations to China and other risk-tolerant nations.[98]

EcoHealth Alliance, meanwhile, has worked with the Wuhan lab for more than fifteen years, pulling bats out of Chinese caves and anally swabbing them to find more coronaviruses to turn into chimeras. The ostensible purpose of this research is to develop vaccines in preparation for hypothetical future pandemics.[99]

Notably, Gates, Fauci, and others affiliated with the Wuhan lab and Eco-Health sided with the Chinese government (which they repeatedly praised for its response) on the lab leak versus natural origin debate, and allied outlets were quick to dismiss the lab leak theory as xenophobic conspiracy theories.[100]

Thousands of coronaviruses have been discovered since SARS, but thus far only seven have been found to infect humans. In addition to the original SARS virus and the newer one that causes COVID-19, other human-afflicting coronaviruses include the Middle East Respiratory Syndrome (MERS) virus, as well as others ranging from the mild virus that causes the common cold to the often-fatal pneumonia virus (Gates has funded research into these coronaviruses for well over a decade).[101]

One institute that the Gates Foundation funded was able to patent several methods for administering coronavirus vaccines for livestock in 2014. The institute has stated that the Gates Foundation did not fund the specific patents, a distinction with minimal difference. And while Gates was funneling cash into virus research, he was also funding a novel way to treat them.[102]

CEPI became one of the channels for Gates's decades-long interest in viruses and vaccines. The coalition was conceived in 2015 (by at least one scientist closely tied to Gates and EcoHealth Alliance), and soon Gates became the key backer. In January 2017, Gates announced during his WEF keynote speech in Davos that the coalition had secured nearly half a billion dollars in funding.[103]

CEPI was effectively a slush fund for global vaccine development that would provide grants, loans, and other financial incentives to large pharmaceutical companies in order to help speed up the mass rollout of vaccines. In addition to the Gates Foundation, CEPI's funding partners include the WEF, the governments of Germany and Japan, and the Wellcome Trust, one of the world's most influential NGOs, which describes itself as a "biomedical research charity."[104]

A frequent Gates partner, the Wellcome Trust is closely affiliated with the British Royal Family, and Her Majesty the Queen officially opened its London headquarters in late 2004.[105]

Thanks to the Gates Foundation and CEPI, it did not take years or even months to design the Moderna and Pfizer mRNA gene therapies. It did not even take a week. It took only a couple of *days* for Moderna (and just three *hours* for Inovio) after learning the genetic sequence of the virus. *How was it possible to do this so quickly?* The answer was provided by none other than Bill Gates.[106]

In an April 2020 interview that was broadcast on the Microsoft-owned LinkedIn social media platform, Gates explained that he had knowledge that his audience could not comprehend because, unlike him, they "haven't spent much time on these issues." The secret that Gates knew was that an unproven new technology was in the works that, while risky, could revolutionize the billion-dollar vaccine industry.[107]

In Gates's experience, developing traditional vaccines (using a dead or weakened form of the virus) can take a decade or more. As everyone knows, there are many viral diseases (especially prior coronaviruses, such as SARS, and even the common cold) for which there are no vaccines, despite considerable funding from Gates and Rockefeller types. That is far too long for an impatient innovator such as Gates, which is why he has plowed billions of dollars into a new technology called mRNA gene therapy.

Gates was proud of his effort to finance mRNA solutions to COVID-19 and told his audience so:

> There's about a hundred efforts in the world, of which about eight to ten are very promising. And we have to back all of these. About four of them are based on a new approach—which is RNA/DNA—and that's like CureVac, Moderna, BioNTech, Inovio—all of these are people funded by the Gates Foundation because we were going to use that platform to make vaccines for things like malaria, and we've always known that investing in this both directly and through a group we created called CEPI . . . would get the world to be more ready for the pandemic.[108]

The speed with which the jabs were developed was bewildering. There were no human trials for long-term safety or efficacy. Equally bizarre was the *way* the jabs were developed. "On January 11, 2020, the Chinese authorities shared the genetic sequence of the novel coronavirus," Moderna stated in a filing with the Securities and Exchange Commission (SEC). Within forty-eight hours, Moderna had "mobilized toward clinical manufacture," and Dr. Fauci's institute within the National Institutes of Health was ready to conduct Phase I trials.[109]

But Moderna had been working on delivering proof of concept for the revolutionary new mRNA technology well before the pandemic even began. Moderna's chief medical officer explained the technology in a December 2017 TED Talk titled "The Disease-Eradicating Potential of Gene Editing." Moderna's gene therapies were "hacking the software of life." The ambitious goal for mRNA was to eliminate every disease from Alzheimer's to Zika and especially every form of cancer.[110]

In October 2019, Dr. Fauci appeared on a panel with fellow immunologist Dr. Rick Bright to discuss the future of vaccines. Over the course of the panel, Fauci said that traditional vaccines take too long and pushed repeatedly for a "much better" system: mRNA. Bright, who had previously worked on Gates-funded research (and for the CDC, Novavax, and PATH), issued this stunning hypothetical:

> It is not too crazy to think that an outbreak of a novel avian virus could occur in China somewhere. We could get the RNA sequence from that and beam it to a number of regional centers, if not local, if not even in your home at some point, and print those vaccines on a patch to be self-administered.[111]

Less than seventy-five days later, that is exactly what happened (sans the print-at-home vaccine patches). As Moderna told its investors, the Chinese authorities *did* beam the coronavirus gene sequences around the world and the pharmaceutical companies were off to the races. The transdermal vaccine "patches" are likely coming—Gates has made major grants to the research and owns stakes in the corporate patent holders.[112]

In theory, the COVID-19 jabs would spread synthetic mRNA throughout the human body to program the human cells to act like antibody factories. As fear was spreading throughout the world in early 2020, many began to look to Gates as a savior. The executives at Pfizer, Moderna, and other mRNA producers were not giving highly publicized and reassuring interviews that demystified this unproven technology. But Gates was.[113]

"You essentially turn your body into its own vaccine manufacturing unit," Gates explained on his blog in April 2020. "There's a catch, though," he warned. "We don't know for sure yet if RNA is a viable platform for vaccines." The world was about to find out.[114]

In simplified terms, mRNA is a software update for the human body. It can encourage or discourage bodily functions by reprogramming the human body's response to exterior influences. Billionaire futurist Elon Musk took the exciting promise of mRNA miracles a step further and suggested that mRNA gene therapies could hack aging—"like a computer program," he said—and possibly even cure death.[115]

The Controligarchs seem to think that this miraculous medicine could, in the words of the Gates-funded British Broadcasting Corporation (BBC), "make us superhuman."[116]

If it sounds like these billionaires and bureaucrats are playing God, it is because that is exactly what they are doing.[117]

Gates's Final Form: Programmer of Human Genetics

Thanks in large part to his parents' connections, Bill Gates has lived several lives. The first life was Bill Gates, the hard-nosed capitalist and computer monopolist. The second life was Bill Gates, the zealous billionaire philanthropist. And the third life is Bill Gates, the population control fanatic masquerading as a global health expert. His ruthless zeal in each of these endeavors could be rivaled only by that of the Rockefellers (whom Gates considered role models and mentors).

As Gates preached his vaccine evangel, few outside the very small world of epidemiology could have fathomed that a coronavirus vaccine would be available within a matter of months. Most existing vaccines had taken years or even decades to develop—and even longer to test for safety and efficacy and, finally, to manufacture.

As time went on, study after study confirmed suspicions that the mRNA jabs could come with more than a few devastating side effects. Scientists and doctors from leading medical institutions such as Johns Hopkins and MIT (and even a Nobel Prize winner) linked the jabs to serious heart problems such as myocarditis, stroke-inducing blood clots, and perhaps the most frightening side effect of all: signs of fertility issues in both men and women.[118]

But Gates maintained that vaccine injuries, which would have been discovered earlier with more robust safety trials, were rare even as reports of adverse events surged. When parliamentarians in the European Union questioned Pfizer's representative about the lack of safety testing, the Pfizer rep claimed that mRNA jab manufacturers were moving "at the speed of science." One parliamentarian described the admissions as "shocking, even criminal."[119]

It turns out that vaccinating in the middle of a pandemic (rather than before) may be futile, at best. Many viruses—especially fast-mutating coronaviruses like the one that causes the "common cold"—have proved impossible to vaccinate against despite billions of dollars spent over decades of research (recall that the Rockefellers had spent forty years attempting to eradicate yellow fever, unsuccessfully, and Gates and company have spent roughly the same amount of time trying to create an HIV vaccine).[120]

The tricky nature of coronaviruses and the fact that there had never been a coronavirus vaccine make Gates's insistence that the world vaccinate its way out of the pandemic so bizarre. The mRNA jabs (with their seemingly endless "booster" regimen) have been extremely profitable—Pfizer set a revenue record by bringing in more than $100 billion in 2022. And Moderna is now projected to become the first trillion-dollar drug company.[121]

But was profitability the only driver behind Gates's efforts? Surely not. Population control is also a big motivator for Gates, especially considering his status as a founding member of the Good Club. And in addition to calling vaccines his greatest investment, Gates has repeatedly claimed that inoculations help to curb population growth.

It did not take long for billionaires and multinational corporations around the world to follow Gates's lead and demand mRNA-jab mandates. How were they all on the same page? One organization in Davos, Switzerland, may hold the key.

When Gates took the stage in Davos to announce the new international CEPI vaccine slush fund in January 2017, hardly anyone knew that the World Economic Forum would become ground zero for all things pandemic-related. When Gates again partnered with the WEF for a pandemic exercise in October 2019—just weeks before the coronavirus escaped either nature or the Wuhan lab—again, almost no one noticed.

But soon, many people recognized that higher-ups within the WEF had more sweeping designs—not just related to international health policy but also affecting nearly every facet of human life—that would hand more power to men such as Bill Gates.

It was called the Great Reset.

3

The Great Reset

I don't know how it will play out in November [2020], but what we
know is that we will end up with many more unemployed. . . . So, we
will see definitively a lot of anger . . . because this crisis will be with
us until we really have found a remedy. So, we have to prepare for a
more angry world. . . . I see the need for action. I see the need
for a Great Reset.[1]

—*Klaus Schwab, WEF founder, July 2020*

When an exotic Chinese virus first appeared in the United States
in January 2020, most Americans were blissfully unaware of the
new contagion. Soon, however, SARS-CoV-2, and the disease that it caused,
COVID-19, would be all that anyone could think about. Some believed that it
was the next plague—capable of wiping out tens of millions of people. Others
believed that it was no worse than the common cold.

But like Bill Gates, a few Controligarchs saw it as an opportunity. Notable
among them was a man named Klaus Schwab, a little-known German business
professor for whom the arrival of COVID was a true meeting of a man
and his moment. Schwab had spent decades developing a grand theory for
reordering the world, and now, he believed, the world was ready to embrace it.

In July 2020, six months after the first American COVID patient was
hospitalized, the global outlook was grim. There was no clear and convincing consensus coming from such health experts as Dr. Anthony Fauci and
his colleagues about the *true* mortality rate of the coronavirus. Worse than

the uncertainty about COVID's lethality, perhaps, was the experts' certainty that draconian control measures would work. These measures—including lockdowns and the designation of people into "essential" and "nonessential" categories—appeared to be taking a greater toll than that of the virus itself. People wondered: *What happens if I can't work? How will I feed my family?*

It was at this critical moment that Schwab stepped onto the world stage.

Situated in front of a sky-blue World Economic Forum logo at a virtual event in July 2020, the man who promised to save the world hardly seemed an imposing figure. Schwab is an elderly man with a slight paunch, a deeply wrinkled face, and sagging eyes that sit behind rimless spectacles. His shaved head and thick German accent evoke a parody of a movie villain.

But Schwab is anything but funny. Indeed, people who matter—from kings to presidents to titans of industry—take the professor and WEF founder quite seriously. The television reporter running the interview—CNBC's Karen Tso—effectively surrendered the microphone to her subject. Schwab said that he could not guess who would win the American presidential election in a few months, but he knew that whatever the outcome, stormy times lay ahead. He predicted massive unemployment, "so we will see definitively a lot of anger." Many industries, he continued, "will have difficulties to survive."[2]

But Schwab proposed a remedy: "I see the need for a Great Reset."[3]

The Great Reset turned the COVID-19 chaos into an opportunity for the Controligarchs. As Schwab put it, to "tie government aid to the green economy" and to "revolutionize" and "digitalize" everything. He called the virus a "call for action" to address global warming and hoped that "this COVID crisis will create sufficient drive for each government to be more open for global cooperation." Schwab assured his audience that his "Great Reset" was a way to "recreate a global framework which really is in line with the requirements of a society in the twenty-first century."[4]

The average person, especially in the United States, had never heard of Schwab. But global leaders, corporate titans, and Big Tech oligarchs—many of whom are among the more than 1,400 WEF members collectively worth trillions of dollars and counting—feel his influence. This positions him perfectly to steer global operations without compromising his public image.

Schwab identified at least five major opportunities that COVID presented to the world. First, the world could redefine the social contract to be "more inclusive." Second, the pandemic could be used to "decarbonize the economy." Third, "everything that can be digitalized must be digitalized" under something Schwab termed the "Fourth Industrial Revolution." Fourth, companies could use the pandemic to rethink their profit motive and transition to a new system he called "stakeholder capitalism." And finally, the Great Reset meant more global cooperation or "global governance."[5]

To his audience and those paying close attention, the tenets of Schwab's Great Reset had a ring of familiarity. That is because the WEF and its affiliated organizations, such as the United Nations and the Club of Rome, had been sounding such themes for years (in fact, the Club of Rome's co-president co-wrote an appeal for a post-pandemic green energy transition that the WEF published before Schwab announced his book on the topic).[6]

Evidence of the pervasiveness of Schwab's ideas among the international elite could be seen in then presidential candidate Joe Biden's announcement of a plan to "Build Back Better," whose proposals were eerily similar to Schwab's Great Reset agenda. From then on, at campaign stops and on social media, Biden insisted that Build Back Better was *his plan*. It was not. Biden was not even the first world leader to utter the mantra.[7]

On May 28, 2020—forty-two days before Biden announced the new campaign slogan—British prime minister Boris Johnson proudly announced that "we owe it to future generations to build back better," which he said meant rebuilding a "fairer, greener, and more resilient global economy." So, Johnson used the slogan before Biden and later admitted that he had "nicked it from someone else."[8]

Johnson was no stranger to Schwab's economic agenda. A decade earlier, while mayor of London, Johnson had spoken at a WEF event for Schwab's Forum of Young Global Leaders, an incubator of sorts for rising political stars.[9]

Johnson's Davos connections could help to explain why he boasted that his country had become the largest single donor to CEPI, the global vaccine consortium backed by the WEF, Bill Gates's foundation, Pfizer, Johnson & Johnson, and the WHO, among others.[10]

Under Schwab's leadership, the WEF has declared a bold agenda. Among its ambitions are the abolition of private property and personal privacy, the elimination of fossil fuels, and a global transition away from animal protein to an insect-based food system. "You'll own nothing," the WEF has famously assured, ominously adding, "and you'll be happy."[11]

The forum has been very open about its plans for the entire world to eliminate cash in favor of a tightly controlled digital financial system. The complementary digital identification regime that the WEF has long demanded seemed like a solution in search of a problem—until COVID created an opening for unforgeable vaccine passports.[12]

For decades, the WEF was known simply as "Davos," after the glitzy town in the Swiss Alps where these global elites flock for the forum's annual retreat. The Davos Man (the prototypical attendee) is an individual who possesses the "Davos Spirit." The price of attendance to schmooze with Team Schwab is wealth, power, or prestige—or, ideally, all three. Mere "members" pay around $65,000 for the privilege while esteemed "partners" can pay $650,000 or more.[13]

Davos Man's reasons for his alpine pilgrimage are many. But at its most basic level, Davos provides a venue for worldly bureaucrats and plutocrats to hobnob and strike deals—far from the prying eyes of their constituents and haters—all with the stated purpose of saving the planet. Even the Davos attendees who may not support its global governance technocratic agenda admit that they go for a very simple reason: to wheel and deal.[14]

To people such as Schwab, the WEF, and our Good Club members from Chapter One (most of whom help set the WEF agenda), COVID-19 was an opportunity to help save the world from itself. We could all build back as a stakeholder utopia, together, better than any system ever.

The Great Reset was for our own good.

The Nazi Road to World Citizenship

Like Rockefeller and Gates, Schwab had power that was not created in a vacuum.

Klaus Martin Schwab was born on March 30, 1938, in Ravensburg, southern Germany—roughly halfway between Munich and Zurich and close to the Swiss border. At the time, Ravensburg was the epicenter of the early Nazi eugenics program and became the first city to forcibly sterilize citizens by the hundreds.[15]

Schwab's father, Eugen Wilhelm Schwab, was the managing director of a Zurich-based subsidiary of an engineering firm called Escher Wyss, which was a major supplier in the Nazi war effort and one of Adolf Hitler's Nationalsozialistischer Musterbetrieb, or a "model" Nazi company.[16]

Eugen Schwab was, himself, a Nazi collaborator. He belonged to several German National Socialist groups, including two of the most prominent pro-Nazi organizations: the German Labour Front and the National Socialist People's Welfare. His Ravensburg branch of Escher Wyss used war prisoner slave labor to manufacture industrial war machinery.[17]

Working for Escher Wyss, Eugen represented Swiss interests in Germany while the engineering firm had business contracts with Nazi mineral companies and for the manufacture of flamethrowers, presumably for use against Allied soldiers. The firm had an impressive technological track record and even built a turbine for a plutonium nuclear reactor—one of the first in the world—for Nazi military use.[18]

During his father's tenure working with the Nazis, Klaus was too young for involvement in Hitler's regime. But growing up in wartime Germany almost surely left a lasting mark on the boy. It seems that he was unable to associate his national identity with Germany amid the chaos of the failed Nazi regime, and so instead he became a citizen of the world.[19]

Klaus Schwab followed his father's footsteps and became an engineer. He credited his parents for teaching him the value of education, collaboration, and the idea that would become central to his worldview: the "stakeholder principle."[20]

After graduating from high school in 1957 and college in 1962 with a degree in mechanical engineering, Schwab landed his first major gig in 1963 as a personal assistant to the managing director of the German Machine-Building Association. He worked there until 1966 and earned a PhD at the Swiss Federal Institute of Technology that same year.[21]

Schwab received an economics doctorate the following year at the University of Freiburg and a master's in public administration from Harvard's John F. Kennedy School of Government. It was at Harvard that Schwab met one of his earliest and most powerful mentors: US foreign policy author Henry Kissinger (a close friend, confidante, and handsomely paid advisor to the Rockefellers).[22]

Soon, Schwab's career took off. In 1967, Schwab joined the management board of Sulzer-Escher Wyss AG, a merged successor entity of the Nazi wartime supplier where his father worked in Zurich.[23]

While still working for the Swiss engineering firm, his former employer— the German Machine-Building Association—commissioned Schwab to write his first book: a manifesto on modern management techniques in mechanical engineering. The book, published in 1971, was designed to address management methods and their applications to competition and opens with the following words from a member of the association's executive board:

> No war, no strike, however long, no serious economic crisis can restrict the development opportunities of a national industrial sector as much as modern, more successful management methods in the hands of the competitive industries in other countries.[24]

Schwab argued that as companies grow, they can reduce costs but warns that similar innovation by corporate rivals "often results in fierce price competition, which depending on the severity and duration of this competition can squeeze profits or even cause losses." If a company wants to increase its market share, one of Schwab's recommendations is the "temporary or complete elimination of competitors."[25]

The book also laid out the earliest version of Schwab's "stakeholder economy," which is the first pillar of the Great Reset. This theory contends that companies should be responsible not solely to shareholders but rather to an amorphous group of "stakeholders."[26]

Schwab described the theory in a 2010 *Wall Street Journal* op-ed:

> Almost 40 years ago, I first developed the "stakeholder theory" for businesses at the World Economic Forum in Davos, Switzerland. This considers the enterprise as a community with a number of stakeholders—in other words, social groups that are directly and indirectly connected to the enterprise and that are dependent on its success and prosperity. These groups include employees, customers, suppliers, the state and especially the society in which the enterprise is active.[27]

Schwab adapted this stakeholder concept into a brand-new economic system he calls stakeholder capitalism. It seems like a humane idea, on its face; after all, it is true that a business's fortunes impact people, entities, and communities far beyond its own corridors. But what is new, and slightly diabolical, about Schwab's formulation is its subtle but profound reordering of the dynamics between business and its community stakeholders.

Under traditional free-market capitalism, the top priority for business is profit for itself and shareholders; and benefits to the "stakeholder community" flow from that in the form of jobs, revenue generation, et cetera. But if the profit motive is mitigated by the elevation of the "community good" as a prime consideration, then someone must decide what that is. Thus, this gave rise to a powerful new class of experts whose prescriptions for the community good naturally reflect their own ideological agendas.

Stakeholder capitalism looks strikingly like China's tyrannical "state capitalism" model (which was actually developed with the help of Kissinger, Rockefeller, and the WEF) and is enjoying popularity among governments

worldwide, particularly in the area of a corporate social-credit system commonly known as Environmental, Social, and Governance (or ESG) scores.
More on these later.[28]

Schwab's work in the private sector for the Swiss engineering firm was
short lived, and although nearly fifty years would pass before Schwab
penned his next stakeholder manifesto, he spent that time building a multinational machine—the WEF—that would become the primary driving force
for the replacement of democracy and capitalism with a far more radical
system.[29]

Schwab found a receptive audience for his vision among powerful internationalists, including his Harvard mentor, Kissinger—a regular WEF attendee and keynote speaker. Industry titans like the Rockefellers and Bill
Gates had already formed more secretive groups such as the Good Club, the
Trilateral Commission, the Bilderberg Group, the Council on Foreign Relations, and the Club of Rome. These key global influencers were early supporters of the WEF and among its first contributors.[30]

Schwab created the Davos forum in 1971 to promote his stakeholder
system and headquartered it in Geneva, Switzerland. The WEF's self-
proclaimed mission is to "shape global, regional and industry agendas" and
does so thanks to its "unique institutional culture founded on the stakeholder theory, which asserts that an organization is accountable to all parts
of society."[31]

The Davos forum began as an excuse for wealthy business executives
to take "a delightful vacation on the expense account," according to *Time*
magazine in 1981. But with every passing year, the forum's cachet grew along
with the prestige of its membership, and by the 1990s, its cheerleading for
globalization earned the WEF a strongly positive reputation among globalist decision-makers and multinational corporations alike.[32]

Not long before Clinton made him one of America's top diplomats, renowned globalist Strobe Talbott declared in 1992 that "nationhood as we
know it will be obsolete; all states will recognize a single, global authority.
A phrase briefly fashionable in the mid-twentieth century—'citizen of the

world'—will have assumed real meaning by the end of the twenty-first."
There can be little doubt that Talbott and other supporters of a single, global
authority came to view the WEF (which Talbott later commended for its
"high-powered commission on global governance") as the entity that could
make nationhood obsolete.[33]

For the corporate elite around the world, Davos became an opportunity
to virtue signal. Spending a few days participating in group therapy sessions
on global warming made them feel better about their private jet use each
year. *New York Times* reporter and Davos Man biographer Peter S. Goodman explains the phenomenon this way:

> Schwab has constructed a refuge for the outlandishly wealthy, an
> exclusive zone where they are free to pursue deals and sundry she-
> nanigans while enjoying the cover of participating in a virtuous under-
> taking. Their mere presence in Davos at the Forum signals their
> empathy and sensitivity.[34]

The WEF Champions a Death to Democracy

For Americans and for much of the free world, Schwab's stakeholder capitalism has one major flaw that Davos Men prefer to gloss over. While stakeholder capitalism promises a technocratic, utopian future, it is inherently
antidemocratic.

Technocracy is a form of government where the leaders are not elected
but selected based on their expertise. Therefore, technocratic leaders are
not beholden to voters. In recent years, they have mastered the use of go-to
phrases such as the increasingly popular "Trust the science," whereby voters are encouraged to not question the so-called experts.

The WEF does not, however, care to hide this fact. In one early 2018 post
titled "It's Time for a New Social Contract," the WEF contributor states
rather ominously that "democracy is becoming collateral damage in a world
where global risks have been ignored or exacerbated by those with the

power to act." The post was an oblique shot at then president Donald Trump, and the author bemoaned the closure of borders and the "rising wave of misogyny," while he praised the corporate executives who committed to the UN's Sustainable Development Goals and Paris climate accords (both of which the American president eschewed).[35]

In another WEF post titled "How Do People View Democracy?," WEF-affiliated pollsters from the Pew Research Center write favorably on technocracy as a system "in which experts, not elected officials, make decisions." In addition, the WEF collaborators claim to have polling data showing that public opinion prefers (overwhelmingly, in some cases) a technocratic system.[36]

As the root words imply, a technocratic system relies on technical expertise, especially in the management of systems, processes, and people. The evolution of technology—particularly computers that can process large data sets upon which the "experts" can base their decisions—has led to a technocratic renaissance. It should come as no surprise that the rise of computers tracks closely with the rise of technocratic WEF proposals and directives.

The WEF, Rockefeller, and the Persistent Overpopulation Myth

The WEF's technocratic dreams began like so many of the technological advances in the twentieth century: with Rockefeller funding.

In the 1930s, Rockefeller developed some of the first computer technology that resulted in the Rockefeller Differential Analyzer. In 1971, the president of the Rockefeller Brothers Fund approached a computing pioneer, MIT systems engineer Jay Forrester, at a North Atlantic Treaty Organization (NATO) conference and offered to fund his work directly.[37]

Forrester's analysis led to *The Limits to Growth* (*"Limits"*), a report published in 1972 by the Rockefeller- and WEF-linked Club of Rome. And Schwab's early Davos precursor, the European Management Symposium, heavily promoted the *Limits* report. A decade before Bill Gates's Microsoft unveiled even the rawest version of the analytical Excel spreadsheet, Forrester's crude computer models predicted dire outcomes for the planet unless its preconceived solutions were immediately implemented.[38]

Even though *Limits* was quickly and credibly refuted by independent scientists who blasted the report for its faulty modeling techniques, the report refused to die. Thanks to its proponents and media mouthpieces, the report continues to serve as a tool to bludgeon laypeople into accepting technocratic solutions to every global crisis from poverty to climate change.[39]

Through the WEF, Schwab has repeatedly touted the *Limits* theses. And his Great Reset plan marched in lockstep with the Club of Rome's parallel agenda. For example, when CoR called for a post-pandemic "Green Reboot"—a mere two weeks after the pandemic began and months before Schwab announced his Great Reset—the CoR again touted the *Limits* report and completely ignored its failed predictions.[40]

Forrester's "business as usual" model predicted that failure to implement technocratic policies ensured dire outcomes for planet Earth—primarily a total collapse of civilization due to the overconsumption of resources. The "stabilized world" model was the ideal scenario—one in which global leaders channeled the Davos Spirit (and adopted Schwab's playbook) with a familiar ruthless zeal.[41]

The Achilles heel of *Limits'* conclusions—and all doomsday predictions—is that its models fail to account for two things: first, discoveries of new resources and new technologies and, second, the most valuable resource of all: human ingenuity, which leads to adaptation. The omission of mankind's adaptability is a *fundamental* flaw that continues to plague doomsday prophets at the WEF and CoR today.

The Limits to Growth spilled considerable ink discussing population (or birth) control. The authors devised a formula for calculating a family's decision whether to have children. They assigned variables that allowed them to estimate the "value" of a child compared with the "cost." According to the report:

The "value" of a child includes monetary considerations, such as the child's labor contribution to the family farm or business and the eventual dependence on the child's support when the parents reach old age. As a country becomes industrialized, child labor laws, compulsory education, and social security provisions all reduce the potential monetary value of a child.

The cost of a child was determined by factors such as "financial outlays" and the "opportunity costs of the mother's time devoted to child care," as well as the "increased responsibility and decreased freedom of the family as a whole." If the value decreases and the (perceived) cost increases, this reasoning held, families will have fewer children.[42]

As new resources were discovered, the idea that the overconsumption of resources would lead to civilization's collapse fell out of fashion. In response, the Club of Rome promoted a new model that doubled its previous peak resource assumptions. In the *Limits* updates—published decades later—society still was predicted to collapse but not because of a lack of resources.[43]

The new downfall was due to catastrophic "global warming"—a term that does not appear in the 1972 *Limits* manifesto and only begins to surface in obscure Controligarch-backed studies several years later.[44]

The pivot from apocalyptic resource depletion to apocalyptic global warming was significant and enduring. Hyping pollution as a global cataclysmic threat kicked off the "climate change" hysteria that has reached a fever pitch in recent years. The 1991 CoR report had uttered the quiet part aloud: "We came up with the idea that pollution, the threat of global warming, water shortages, famine and the like, would fit the bill. . . . The real enemy then is humanity itself."[45]

It is much easier to generate fear about pollution than it is to persuade the world that resources are running out. After all, starvation-level poverty has been on a steady decline for decades, and the earth is covered in water. Human ingenuity and adaptation, as mentioned, can solve resource shortages with innovations in agriculture and water desalinization technology.

Pollution as a global common enemy has the added marketing benefit of frightening optics, such as smog-belching factories, so-called holes in the ozone layer, starving polar bears trapped on melting icebergs, and plastic straws stuck in the nostrils of sea turtles. And as each terrifying image inevitably loses its shock value—new carbon scrubbers filter pollutants emitted from smokestacks, the ozone layer appears to be fine, ice caps are growing, the polar bear population is stable, and the massive "garbage patch" floating in the Pacific is teeming with biodiversity—new terrors arise.

Today's climate alarmism relies on an endless fear-based media cycle. Common historical weather events—such as forest fires, hurricanes, heat waves, and even snowstorms—are used as evidence that humans cause climate change.[46]

The Limits manifesto is conveniently updated on an ongoing basis. The models and algorithms are tweaked to ensure that new arbitrary data sets result in the same dire outcomes. *Limits to Growth: The 30-Year Update*, published in 2004, concluded:

> We do not have another 30 years to dither. Much will have to change
> if the ongoing overshoot is not to be followed by collapse during the
> twenty-first century.[47]

And the most recent update, in May 2022, titled *The Limits to Growth Model: Still Prescient 50 Years Later*, completely whitewashed the failures of its previous models, which were simply and innocently "recalibrated." Despite all the ecological progress that has been made since the original 1972 report, the 2022 authors lamented that the Club of Rome's and WEF's technocratic diktats have been "ignored" and have thus left "humanity [still] on the brink of collapse." The "battle for humanity's soul" will be lost if the world does not immediately adopt the CoR-WEF agenda.[48]

The WEF agenda manifests itself as innocuous-sounding policy prescriptions that are peddled under the aegis of the United Nations. The UN gives a patina of legitimacy to the multinational corporations' demands for technocracy and implies that WEF policy prescriptions are, like the UN it-self, for the good of mankind.

The Evolving Agenda to Use
Crises for Control

The first major WEF policy prescription scheme laundered through the UN was called Agenda 21—a 1992 plan to reset the trajectory of the twenty-first century and included scores of action items and goals, ostensibly to avert global catastrophes.[49]

Predictably, Agenda 21 was all about control and touched on the follow-ing: drought control; desertification control; agriculture control; erosion control; control of land use; chemical control; pollution and effluent (or sew-age) control; coastal erosion control; biological, physical, and cultural con-trol; resource control systems; oil and gas platform control; border control; and disease control.[50]

Agenda 21 also pushed for the development of "new drugs" and robust immunization- and vaccination-control schemes. Several years after the 1992 Agenda 21 was set, Bill Gates, a frequent WEF contributor and then the world's wealthiest man, would latch on to this immunization aspect of global control with the creation of his eponymous foundation.[51]

Unlike the WEF, the UN has the authority to implement these controls under global conventions and treaties like the "United Nations Convention on the Law of the Sea." While the forum does not have the power to regulate policies such as emissions and pollution, individual governments do. Push-ing the WEF's control measures through UN conventions is a clever way to tie governments' hands and push them to implement the Davos agenda. In fact, without the UN's imprimatur, Schwab is mostly powerless.[52]

In 2000, the United Nations followed up Agenda 21 with the much more streamlined "Millennium Development Goals."[53]

The list was simple if not bromidic:

1. Eradicate extreme poverty and hunger;

2. Achieve universal primary education;

3. Promote gender equality and empower women;

4. Reduce child mortality;

5. Improve maternal health;

6. Combat HIV/AIDS, malaria, and other diseases;

7. Ensure environmental sustainability; and

8. Create a global partnership for development.

While these goals sound admirable, they are euphemisms for systems of control. Just as the Rockefellers' PR agents determined that birth control should be rebranded as "maternal health," the WEF and the United Nations decided to rebrand food control as "ending poverty and hunger." For the second goal, "universal primary education" means curricula control.

"Gender equality and empower[ing] women," "child mortality," and "maternal health" all fall under the birth/population-control umbrella. "Disease eradication" (as Rockefeller discovered) means control over global health policy. "Environmental sustainability" refers to energy control. And "global partnership for development" is that familiar global governance we keep hearing about.

The new goals were supposed to be implemented by the year 2015 (presumably to avert a global catastrophe), but certain factions within countries around the world were reluctant to surrender their nation's autonomy to the United Nations and the interests behind it, such as the WEF. As it happens, implementing the technocratic agenda is costly. People love affordable fossil fuels, and not everyone loves the idea of "common core" curricula. To many, Agenda 21 soon became synonymous with the "New World Order" (another catchphrase that the Davos crowd abandoned after it became toxic).[54]

Undeterred, the UN rebranded the WEF agenda once again in 2015.

Agenda 21 became Agenda 2030 and the Millennium Development Goals became the Sustainable Development Goals.[55]

The tenets of Agenda 2030 and the Sustainable Development Goals are nearly identical to those bromides listed above. And the millennium goals have grown from a list of seven euphemisms for control to a list of seventeen Sustainable Development Goals with similarly platitudinal objectives, such as:

- End poverty in all its forms everywhere;

- Reduce inequality within and among countries;

- Take urgent action to combat climate change and its impacts; and

- Strengthen the means of implementation and revitalize the Global Partnership for Sustainable Development.[56]

As usual, there are countless reports from the WEF, the Club of Rome, and dozens of other allied think tanks and NGOs, a seemingly bottomless bowl of alphabet soup acronyms that predict the same dire outcomes if their agendas and goals are not immediately implemented. It seems as if fear is the central component of the globalist business model.[57]

Crucially, while the branding continues to change, the solutions remain largely the same and can be summed up simply: the entire world must adopt Klaus Schwab's stakeholder capitalism model and the WEF's technocratic global governance political structure, or we could all perish. And nearly every Davos Man—a globalist through and through—has found his way to benefit from the taxpayer-financed WEF agenda.

Schwab's Great Reset manifesto distills Agenda 2030 and the sustainable goals down to three basic categories: stakeholder capitalism, ESG scores, and the Fourth Industrial Revolution. Each is more alarming than the last.

Stakeholder Capitalism or Crony Fascism?

Stakeholder capitalism is the first pillar of the Great Reset. While the term sounds innocent enough, the economic system that Schwab envisions is neither capitalist nor accountable to any non-WEF stakeholders. Effectively, stakeholder capitalism gives Schwab and his technocrat associates a seat on every board, much like the state-run capitalist system in Communist China, where party officials dictate outcomes and enforce orthodoxy. And there is a reason why Schwab's stakeholder capitalism model closely resembles China's: the WEF helped create China's economic system nearly fifty years ago.

Beginning in the late 1970s, Schwab and the WEF actively influenced China's economic reforms. The WEF's own records tout its role in China throughout the organization's history, especially as China modernized its society and the nation grew in importance.[58]

In 1979, Schwab traveled to Beijing to personally invite the new leader of the Chinese Communist Party (CCP), Deng Xiaoping (whom Schwab had been following "with great interest"), to speak at an early symposium in Davos. And soon after, twenty European CEOs followed WEF to China to develop the fledgling economy. While Deng declined to attend WEF personally, he sent a delegation of his economic reformers, which signaled to Schwab that the new CCP ruler was open to doing business.[59]

Beijing and Washington had been ruthless opponents in the recent Vietnam stalemate, so business contacts were largely off-limits, but Switzerland was a neutral zone where both sides could quietly interact. After the Chinese delegation visited Davos, the WEF and the CCP formed a partnership and began hosting mutual economic exchange events beginning in 1981.[60]

Next, the WEF began exporting Western economic concepts—such as joint-stock companies (rather than communal ones)—to China. The WEF's economic training in China ramped up throughout the 1980s, and in 1989, the WEF had to decide whether to hold its annual summer event after the CCP's brutal murder of student activists in Tiananmen Square. In deference to the CCP, the event "went ahead as scheduled." So, as most of the Western world shunned China after the Tiananmen Square slaughter, the WEF never wavered and helped Beijing reestablish diplomatic relations with the West.[61]

In 1997, Schwab visited China as a distinguished guest of honor, and in 2006, he opened an office in Beijing. The CCP leveraged its relationship with the WEF to burnish its image and raise its profile in the international community. Schwab and his forum were so instrumental in turning China into an economic powerhouse that it might be more accurate to say that China adopted Schwab's model rather than the other way around.[62]

Today, China is a regular participant at Davos, despite being an authoritarian Communist state. In addition, "Summer Davos" has been held annually in the People's Republic since 2007. For his part, Schwab has received lavish praise from the Chinese Communists. And CCP leader Xi Jinping awarded Schwab the Friendship Medal in 2018 for his outstanding contributions in shaping China's policies over the past four decades.[63]

Schwab's stakeholder capitalism system not only requires world governments to dramatically adjust their respective economies as needed but is also a radical departure from the free-market capitalist system that has worked well for centuries. The Controligarchs' agenda relies instead on a social-credit-score system for corporations called ESG.

Creeping Social Credit Scores: The Woke Investing ESG Scheme

Out of the stakeholder capitalism model grew ESG scores—the second pillar of the Great Reset. ESG represents the three major lines of attack that the WEF plans to wage against companies who do not possess the Davos Spirit—in other words, Davos Man's competitors.

The E in ESG means that a company must comply with the WEF's climate change agenda. The S means compliance with the WEF's social agenda (rainbow flag logos during LGBTQIA+ Pride Month, for example). However, the G (or "governance") is a bit harder to define.[64]

Since Schwab announced the importance of ESG scores in mid-2020, the results have been astonishing. As of June 2022, more than $35 trillion in worldwide assets are invested in ESG-compliant companies.[65]

Less than one year after the Great Reset was announced, banks began to "choke off" funds from fossil fuel companies (presumably those who had not yet begun to embrace the *E* and pivot toward "greener" product lines). Not only were lenders encouraged to withhold loans to oil and gas companies, but they were also urged to leverage their "most powerful tools" (such as interest rates) to coerce any clients engaged in nongreen activities and force a transition to "sustainable business models," according to a senior director at the Environmental Defense Fund. On the consumer side, shareholders could apply pressure to a financial institution that is either unwilling or slow to adopt the greener model.[66]

The *S* in ESG has led to what some are calling "woke investing"—which is apparently catching on and is even paying off in some cases. Following the 2020 George Floyd riots, institutional investors (including the $250 billion California State Teachers' Retirement System) began targeting public corporations and pressuring them to "undergo racial equity audits" and to "prioritize racial diversity issues."[67]

Certain willing and clever corporate executives have learned how to game this system. *The Intercept* reported that private prison corporations—typically not the darlings of the socially conscious Left—have been using ESG scores to their advantage by voluntarily submitting to racial equity audits.

As structured, the ESG system ensures that companies with nonwhite, nonmale, and LGBTQ leadership score higher in the equity audits. And having a "diversity, equity, and inclusion" (DEI) report can also boost a company's ESG score. Here is how it works: receiving a favorable racial equity audit and submitting a DEI report (with a corresponding ESG score) can lead to more funding from Wall Street backers seeking to invest in "socially responsible" companies.[68]

ESG scores are a test to see how well a company is complying with the WEF's technocratic agenda. Of the surveyed Fortune 100 corporations,

98 percent participate in the ESG scheme. Many seem to be true believers in Schwab's vision. Bank of America's CEO, for example, defends ESG and stakeholder capitalism as the prioritization of "profits *and* purpose."[69]

Some corporations that may not be true adherents of Schwab's vision appear to be using ESG as a way to escape bad press. Companies that could use a boost in reputation include Philip Morris, which sells 700 billion cigarettes each year, and Coca-Cola and PepsiCo, which contribute to the US diabetes crisis costing over $300 billion annually. A sizable portion of major corporations (particularly energy and finance companies) seem to be cautious about opening themselves to legal actions resulting from failure to comply with shifting ESG requirements and the omnipresent threat of losing favor with clients, lenders, and/or regulators. FTX is one example of a company whose glowing ESG score may have been a reason why it was able to avoid scrutiny.[70]

Several states across the country have taken a stand against the implementation of ESG scores. In January 2022, New Hampshire was one of the first to introduce a bill banning the use of ESG scores. One "Live Free or Die" lawmaker criticized the "self-appointed financial elite" and the "godless elites," which he claimed had "weaponized a 30-year social investing strategy and turned it into a tool of economic coercion similar to China."[71]

Since then, more than twenty-five states—including Florida, Michigan, Tennessee, Texas, Utah, Wyoming, and West Virginia—have taken similar steps to stymie the ESG scoring system. Efforts include drafting and passing legislation to ban ESG scores and divesting state pension funds from financial institutions such as BlackRock, which are pushing ESG and are closely aligned with the WEF.[72]

Creeping Dystopia: Klaus Schwab's "Fourth Industrial Revolution"

The third and final pillar of the Great Reset is to unleash what Schwab calls "the Fourth Industrial Revolution." In his book with that title, Schwab describes the "staggering confluence" of new technologies that will make his new revolution possible, including "artificial intelligence (AI), robotics, the internet of things (IoT), autonomous vehicles, 3D printing, nanotechnology, biotechnology, materials science, energy storage and quantum computing."[73] These technologies could be used to supplement increases in work-from-home arrangements, in telemedicine, as biotech solutions to illnesses, for disease surveillance, and in digital vaccine passports.

Schwab predicted that "the most recent biotechnology techniques using RNA and DNA platforms make it possible to develop vaccines faster than ever." At the time, neither Pfizer nor Moderna nor Johnson & Johnson had yet released a vaccine. And very few outside of the relatively tiny world of epidemiology guessed that untested mRNA vaccines would be the solution that technocrats such as Schwab would propose as a way to return to normalcy.

One of the WEF's agenda contributors on the Fourth Industrial Revolution technology (and someone that Schwab quotes at length in *The Great Reset*) is a man named Yuval Noah Harari. Schwab introduces Harari in a section called "The Risk of Dystopia." Realizing that his Fourth Industrial Revolution fantasies might come across like some futuristic dystopian television show (he specifically mentions the popular novel *The Handmaid's Tale* and the Netflix series *Black Mirror*), Schwab assures the public that it does not need to "fear the grip of technology on personal freedom." Schwab added that WEF-minded thinkers such as Harari carefully weigh the "fundamental choice to make between totalitarian surveillance and citizen empowerment."[74]

As a WEF agenda contributor, Harari has his vision of the future spelled out across the pages of the forum's website. He promotes innovations such as brain microchips (Elon Musk's Neuralink), virtual-reality existences (Mark Zuckerberg's metaverse), "happy pill"-style complacency drugs (Pfizer's Zoloft), and eugenics-style gene editing (Rockefeller's and Gates's CRISPR endeavors).[75]

Like Schwab, Harari has said that the COVID-19 pandemic presented a

massive opportunity to implement technocratic solutions. Biometric surveillance, for example, is a solution that few were begging for. But according
to Harari:

> COVID is critical because this is what convinces people to accept [and]
> to legitimize total biometric surveillance. If you want to stop this epi-
> demic, we need not just to monitor people, we need to monitor what's
> happening under their skin.[76]

But subdermal microchips are just the beginning. Harari has also said
that the entire human body can be "hacked" and that in the future, humans
may be able to purchase immortality through biotechnological upgrades.
For all human history, "death was the great equalizer," Harari said in an
interview. But a few generations from now, there may be a new class structure in which poor people still die but rich people "in addition to all the
other things they get, also get an exemption from death."[77]

At a 2018 forum, Harari elaborated on his prediction that human bodies
and minds will be the commodities of the future. The identity of "the future
masters of the planet," Harari said at Davos, "will be decided by the people
who own the data. Those who control the data control the future—not just
of humanity but the future of life itself."[78]

It's no wonder that those who control much of the world's data—Bill
Gates, Google's Sergey Brin, Facebook's Mark Zuckerberg, and Twitter cofounder Jack Dorsey—have all expressed an appreciation for Harari and his
writings.[79]

Harari seems particularly enthused about artificial intelligence. "We'll
soon have the power to re-engineer our bodies and brains—whether it is
with genetic engineering or by directly connecting brains to computers or
by creating completely non-organic entities [such as] artificial intelligence,"
Harari declared, adding that "these technologies are developing at break-
neck speed."[80]

Harari predicts that artificial intelligence and genetic engineering will "enable parents to create smarter or more attractive children." Harari acknowledges that these technological advancements will potentially create a new caste system when only the rich are able to genetically hack their biology and create new superhumans. He concedes that "biological inequality" could lead to more "inequality than in any previous time in history."[81]

Harari expects that humanity will face a crisis over what to do with non-elites. "The biggest question maybe in economics and politics in the coming decades will be *what to do with all these useless people*" (emphasis added).[82]

These twenty-first century "useless people" are not disabled or unfit; they are simply bored and superfluous. Not to worry, video games, TikTok, Netflix, and drugs will be able to placate them. In fact, Harari says, that is exactly what is happening now:

> The problem is more boredom, and what to do with people, and how will they find some sense of meaning in life when they are basically meaningless, worthless. My best guess at present is a combination of drugs and computer games as a solution for most . . . It's already happening.[83]

Another Controligarch solution to the useless-people problem is to simply create digital existences for them, such as Facebook founder Mark Zuckerberg's newest invention: the virtual world that he calls "the metaverse" (accessed with a virtual reality headset) in which the WEF is a major partner—more on that in Chapter Nine. As an example of this solution already in practice, Harari pointed to Japan and the phenomena of "virtual spouses" and "people who never leave the house and just live through computers."[84]

Harari is not just some fringe futurist. His books have sold more than thirty-five million copies worldwide and have been translated into sixty-five different languages. Barack Obama has promoted Harari's work, and CNN's Anderson Cooper calls Harari "one of the most popular writers and thinkers on the planet."[85]

In an interview with Cooper, Harari argues that AI will have no consciousness (nor conscience) and will therefore make decisions without the burden of human ethics. "And they will have power over us?" asked Cooper. "They are already gaining power over us," replied Harari. As an example, some financial lenders use algorithms to make loans.

"It's not just dystopian, it's also utopian," Harari says of biometric surveillance, since it can "enable us to create the best health care system in history."

COOPER: What does Pfizer want the [biometric] data of all Israelis for?

HARARI: To develop new medicines, new treatments, you need the medical data . . . And, of course, it's not all bad!

Harari acknowledges that Silicon Valley's tech oligarchs are "a bit afraid of their own power—that they have realized the immense influence they have over the world, over the course of evolution really[,] and I think that spooks, at least some of them . . . And this is why they are kind of to some extent open to listening."

The companies with the most data will control the world, according to Harari: "Data is worth much more than money." Harari used Facebook's purchase of WhatsApp and Instagram for billions of dollars as an example. Why would they do this? Because data is power. Biometric data is the crown jewel, and Harari predicts that biometric data trackers will someday be implanted beneath people's skin.

In one lecture, Harari described a future where "Netflix tells us what to watch, and Amazon tells us what to buy. Eventually within ten or twenty or thirty years, such algorithms could also tell you what to study at college, and where to work, and whom to marry, and even for whom to vote."

Harari has said that to "hack" human beings, one must get to know them better than they know themselves. He also said that Facebook or Amazon can know if a teenager is gay even before that person does by analyzing his patterns. And he added that for those citizens who live in Iran or Russia or some other homophobic country, the police could also know if a person is gay before she does.

"We are at the point when we need global cooperation. You cannot regulate the explosive power of artificial intelligence on a national level." COVID-19 seemed to validate Harari's view, much as it did those of Schwab and other Controligarchs.[86]

And to any useless peasants thinking about a revolt, do not bother. As Harari says:

> We are used to thinking about the masses as powerful, but this is basically a nineteenth-century and twentieth-century phenomenon . . . I don't think that the masses even if they somehow organize themselves stand much of a chance; we are not . . . in nineteenth-century Europe.[87]

Penetrating the World: How Schwab Grooms Political Elites

In 2004, Klaus Schwab founded another forum under the aegis of the WEF: the Forum of Young Global Leaders. Schwab's Young Global Leaders were a combination of future heads of state, industrialists, titans of business, and tech entrepreneurs. Among the very first Young Global Leaders chosen were US Senator John Sununu, then author Samantha Power (many years before she became a top advisor to both Presidents Obama and Biden), and Google cofounders Larry Page and Sergey Brin.

Within two years, Schwab had collected more than four hundred young leaders, and he chose nearly twice as many corporate players as government leaders for his 2006 class. And, as it turned out, the harshest mandates during the pandemic came from Schwab's Young Global Leaders.[88]

Schwab boasts of the WEF's ability to infiltrate world governments (in his words, "we penetrate the cabinets"). The WEF penetrated Canada long before the pandemic, but its influence there was not fully apparent until Prime Minister Justin Trudeau and his economic czar, Chrystia Freeland, began rolling out draconian lockdowns and unilaterally abolishing basic civil rights.[89]

In New Zealand, Prime Minister Jacinda Ardern implemented some of the most stringent COVID-19 policies in the world, from curfews to school lockdowns—all under the threat of brutal police physicality. Ardern was among the first world leaders to require vaccine passports of those wishing to participate in society. "If you've got a vaccine pass, you can do everything," Ardern said with a sinister grin. She was granted a Young Global Leader appointment in 2022.[90]

Today, Schwab's Young Leaders are among the most powerful people in the world: Facebook's Mark Zuckerberg, Palantir's Peter Thiel (cofounder of PayPal), Wikipedia founder Jimmy Wales, Rockefeller Foundation president Rajiv Shah, and YouTube cofounder Chad Hurley, to name a few.[91]

And in the United States, Schwab tapped young leaders from the Democratic Party like former congresswoman Tulsi Gabbard, current US transportation secretary Pete Buttigieg, and Chelsea Clinton. But Schwab did not exclusively select Democrats; he also chose US Senator Tom Cotton, Congressman Dan Crenshaw, and Ivanka Trump. It is not clear why these seemingly staunch conservatives accepted Schwab's Young Global Leader invitation, but none of them has been a very vocal opponent of the WEF's globalist worldview.[92]

Schwab also tapped Obama's surgeon general, Vivek Murthy, to be a 2015 Young Global Leader. President Trump fired Murthy in April 2017 after the "vaccine champion" refused to resign, but he was rehired by Biden in early 2021 to serve as both surgeon general and a member of Biden's COVID-19 Response Team along with Dr. Anthony Fauci and Dr. Rochelle Walensky, among others.[93]

The WEF Pandemic Prophecies

The World Economic Forum had been involved in pandemic response plans for years. In fact, the WEF promoted *two pandemic exercises in less than two years* before the Wuhan outbreak: the Clade X and Event 201.

In 2018, for example, the WEF cited the results of a pandemic simulation hosted by Johns Hopkins. It ended in terrifying fashion. Up to forty million Americans died from the novel virus (which had been made more lethal using gain-of-function bioengineering) and close to one billion died worldwide—roughly 12 percent of the global population.[94]

The October 2019 Event 201 pandemic simulation, which Johns Hopkins conducted in partnership with the WEF and the Bill & Melinda Gates Foundation, produced less extreme results. The novel coronavirus used in the exercise bore much closer resemblance to the SARS-CoV-2 virus that would officially begin its march across the world just weeks later. The pandemic planners were even preparing for the possibility of a spread with mild symptoms, which coincidentally became a major concern with COVID-19.[95]

The two exercises left no stone unturned in terms of eventualities in a potential global pandemic. The exercises covered lockdowns and quarantines, the shuttering of small businesses and mass job losses, widespread protests and riots, and the implementation of surveillance measures and biometric IDs.

Perhaps the most unsettling item on the agenda was the role of news and social media companies: mass censorship to "combat mis- and disinformation." Event 201 especially emphasized the need to "flood" social and mainstream news media to ensure that "authoritative messages are prioritized and that false messages are suppressed." The simulations revealed a powerful drive among decision-makers toward censorship. And during the COVID crisis, social media companies shut down many accounts that dared to question official COVID narratives.[96]

Politicians attempted to control information flow as well. Prime Minister Ardern admonished New Zealanders in March 2020 that the government "will continue to be *your single source of truth*." Later, she added, "Unless you hear it from us, it is not the truth."[97]

In July 2021, Joe Biden accused Facebook of "killing people" for not censoring more COVID-related content. His Department of Homeland Security (DHS) attempted to set up in April 2022 something called the "Disinformation Governance Board" to track citizens believed to be spreading unapproved

COVID narratives, but the plan floundered after widespread criticism alleging that the disinformation board was nothing more than an oblique version of the sinister Ministry of Truth in George Orwell's *Nineteen Eighty-Four*.[98]

Almost predictably, its defenders alleged that the Disinformation Governance Board was defeated by disinformation—ironically, the very thing that the board was purportedly supposed to control. And while the board was disbanded, the administration's mission to stifle unapproved narratives lived on.[99]

In addition to predicting a need for robust censorship, Event 201 foresaw great turmoil. "The next severe pandemic will not only cause great illness and loss of life but could also trigger major cascading economic and societal consequences that could contribute greatly to global impact and suffering," the organizers presciently concluded.[100]

The implications were obvious: a global pandemic would be chaotic and terrifying. But the Controligarchs were preparing to meet the challenges such a crisis could present.

With so much preparation, how could the Controligarchs get the COVID response so wrong? Why did the Controligarch-backed response seem to benefit only the rich and powerful—more money, more power, more control—while leaching the same from the less privileged?

Perhaps these questions answer themselves.

The COVID Fallout: Crisis Equals Control

The economic outcomes of the pandemic have been dramatic and undeniable: the Controligarchs won, and everyone else lost. The pandemic created a new billionaire roughly every thirty hours—many of them WEF attendees. They profited from the pain at our expense. And worst of all, they appear to be getting away with it.[101]

During the pandemic, global supply chains broke down, central banks flooded the economy with cash, and inflation soared. Countries that have adopted economic policies pushed by Schwab felt their painful effects in less than two years. The Western world has allocated more than $977.5 billion (which they could not afford) to implement green policies. The resultant crippling of their fuel-intensive agriculture industries (and their inability to get gasoline) has led to predictions of massive food shortages.[102]

Despite all of this, Joe Biden pushed his Build Back Better program, which would turn the US away from fossil fuels toward green energy sources. When gas prices soared in the US in 2022—after Russia invaded Ukraine—the war between the two major gas suppliers was widely blamed. But there was another, less-remarked-on reality in play, too: the green transition that had begun long before the conflict. The inflationary effects of the expensive green energy policies in Biden's Build Back Better program fuel inflation and thus reduce the value of currency and consumers' purchasing power.

And the US wasn't alone. What many fail to acknowledge is that every country experiencing inflation today follows the same "print and spend" approach. This profligate spending is backed by many Controligarchs—because it benefits them at our expense.

4

The Power Grab

You never want a serious crisis to go to waste ... For a long time our entire energy policy came down to cheap oil ... This crisis provides the opportunity ... to do things that you could not do before.[1]

—*Rahm Emanuel, advisor to Presidents Clinton and Obama, November 2008*

In the weeks and months following Klaus Schwab's call to action for a Great Reset, allied world leaders, NGOs, corporations, and media conglomerates heeded the Davos rallying cry and seized on the coronavirus opportunity to build back a better, greener economy.

In the preceding decades, the Controligarchs and their environmental doomsayers' steady drumbeat of apocalyptic predictions about resource exhaustion and the limits to growth had been omnipresent. But their warnings of a *distant* doom were more subdued—mostly discussed in the halls of the UN and WEF and at Rockefeller Foundation working groups. Much of the public had responded, for decades, with a collective shrug.

The Great Reset and the switch to a zero-carbon global energy system (which the Davos crowd began to call "the transition") relied on fear—not about resource exhaustion but rather about killing the planet. The crisis was now.

"This is Code Red," Joe Biden declared forcefully at a September 2021 press conference in New York City, which had just been hit by Hurricane

Ida. With uncharacteristic vigor, Biden emphasized that "the storms are going to get worse and worse and worse."[2]

The president was wearing his signature aviator sunglasses, so people knew that he meant business. The sleeves on his crisp, blue-and-white striped, oxford-style shirt were rolled up. No jacket, no tie. Biden was ready to get to work.

Citing "the scientists," as well as the economists and even the national-security experts, Biden expressed certainty that the world was in grave climate peril. This claim was "not hyperbole," he warned the crowd. "That. Is. A. Fact." Biden accentuated every syllable. He was practically shouting.

US senator Chuck Schumer (D-NY), New York governor Kathy Hochul, and lame-duck mayor Bill de Blasio crowded around Biden at the podium. Their mask-clad faces nodded in unison, signaling their agreement.

Biden insisted that the extreme weather prophecies from years (or decades) past had finally arrived—America was "living it in real time now."[3] Fires, floods, diseases, devastation to transportation, supply chains, and crops—Biden attributed all to the existential threat known as climate change. But Biden had a solution:

> When I talk about building back better . . . I mean, you can't build to what it was before this last storm. You've got to build better, so if the storm occurred again, there would be no damage.[4]

Hurricane Ida had presented a crisis, and the president was in New York that day, not letting that crisis go to waste. Biden took advantage of the opportunity to promote his Build Back Better green infrastructure blueprint.

He pledged that if his plan were approved, "there would be no [storm] damage," and that it would even prevent fires, floods, and diseases while creating untold numbers of jobs—"union jobs."[5]

How could spending trillions of the taxpayers' dollars eliminate storm damage and prevent disasters? Biden did not elaborate. But even after he signed the bill and began disbursing the funds, storms and disasters proceeded unimpeded. And the Biden administration could not *respond* adequately when disasters struck. America's infrastructure (which Biden had promised to rebuild with a *separate* trillion-dollar bill) continued to crumble, which led to massive chemical disasters in America's heartland. Two big spending bills in two years. Numerous promises. Unacceptable results.

Furthermore, these gargantuan bills were not even the first ones that Biden had used to promise unlikely results.[6]

Twelve years prior, Vice President Biden proudly announced a big loan guarantee—the first "green" outlay from the near-trillion-dollar American Recovery and Reinvestment Act. Biden boasted of the "unprecedented investment" in "renewable energy" as the administration gave a whopping $535-million loan guarantee for a solar panel start-up called Solyndra.[7]

Like the promises he would make more than a decade later, Biden claimed that the taxpayers' handout to Solyndra would create thousands of jobs, while Obama's Energy secretary assured that the Solyndra "investment" would end dependence on foreign oil and cut carbon emissions. Roughly two years later, Solyndra went belly-up and laid off more than one thousand workers.[8]

The taxpayers' loss was Silicon Valley's gain. Solyndra's investors happened to be major fundraisers for Obama and Biden's campaign. The company spent nearly $2 million on lobbying, and Solyndra's top investor visited the White House more than a dozen times, before and after the $535 million cash infusion was approved. Ironically, Solyndra's largest investor and multiple directors were major players in the fossil fuel industry.[9]

Solyndra's billionaire backers recouped most of their investment. The taxpayers did not. Later, Solyndra's best assets—namely, its California real estate and its factory adjacent to San Francisco Bay—were scooped up for a fraction of the price by the Silicon Valley–based tech company Seagate, which happened to be linked to Gates's foundation and supplied hard drives for Microsoft's Xbox game player.

Solyndra was Obama and Biden's first green energy handout to one of their cronies, but it would not be their last. Following Solyndra's collapse, a *Washington Post* analysis found that the Obama-Biden administration gave nearly $4 billion in federal grants and other funding to twenty-one green energy cronies. A couple of years later, a separate analysis revealed that more than $1.5 billion in taxpayer monies had been wasted on corporate welfare to solar and other green energy companies that later went bankrupt (or otherwise failed).[10]

The fiasco of the Solyndra case (and the other taxpayer-funded green energy companies that swiftly failed) provided an instructive blueprint that would be recycled a decade later: Biden's Build Back Better plan was also loaded with handouts to politically connected players and crony corporations.

The Build Back Better behemoth—*more than $4 trillion*—initially failed to secure enough votes in Congress, but its critical components survived and were passed piecemeal in subsequent bills. One of these, the Inflation Reduction Act, which Biden signed in August 2022, had among its biggest winners Biden donors, insiders, and Democratic allies. It also had clear losers: the middle and lower classes, who had to finance Biden's boondoggles. By the time the "inflation reduction" act passed, the pork-laden act had become widely known as Biden's "climate bill."[11] Biden's climate bill was also referred to as "Biden's health and tax bill," even though it was a series of energy handouts. Why? Because taxpayers and the pharmaceutical companies were paying for it.[12]

Buried deep within the climate bill were at least half a dozen new taxes, including a $6.5 billion natural gas tax, a $12 billion crude oil tax, and a $1.2 billion coal tax—all of which would increase household energy bills, gas prices, or both. There was also a $52 billion tax hike on family and medium-sized businesses and a $74 billion stock tax, which was expected to affect retirement plans substantially. Naturally, these taxes hit the middle class especially hard.[13]

Perhaps the most controversial aspects of the legislation were a potential tax on pharmaceutical companies and almost $80 billion in IRS spending to hire nearly eighty-seven thousand federal tax agents to enforce the new tax increases.[14]

The law was hailed by Biden's allies as a major pre-midterm election win for Democrats and the administration, but it was a scam.

With hundreds of billions in new green energy spending—almost entirely paid for by the middle class—destined for Biden's donors, Democratic allies, and billionaire climate activists, many already-struggling American taxpayers were alarmed at the new, heavily funded IRS, and *The Wall Street Journal*'s editorial board warned that the federal tax collector was going into "beast mode."[15] And new IRS job postings listed "be willing to use deadly force, if necessary" among the requirements.[16] After much criticism, the tax agency hastily deleted the lethal-force requirement from its posting.

But plundering the Treasury, printing trillions of dollars (thereby accelerating the already record-high inflation rate), and dispatching armed federal agents to pursue taxpayers were not the only concerns that citizens had with the Build Back Better plan and "Code Red" climate change bill. Biden and his green energy Controligarch backers' ruthless zeal to "save the planet" meant that sacrifices would have to be made. Every man, woman, and child's life would have to change.

How Oil Kings Created a Climate Panic for Profit

Long before the war on climate change, the Rockefellers became the undisputed kings of cheap energy and, later, green energy.

One hundred and fifty years ago, John D. Rockefeller Sr. discovered the secret of abundant energy, and it made him one of the richest men in history. The secret was simple: deliver the best product for the lowest price. Most of Senior's customers were the middle and lower classes—the working men and women of America—and he was relentless in his quest to deliver affordable petroleum-based products.

To dominate the market, Senior's products had to be superior, but most of all, oil had to be cheap. And it was. Rockefeller made lighting homes and businesses with Standard Oil kerosene so affordable in fact that consumers chose Rockefeller's products over whale-based lamp oil and even the much newer electric lighting.[17]

Along the way, Senior and his descendants learned that once they controlled the oil supply, they had greater influence over the price. Their unmatched market power meant that they could buy out any competitor to ensure a near-monopoly. These tactics got Standard into trouble with antitrust regulators. By controlling the price of energy, the Rockefellers had outsized influence over the price of many other things—transportation, manufacturing, and consumer utilities, for example.

After the Justice Department broke up The Standard into thirty-four different companies in 1911, the largest became the oil giants of today, including Exxon, Mobil, Amoco, and Chevron. After the breakup, Rockefeller was able to own up to 25 percent of each of the resulting companies, and became even richer.[18]

For more than fifty years, as the oil industry grew, energy costs got cheaper; the automobile (and all the freedom that it afforded) became ubiquitous. America flourished and the world followed.

A geologist and petroleum industry researcher named Marion King Hubbert introduced the term "peak oil" in 1956—a prediction that oil production would peak in the early 1970s and then begin to decline. Hubbert was a technocrat (he cofounded the Technocracy Incorporated movement in the early 1930s) and received the Rockefeller "Public Service Award" in 1977. Hubbert's alarmist energy theories ultimately proved false.[19]

Peak-oil alarmism became a way to artificially limit the supply and accelerate a "transition" to alternative sources of energy. When supply is artificially restricted, profits soar.[20] As it turned out, forecasting peak oil was decidedly a fool's errand, and every time a peak-oil alarmist—including executives from the largest oil companies in the world—said that the world would run out of oil, human innovations created new technologies to discover fresh oil fields and more ways to extract it. While oil flows, scarcity is harder to manufacture.[21]

It was around the time that peak-oil predictions failed to materialize that the Club of Rome and the WEF began pushing the *problematique*—or "the predicament of mankind"—that kicked off the top-down environmental movement. Eventually, Schwab and his forum helped push this idea into the mainstream.

The Rockefellers had dominated the twentieth century with oil, and they were positioning themselves to dominate the twenty-first century with something cleaner. In a timely move for the new century, the Rockefeller brothers (Senior's offspring) began their transition to climate-friendly investments. They called their investments in renewable energy, agriculture, transportation, and other green technologies "impact investing," which they began to ramp up in the 2010s.[22]

Naturally, the Rockefeller "impact investments" were fully compliant with the UN Sustainable Development Goals and the Davos-backed ESG woke capital scheme. It was only *after* the Rockefellers began pouring more than $200 million into climate-compliant enterprises that they fully divested from their old friends, the fossil fuels.[23]

It seems that every time a predication fails to come to pass, the Controligarchs ring new climate alarm bells. After all, catastrophes present opportunities. And an impending climate apocalypse presents perhaps the greatest opportunities of all.

The solution to a climate catastrophe, "green energy," not only presents opportunities for Controligarchs such as Gates—with his solar, wind, and nuclear projects—to profit substantially but also leads to the inevitable centralization of political power. And concerns about the size of one's "carbon footprint" have led to proposed solutions such as a "carbon credit trading program" to offset one's carbon footprint, which gives more control to the people running the program.[24]

Green energy is an inherently more centralized system than carbon-based energy. Generating power from solar, wind, and nuclear sources presents near-insurmountable barriers to entry for competitive entrepreneurs. In essence, there can be neither scrappy wildcatters nor lucky Jedd Clampetts of the solar, wind, or nuclear power industries. Success in each of those industries relies on good government relations. Carbon-based power companies have been highly monopolized for a century. Green energy and the precisely controlled "smart grids" that distribute this new green energy can ensure monopolies for another century.

Thus, upon further examination, the green energy "revolution" begins to look increasingly like a power grab by Controligarchs, who often demonstrate minimal personal commitment to living a greener lifestyle, given their energy-intensive mansions and frequent private jet travel.

To be sure, not all advocates of green energy are looking to control the energy sector—but many do desire to change human behavior. There are plenty of sincere advocates who believe that climate *does* pose an existential and earth-ending crisis. The Rockefeller family, for example, has publicly split with several heirs attacking Standard Oil's legacy.

David Rockefeller's granddaughter, Ariana, defends Exxon's timely pivot toward renewables, while a cousin and Senator Jay Rockefeller's daughter, Valerie, blasted their family's legacy. These greener Rockefellers promoted a campaign titled #ExxonKnew (about the company's alleged role in changing Earth's climate) and have sought fraud and racketeering charges under the RICO statute.[25]

Proving whether theories of catastrophic anthropogenic (human-caused) climate change are entirely with or without merit exceeds the scope of this book. But it is worth noting that each of the predictions of climate doom in the last half century have been wrong—from the population bomb (running out of resources) in the 1960s to global cooling in the 1970s and 1980s to holes in the ozone layer in the 1980s and 1990s to global warming and sea-level rise through the 2000s—or have at least been dramatically revised.[26]

And when predictions have failed to materialize, climate scientists have walked back the predictions and the UN's Intergovernmental Panel on Climate Change (IPCC) has recast its data on more than one occasion.[27]

But rather than apologize for pushing fear based on faulty data, the scientific community rallied around the IPCC and attacked the whistleblowers, who critics smeared as "climate change deniers." As a whole, green energy Controligarchs and the politicians that cater to their interests have rarely, if ever, acknowledged the dozens of failed predictions from the past fifty years.[28]

Predictions that made them very, very rich.

The More Pain, the More Profit

Since the second half of 2020, the timely investments made by global political leaders, major banks, and multinational corporations have paid off in spectacular fashion.

Jet-setting billionaires such as Bill Gates, Jeff Bezos, Michael Bloomberg, George Soros, Mark Zuckerberg, and Elon Musk hold tens of billions of dollars in solar and wind power companies, electric vehicle (EV) manufacturers, rechargeable lithium battery technology, and the software that could use green energy smart grids as a tool for behavioral control.[29]

Politicians such as Joe Biden are downstream from these massive financial interests, and many of them are true believers in the endless studies produced by the billionaire-funded climate change think tanks. "The science" that Biden and the bureaucrats frequently invoke has been effectively trademarked and weaponized.

On the 2020 campaign trail, Biden repeatedly promised to work toward the complete elimination of fossil fuels. In fact, he "guaranteed" it. Once president, he signed multiple executive orders that systematically dismantled his predecessor's "full spectrum American energy dominance" doctrine that had launched the United States past its once-elusive goal of energy independence to become—for the first time in a long time—a net exporter of fuel.[30]

For the Biden administration, solving climate change was more important than securing cheap fuel for Americans. In addition to the carrots (trillions of dollars in corporate welfare), bureaucrats also planned to wield more
than a few sticks—mostly in the form of higher prices and taxes.

Citizens would have to start paying more to heat and cool their homes as
electrical grid regulators in multiple states raised prices and even told residents to limit their electricity usage, which meant turning their thermostats
up or down depending on the season. For example, utility companies in California (increasingly wind- and solar-powered) issued half a dozen "Flex
Alerts" in the summer of 2021 to motivate customers to decrease their electricity consumption.[31]

Months earlier, during the winter, hundreds of Texans reportedly *froze
to death* as the power grid collapsed in the worst rolling blackout in American history, which left more than ten million residents without power and
critical infrastructure.[32]

How could an oil-rich state such as Texas—with enough liquid gold to
power the state for decades—suffer such a catastrophe? The answer depends
on who you ask.

Climate change alarmists at the WEF were eager to blame something
called "Arctic warming" for the freezing Texas temperatures. The unproven
theory is that global warming had caused a "ripple" effect that carried freezing winds from the North Pole to Texas and thus overwhelmed the power
grid.[33]

The Texas freeze was possibly the most expensive energy disaster in
Texas history and resulted in nearly $200 billion in damages. The utility
companies charged up to $9,000 per megawatt hour (wholesale) during the
surge—up from just $22 per megawatt hour on average. That meant that
consumers' home utility bills skyrocketed, with multiple customers reporting a $5,000 charge for just five days of service.[34]

The Texas power grid operator had been touting the green energy transition for nearly a decade, but it was still unable to prevent the blackouts. After
the crisis, six of its board members and all three public-utility commission-

ers resigned amid allegations of incompetence or unethical practices with utility investors.[35]

In addition to paying higher electricity rates, the green "transition" meant that automobile travel could become far less convenient. Rising fuel prices would make road trips a luxury for anyone who could not afford a new electric vehicle.[36]

"The more pain we are all experiencing from the high price of gas, the more benefit there is for those who can access electric vehicles," Biden's transportation secretary Pete Buttigieg blurted out in a moment of candor in July 2022.[37]

Climate change meant sweating it out in the summer and maintaining a chilly home in the winter. At one point, Biden proposed taxing gas-powered automobile owners for every mile they drove, and in one of his more extreme proposals, he even suggested that throwing fossil fuel executives in jail might be a solution to combat pollution or climate change.[38]

Fuel price increases—especially artificial ones such as Biden's per-mile gas tax—are something that Bill Gates likes to call "green premiums." He defines the term as "the difference in cost between a product that involves emitting carbon and an alternative that doesn't." Gates compared the average price of standard jet fuel with the average price of biofuels (the latter carries a 140 percent "green premium").

Gates acknowledges that customers would "balk" at resulting airfare increases, so his solution is to "find ways to either make [biofuels] cheaper or make jet fuel more expensive"—or perhaps some combination of the two. Calculating green premiums is not an exact science, Gates admits.[39]

Gates also suggests that green premiums are a way to reduce emissions in the most carbon-heavy sectors, including electricity production, agriculture, manufacturing, heating and air-conditioning, and transportation. In other words, every facet of human existence must become more expensive to achieve the WEF and UN's Agenda 2030 emission reductions. As Buttigieg said, the simplest way to view green premiums is more pain equals more benefit.[40]

The United Nations and its affiliates (such as the IPCC) allege that "in order to avert the worst impacts of climate change and preserve a livable planet, global temperature increase needs to be limited to 1.5° [Celsius] above pre-industrial levels."

The UN claims that the earth has warmed about 1.1 degrees Celsius since the late 1800s, when the Second Industrial Revolution was taking place, meaning that a further 0.4-degree increase would make planet Earth unlivable. To avoid this, it claims, humans must reduce global carbon emissions by 45 percent by the year 2030 and completely eliminate them by 2050.[41]

In other words, there is no time to wait and see if the UN's hypothesis is correct. The only option is to do exactly what the UN says *immediately*.

Gates's Big Green Payday

One November day in 2021, at a UN event in Glasgow, Scotland, Bill Gates took to the podium to announce his third career: he was now a revolutionary (and a climatologist).

Beginning in the summer of 2022, he sought to leverage the rapidly increasing carbon-based energy prices and get a piece of the green premium action. Gates's proposed system offered potential to control human behavior.[42]

"Together, we must build a green industrial revolution—one that stops climate change, protects vulnerable communities, and puts the world on a path to progress," Gates said. The populist bromides were tactical. Invoking "vulnerable communities" personalized the issue.[43]

Gates's climate revolution began to materialize less than one year later with the implementation of Biden's climate bill—the third installment in his multitrillion-dollar Build Back Better plan. The Democrats controlled Congress, but only barely, and one pesky senator from carbon-rich West Virginia was anything but a sure vote.[44]

Throughout the summer of 2022, Gates feverishly called lawmakers, pressuring them to pass Biden's pricey climate bill (which was eventually called the Inflation Reduction Act—a not-so-clever misnomer at a time when inflation was surging).[45]

Senate majority leader Chuck Schumer commiserated with Gates over the fact that the deciding vote—Senator Joe Manchin (D-WV)—might be a problem. But Gates is more powerful than any lobbyist and is a master of backroom deals. Multiple times before the final vote in August 2022, Gates picked up the phone and lobbied the West Virginia senator. Recordings published by Bloomberg News revealed that Gates came away from the call feeling optimistic. The mainstream media coverage of moments such as this one—a billionaire calling a US senator and pressuring him to pass a controversial piece of legislation—might have been critical twenty years ago. But those days were over.[46] Instead, Bloomberg News called it the "Secret Push to Save Biden's Climate Bill."[47]

Gates and his foundation have spent billions of dollars hyping the threat of climate change for decades—more than $4.1 billion since 2021 alone. The climate bill presented a timely opportunity to realize a return on that investment. So, what did Gates and his billionaire buddies get from the climate bill?

Consider the case of Gates's Seattle-area nuclear energy start-up Terra-Power, which endeavors to put small modular reactors in towns and homes across America. The solution to climate change is the elimination of traditional carbon-based fuels. What will replace fossil fuels? Nuclear, in addition to wind and solar, energy.

On top of the benefits provided by Gates's investments and the grants from his tax-exempt foundation, TerraPower also benefits from direct taxpayer cash infusions in the form of Department of Energy grants. In June 2018, TerraPower and its partners won a combined $4.8 million from the department for nuclear projects in North Carolina and New York. In October 2020, the Department of Energy again awarded TerraPower taxpayer money—this time a staggering $80 million in initial funding to build a nuclear reactor.[48]

In November 2021, TerraPower announced that it would be building an advanced nuclear reactor in Wyoming. The plant had a stunning $4 billion price tag, and while TerraPower would be funding half of it, American tax-payers would be picking up the other half of the tab. If and when completed, the plant will be operated by a subsidiary of Warren Buffett's Berkshire Hath-away, where Gates served as a board member for more than a decade.[49]

Five months prior to TerraPower's announcement, Buffett funneled over $3.2 billion to the Gates Foundation, where he had served as a trustee for fifteen years (Buffett once pledged more than $30 billion to the Gates Foun-dation, which was the largest charitable pledge in history). Buffett's whop-ping multibillion-dollar donation to the Gates Foundation was announced as he resigned as trustee. In March 2022, TerraPower landed another taxpayer-funded grant. This one was for $8.55 million and was the largest in a package of eleven grants announced by Biden's energy secretary Jennifer Granholm.[50]

Later that year, in November 2022, Granholm participated in a "fireside chat" with TerraPower's president and CEO at the UN's climate summit called COP27. And at that event, Biden climate envoy John Kerry announced a new effort called Project Phoenix. Standing beside TerraPower's presi-dent and CEO and the Ukrainian energy minister, Kerry stated that Project Phoenix would "provide direct US support" for a coal-to-nuclear transition across Central and Eastern Europe. American taxpayers would be funding Europe's clean energy transition, and Gates's nuclear power company boasted of its involvement.[51]

Gates's green energy gambit illustrates the Controligarch business model: profit mightily through corporate welfare while avoiding taxes. Green Con-troligarchs such as Elon Musk, George Soros, Warren Buffett, Michael Bloomberg, and Jeff Bezos—among others—profit while paying minimal in-come taxes. They, like Gates, do so by moving their personal funds to their tax-exempt foundations.[52]

Like the Rockefellers, generosity plays a marginal role in the modern Controligarchs' legal tax-avoidance schemes. Their billionaire lifestyles en-dure, no matter how much they transfer to tax-exempt foundations. Fur-ther, their foundations serve their own financial interests as vehicles to promote their for-profit endeavors. The profit cycle comes full circle when the Controligarchs finance seminars and white papers that supply talking points to political operatives, which, in turn, pressure governments to subsidize these business interests with taxpayer funds.

With hundreds of billions earmarked for green energy, Biden's 2022 climate bill had the potential to make TerraPower's previous federal awards look like pocket change. Eight days after the Senate passed Biden's climate bill, TerraPower announced that it had received $750 million in new private funding.[53]

Gates's investment in America's second-largest waste management company, Republic Services, is another example of how Gates, his foundation, and the federal government work to enrich him—at the expense of others. In 2007, Gates, his foundation, and his vehicle, Cascade Investment, purchased tens of millions of shares in Republic Services. Since then, the company has engaged in a variety of antiworker behaviors, including charging customers to *not* have their trash collected during an employee labor strike.[54]

Since 1998, Republic Services had used diesel vehicles for their waste management operations. But following Gates's investment, Republic Services began exploring taxpayer-funded opportunities to replace their fleet with trucks that use cleaner fuel. In 2009, President Obama signed the American Recovery and Reinvestment Act, which provided nearly $1 trillion in stimulus funds for progressive priorities, and Republic Services was an early beneficiary.[55]

On June 17, 2014, Cascade purchased 205,300 shares in the waste management company for just over $7.5 million. Less than two months later, the Obama Department of Energy announced that Republic Services had been accepted into the National Clean Fleets Partnership, which would provide Gates's investment with taxpayer-funded refueling assistance, route-mapping services, "specialized resources," and "other technical assistance."[56]

Gates has pushed for policies such as carbon taxes that would dramatically hurt his competitors. This is the "extinguish" phase of the Embrace-

Extend-Extinguish strategy akin to taxing non-Microsoft operating systems or banning competing apps from a Gates-controlled platform.[57]

In 2018, one of Republic Services' competitors filed a lawsuit stating that the Gates-funded company had "aggressively abused their position" and had been doing it for years "behind the scenes." Six months later, the competitor declared bankruptcy, leaving many customers "in the dark." Since 2008, Republic Services has been repeatedly sued for unethical business practices and various forms of contamination, including improper handling of hazardous waste, among other things. Republic Services has been ordered to pay more than $10 million to settle various claims against the company and a major class-action lawsuit filed in 2022 remains ongoing.[58]

But not all of Gates's green energy projects are winners. Sapphire Energy, which endeavored to make biofuel from plant algae, is another one of Gates's green energy ventures that secured federal funding. In September 2008, Gates joined the Rockefellers' investment vehicle, Venrock, and other big backers (Wellcome Trust and ARCH Venture Partners) to funnel $100 million into Sapphire Energy. The following year, the Agriculture Department approved a $54.5 million federal loan guarantee for the company.[59]

The Department of Energy touted Sapphire Energy as a "success story" in 2014, and the company insinuated that it could be producing five thousand barrels of biofuel per day within a few years. In 2017, the Department of Energy announced another $8 million for Sapphire Energy and two other algae-based-fuel companies (though any update on the promises to be producing thousands of barrels of biofuel per day was noticeably absent).[60]

Like most pie-in-the-sky green energy fantasies, Gates's dream of replacing oil with algae eventually crashed into reality. By 2019, Sapphire Energy had abandoned its biofuel efforts and sold off its biorefinery to a company making livestock feed, and it appears that the company is now defunct. There is no evidence that American taxpayers were ever reimbursed for their investment in Gates's algae company.[61]

Climate Saviors: The Gas, Coal, and Oil Men behind the Curtain

Michael Bloomberg is another climate profiteer concerned about overpopulation. One of New York City's longest-serving mayors, Bloomberg is also among the largest billionaire backers of the energy control agenda. With a net worth exceeding $90 billion—up from his pre-pandemic valuation of $48 billion—Bloomberg is the ninth-richest man in the world.[62]

Bloomberg has portrayed himself as a climate savior for decades, and his efforts to implement emission control measures in New York City were undeniable. In June 2019, Bloomberg pledged $500 million to wage war on coal and later claimed that his crusade as mayor to reduce coal power consumption helped "cut New York City's carbon footprint twice as much as [that of] the rest of the country."[63]

But like most billionaire climate activists, Bloomberg held investments in the greener energy systems that he was pushing.[64]

In November 2019, Bloomberg announced that he was running for president. But the climate plan that he presented ahead of the 2020 campaign was not good enough for his constituents. It simply was not sufficiently punitive on fossil fuels and fracking. He also criticized controversial plans such as the Green New Deal. As a result, Greenpeace USA ranked Bloomberg's plan last among the Democratic hopefuls, and a spokesperson for the environmental organization stated that Bloomberg had "committed to doing less than other candidates in the race."[65]

Then, his campaign fell apart. As a 2020 presidential candidate, Bloomberg was required to disclose all his investments, but he was able to evade disclosure long enough to drop out, and the disclosure requirement became moot. According to the watchdog group Center for Public Integrity, Bloomberg essentially "ran out the clock on transparency."[66]

One reason that Bloomberg may not have wanted to reveal his holdings is that he owned sizable investments in natural gas, which had become the most viable alternative to coal. "We are natural gas bulls," a senior investment manager at Bloomberg's personal and philanthropic wealth management company (Willett Advisors) told a trade publication in 2013.[67]

As Bloomberg was waging war on coal, his company was investing in fracking companies such as Oklahoma oil and gas producer White Star Petroleum, and another investment manager stated in 2015 that Bloomberg's company invested in "North Dakota and other places like that."[68]

Bloomberg was profiting from fossil fuels while pushing green energy policies that would disproportionately affect the family budgets of the lower and middle classes—hardly a unique feature among the Controligarchs. Climate activist billionaires are frequently accused of holding double standards—such as when they fly around on private jets between their power-sucking mansions—but that rarely stops them from pushing coercive energy policies on others. But this time Bloomberg's hypocrisy was impossible to hide, crashing his presidential ambitions.

Bloomberg's failed campaign taught a crucial lesson: climate activist billionaires will have more luck winning energy control from a private perch.

Currency speculator and national bank breaker George Soros is the type of billionaire who does not need to run for president. He wields power and exerts control behind the scenes.

Soros invests in far more than mere commodities. Like Klaus Schwab, Soros invests in *powerful people and concepts*—such as "open societies" and "social justice"—and that word that many politicians like to throw around: *democracy.*[69]

For much of his life, Soros had been conspicuously quiet on the issue of climate change. Naturally, that was when he made the most money on fossil fuels. But as Soros began investing in cleaner energy sources, his support for green energy grew louder.[70]

Soros helped the Obama-Biden administration crush the coal industry. Their war on coal appeared passionately ideological, but Soros's motives were unmistakably profit driven: he shorted coal stocks as the administration smashed the industry. Soros then grabbed the coal stocks for pennies on the dollar. A *Forbes* financial analyst stated, "I think George Soros used the government like a blunt object to beat down coal stocks and make money shorting them."[71]

Soros poured his money into green energy projects (pledging a $1 billion investment) around the same time when the Obama-Biden administration was rolling out its stimulus program.[72]

By 2016, Soros was investing hundreds of millions in solar projects and bailed out Elon Musk's floundering Tesla-charging solar company, Solar-City, in a financing deal worth more than $300 million.[73]

That year, Musk was worth just north of $10.5 billion, making him the thirty-fourth-richest person in the world. Over the next six years, Musk's net worth skyrocketed by roughly 1,800 percent (mostly during COVID) to around $200 billion: the world's richest person.[74]

After Soros began investing in massive green energy projects, he ramped up his green politicking. Soros pushed policies that benefited his financial interests. He plunged $1.1 billion into environmentalist think tanks, such as Friends of the Earth, Alliance for Climate Protection, Earthjustice, the Earth Island Institute, Green for All, and the Natural Resources Defense Council, which effectively exist to ring the alarm bells on climate change.[75]

The Center for American Progress, founded by Clinton operative John Podesta with funding from Soros, aggressively sought to take down fossil fuels. At the January 2020 World Economic Forum in Davos, Soros gave a keynote address wherein he committed an additional $1 billion to start a *global* university to fight climate change, among other things.[76]

"Taking into account the climate emergency and worldwide unrest," Soros predicted that the next few years would determine "the fate of the world." He, of course, had advanced (and likely helped devise) some of the UN's Sustainable Development Goals and was a major backer of ESG scores.[77]

Days before Biden signed the Inflation Reduction Act, Soros spent more than $20 million on 29,883 Tesla shares. The tech-heavy stock exchange Nasdaq declared Tesla "the biggest winner" of the Biden climate deal.[78]

California governor Gavin Newsom, who has received money from Soros, implemented numerous coercive steps that would enrich climate billionaires like Soros and Musk at the expense of average citizens.[79]

As Soros, Musk, Gates, and other Controligarchs increased funding for EV manufacturers and charging stations, Newsom was preparing to ban the competition.

On August 25, 2022, California officials unanimously voted to do away with gas-powered vehicles. "Our kids are going to act like it's a rotary phone, or changing the channel on a television," Governor Newsom said of gas-powered vehicles. California plans to phase out the sale of new gas-powered vehicles by the year 2035.[80]

In an ironic twist just twenty-four hours later, California's grid operator announced a warning to its customers: charging electric vehicles—or even just running the home air-conditioning—would place too much strain on the increasingly green power grid.[81]

Teslas and Technocracy: Beneath Elon Musk's Freedom-Loving Exterior

When Biden announced his $2 trillion infrastructure spending bill in March 2021, analysts immediately began predicting the winners and losers. Controligarch-backed green technology and electric vehicle companies were expected to benefit greatly, and America's largest EV manufacturer, Tesla, was projected to be one of the biggest winners.[82]

But Tesla's CEO came out against Biden's plan, which was loaded with rebates and tax credits that would have dramatically increased Tesla's profits. Why? A likely reason is that Tesla's competitors would also qualify for the rebates and Tesla, having already hit a two-hundred-thousand-vehicle cap placed on EV manufacturers under previous legislation, might not.[83]

"We don't need the $7,500 tax credit. . . . I would just can this whole bill. Don't pass it," Musk said in December 2021 about Biden's infrastructure bill.

"Not obvious how this serves American taxpayers," the Tesla CEO said about a subsequent Biden proposal to expand tax credits for EVs built using union labor. "This is written by Ford/UAW lobbyists," Musk said, while also criticizing his competitors for outsourcing parts of their operations to Mexico.[84]

Musk has always been a bit of an enigma. With one foot in the libertarian camp and the other foot firmly planted in the green energy futurism camp, Musk is politically hard to pin down. But since he denounced the Biden administration and ascended as a free-speech warrior as Twitter's new owner, he has been widely praised and almost deified by his die-hard fans—the "Musketeers."[85]

Ultimately, though, Musk's wealth is tied to the green energy revolution and surges when climate change becomes a government spending priority. As with many other Controligarchs, Musk relies on corporate welfare— taxpayer subsidies and government contracts—to get rich.

In addition to his more famous projects, such as Tesla and space tourism company SpaceX, Musk has founded numerous ventures that range from a microsatellite global internet provider (Starlink) to an underground-highway-tunneling venture (The Boring Company) to an artificial intelligence project (OpenAI, which partnered with Microsoft to create ChatGPT) to perhaps the most controversial: a brain-microchipping company (Neuralink).[86]

Musk has cultivated a reputation as a man of the people—and it costs a lot of money to maintain. He was the CEO of digital payment service PayPal in the company's early days and has been a major advocate for cryptocurrencies—a decentralized form of money—which proponents claim will decrease the power of governments and central banks around the world.[87]

Musk differs in a few key ways from Bill Gates and other Controligarch tech billionaires. He promotes open-source technologies and promised in 2014 that he will not patent his Tesla inventions.[88]

Musk appears to be a climate change realist and has stated that without continued oil and gas usage for the immediate future, "civilization will crumble." And while other billionaires, such as Gates, seek to decrease global birth rates, Musk (a father of at least eight children) has warned that current rates are dangerously and unsustainably low.[89]

On the other hand, Musk is cut from the same cloth as Gates and the other Controligarchs: government contracts and subsidies helped launch and propel his businesses into the stratosphere. And like the others, Musk has a clear technocratic streak. His brain-microchip and AI companies present potential opportunities for totalitarians seeking to control human thoughts and behaviors. These are dangers that, to his credit, Musk's occasional business partner Soros has denounced.[90]

Musk is a tri-citizen—a South African by birth who immigrated to the United States via Canada thanks to his mother's Canadian citizenship. Thus, like Schwab, Soros, and other rootless technocrats, Musk is somewhat of a citizen of the world.

His greatest influence may have come from his maternal grandfather. "My parents were very famous," Elon's mother, Maye Musk, said, while clarifying that they were "never snobs." Her father was a Canadian public figure named Joshua Haldeman.[91]

Haldeman was born in 1902. His father, John Elon, was the Tesla scion's namesake, and his mother was one of Canada's first chiropractors. Haldeman followed in his mother's footsteps, and his influence in the medical community translated into political power. From 1936 until 1941, Haldeman was a leader of Technocracy Incorporated in Canada. He was also the national chairman of Canada's Social Credit Party, which endeavored to create its own utopia.[92]

Musk's grandfather and his technocratic comrades hoped to replace democracy with a new form of government ruled by scientists with autocratic decision-making power. They fought to replace capitalism and the dollar by issuing a new form of universal currency based on energy measurements called ergs.[93]

The Canadian government saw the technocracy movement as a radical threat to democracy and began to crack down on its leaders. Elon's grandfather was arrested on October 13, 1940, for his radical beliefs, and eventually, he and his family fled Canada for South Africa.[94]

Today, Musk seems to follow in his grandfather's footsteps, who held that human behavior can be calculated and ultimately controlled.

Indeed, Musk often presents technocratic solutions to present-day dreams—from colonizing Mars to microchipping the human brain.

During the pandemic, Musk's net worth surged mostly because of Tesla's exploding stock price. In May 2019, Tesla was trading at approximately $200 per share, and Musk was worth just $22.3 billion that year.[95]

In July 2020, Tesla's share price was around $100 per share. Tesla's share price rebounded and surged higher and higher through 2020 and 2021 after Biden had begun to deliver on his campaign promise to use EV subsidies to help "end fossil fuels."[96]

Beyond the Great Reset and Biden's energy policies, Musk benefited from the pandemic in another unexpected way: Tesla's main plant in California was forced to shut down for a couple of months, but that was not the case for its new plant in Shanghai, China.[97]

By 2021, Tesla had decided to make Shanghai its new "export hub" (replacing the hub in Fremont, California) because of China's lack of coronavirus lockdowns at the time, cheaper labor and material costs, and no import tariffs. In short, Musk became the world's richest man in 2021 largely because of a sweetheart deal with China, which he has praised for its authoritarianism.[98]

Like his deals with Communist China, Musk's political spending is opportunistic and favors whoever can best assist his business, as is most political spending by the billionaire class. In 2014, Musk spent up to $445,000 lobbying and contributing to state legislators who could help fund a Texas launchpad for SpaceX. Musk's return on investment was significant—the same Texas lawmakers who Musk donated to secured him "a $15 million budget rider" for SpaceX.[99]

But unlike most Controligarchs, Musk seems to prefer Republican leadership. He reportedly hangs out with top House Republican Kevin McCarthy and has publicly denounced the Biden administration on multiple occasions.[100]

When Biden announced his 2022 climate bill, Musk was unusually quiet. He tweeted a lukewarm criticism of the bill's nearly $80 billion earmarked IRS expansion—"seems high," he wrote. But beyond that, Musk said little of the bill expected to dramatically boost the EV industry. Musk had previously blasted the Biden White House for snubbing Tesla on more than one occasion. Counterintuitively, Musk once criticized EV tax credits, and favored a coercive "carbon tax" approach to addressing climate change.[101]

But soon it became clear that Tesla would be a huge winner of the Inflation Reduction Act, which removed the cap on tax credits, and Biden's climate bill also allowed Musk to launch a new line of electric semitrucks.[102]

As we will see in later chapters, Musk has done admirable work to give control back to average citizens over their lives—especially with his takeover of Twitter, which broke a Big Tech information stranglehold. But he has also advanced major Controligarch priorities, and the green energy power grab is among the most critical of those priorities. However, Musk is not the only billionaire seeking to capitalize on EVs.

Conflicts of Interest:
Putting the "EV" in Revolving Door

In January 2021, as gas prices surged skyward, Biden and his officials repeatedly told Americans that the solution to pain at the pump was to buy an EV.[103]

Transportation Secretary Pete Buttigieg, Energy Secretary Jennifer Granholm, and others were slammed as being "out of touch" for telling increasingly cash-strapped consumers to buy vehicles with an average price tag near $56,000.[104]

In his confirmation disclosure, Buttigieg said that COVID was an opportunity to "build back better." It is also worth noting that prior to becoming transportation secretary, Buttigieg ran for president in 2020 and capitalized on the spotlight to rake in large book and media payments—$800,000 to $1,800,000 over a two-year period—according to his financial disclosures.[105]

While it is the most popular, Tesla is not the only EV company making a mint off climate change hysteria. Major vehicle manufacturers such as Ford, Cadillac, and General Motors (GM), among others, have raced to get into the market and grab the taxpayer funds that subsidize EVs. Tesla's success is undeniable, while other EVs have been underwhelming at best and worse: dangerous disasters.

When GM announced an EV called the Chevrolet (Chevy) Volt to rival Tesla, opponents of gas-powered vehicles were thrilled. Soon after, the Obama-Biden administration began funneling gigantic sums—ultimately some $50 billion—to bail out GM. With the taxpayers' money in hand, GM needed to deliver on the promises of an EV future.[106]

The Detroit-based auto manufacturer received nearly $130 million in taxpayer funds as part of the administration's green energy stimulus. GM was praised by the Obama-Biden administration for putting its corporate welfare toward solving climate change. Everyone celebrated the Chevy Volt—from Jennifer Granholm (then governor of Michigan) to Biden's top climate advisor (previously Obama's Environmental Protection Agency head) to even Biden himself.[107]

The Chevy Volt was immediately awarded *MotorTrend*'s "Car of the Year" in 2011 and received other prestigious awards—some before it even hit the road. (*MotorTrend* later commented, "In the 61-year history of the Car of the Year award, there have been few contenders as hyped—or as controversial—as the Chevrolet Volt.")[108]

The car flopped with consumers owing to its $41,000 price tag ($33,500 with a federal EV tax credit) and an abysmal battery life that could only take drivers forty miles before requiring its *gas-powered* generator to kick in. But a pitiful battery life was only the beginning of the Volt's woes. Eventually, the Volt was scrapped, and Chevy began promoting a new EV: the Bolt.[109]

After touting the failed Volt, Biden, a self-described "car guy," hyped the new Bolt. Less than two months later, GM recalled the Bolt for spontaneous combustion—a problem that has led to at least four other companies recalling their EVs. GM tried to fix the Bolt's exploding battery problem but discontinued it after multiple smoke-inhalation injuries.[110]

After Granholm hyped the doomed Chevy Volt as Michigan governor, she weaved through the revolving door and joined the board of an EV company called Proterra in 2017. At Proterra, Granholm received $5 million in vested stock options and 61,042 unvested stock options with a value that was "not readily ascertainable." She kept her Proterra stocks when she became energy secretary—a controversial decision as the administration began boosting the company. One week after Biden promoted the company with a virtual tour in April 2021, a leading Republican called for an investigation into Granholm's potential conflict of interest.[111]

The energy secretary sold her Proterra stocks in May 2021 but did so only *after* Biden had promoted the company. Further, Granholm had promised to recuse herself from any matters relating to Proterra, but later that year, both Vice President Harris and Granholm announced $127 million in grants and subsidies *while at a Proterra event.*[112]

For its part, Proterra spent at least $680,000 lobbying Granholm's agency and others on issues, such as Biden's climate bill, in the first two years of his administration. In August 2023, Proterra filed for bankruptcy.[113]

Other car manufacturers have tried (and failed) to capitalize on the global effort to reduce emissions. Volkswagen created a device that tricked consumers into thinking that their carbon footprint was lower than it actually was. After the elaborate ruse was exposed, the US Department of Justice charged the German automaker's former board chairman with conspiracy and wire fraud in 2018 for the long-running emissions reduction scheme.[114]

Controligarchs such as George Soros and Jeff Bezos (through his Amazon online retailer) invested in another EV start-up called Rivian. After Bezos was blasted for buying twenty thousand fossil fuel–powered vehicles, he announced that Amazon would buy one hundred thousand electric delivery vans. The 2019 announcement put Rivian on the map and provided much-needed credibility. Subsequent news of Amazon's rollout of the electric trucks caused Rivian's stock price to surge.[115]

Soros bought twenty million Rivian shares in late 2021 for approximately $2 billion, and the EV start-up became the largest single holding in his portfolio (Amazon was his second largest).[116]

In early 2022, Soros bought six hundred thousand shares in another EV start-up, Silicon Valley–based Lucid Motors, which was developed by a former Tesla engineer and backed by the Rockefellers' Venrock fund. At the same time, Soros bought roughly one hundred million shares of Chinese EV start-up Nio.[117]

Soon, however, reality caught up with all the EV hype. The share prices of Rivian, Lucid, Nio, and many other EVs plummeted throughout 2022. The high price tags and low battery ranges amid a looming recession (along with lower-than-expected deliveries) sunk Nio's and Lucid's share prices by more than half. Rivian's cratered, losing more than 75 percent. By May, Soros had lost a projected $1.5 billion. In August 2022, he dumped millions of Rivian shares to stanch the bleeding and continued to decrease his exposure into 2023.[118]

As the billionaire backers of EV companies were losing their shirts in 2022, Gavin Newsom announced his plan to phase out gas-powered vehicle sales by 2035. Earlier that year, Newsom granted a staggering $10 billion EV handout.[119]

Just days after Newsom declared the gas vehicle plan, California energy officials warned residents not to charge their electric vehicles during Labor Day weekend. More outrageously, residents had to stop cooling their homes to their desired temperatures. This was all part of another "Flex Alert" from the grid operator, which told Newsom's constituents to raise home temperatures to *"78 degrees or higher"* (emphasis added).[120]

Adding insult to injury, Newsom wore a fleece coat and a baseball cap (in the height of summer) in his own chilly indoor environment as he lectured California residents about indoor temperatures.[121]

Newsom and others blamed climate change for the discomfort that

Californians now had to endure. The truth is that California's power grid did not have the power that consumers needed, in part because it was *too green.*

Smart Homes, Smart Cities, and the Internet of (Controlled) Things

Fourteen months before California's power grid began to fail in August 2022, some residents in the Houston, Texas, area were faced with an even scarier loss of personal control: the utility companies remotely adjusted their air-conditioning. Utilities can now override some customers' home thermostats, change the temperature in their homes, and force unsuspecting residents to wake up drenched in sweat.[122]

Also that summer, tens of thousands of Coloradans found themselves in a similar situation when their utility company restricted thermostat usage during an "energy emergency." These customers, according to the energy company, had agreed to be part of a rewards program that allowed it to control their smart thermostats remotely in exchange for discounts on their energy bills. Still, many customers said they had always been able to override the system. Now, some customers reported, there was nothing they could do as their thermostats locked at 78 or 79 degrees and the temperature in some homes rose into the eighties.[123]

How is this possible? the residents wondered.

The answer is that smart thermostats, while attractive on the surface for their convenience, come with more significant risks and potential drawbacks than advertised. Oligarch-run companies like Amazon and Google are selling their digital, Wi-Fi-enabled smart thermostats as an innovative way to change home temperatures remotely, and utilities across the United States are offering discounts and rebates for those who get them installed. The pitch goes like this: "Did you forget to turn off your A/C before you left the house, or do you want to return from work to a cool home? Set your smart thermostat from the road or office!"[124]

But the programs that enable a utility company to remotely adjust smart thermostats during heat waves seem not to have been clearly advertised, nor were the hacking risks, even though the Federal Bureau of Investigation (FBI) and various security researchers have raised concerns. If the real cost of smart devices like these were more clear, many residents likely would never have installed them. And thermostats are not the only smart devices the Controli-garchs are pushing: entire homes can now be "smart." Most people hear "smart home" and think of their Google Nest or Amazon Echo or Apple HomePod, when they can speak the words "Okay, Google, what's the weather like today?" and then a robotic voice that sounds uncannily human will in-form them that it is the second-hottest day on record. After that, one could say, "Hello Siri, I'm too warm," and the air-conditioning would kick on.[125]

Smart homes can also be equipped with lighting, heating, and electronic devices that can be controlled remotely by smartphone or computer. So it should come as no surprise that Bill Gates has long been a big fan of smart homes and "smart cities." In 2017, he dropped $80 million on nearly 25,000 acres outside Phoenix, Arizona. He planned to build a smart city that would be called Belmont.[126]

From the start, Belmont would be planned from the top down to be a utopia. In addition to smart homes and smart businesses, Belmont would have driverless smart cars and maybe even smart ice-cream trucks. Ap-proximately 4,300 acres have been set aside for commercial purposes, retail space, offices, and public schools.[127]

While Belmont has not yet been built, Gates and Microsoft are commit-ted to turning every city into a smart city. Today there are more than one thousand (and counting) smart-city projects around the world.[128]

As it happens, the technologies that make homes "smart" are major prior-ities for Schwab and his Great Reset—digital ID, contactless payments, and the "Internet of Things" (IoT). "In its simplest form," Schwab says, IoT "can be described as a relationship between things (products, services, places, etc.) and people that is made possible by connected technologies and various platforms."[129]

The IoT is, in other words, a fun way to refer to "smart devices" that are connected to the internet. From your refrigerator to your washing machine to your keychain to even your pet cat—all those things can now be internet-enabled devices.

"Hey, Alexa! Where's Mittens?" you ask your smart watch. "Mittens is asleep on top of Pocket Lint [the name of your smart washing machine]," your smart watch chirps back. *That little rascal,* you chuckle.

IoT feels innocent—certainly convenient—and it may even help to save the planet, its proponents say. You can monitor everything you own (this author just got a notification that the litter box is full). But the IoT also gives Controligarchs increasing amounts of control over the operation and content of those connected things. In May 2023, for example, an Amazon customer claimed that he was locked out of his account and Alexa-enabled smart home devices after a delivery driver falsely accused him of hurling a racist slur through a smart doorbell intercom. (Bezos's company had acquired its own smart doorbell camera, Ring, for more than $1.2 billion in 2018.)[130]

Now imagine this potential digital suffocation on the scale of an entire smart city, connected and run by Microsoft, Amazon, Google, and the like.

Perhaps even more concerning than these billionaires' controlling transportation or home energy consumption is their growing investment in the agriculture and food production industries—under the guise of "saving the planet," naturally.

5

The War on Farmers

But we can cut down on meat eating while still enjoying the taste of meat. One option is plant-based meat: plant products that have been processed in various ways to mimic the taste of meat. I've been an investor in two companies that have plant-based meat products on the market right now—Beyond Meat and Impossible Foods—so I'm biased, but I have to say that artificial meat is pretty good.[1]

—*Bill Gates*, How to Avoid a Climate Disaster, *2021*

I n the summer of 2022, farmers around the world formed angry mobs to protest new emissions restrictions targeting their fertilizer usage and livestock waste. The fertilizer restrictions were the result of the latest Agenda 2030 priority concocted by the World Economic Forum, the United Nations, and the Controligarchs, who wield increasing power over global food production through their aggressive plans to ameliorate climate change.[2]

The Controligarchs insisted that humanity had little chance of surviving unless it embraced the Sustainable Development Goals of the United Nations and the WEF, which would allow the world to avoid climate crisis if implemented by the target year of 2030. "Goals" become dictates when they are imposed by governments, which is precisely what began to happen around the world.[3]

So when in June 2022 the Dutch government implemented its plan to cut agriculture emissions by as much as 70 percent before 2030, agriculture workers erupted into widespread protests that wreaked havoc on the country's infrastructure.[4]

The Dutch farmers stopped deliveries to grocery stores and formed trac- tor convoys that stretched for miles, using hay bales and other objects to gridlock highways. Dairymen brought their cows to government buildings, threatening to slaughter the livestock in front of parliament, while others flung cow manure at the minister of agriculture's private residence.[5]

Not typically known for their political activism, the Dutch farmers had finally had enough of the Great Reset (or as their government now called it, an "unavoidable transition" to a greener economy).

As one of the most productive and densely farmed countries in the world, the Netherlands was a rich target for attempts at controlling emissions in agriculture. The country's looming fertilizer reduction was, by far, the most extreme of all Western countries, but plans for similar cuts had been rolling out elsewhere for months.[6]

Canadian prime minister Justin Trudeau—one of the WEF's Young Global Leaders—followed suit and put in place similar restrictions on fertil- izer usage, demanding a 30 percent restriction by the year 2030. Farmers across Canada staged protests despite Trudeau's brutal crackdown on a Canadian trucker convoy a few months prior.[7]

In November 2021, the government in Ireland had announced a plan to reduce emissions by up to 30 percent. Irish farmers formed long tractor convoys and disrupted traffic in Dublin's city center. The farmers said that the government promised financial support, but instead it was "legislating us out of the sector." These workers feared the impending death of family farms and warned that emissions cuts were putting small-scale farming at risk of extinction.[8]

There was a reason that governments around the world set the deadline for their new fertilizer emission targets for the year 2030: the Controligarchs wanted it that way.[9]

The Rockefeller Foundation and a consortium of other billionaire-backed foundations declared that solving the world's most critical problems via Agenda 2030 would not be possible without an immense influx of cash (they estimated trillions of dollars) and put up at least $60 million of their own money in March 2019 to fund "promising new ventures that help close the SDG funding gap."[10]

Following the Rockefeller imperative, in June 2019, the WEF's Klaus Schwab and the UN's secretary general, António Guterres, signed a memorandum of understanding pledging a strategic partnership between their two organizations. The goal: accelerate the implementation of Agenda 2030 by, among other things, providing the funding that the Rockefeller consortium had called for.[11]

And when Schwab announced the Great Reset's green priorities, governments around the world began to fall in line.

Key players in the Davos crowd applauded the new urgency behind Agenda 2030 and committed to help it along. The Rockefeller Foundation, for example, hailed the "incredible energy being mobilized" amid the Great Reset and the opportunity that it provided for Agenda 2030's success.[12]

The UN's food and agriculture subagency had specifically identified "excessive use of nitrogen fertilizer" as "a major cause of water pollution and greenhouse gas emissions." For independent farmers who are not Davos Men, this was bad news. It meant that their entire business model was about to be turned upside down.[13]

Slashing fertilizer usage meant either smaller crop yields, increased input costs for newer fertilization technologies, or both. Cutting methane emissions from livestock did not seem to have an easy solution. Agenda 2030 was and is directly harming the lives and livelihoods of agricultural workers (and food consumers) around the world.

Farmers everywhere worried whether Agenda 2030's climate change restrictions would force them to allow their fields to go fallow and slaughter their livestock. Meanwhile, Controligarchs such as Bill Gates and WEF-aligned conglomerates—historically some of the worst polluters on the planet—had been looking for ways to contribute to, and profit off of, the climate-friendly revolution in agricultural techniques.[14]

The food of the future is already patented.[15]

A bitter irony is that some of the same Controligarchs who profit from

Agenda 2030–compliant farming techniques had previously profited from the "dirty" agricultural technologies that they now decry. For decades, Rockefeller interests had secured dozens of patents relating to nitrogen fertilizer production. But those patents had expired.[16]

Dutch multinational chemical giant Royal DSM was one company that seemed well positioned to profit from the 2030 goals. Royal DSM—which the Gates Foundation frequently partnered with and had once invested millions in—had prepared for nitrogen reductions with new synthetic fertilizers, developed alternative proteins from canola, and even patented a solution to cow flatulence.[17]

Unlike the protesting farmers, Royal DSM was a WEF partner and an advocate of Agenda 2030.[18]

German multinational pharmaceutical conglomerate Bayer AG (a WEF partner) was also ready to capitalize on the new fertilizer and emissions reductions. Several years before the Great Reset, Bayer began acquiring the notorious seed designer Monsanto in hope of harnessing the latter's CRISPR gene-edited crop technology. Next, Bayer teamed up with a Gates-funded biotech company to genetically modify plants and turn them into self-fertilizing crops. This was the kind of patented breakthrough that could disrupt the livelihoods of independent farmers everywhere.[19]

The Controligarchs also began purchasing farms that could rapidly integrate the new fertilizers and so-called sustainable agricultural technologies. Several billionaires—particularly Good Club members Ted Turner and Bill Gates along with Jeff Bezos—had been quietly and systematically amassing millions of acres of prime ranchland and farmland in the United States.[20]

In addition to investing in new forms of synthetic fertilizers and purchasing massive quantities of arable American acreage, climate alarmists are also funding a variety of alternative proteins to replace more conventional forms of food. These range from synthetic (meaning lab-grown or plant-based) beef, pork, and chicken to fermented fungi and, most disturbingly, insects and maggots. Livestock such as pigs and cows are allegedly major emitters of methane, which the United Nations and Controligarchs consider a harmful greenhouse gas. So, naturally, Gates-funded substitutes must be provided.

As Gates and other billionaires, particularly from the Big Tech industry, secured sizable investments in the food and agriculture sectors, they began aggressively hyping the "transition" to greener agriculture and fake meats.[21]

The Rockefellers' Food Takeover Playbook

The takeover of the food system, like so many other control schemes described in this book, began with the Rockefellers and was advanced by Bill Gates. As with most of their monopolies—from oil to software and eventually to biotechnology—Controligarchs secure increasing amounts of control over the intellectual property of food production through trademarks, copyrights, and patents.

Food production (on any scale) used to be relatively simple: farmers grow crops and raise livestock. Natural disasters such as droughts and plagues of insects have periodically destroyed crops and caused famines. But then the UN and the WEF declared that "man-made" problems could only be solved with systemic, Controligarch-backed solutions. Their interventions threaten to replace what had worked for millennia: family-owned farms.

Decades ago, starting in the 1940s, the Rockefellers initiated a project called the "Green Revolution" to respond to the very real crises of poverty and starvation. The agricultural advances made possible by Rockefeller-funded research and design deserve credit and helped to feed millions of starving people as the global population rapidly increased. But the side effects also poisoned both people and resources (such as soil and water).[22]

Crucially, the Green Revolution upended mankind's most ancient vocation—working the land—and created a new system of corporate-controlled farming that made independent farmers dependent on multinational corporations for genetically modified organisms (GMOs), mostly seeds, toxic pesticides, and synthetic chemical fertilizers.

GMO seeds gave the Rockefellers and their allies control over the GMO seed patents, which, in turn, gave them control over the crops. An added benefit was controlling the types of conditions under which those seeds could flourish—primarily heavy usage of toxic pesticides such as DDT and chemical fertilizers.[23]

The program started in Mexico shortly after World War II, and at first the results seemed wonderful. Crop yields increased dramatically. But the program led to a consolidation of farm ownership—so independent farms shrank, and corporate-controlled farms got bigger. The Rockefeller seeds and pesticides ultimately hurt independent farmers, and after a decades-long campaign, Mexico banned GMO seeds and began to phase out the controversial pesticide glyphosate.[24]

The negative effects of the Green Revolution in Mexico eventually spilled over into the United States. Over time, the Rockefellers' revolutionary package of seeds, fertilizers, and pesticides allowed Mexico to increase its food exports, and that helped to drive down revenues for American farmers to unsustainable levels. In 1977, farmers went on strike and began protesting nationwide. They formed an angry convoy of five thousand tractors (sound familiar?) and drove all the way to Washington, DC. At one point, things got violent.[25]

Farmers demanded a "country of origin" label and some passionate protesting farmers were tear-gassed and jailed by authorities. "We were sick and tired of the double standard," one such American farmer recalled. "Mexico was sending their produce across the border treated with DDT and other chemicals that we weren't allowed to use," he said.[26]

Ultimately, the Green Revolution's assault on small-scale farming in Mexico, among many other problems there, forced mass migration north of the border into the United States, where wages would be meager but better. Today, nearly 73 percent of American farm laborers are undocumented immigrants, mostly from south of the border.[27]

Claiming to have solved the crises of low crop yields and poverty in Mexico, the Rockefellers then set their sights on the famine crisis in India. As in

Mexico, the Rockefeller package of seeds, pesticides, and fertilizers were effective. Strains of "miracle rice" and "golden wheat" helped solve the hunger crisis. But as in Mexico, there were huge negative consequences.[28]

"At first, the Green Revolution was wonderful," admitted Indian agricultural geneticist and environmentalist Suman Sahai. But the miracle crops required an unsustainable amount of water and caused long-term toxic contamination of some of the earth's best farmland and its water supply, "and it should have ended long before it did," Sahai lamented.[29]

Africa was the next continent that the Rockefellers set their sights on for a Green Revolution. This time, Bill Gates would help them.

Gates's War on Small Farmers

After Gates set up his foundation, he became a champion of not only human eugenics (via vaccines, abortions, and CRISPR technology) but also crop eugenics. Gates began funding research and development of genetically modified foods in 2005, seeking to pump bananas, rice, and other staples full of "micronutrients."[30]

The following year, 2006, the Gates Foundation partnered with the Rockefeller Foundation to reboot the Green Revolution—which had focused its efforts primarily in Asia and Latin America—calling the joint venture the Alliance for a Green Revolution in Africa (AGRA). They tapped former UN secretary general Kofi Annan to serve as AGRA's first chairman.[31]

Gates and the Rockefellers funneled nearly $1 billion into AGRA with the explicit goals "to develop and deliver better seeds, increase yields, improve soil fertility, upgrade storage facilities, improve market information systems, strengthen farmers' associations, expand access to credit for farmers and suppliers, and advocate for national policies that benefit smallholder farmers." Gates and the Rockefellers claim that AGRA helped the independent African farmers, but many farmers disagree. Some accuse AGRA of being a ploy for the corporate takeover of independent farms.[32]

AGRA's private sector partners include the usual WEF-allied multinational corporations, such as Mastercard, Microsoft, Monsanto (Bayer), Nestlé, and Syngenta.[33]

By partnering with the veteran agriculture NGOs such as the Rockefeller Foundation and its affiliated food research institutes, Gates asserted that he could help ameliorate hunger in Africa. This crisis offered Gates an opening to begin investing in food technology companies that could supplant independent producers. Hunger was the *problem*; the African governments' *reaction* was to let Gates and the Rockefellers take over their agriculture policies to implement their *solution*: yet another Controligarch takeover of small-scale farming.[34]

Just as Gates did with his funding of the World Health Organization to consolidate control over global COVID policy, he also sought to consolidate control over global food policy under one organization: the Rockefeller-founded global seed bank called Consultative Group on International Agricultural Research (CGIAR). The UN and the WEF were also partners in this quest to solve both world hunger and climate change.[35]

In June 2019, the WEF and the United Nations formed their strategic partnership to accelerate Agenda 2030, and three months later, in September 2019, the Gates Foundation teamed up with the World Bank and several European governments to provide more than $650 million in funding to the CGIAR seed bank.[36]

The donation from Gates and his allies was part of "a broader commitment of more than US $790 million to address the impact of climate change on food and agriculture."[37]

In January 2020, Gates announced a new venture, Bill & Melinda Gates Agricultural Innovations, nicknamed Gates Ag One. Its stated purpose was to "provide smallholder farmers in developing countries, many of whom are women, with access to the affordable tools and innovations they need to sustainably improve crop productivity and adapt to the effects of climate change."[38]

Gates chose a seed engineer named Joe Cornelius to be the leader of Gates

Ag One. Cornelius was previously the director of the Global Growth and Opportunity division at the Gates Foundation, and before that he worked on
"cutting edge life-science research and development" for Monsanto, Bayer,
and Pfizer.[39]

As a signal that Gates Ag One planned to retain control over its crop innovations, the venture had its own in-house "patent agent" (registered with the
US Patent and Trademark Office) ready to stake Gates's claims.[40]

Once again, the fallout of the COVID pandemic gave Gates and his associates the opportunity to consolidate control over major industries like agriculture. Just a few months into the pandemic, Gates and the technocrats at
the WEF and the United Nations sought to unite more than a dozen "legally
independent" crop research centers and seed banks under the CGIAR in
a plan called One CGIAR. Predictably, the need to consolidate control of
agriculture was urgent, Gates and his allies claimed, due to climate change
and the supposed need for a fundamental reset presented by COVID.[41]

A progressive organization called the International Panel of Experts on
Sustainable Food Systems noticed the obvious, criticizing the plan as "coercive" and warning that it risked "exacerbating power imbalances" with too
many wealthy white men from the Global North effectively recolonizing
the Global South.[42]

In addition to financing the development of genetically modified seeds
and the CGIAR consolidation, Gates and his allies have funded something
called the Crop Trust, which has stockpiled a staggering 1.1 million seed
varieties in a "vast 'doomsday' vault" located on an archipelago in the Arctic
Ocean.[43]

The Green Revolution was simultaneous proof that problems such as poverty and famine could be solved through human innovation and that the
solutions, such as pesticide-resistant GMO crops, can present new problems,
such as pollution, resource exhaustion, and the consolidation of small-scale
and family-owned farms into giant corporate-controlled farms. But rather
than take responsibility, the Rockefellers hyped the crop abundance while
blaming the new problems on the convenient scapegoat of climate change.[44]

Now the Controligarchs claim they can solve the climate crisis with *new* patented miracle products, which also just happen to make themselves even richer and, once again, at the expense of independent farmers.

Embrace Farming, Extend Corporate Ownership, and Extinguish Family Farms

Gates has never been shy about his passion for the "magical innovation" of fertilizer. He credits fertilizer with saving millions of lives and lifting millions more out of poverty, famously claiming that "two out of every five people on Earth today owe their lives to [fertilizer]." Gates would be a leading figure in the push for new synthetic fertilizers, and he had powerful partners.[45]

In addition to his philanthropic efforts in Africa, Gates has personally invested hundreds of millions in the fertilizer industry, but he learned early on that he would need to back companies with less baggage than some of the world's largest agrichemical giants whose past dirty deeds could present a public-relations headache.[46]

For example, when Gates invested $23 million in Monsanto in 2010, the media backlash was immediate. "The Bill and Melinda Gates Foundation's investments in Monsanto . . . have come under heavy criticism," *The Guardian* declared before asking, "Is it time for the foundation to come clean on its visions for agriculture in developing countries?"[47]

Shortly thereafter, Gates divested his stock holdings in Monsanto—one of the world's most powerful agrichemical companies and manufacturers of controversial agents such as DDT and glyphosate.[48]

However, he continued to profit from the Monsanto relationship through a genetically modified fertilizer joint venture. His foundation continued to partner with the agrichemical giant, and Gates has publicly criticized Monsanto's competition: "organic" fruits and vegetables, which use less pesticides. Gates has derided organic foods for failing to reduce climate change and claimed that growing produce organically requires too much land.[49]

When Monsanto sold out to Bayer AG for $63 billion in 2018, it was the largest merger and acquisition deal in Germany's postwar history. The deal brought together two corporations whose products, intentionally or not, were some of the deadliest in world history: Bayer, as part of IG Farben, manufactured the poisonous Zyklon B used in Nazi gas chambers, and Agent Orange–manufacturer Monsanto, which Greenpeace has called "perhaps the world's most reviled environmental villain."[50]

The merger with Monsanto allowed Bayer to pioneer and patent new genetic-modification technologies, and soon the chemical company formed a joint venture with a Gates-backed start-up called Joyn Bio. This venture sought to genetically modify crops to require less traditional synthetic fertilizer. But Gates had learned not to put all his eggs in Monsanto's much-loathed basket.[51]

Between 2010 and 2020, Gates and his co-investors poured more than $1.6 billion into various synthetic fertilizer start-ups, such as Joyn Bio, Pivot Bio, Ginkgo Bioworks, and Allonnia, which held fresh patents on genetic-modification technologies. And Gates and his allies invested at least $40 million into researching feces- and urine-based commercial fertilizers.[52]

In a 2018 event titled the "Reinvented Toilet Expo," in Beijing, Gates praised Xi Jinping's "Toilet Revolution" and proceeded to list all the ways that China's sanitation efforts could change the world. Gates boasted of his and his partners' efforts to "develop a small-scale treatment plant to process fecal sludge and biosolids from pit latrines, septic tanks, and sewers." He and his partners created the Omni Processor, which "converts the resulting materials into products with potential commercial value—like clean water, electricity, and fertilizer."[53]

Through its agricultural projects in Africa, Gates's foundation formed powerful relationships with fertilizer interest groups, in the United States and around the world, which would be his allies in the push for choking off the air supply to traditional fertilizer competitors. The Fertilizer Institute, for example, is an American advocacy organization based in Washington, DC, which aligns itself with Gates's goals and methods.[54]

In addition to being a big fan of Bill Gates, the Fertilizer Institute is ideo-logically in sync with the Controligarchs and proudly supports the UN's Sustainable Development Goals. The institute has multiple associates work-ing to train fertilizer companies in how to navigate the ESG corporate social-credit-score system and has pushed for the restrictions on traditional fertilizers that now have farmers up in arms. Over the past decade, the Fer-tilizer Institute has spent a total of $1.1 million to influence US agriculture policy.[55]

Internationally, Gates has partnered with a multinational fertilizer con-glomerate called Yara for more than a decade. Yara is a major sponsor of the Gates- and Rockefeller-backed African Green Revolution Forum (as are other crop and agrichemical giants such as Monsanto, Syngenta, and the CGIAR seed bank). Along with the Gates and Rockefeller foundations, Yara has been among the largest funders of the African Green Revolution.[56]

Purported environmentalists have lauded Yara for its new "green" fertil-izer efforts, but it has long been accused by watchdog organizations of caus-ing devastating pollution and fueling a "climate catastrophe." The WEF, for example, extols Yara's virtues on its website despite Yara's sordid history, which includes massive worldwide pollution and bribing officials in coun-tries such as Libya, Russia, and India. According to the WEF, the Gates-allied multinational fertilizer company "delivers solutions for sustainable agriculture and is guided by the ambition to grow a nature-positive food future."[57]

In 2021, Biden's "climate czar" John Kerry honored Yara as one of the founding members of something called the First Movers Coalition, which is a group of over twenty-five multinational corporations—including nu-merous WEF partners—committed to the UN's "net zero" emission goals and marching in lockstep to the 2030 agenda.[58]

Why? Because Yara has bought into the 2030 agenda, net zero, and has even patented new "greenhouse gas reducing" technologies. And now that Yara is well positioned to profit from Agenda 2030, a subsidiary of the Norway-based conglomerate is pouring money into the US political system.

Since 2015, Yara North America Inc. has spent more than $1 million lobbying American officials on fertilizer issues, including for favorable "regulatory treatment of fertilizer" and "sustainable agriculture."[59]

Gates's other fertilizer partners—Monsanto and Bayer—have consistently been the largest lobbying spenders in the United States, spending a whopping $120 million in just ten years (leading up to their merger). They, too, benefit from the new Agenda 2030 fertilizer restrictions.[60]

By partnering with the agrichemical companies that had wreaked havoc on the environment in the first place, Gates became one of the world's preeminent experts and most high-profile investors in the new fertilizers— those that would supposedly fix the problems that companies such as Yara and Monsanto had created.

Gates's investment in and takeover of the fertilizer market was the agricultural version of Microsoft's Embrace-Extend-Extinguish strategy.

Gates's Great American Land Grab

For more than a decade, as Bill Gates has been targeting the fertilizer industry, he has also been quietly buying up large swaths of American farmland. In June 2022, he hit his first speed bump on his journey to become America's largest farmland owner. Residents across the state of North Dakota were "livid" when they learned that the billionaire had purchased Campbell Farms, which owned 2,100 acres of prime farmland, for $13.5 million in late 2021. They demanded that their attorney general intervene.

The state attorney general, having gotten a "big earful" from his fellow Dakotans, sent a letter to Gates's holding company, Red River Trust. He wanted to know what the purpose of Gates's purchase was and whether the sale complied with an anticorporate farming law supposedly in place to prohibit exactly the type of takeover that Gates had just initiated.

The North Dakota governor was noticeably silent on the controversy, which some of his constituents attributed to his history as a former Microsoft executive and recipient of $100,000 in campaign cash from his former employer. Ultimately, the North Dakota attorney general found that Gates's purchase of the Campbell family farm fell into a legal loophole, and the deal was approved.[61]

The loophole was instructive: while Gates would not have been allowed to purchase the farm with his holding company for its own agricultural purposes, his company was allowed to *own* the land if it planned to *lease* it. Gates's holding company confirmed that it would be the landowner and that the Campbell family would lease the land they previously owned.[62]

The North Dakota land grab was only the latest in a long line of Gates-backed takeovers of American farmland that saw Gates's agriculture holdings surge from negligible acreage in 2011 to at least 270,000 acres in 2022. Spread across eighteen states, Gates's land now makes up a combined chunk of America larger than the area of New York City.[63]

Gates began his farmland buying spree in December 2012—nearly one decade prior to the Campbell farm takeover in North Dakota. Gates's holding company completed the purchases of Georgia-based Coggins and Stanley Farms in 2013 and 2014, respectively. "The investment in the farm is not a foundation investment and doesn't have anything to do with foundation work," said Christopher Williams, Gates Foundation spokesman.[64]

In 2016, the two farms (both third-generation family-run operations) merged to form Generation Farms and combined their thousands of acres across Florida and Georgia. The following year, Gates achieved his largest land purchase yet when he snapped up sixty-one properties in one fell swoop (dropping more than half a billion dollars in the deal).[65]

Today, Gates's largest farmland holdings are in northern Louisiana, where his companies own nearly 70,000 acres growing corn, cotton, rice, and soybeans. Gates's second-largest agricultural holding is in Arkansas with approximately 47,000 acres. In Nebraska, Gates's companies grow soybeans and other crops across roughly 20,000 acres.[66]

And in Gates's home state of Washington, his 14,500-acre potato farm—called 100 Circles Farm—is visible from space and pulls between one thousand and two thousand *tons* of potatoes out of the ground every day. Gates bought the massive potato farm—a major supplier for fast-food leader Mc-Donald's and previously run by Conagra—for $171 million in 2018.[67]

All told, Gates has spent over $1 billion on farm acquisitions and the Agenda 2030–compliant technologies his farms now employ (not including the $850 million in John Deere stock holdings he transferred to Melinda Gates in May 2021 amid their divorce negotiations). Gates's total funding toward his global food and agriculture agenda tops $11.7 billion.[68]

Gates has remained mostly silent on his farmland acquisitions. He was asked, "Why are you buying so much farmland?" on the internet forum Reddit, and his response was cryptic:

> My investment group chose to do this. It is not connected to climate. The agriculture sector is important. With more productive seeds we can avoid deforestation and help Africa deal with the climate difficulty they already face. It is unclear how cheap biofuels can be but if they are cheap, it can solve the aviation and truck emissions [problem].[69]

Gates's response to his alleged takeover of American farmlands appeared contradictory. He claimed that his farmland purchases were not his decisions and that the purchases were "not connected to climate" (his professed passion), but then proceeded to give his reasons why the agricultural sectors that he does invest in (seeds, biofuels) are important for dealing with "climate difficulty" and solving emissions. And while Gates was publicly advocating for a Green Revolution, he was quietly grabbing the farmland from family-run farms that have found it increasingly difficult to survive.[70]

Gates and his affiliates already control the commercial inputs (and intellectual property) of agriculture—the genetically modified seeds, the fertilizers, and the herbicides and pesticides. Now he wants the land.[71]

When Gates buys tens of thousands of acres, he is not just buying the land—he is also buying the rights to water below the ground. In addition to farms (and irrigation) and fertilizer, Gates has been hunting for sizable interests in water and water treatment—a crucial component of the agriculture industry.[72]

Gates first bought a large chunk of food-services conglomerate Ecolab in 2008. Taking a 25 percent ownership stake in the multibillion-dollar company—which has commercial, residential, and agricultural operations—required board approval.[73]

Ecolab's board approved Gates's purchase, and he has continued to purchase huge numbers of Ecolab stocks since then—both personally (through Cascade Investment) and through the Bill & Melinda Gates Foundation Trust. Notably, Gates investment guru Michael Larson has been on the Ecolab board since 2012.[74]

Ecolab is another multinational conglomerate and WEF partner that pollutes the environment but purchases absolution from Davos through ESG commitments. Since 2008, Ecolab and its subsidiaries have spent more than $15.6 million lobbying for favorable treatment on issues such as climate change, pesticides, fertilizers, and "sustainability." Ecolab provides water treatment services to both farms and the food industry, so Gates's interest in the company—valued at more than $6 billion—appears to complement his fertilizer and farmland endeavors.[75]

In 2012, Gates also began buying up pristine farmland land atop Florida's legendary aquifer. By 2014, Gates had spent nearly $30 million buying up almost five thousand acres. A subsidiary of Gates's Cascade Investment vehicle, called Lakeland Sands, pumps twenty million gallons of groundwater out of Florida's aquifer every single day and is, in the words of a Florida Springs councilman, "compromising the health and welfare of North Florida."[76]

Gates (or his investment group) chose folksy and benign-sounding names for his agriculture landholding companies (such as Oak River, Midwest, Suwannee, and Generation Farms and Red River Trust, Mt. Lemmon Holdings, and Cottonwood Ag Management), but his intentions appear anything but benign.

In 2020, a nonprofit agricultural consortium called Leading Harvest revealed what Gates and his partners had in store. According to the press release:

Today, Earth Day, a group of forward-looking farmers, conservation-
ists, landowners, managers and investors are launching Leading Harvest, an agriculture sustainability venture providing the first scalable,
industry-wide solution to urgent issues facing us—from climate change
and biodiversity to the resilience of our croplands and communities.

Farmers and the supply chain for too long have had to manage a
complex landscape of sustainability platforms, each using different
data tools, metrics and scorecards to address a single crop, issue area,
or stakeholder interest. Instead of improving outcomes, this approach
has both discouraged participation in critical sustainability efforts and
underperformed consumer expectations for tangible assurances of
proper stewardship of our agricultural lands.

Leading Harvest resolves this stubborn barrier to sustainability
with a universal standard that can be applied across all crops and geog-
raphies while addressing a uniquely broad spectrum of societal interests.[77]

Gates's Cottonwood Ag Management was one of the inaugural members
in Leading Harvest's effort to create a "sustainability standard," and Gates's
Oak River Farms properties are committed participants. The Leading Harvest standard lists thirteen "Sustainability Principles" that look suspiciously
similar to the UN's Sustainable Development Goals.[78]

Creating a "standard" is a critical component in step one of the Embrace-
Extend-Extinguish strategy that the Justice Department accused Microsoft
of using to exterminate its competitors. Leading Harvest began as a voluntary sustainability pledge and eventually formalized this pledge by adopting
what it calls the Leading Harvest Farmland Management Standard.[79]

According to this standard, Leading Harvest would next extend its reach
within the agricultural industry and encourage farms not owned by Gates
to "share and adopt better practices now," which means committing to the
Leading Harvest standard.[80]

Leading Harvest now appears to have reached the Extend phase as it boasts more than two million acres (and counting) committed to its standard. For a sense of what the Extinguish phase might look like, just ask the Dutch farmers.[81]

Meanwhile, Microsoft's angel investor, IBM, is creating a network called Food Trust that endeavors to use AI to track and control the global food supply.[82]

Gates has funded another produce preservative company called Apeel, which manufactures a fatty, waxy, and edible coating that allows fruits and vegetables to look fresh for longer. The FDA accepted Apeel's application for a "Generally Recognized as Safe" classification, but some still have concerns about consuming the coating, which they say cannot be washed off.[83]

And if that does not seem like enough playing with the food you eat, in 2013, Gates boldly declared that the "future of food" was fake meat and dairy.[84]

Fake Dairy, Fake Eggs, and Fake Breast Milk

The Controligarchs have been working on revolutionizing dairy products for decades.

In 1993, the FDA approved Monsanto's artificial growth hormone, Posilac, which was used to increase cow milk production by approximately one gallon per cow per day. The synthetic hormone was controversial for its feared link to diseases in both cows and humans.[85]

As consumers grew wise to the effects of artificial growth hormones in their dairy products, grocery stores began selling "hormone free" options, and Monsanto sold the artificial Posilac hormone to Eli Lilly.[86]

Consumers' rejection of cow milk pumped full of Monsanto's artificial hormones also led to the rise of alternative dairy products like soy-based and nut-based milk alternatives. The Silk brand of soy milk traces its roots to the late 1970s, but the concept of soy milk really took off among vegans and the lactose intolerant in the late 1990s. The company's revenue more than doubled in a single year—from $29.6 million in 2000 to an astonishing $81 million in 2001.[87]

The following year, America's largest dairy conglomerate, Dean Foods, acquired the Silk producer for a combined investment topping $200 million.[88] And in 2016, the France-based multinational food conglomerate Danone purchased the Silk brand in a deal that exceeded $10 billion.[89]

Danone is a major WEF partner and has spent more than $3.5 million in the last five years lobbying American politicians for favorable legislation on topics like "sustainable agriculture." The Controligarch-aligned foreign food conglomerate continues to roll out new, *patented* fake milks, such as Silk Nextmilk, which was released in January 2022.[90]

While soy- and nut-based dairy alternatives like Silk have been around for decades, egg alternatives are relatively new. In 2011, an entrepreneur and former UN-affiliated activist named Josh Tetrick founded a company that hoped to flip the egg industry upside down. Gates was an early investor.[91]

Tetrick's Hampton Creek became embroiled in scandal when allegations surfaced that the company had been buying its own product en masse to boost sales numbers. In a crushing blow, Target removed the fake egg products from its shelves because of safety concerns.[92]

Hampton Creek's Controligarch investors—such as Bill Gates and Peter Thiel—were left with (fake) egg on their faces.

But it's not just your protein sources that Bill Gates is trying to disrupt. He wants to change the diet of babies, too. In 2020, Gates's climate change–focused investment firm, Breakthrough Energy Ventures, became one of the first investors (leading a $3.5 million funding round) in a company called Biomilq, which was described by CNBC as "a North Carolina-based start-up that's targeting infant nutrition by attempting to reproduce mother's breast milk in a lab."[93]

Biomilq's CEO and cofounder is a Gates Foundation alum and former food scientist at the General Mills conglomerate. As partners in Gates's Breakthrough Energy Venture, other Good Club members and WEF-aligned billionaires such as Jeff Bezos, Mark Zuckerberg, Richard Branson, and Michael Bloomberg backed the mother's milk substitute.[94]

Gates's investment in Biomilq made headlines in 2022 when a devastating baby formula shortage struck the United States and the synthetic baby food company was seen as a beneficiary of the crisis. The culprit for the shortage was Biden's FDA—which had shut down the largest formula production plant in the United States—for what was effectively a false contamination alarm. Biomilq hadn't even hit the market yet. Nonetheless, the fiasco raised the profile of Gates's synthetic breast milk investment and, as they say, there is no such thing as bad press.[95]

At this point, it was clear that Bill Gates was leading the investments into alternative proteins—including things like edible insects and lab-grown "meats." But other Controligarchs wanted to bring lab-grown meats to market as well.

The Rise of Alternative Proteins and Lab-Grown Meats

In an obscure 1931 *Strand Magazine* editorial, British prime minister Winston Churchill predicted the rise of lab-grown meats. Though he did not mention the word *lab*, Churchill anticipated that meats such as chicken breasts would be produced in "a suitable medium." In the piece, titled "Fifty Years Hence," Churchill wrote:

> With a greater knowledge of what are called hormones, i.e., the chemical messengers in our blood, it will be possible to control growth. We shall escape the absurdity of growing a whole chicken in order to eat the breast or wing, by growing these parts separately under a suitable medium.[96]

Though lab-grown meats were not quite ready by the 1980s as Churchill predicted, he was not far off. A prisoner-of-war camp survivor named Willem van Eelen reimagined the idea of lab-grown meat after spending time in a Japanese internment camp and, fifty years later, applied for the first lab-grown meat patent in 1994. In 2017, the Eat Just fake-egg company purchased the patent from Eelen's estate and named his daughter, Ira, an advisor.[97]

Decades after Churchill's prediction, Google's Sergey Brin was perhaps the first Controligarch to bring synthetic meat to fruition, after he quietly spent $330,000 to grow the world's first "hamburger" in a Dutch lab. Scientists created the synthetic beef by harvesting stem cells from cows and growing them in a similar way to how stem cells are used for growing human organs.[98]

The BBC described the petri dish–to-plate process thusly:

> [Professor Mark Post] starts with stem cells extracted from cow muscle tissue. In the laboratory, these are cultured with nutrients and growth-promoting chemicals to help them develop and multiply. Three weeks later, there are more than a million stem cells, which are put into smaller dishes where they coalesce into small strips of muscle about a centimetre long and a few millimetres thick.[99]

The initial result was small white "beef" pellets, which were collected, smooshed, and placed into a freezer to be cooked at a later date. The white color of the fake beef—made with something called "fetal bovine serum" harvested from baby cows—was decidedly unpalatable, so the scientists dyed the "meat" red with beetroot juice. PETA was thrilled.[100]

The Maastricht University scientist who developed the burger, Mark Post, went on to cofound a company called Mosa Meat and promised that the price of the synthetic burger would come down. Post was a distinguished speaker at the WEF's Annual Meeting of the New Champions 2015, where he hyped the crowd on lab-grown meats. Despite nearly $100 million in funding and adding celebrities such as Leonardo DiCaprio to its board, thus far, Mosa has found that its *patented* lab-grown meat has been difficult to scale.[101]

One of the problems with lab-grown meat (beyond its ludicrous price) is its unnatural flavor. But recent studies have shown that the ingredients in animal blood—primarily myoglobin and hemoglobin—can be harvested from cows, horses, and even wild boars to give fake meat a more real taste.

Additionally, the "heme protein" in soy and other plants (including tobacco) can be added to the lab beef to produce a more meat-y taste.[102]

In 2018, Gates and other wealthy investors—including Kimbal Musk (Elon Musk's brother), Virgin Group billionaire Richard Branson, and General Electric's former CEO Jack Welch—poured $17 million into a company called Memphis Meats. The company engineered a unique form of climate-friendly synthetic meat and boasted the creation of the "world's first clean meatball" and the world's first "clean poultry" in 2016 and 2017, respectively.[103]

In January 2020, Gates, Branson, Musk, and other investors joined with food behemoths Cargill and Tyson Foods to provide Memphis Meats an additional $161 million in funding. Like other synthetic-meat companies that Gates had invested in, Upside Foods—the new name for Memphis Meats—holds numerous patents.[104]

Upside Foods and other companies hoping to grow meat in a lab—like Mosa Meat—have had trouble making their synthetic meats cost-effective. In 2016, the Upside Foods CEO admitted that the company's fake ground beef costs approximately $3,300 per gram. This would mean that one average-sized meatball would cost nearly $375,000, and a plate of spaghetti with four meatballs could cost over $1 million.[105]

The Upside CEO claimed that within three years (i.e., by 2019) the cost would plummet to just five dollars per gram, and by 2021, Upside's fake beef would be two cents per gram. "That has yet to happen," *Business Insider* reported in 2021.

That same year, two of Upside's top executives—including its chief science officer and cofounder as well as the vice president and co-inventor of the synthetic technology behind some of Upside's products—left the company, dealing Upside a major blow. It seems that lab-grown meats have yet to prove as popular and viable as early investors (and inventors) had hoped.[106]

Still, the US Department of Agriculture and the FDA have agreed to legitimize the market for lab-grown meat, and financial analysts have projected lab-grown meats to balloon into a half-billion-dollar per year industry by the year 2030.[107]

The World Economic Forum is fully behind lab-grown foods and has promoted a company called Modern Meadow, which has taken the lab-grown concept a step further by biofabricating, or 3D-printing, meat (based on its 3D-printed human organ concept).[108] Around the same time Ginkgo Bioworks was founded, another genetically modified food company, called Beyond Meat, started up as well.[109]

And Gates soon enlisted them in fighting the good fight. Since 2013, Gates had been casually discussing replacing "very inefficient" natural meat with meat alternatives and teased "alternatives to meat." But as he locked in ownership stakes in at least half a dozen synthetic-meat companies, he decided that it was time to pressure the world into making his investments more profitable.[110]

In an interview with *MIT Technology Review* promoting his 2021 book, *How to Avoid a Climate Disaster*, Gates made the shocking claim that "all rich countries should move to 100% synthetic beef." Anticipating pushback, Gates assured that people will "get used to the taste difference," before promising that attempts to "make it taste even better over time" were underway.[111]

"Impossible and Beyond have a road map, a quality road map and a cost road map, that makes them totally competitive," said Gates, referring to the fake-meat companies in which he had invested. "As for scale today, they don't represent 1% of the meat in the world, but they're on their way," Gates said. "Eventually, that green premium is modest enough that you can sort of change the [behavior of] people or use regulation to totally shift the demand," Gates said. "So, for meat in the middle-income-and-above countries, I do think it's possible."[112]

Beyond Meat and Impossible Foods, both of which were founded in 2011, were lucky enough to count Bill Gates as an angel investor. Now they are two of the world's largest plant-based meat companies.

Beyond Meat was incorporated on April 8, 2011, and Gates first invested in the company on January 10, 2012. The Beyond Meat founder was so broke that he could not afford a hotel room when Gates first met with him. As Beyond Meat secured dozens of trademarks and patents, Gates continued to up his investment and even began publishing recipes for Beyond "chicken" tikka masala and grilled "chicken" salad. The Beyond Meat founder is now a multimillionaire.[113]

And Gates timed his investment almost perfectly: he quietly dumped millions of dollars in Beyond Meat stock just before the company had an "epic crash."[114]

Shortly after its May 6, 2019, initial public stock offering, Beyond Meat's stock peaked at $234.90 per share. The month of its peak (July 2019), according to documents filed with the SEC on July 31, 2019, Gates owned 1,688,971 shares, putting his total investment at $396,739,288. Gates sold 128,737 shares, pulling a potential $30 million out of the company.[115]

While not an exhaustive sell-off, it indicated a bearish view of the stock's future. And it was well-timed. Fast-food partners McDonald's, Dunkin' Donuts, Panda Express, Taco Bell, and others eventually dropped their Beyond Meat products because of low enthusiasm. Beyond Meat's stock tumbled more than 50 percent and led to layoffs in August 2022. Some analysts called it a "zombie stock" that could drop to zero, bankrupting the company.[116]

Impossible Foods is also failing with consumers. Burger King started offering the Impossible Burger in 2019. Less than two years later, sales dropped precipitously, and Burger King was forced to drastically cut the price. The company also faced legal troubles, suing rival Motif FoodWorks, which had implored the US Patent and Trademark Office to revoke an Impossible Foods patent.[117]

It turns out, fake foods are not popular with consumers. The billionaire-backed alternative proteins (fake dairy, fake eggs, and fake meats) are either genetically engineered, genetically modified, or heavily processed (or some combination of all three). And foods designed in a lab taste unnatural.[118]

One of Beyond Meat's first investors was Big Tech mogul and vegan activist Christopher Isaac "Biz" Stone (who had cofounded Twitter with Jack Dorsey and held a senior position at Google). In May 2013, Beyond Meat announced a new wave of funds, and by 2014 Bill Gates had joined the Twitter cofounder, becoming one of Beyond Meat's earliest and largest investors.[119]

Just over a year later, Gates increased his Beyond Meat investment. The total funding amount was undisclosed. Filings with the SEC indicate Gates held at least 650,000 shares by October 2018. The following year, Beyond Meat's initial public offering caused Gates's investment to nearly triple.[120]

Impossible Foods was founded the same year as Beyond Meat with the audacious goal of using genetically modified yeast to create a vegan burger that tastes (and even "bleeds") like meat. Impossible filed its first patent on July 12, 2013, and just four days later, Gates became one of the first major investors in a $25 million funding round. Impossible received its first patent in July 2017 and that same month, Gates poured in more money in a $75 million funding round.[121]

Impossible has secured more than two dozen patents for its fake meat (and fake dairy) products and has more than one hundred patents pending.[122]

Around the time Gates was considering cashing in some of his Beyond Meat stock, he began investing in yet another fake-meat competitor, Ginkgo Bioworks. Ginkgo (which had created the Joyn Bio partnership with Bayer to genetically modify crops that could produce their own nitrogen fertilizer) spun out another company called Motif FoodWorks in 2019.[123]

Motif FoodWorks quickly raised nearly $350 million and would soon become a rival to other fake-meat companies. Gates's Breakthrough Energy Ventures—a coalition of the usual Controligarch suspects including Bezos, Bloomberg, Branson, Zuckerberg, and others—funded Motif FoodWorks, and the company added the BlackRock financial behemoth (and WEF darling) to this high-profile list of backers.[124]

In 2022, Gates continued to promote his Motif investment (even as Motif was engaged in a bitter legal battle with the other Gates-backed fake-meat producer, Impossible Foods). Motif publicly thanked Gates for his support.[125]

Eat the Maggots, Peasants!

Other oligarchs rushed to get a piece of the action. Billionaires Zuckerberg (and his sister), Bloomberg, Branson, and others have, like Gates, invested millions in alternative proteins. While plant-based and lab-grown meats have received the bulk of the attention, new alternative proteins have captured the Controligarchs' attention: microbes and maggots.[126]

Amazon billionaire Jeff Bezos and former vice president Al Gore (both climate activists) joined forces with Bill Gates to fund a microbe-based protein company called Nature's Fynd (which the company says could be "planet-saving").[127]

Nature's Fynd microbes are technically fungi but are nothing like an average portobello mushroom. Rather, Fy, a protein whose name is an acronym for the fusaria of Yellowstone National Park, are closer to bacteria, and they thrive in Yellowstone's volcanic hot springs.[128]

Despite all the talk about saving the planet, the bottom line for Gates's investment team is obviously money. "We think the Nature's Fynd model can undercut costs of traditional protein sources," a spokesperson said. "That's what really sold us on this opportunity."[129]

As if microbe-based and lab-grown meats and dairy products were not unappetizing enough, the United Nations, the WEF, Bill Gates, and other ideologically aligned climate capitalists decided to take their environmentally friendly food offerings a step further: they began pushing insect-based foods.[130]

In 2013, a 201-page UN report titled *Edible Insects—Future Prospects for Food and Feed Security* concluded that more conventional protein farming (such as beef, pork, poultry, and dairy) will "destroy the planet" and must be replaced by alternative and insect-based proteins.[131]

Just over a year later, in 2015, *The Late Late Show* host James Corden, actress Anna Farris (famous for starring in the *Scary Movie* franchise and the highly rated sitcom, *Mom*), and *Unbreakable Kimmy Schmidt* actor Tituss Burgess made headlines for sampling a smattering of gourmet bug-based snacks.

The late-night show segment was entirely bug positive, and the second-tier celebrities (minus Burgess) were praised for being "more than willing to chomp on the alternative to the classic [ants-on-a-log] kids' snack as soon as they heard [that real] ants 'increase sexual vigor.'"[132]

In 2018, *Vanity Fair* produced a video titled *Nicole Kidman Eats Bugs* as part of a series about Hollywood celebrities' "secret talents." Kidman seductively ate a four-course meal of all maggots, grubs, and grasshoppers. "Mm, extraordinary," the actress gushed, licking the hornworms from her chopsticks. "Two billion people in the world eat bugs, and I am one of them," Kidman said, before diving into course two (mealworms), which had a "fruity taste." She said, "I'd recommend it," multiple times in the bizarre video.[133]

Apparently, *Vanity Fair* thought that the "sex sells" marketing strategy would work on insects, though the comments on the YouTube video suggest otherwise.[134]

The actress Angelina Jolie revealed that she and her children regularly eat insects. Justin Timberlake partnered with American Express (a major WEF partner) for his *Man of the Woods* album-release party. On the menu? Ants and grasshoppers. Numerous other celebs have likewise put out favorable videos attempting to normalize eating bugs.[135]

In concert with Davos, the media seems to be pushing maggots as a food source. The WEF and the billionaire-backed *Economist* magazine (and many others) have produced an unending stream of content extolling the future of insect-based foods, and most mainstream media outlets have likewise issued pro-bug propaganda.[136]

After the Super Bowl in February 2021, *Iron Man* actor Robert Downey Jr. went on late-night television's *The Late Show with Stephen Colbert* to promote a company into which he had put a staggering $224 million: Ÿnsect, an insect-based protein and fertilizer company.[137]

"What is this . . . You're not just getting me to eat dirt?," the late-night host asked after taking a deep whiff of the brown powder–filled jar. "Nah, man, I wouldn't play you, bro," replied the actor and boasted that it had just been approved in the European Union for human consumption.

"I could put this in a smoothie?" Colbert asked. "I'm tellin' ya—yup—and they're going to be making all kinds of stuff out of it," Downey Jr. replied, before touting the amount of agriculture emissions insect powder could dramatically reduce.[138]

The WEF had tapped Ÿnsect to join the Forum's "Global Innovators" program one month before Colbert's Super Bowl special, and the WEF quickly began publishing pro-Ÿnsect propaganda. Ÿnsect had raised $435 million and pledged to build "a more sustainable future."[139]

"With climate change and increasing populations worldwide, we need to produce more food with less available land and fewer resources," said Ÿnsect's cofounder, president, and CEO, who was "thrilled" to receive the WEF's "prestigious" invitation and proud to become a contributor to the Davos agenda.[140]

The Gates Foundation, as usual, was ahead of the curve vis-à-vis insect-based food sources and awarded two grants to a maggot-based protein company called AgriProtein.[141]

AgriProtein grows maggots from black soldier flies, which eat organic food waste from restaurants and breweries and can reduce human excrement called fecal sludge. The Gates-backed company won an award from the United Nations in 2013 and hopes to feed its "MagMeal" product to livestock and house pets alike.[142]

Insect-based protein companies are facing some pushback as consumers grow increasingly wary of the motives of Gates, the UN, and the WEF for pushing alternative proteins. "Everybody thinks that we're working for Bill Gates—somehow we're all Bill Gates conspiracy theorists," said one cricket-based protein powder producer.[143]

The War on Farmers Is a War on You

The UN and WEF's acceleration of Agenda 2030 and the Sustainable Development Goals in the name of "reducing climate change" amounts to a war on family-run farms. In typical Schwabian fashion, the emission restrictions followed the familiar problem-reaction-solution playbook.

The problem, 2030 agenda setters declared, is that agriculture in its current form consumes too many resources while producing too many emissions (in the form of dirty fertilizers, methane from cow flatulence, and carbon dioxide from heavy farm equipment). Their solution seems to be to revolutionize agriculture into a patented system of control.

And it should come as no surprise that while the peasants are expected to eat fermented fungal patties, lab-grown meats, and maggot milkshakes, the Controligarchs—with their private chefs—have no intention of doing the same if recent behavior is any indicator.

Bill Gates and Warren Buffett famously love eating beef burgers and steaks when Gates visits his mentor in Omaha. Mark Zuckerberg likes smoking beef brisket and grilling pork ribs (from real cows and pigs) and says meats taste "doubly better when you hunt an animal for yourself."[144]

Jeff Bezos loves real beef burgers so much that he tasked an Amazon executive with developing something he called the "single-cow burger" purely out of curiosity, wondering if a beef burger tasted better if it came from a single cow. In this case, a one-cow Wagyu burger, it did.[145]

In 2021, Bezos donated a "surprise" $100 million to a charity run by world-famous chef José Andrés, whose Bazaar Meat steakhouses—with locations in Los Angeles, Chicago, and Las Vegas—sell the finest Kobe beefsteaks for more than $65 *per ounce*. Ironically, or perhaps unsurprisingly, the beef merchant used the $100 million to fight climate change.[146]

The good news is that the novelty of fake-protein products seems to be wearing off, and consumers are buying less and less of it. The bad news is that the UN, the WEF, Gates, and other Controligarchs seem committed to pushing them on us anyway. After all, the Controligarchs have a lot of money riding on these creepy cuisines.[147]

Billionaire George Soros is yet another Controligarch who, like Bill Gates and Jeff Bezos, has invested heavily in the food and agriculture industries. But instead of waging war on farmers, Soros wages silent ideological and financial wars on entire countries.

6

The Open Society Scheme

I fancied myself as some kind of god . . . If truth be known, I carried some rather potent messianic fantasies with me from childhood, which I felt I had to control . . . It is a sort of disease when you consider yourself some kind of god, the creator of everything, but I feel comfortable about it now since I began to live it out.[1]

—*George Soros, as quoted in the* Los Angeles Times, *October 2004*

One cool afternoon in May 2022, global financial speculator George Soros took the stage at the annual World Economic Forum confab to deliver an alarming address.[2]

Soros, then into his nineties and showing it, wanted to address a world on fire—a fire that, as we will see, he had helped build, kindle, and douse with gasoline.[3]

"Since the last Davos meeting the course of history has changed dramatically," Soros began. "Russia invaded Ukraine," he added, and this development had "shaken Europe to its core." There would be no coming back from this new crisis, according to Soros. A new normal was taking shape.

"The invasion may have been the beginning of the Third World War," Soros declared, "and our civilization may not survive it." This would be the subject of his address. The Davos Men and Women in his audience chuckled, nervously.

Russia's invasion of its sistering land, Ukraine, did not "come out of the blue," Soros admitted. This conflict had been long in the making. In a way,

Soros had played a role. It was no secret that Soros was Russia's public enemy number one, and he and his philanthropic outfits were famously ban-
ished from that country. Soros had done more, perhaps, than any one person
(including President Obama's "point man" on Ukraine, then vice president
Biden) to steer Ukraine away from Russia and toward the neoliberal Western
establishment.[4]

In Davos, Soros acknowledged that the West—particularly the European
Union—had failed in its design to keep peace across Europe. In a way, it was
an admission of his own failures. Soros, along with the WEF, had been instrumental in helping establish the European Union (or EU, which he regarded as the embodiment of what he calls "an open society").[5]

And when the United Kingdom had threatened the EU with a British exit
(or "Brexit"), Soros leaped to the EU's defense, vocally and financially, seeking to thwart those efforts.[6]

The Russia-Ukraine conflict of 2022 was the culmination of many failures, not just the EU's, especially for a globalist such as Soros. Not only had
he worked tirelessly for decades on EU expansion, but he had also been a
staunch defender of the North Atlantic Treaty Organization (NATO).[7]

NATO, Soros once wrote in the early 1990s, was critical to his (and
others') plans for what they called a "New World Order."[8]

The New World Order was a name that Soros and other Western thought
leaders coined to describe the state of the world after the Soviet Union fell
in the early 1990s. After a half century of dueling superpowers between the
United States and the Union of Soviet Socialist Republics, the United States
defeated the Soviets to become the world's first "hyperpower."[9]

After World War II, the world order was called the "liberal world order,"
the "liberal international order," and the "international rules-based order"—
all names that returned in recent years after "New World Order" fell out of
favor.[10]

For Soros, the New World Order was not a term invented to describe a
world in which the United States would be dominant. Rather, the New World
Order was to be the transition to a global governance system that now looks

a lot like Klaus Schwab's World Economic Forum with its revolutionary stakeholder capitalism ambitions.

For the New World Order to succeed, there could be no hyperpowers. The United States's role would have to change, substantially. As we will see, Soros has worked very hard to see to that.

Soros's speech to the WEF revealed that he was not like most other Davos Men. Unlike Klaus Schwab and Bill Gates, Soros rarely talks about controlling human behaviors *directly*. In fact, he often indicates his desire to do the opposite. He criticized what he termed "instruments of control" made possible by the pandemic and technology such as artificial intelligence. He said lockdowns had "disastrous consequences."[11]

To his credit, Soros has been very vocal against repressive regimes. He was critical of not only Vladimir Putin's Russia but also the CCP. He has also criticized the Big Tech companies' capacity for manipulation and control. These statements make Soros appear to be an old-school liberal and a borderline sympathetic character.[12]

But don't be fooled: Soros craves power just as much as the rest of his Controligarch peers do.

Soros is not the type of billionaire who seeks to forcibly inject a population with a new drug or tell people what types of foods they can eat. In fact, his statements indicate he wants maximum freedom for the individual and is opposed to such heavy-handed mandates.[13] Instead of forcing behavior, Soros wants to change hearts and minds.

In order to accomplish this, he has for decades engaged in what he calls "political philanthropy." This form of philanthropy is a familiar method of self-enrichment and tax mitigation with the added benefit of purchasing good press.[14]

Just like Bill Gates (and the Rockefellers before him), Soros receives exponentially more in intangible and fringe benefits for every dollar he gives away. Soros then uses some of his proceeds to reinvest in his philanthropy and other proceeds to invest in political decision-makers (who happen to make him more money).

But Soros seems to be more than a simple profit-motivated capitalist like Gates or even the Rockefellers. Soros is a true believer. His intentions behind pouring money into his social justice initiatives, such as Black Lives Matter or electing soft-on-crime prosecutors, are philanthropic. He says that racial grievances have not been fully aired out and that the disparate impact that law enforcement has on minority communities must be rectified by emptying the prisons.[15]

But despite the good intentions woven into his carefully crafted statements, the consequences of Soros's actions and funding cannot be ignored. And those consequences are bigger than the advancing "instruments of control" such as pandemic lockdowns or limiting food preferences. Soros's instruments of control are changing attitudes and behaviors at the societal level—imposing his political will and bending the will of the people to fit his demands.[16]

For decades, Soros has spent his money on initiatives such as influencing society's attitudes on birth control, gun control, drug legalization, criminal justice, the nuclear family, and parents' role in childhood education. If a society comports with Soros's preferences, he declares it "an open society." If it does not, he declares it a "closed society" and seeks to reform it.[17]

Entire books have been written on Soros's role as the global "man behind the curtain," but none have revealed the true extent of his influence on American culture and around the world. The best most can do is speculate about global conspiracies and secret networks. But the facts tell a more nuanced story about his strategies for leveraging crises, his grand vision for society, and the way in which he has amassed global influence and personal wealth for himself and his heirs.

Funding America's Decline

In the United States, Soros has been the single-biggest financier of political causes for decades. In 2022, Soros poured $178.5 million into federal campaigns ($0 went to Republicans), which made him by far the biggest campaign contributor in that cycle.[18] His seemingly endless stream of dark money—flowing through a network of political nonprofit organizations—is unmatched even by the likes of wealthier billionaires like Bill Gates and the Rockefeller family.

In Soros's 1993 speech on the future of NATO, he declared that the United Nations had failed as an organization that could assume control over US troops.[19] Soros was not a fan of "American supremacy." The very idea of American exceptionalism needed to be watered down, and NATO could be the means to do so. Top bureaucrats such as Clinton's secretary of state, Strobe Talbott, agreed with Soros. Talbott believed that "events in our own wondrous and terrible century" had already clinched "the case for world government."[20]

Soros pioneered political philanthropy, creating a new form of political dark money fifty years ago, and has furthered it with tax-exempt entities such as his Open Society Foundations. Ironically, the societies that he builds and shapes are sometimes the most closed of all. Eastern Europe and Asia became the breeding grounds for the radical left-wing activism, regime-changing Color Revolutions, and repressive governance tactics now spreading like a cancer across the West.[21]

To many, Soros's open society—without conflict and without borders—appears admirable. But that is not how any of the societies in which Soros and his allies who have made the rules concerning justice, ethics, morality, and acceptable speech have turned out.

So how does Soros make the rules concerning justice, ethics, morality, and acceptable speech? He partners with the institutions and installs the decision-makers who will implement the requisite changes.

For decades, Soros's foundations have partnered with some of the most powerful public and private organizations in the world—including the World Bank; the WHO; the United Nations; the European Commission; the US State Department (and the British, Swedish, Canadian, Dutch, Swiss, German, and Austrian equivalents); and the Rockefeller, Ford, Carnegie, and Gates foundations, among many others.[22]

Soros also funds some of the most powerful global NGOs that monitor corruption around the world, including Human Rights Watch, the International
Crisis Group, Global Witness, Transparency International, Médecins Sans
Frontières (also known as Doctors Without Borders), the Brennan Center
for Justice, the Media Development Investment Fund, and many others.[23]

These organizations all have missions that, on their face, sound beneficial to society. But they pursue their missions selectively, only enforcing Soros's vision of social progress and attacking those who oppose that vision.

The Man behind the Curtain

Any doubter of Soros's role as the most notable political financier in modern
history would have to account for his circuitous and comingled political
contributions—a vast web of dark money—that are intentionally designed to
influence elections and avoid public scrutiny. The staggering amount of
known donations, with strings attached, along with his shadowy funding
machinations have led some of his critics to call him the man behind the
curtain.

In an open society, do the citizens have a right to know who is funding
their politicians?

According to OpenSecrets.org, a research organization that tracks money
in politics (which happens to be funded by Soros's Open Society Foundations), Soros Fund Management was by far the largest single contributor
in the 2022 midterm elections. The fund ranked first out of 30,777 contributor organizations, with a known war chest of more than $178 million. Not a
single dollar went to a Republican candidate.

The political research group noted that organizations like Soros Fund
Management cannot legally contribute directly to candidates or party com-
mittees. Instead, the fund funneled cash to political affiliates, the largest
being an entity innocuously titled Democracy PAC II. The super PAC's Federal Election Commission (FEC) filing lists Michael Vachon as its treas-
urer.[24]

Vachon has served on boards of left-wing organizations tied to Soros's Open Society Foundations, such as NYC Partners, Democracy Alliance, and Catalist. George Soros's son, Alexander, is the super PAC's president.[25]

To be sure, Republican billionaires use similar methods of manipulating how their dark money flows, but Soros's dizzying political financing network is unparalleled. Other Democracy PAC II affiliates include Color of Change, DNC Services, Justice & Public Safety, Democratic Senatorial Campaign Committee, Democracy PAC, and Forward Majority Action, to name just a few (each with multimillion-dollar budgets).[26]

Notably, the first iteration of Democracy PAC funneled more than $80 million to Democratic groups and candidates in the 2020 election cycle. In a statement to *Politico*, Soros said the massive spend was necessary for "strengthening the infrastructure of American democracy: voting rights and civic participation, civil rights and liberties, and the rule of law."[27]

But Soros is undermining—rather than protecting—those core democratic institutions by advancing a political regime where American democracy is only "open" for his favored groups. What could be more antidemocratic?

Historically, the ninety-three-year-old billionaire megadonor has been remarkably transparent about his political intentions. In a 1995 interview with PBS, Soros explained: "I like to influence policy. I was not able to get to George [H. W.] Bush. But now I think I have succeeded with my influence . . . I do now have great access in [the Clinton] administration. There is no question about this. We actually work together as a team."[28]

The same could not be said during President George W. Bush's first term in office. Soros became so distraught about Bush's leadership that he declared the "central focus" of his life was to defeat Bush in his reelection bid. Soros addressed the National Press Club in Washington, DC, weeks before the 2004 election, saying, "I have never been heavily involved in partisan politics . . . but these are not normal times."[29]

Normal times or no, Soros makes his unparalleled political donations that could save democracy in a manner that, not coincidentally, furthers his own vision, fortune, and influence. If laws were broken (Soros has an insider trading conviction and his dark money organizations have paid hefty fines for assorted campaign finance violations) or innocent people harmed (many allege they have been) or, indeed, if actual democracy is subverted to achieve a Soros-controlled "open society," so be it.[30]

Incidentally, the Soros-linked America Coming Together political action committee was slapped with the third-largest fine in the FEC's history, following the unsuccessful bid to defeat Bush in 2004 and install Senator John Kerry (D-MA) in the White House.

The group's $137 million election effort spanned ninety offices in seventeen states and employed more than twenty-five thousand neighborhood canvassers and election staff members. The FEC unanimously approved a $775,000 fine for using unregulated "soft money" to elect Democrats. The penalty was a pittance of accountability compared to the amount spent, though America Coming Together shuttered operations in 2005.[31]

Soros had also given millions to the progressive MoveOn.org Voter Fund to run television ads attacking President Bush. The FEC fined MoveOn.org $150,000.[32]

The progressive megadonor was an early supporter of Barack Obama. In 2004, Soros held a fundraiser in his New York City home for the community organizer from Chicago and his successful US Senate bid in Illinois. Soros— the smart money in the 2008 Democratic presidential primary—would go on to back Obama over Hillary Clinton.[33]

Ironically, Soros would later say that President Obama was his "greatest disappointment." Why? It was not because Obama failed to deliver on Soros's progressive priorities, but rather because Obama, in Soros's view, "closed the door" on him and left Soros to operate outside the president's inner circle. In a 2018 *New York Times* interview, Soros lamented, "He made one phone call thanking me for my support, which was meant to last for five minutes, and I engaged him, and he had to spend another three minutes with me, so I dragged it out to eight minutes," he said.[34]

In 2016, Soros threw his full weight behind Hillary Clinton, and against Donald Trump, by pouring millions into her presidential election run. FEC filings in the summer of 2016 showed that Soros had personally donated or committed more than $25 million—mostly for her benefit.[35]

But dovetailing his financial interests and Clinton's then-unfathomable electoral defeat would prove expensive. According to *The Wall Street Journal*, Soros lost nearly $1 billion in the aftermath of Trump's stunning election victory as he assumed the progressive political catastrophe was also going to be a market catastrophe.[36]

He was wrong.

"Mr. Soros was cautious about the market going into November and became more bearish immediately after Mr. Trump's election," *The Wall Street Journal* reported. "The stance proved a mistake—the stock market has risen over the past two months on expectations that Mr. Trump's proposed economic policies will boost corporate earnings and the overall economy."[37]

Upon Trump's election, the Soros mission turned to getting rid of the forty-fifth duly elected president of the United States. How that jibed with any honest notion of democracy is anyone's guess.[38]

Framing President Trump as a Russian agent guilty of colluding with Vladimir Putin to cheat Hillary Clinton out of the White House was a Clinton-campaign smear. The associated Steele Dossier, named for the former British spy and Fusion GPS opposition research operative Christopher Steele, was laundered through the law firm Perkins Coie.[39]

According to *The Washington Post*, Perkins Coie represented "the national Democratic Party, its governors, almost all of its members of Congress, and its campaign and fundraising apparatus."[40]

The firm's "Democratic superlawyer" Marc Elias was the Clinton campaign's general counsel. Elias was not only involved in the Steele Dossier fiasco—which the FBI used to obtain a surveillance warrant for the Trump campaign and led to subsequent Foreign Intelligence Surveillance Act (FISA) warrant renewals to spy on the Trump presidency—but was simultaneously paid by George Soros to knock down election integrity laws in swing states.[41]

"Soros has given $5 million to the trust that funds the litigation," Michael Vachon told *The Washington Post*, and "Elias said he has picked his shots with an eye toward 'protecting the Obama coalition' of African Americans, Latinos, and young people."[42]

The thrust of the bogus Russia collusion allegations and the subsequent Mueller probe, named for former FBI director Robert Mueller, helped the Democratic Party take the House of Representatives in the 2018 midterm elections. After the investigation fizzled amid a lackluster final report and an aging Mueller's testimony before Congress—Mueller apparently did not even know what Fusion GPS was—a new line of attack opened.[43]

Flash forward to the 2019 impeachment of President Trump, and Soros surfaced again through his Open Society Foundations' ties to Ukraine and the so-called whistleblower at the center of the controversy, identified by independent media reports as Eric Ciaramella.[44]

Breitbart journalist Aaron Klein found that Ciaramella was reportedly receiving email communications from a top director at Soros's Open Society Foundations:

> The emails informed Ciaramella and a handful of other Obama administration foreign policy officials about Soros's whereabouts, the contents of Soros's private meetings about Ukraine, and a future meeting the billionaire activist was holding with the prime minister of Ukraine.
>
> A primary recipient of the Open Society emails along with Ciaramella was then-Assistant Secretary of State for European Affairs Victoria Nuland, who played a central role in the anti-Trump dossier affair. Nuland, with whom Ciaramella worked closely, received updates on Ukraine issues from dossier author Christopher Steele in addition to her direct role in facilitating the dossier within the Obama administration.[45]

Klein also noted that the Soros-funded Center for Public Integrity was selectively releasing documents to fuel the impeachment narrative that President Trump acted improperly by withholding military aid to Ukraine in exchange for evidence of former vice president Joe Biden's alleged corruption.[46]

Corporate media outlets with a collective loathing for President Trump used the Soros-backed group's assertions to substantiate Democratic House Speaker Nancy Pelosi's impeachment effort. Trump was indeed impeached and later acquitted by the Senate.[47]

Just as in previous elections, Soros reportedly told a group at the WEF in Davos that the 2020 election would determine the "fate of the world." He said Trump was "a con man and a narcissist, who wants the world to revolve around him." Previously at the WEF, Soros claimed Trump was "doing the work of ISIS."[48]

Soros spent $52 million in the 2020 presidential election cycle, according to the FEC filings. But there is no way to know how much dark money and influence originated from the billionaire activist, whether directly or indirectly, via his Open Society Foundations.[49]

Pandemic election changes contributed to a 2020 victory that had been a long time in the making for Soros. After the staggering upset in 2016 that might have quelled someone else, Soros redoubled his efforts to influence political outcomes. He continues to expend immense sums of money to reshape American politics in a way that has profound implications for the state of democracy.

Nightmare from the Third Reich

George Soros uses his vast fortune to exert political leverage and to fundamentally transform America, and indeed the world, in his own image. But the source of his billions is not just a wildly successful investing career. It is also the internal drive of the man himself. And to understand that requires delving into one of the darkest periods in human history.

George Soros was born György Schwartz on August 12, 1930. His parents were prosperous, nonobservant Jews living in Budapest, in what was then the kingdom of Hungary. His father, Tivadar, was a lawyer who had previously escaped Russia during World War I after being taken prisoner by the Red Army. Tivadar Schwartz was also an author and editor of *Literatura*

Mondo, a literary magazine written in Esperanto. The esoteric language, which he taught young György, was intended as a global common language to unite all nations.[50]

As the horror of World War I passed, a new horror was just beginning. Nazi Germany and the evils of anti-Semitism were on the rise. Tivadar Schwartz changed the family name to Soros, a palindrome meaning "designated successor" in Hungarian and "to soar" in Esperanto.[51]

Hitler's Third Reich eventually occupied Hungary. It was a period of unimaginable suffering, when innocent civilians had nowhere to run and terrible choices to make. In 1944, a thirteen-year-old George Soros was tasked with handing out Nazi summonses to Jews.

"I took this piece of paper to my father," Soros recalled in an interview fifty years later. "He instantly recognized it . . . This was a list of Hungarian Jewish lawyers. He said, 'You deliver the slips of paper and tell the people that if they report they will be deported.' I'm not sure to what extent he knew they were going to be gassed. I did what my father said."

George did as he was told. He delivered the notices and urged the recipients not to obey. One man, he later recounted, said, "I am a law-abiding citizen, and I am not going to start breaking the law now."[52]

After his father obtained false documents identifying the family as Christians, George Soros worked for a Nazi collaborator—a "godfather" figure and Tivadar's friend. Young George assumed the name Sandor Kiss and his job was to create inventories of confiscated Jewish property.

In a *60 Minutes* interview centering on Soros's 1990s juggernaut Wall Street success, journalist Steve Kroft asked the billionaire investor if his formative experience as a Nazi tagalong was difficult. "I mean, that's—that sounds like an experience that would send lots of people to the psychiatric couch for many, many years," Kroft said.[53]

Soros responded: "Not at all. Maybe as a child you don't see the connection. But it was—it created no—no problem at all."

"I could be on the other side, or I could be the one from whom the thing is being taken away," he continued. "But there was no sense that I shouldn't be there, because that was—well actually in a funny way, it's just like in markets—that if I weren't there—of course, I wasn't doing it, but somebody else would be taking it away anyhow."[54]

Soros seems to be saying, "If I'm not profiting from harm, someone else will." His apparent failure to grasp the troublesome implications of this type of reasoning is unsettling. Now imagine this amoral logic applied at scale.

Soros immigrated to England in 1947. He found his way to the London School of Economics and finished with three degrees. Not long after, he embarked on a new journey, this time, setting out for a fabled land far from Europe and known for offering immigrants the twin dreams of freedom and prosperity.[55]

He landed in New York City and became an American citizen in 1961. After dabbling in foreign securities and spending three years developing his market philosophy, Soros took a job with the investment company Arnhold and S. Bleichroeder. In 1967, Soros and the firm's chairman, Henry Arnhold, established the First Eagle Fund NV. In 1969, he established the Double Eagle Fund, which was worth $12 million by 1973 and eventually became the Soros Fund. [56]

The Soros Fund became the Quantum Fund in 1978 and was worth approximately $103 million. It was then that Soros founded his first philanthropic foundation, the Open Society Fund.[57]

By 1987, the Quantum Fund had $21.5 billion in assets, and George Soros had amassed $100 million in personal wealth. But it wasn't enough. Because, for him, it seems that there is never enough power, money, and control.[58]

A year later, Soros was caught buying and selling ninety-five thousand shares of Société Générale, a Paris-based multinational bank, after receiving information of a planned corporate raid. He was found guilty of insider trading and became a convicted felon in France. Despite his vast fortune and high-priced lawyers, the highest court in France declined to drop the "felon" designation from his record in 2006.[59]

In 1992, Soros and his Quantum Fund were credited with breaking the Bank of England. He took an enormous short-selling position against the British pound, betting that it would be devalued as the UK raised interest rates. Soros encouraged his chief portfolio manager, Stan Druckenmiller, to "go for the jugular," and they sold pound sterling to anyone who would buy it.[60]

On what came to be known as Black Wednesday, Soros won the siege and netted over $1 billion. The British government could no longer support its currency amid the Soros-driven takedown, and the pound sterling was successfully devalued. The British people, however, lost. "Retirees on fixed incomes saw their pensions diminished and their savings wiped out," attested journalist Stefan Kanfer.[61]

Soros was fully aware of his actions, later recalling, "I was in effect taking money out of the pockets of British taxpayers. But if I had tried to take social consequences into account, it would have thrown off my risk-reward calculation, and my profits would've been refused."[62]

By the close of the decade, Soros was a well-known vulture-capitalist trendsetter. Despite his burgeoning progressive philanthropic profile, the paradoxical harm he was inflicting was not lost on some of the more elitist left-wing personalities.

In 1999, Paul Krugman, the Nobel Prize–winning economist and perennial *New York Times* firebrand, described Soros: "Nobody who has read a business magazine in the last few years can be unaware that these days there really are investors who not only move money in anticipation of a currency crisis, but actually do their best to trigger that crisis for fun and profit. These new actors on the scene do not yet have a standard name; my proposed term is 'Soroi.'"[63]

Soros closed his legendary hedge fund, Soros Fund Management, after the US government passed the omnibus Dodd-Frank financial regulation in 2010. The Dodd-Frank Wall Street Reform and Consumer Protection Act, as it was formally known, was a response to the 2008 financial crisis, the worst since the Great Depression.

Complying with Dodd-Frank meant submitting to new hedge-fund transparency rules related to registration and disclosure requirements. Instead, Soros created a "family office" (worth $24.5 billion), which allowed him to avoid the regulation's intended scrutiny.[64]

In 2017, he made a record $18 billion personal gift to his own nonprofit the Open Society Foundations. Forbes had recently ranked Soros the twentieth richest man in the world, while the Open Society Foundations was rated one of the least transparent philanthropic think tanks in the world.[65]

By that time, the Open Society Foundations had become highly controversial. Critics accused Soros of funding and orchestrating mass chaos in America and across the globe through his NGO network. The stunning $18 billion wealth transfer was to ensure the mission would far outlast George Soros's earthly years. But whom could he trust to manage such vast resources and globalist, Esperanto-level goals? His heirs.

George Soros sired three children with his first wife Annaliese Witschak—Robert, Andrea, and Jonathan—and two more children, Alexander and Gregory, with his second wife, Susan Weber. He married his third wife, Tamiko Bolton, at age eighty-three. She was forty-one and has not borne him any new heirs.

Soros's five adult children are critical to his mission and have run his various enterprises—both for-profit and nonprofit—for decades. And they personally donate to the causes their father is passionate about, such as Planned Parenthood, the Center for Reproductive Rights, and the Brennan Center for Justice.[66]

Alexander "Alex" Soros, born in 1985, is perhaps the most politically ambitious family member aside from his father, George. He joined the Open Society Foundations' board of directors at age twenty-six and currently serves as the globalist organization's deputy chairman. A proud WEF member, Alex founded the Alexander Soros Foundation while working on his PhD at the University of California at Berkley. He has bemoaned his own privilege while also earning his reputation as a progressive megadonor in his own right.

In June 2023, the elder Soros confirmed that he would be handing control of his $25 billion empire to his son, Alex, who described himself as "more political" than his father and promised to use the family money to increase funding for elections and abortions.[67]

If Alex Soros lives to the age of his father and makes no erratic financial decisions (i.e., if he simply allows compound interest to grow the Soros nest egg), the Soros family will have tens of billions to enact their anti-American agenda through the year 2075.

The Soros Justice Warriors

George Soros spends millions to elect radical progressive prosecutors. Does that mean he effectively controls the rule of law in the associated jurisdictions? It is a question worth considering given the explosion of Soros-backed prosecutors and their collective trademark: selective enforcement of the law. Thus, Soros has amassed stunning influence over the criminal justice machines in large cities such as New York, Chicago, St. Louis, and Los Angeles, as well as Orlando, Florida, and Contra Costa, California.

Whereas local district attorney races were traditionally small-dollar affairs that went mostly unnoticed, Soros has spent millions blanketing local political landscapes to replace center-left Democrat candidates with far-left "reform" legal insurgents. The result is surging crime and chaos amid backdoor criminal justice policies that allow criminals to terrorize and destabilize communities.[68]

Consider, for instance, Manhattan district attorney Alvin Bragg. Soros gave $1 million to the Color of Change political action committee, which in turn spent the funds to elect Bragg in November 2021. Upon taking office, Bragg announced that the Manhattan District Attorney's Office would no longer seek pretrial detention or prison sentences for offenses other than homicide, public corruption, and major economic crimes as well as a list of other "extraordinary circumstances." In an early memo titled "Achieving Fairness and Safety," Bragg said, "Data, and my personal experiences, show that reserving incarceration for matters involving significant harm *will make us safer.*" And while Bragg was emptying Manhattan prisons of truly violent criminals, he also used his prosecutorial power to harass nonviolent political opponents. On April 4, 2023, Bragg announced an eye-popping thirty-four-count felony indictment of President Trump for an issue that federal prosecutors had previously investigated and effectively dismissed.[69]

Soros's justice warrior has manufactured a Trump trial and put it on a collision course with the 2024 election.

Open Society Indoctrination

Ancient philosophers knew that those who educate a society's youth would exert a massive influence on the future of that society. "Train up a child in the way he should go, and when he is old, he will not depart from it," King Solomon wrote in the Book of Proverbs. Teach them to think, and they will. Indoctrinate them, and they will destroy. The concept is not lost on tyrants and despots. Mao Zedong created Communist reeducation camps during the largely student-led Chinese Cultural Revolution, where high school and university students were organized into "Red Guards to attack all traditional values." Vladimir Lenin, leader of the early Soviet Union, put it this way: "Give me just one generation of youth, and I'll transform the whole world."

While George Soros is no Communist despot, his commitment to influencing higher education, and by extension the future, is ideological. He has given hundreds of millions of dollars to ostensibly support the goals of human rights, academic freedom, and "open societies." In reality, the Soros education model only allows for his vision of control.

Soros's first foray into higher education came with a grand strategy of churning out waves of ideological recruits in the heart of Europe—namely, the Central European University, based in his birth country of Hungary. Soros founded the university in 1991, after the fall of the Berlin Wall two years earlier. The implosion of European Communism was a gift to humanity, to be sure. But Soros leaped at the opportunity to fill the vacuum.

Previously, he had been committed to changing institutions from within. "After the fall of the Berlin Wall, I changed my mind," he said years later. "A revolution needs new institutions to sustain the ideas that motivated it, I argued with myself. I overcame my aversion toward institutions and yielded to the clamor for a Central European University."[70]

Soros seeded the project with $25 million over its first five years. The "independent" university planned to offer graduate degrees in social sciences and retain campuses in Warsaw, Poland, and Prague, Czech Republic, while being headquartered in Budapest, Hungary. Soros would later leave an endowment of $880 million, making the Central European University one of the wealthiest universities in Europe on a per-student basis.[71]

According to the university's website: "His vision was to recruit professors and students from around the world to build a unique institution, one that would train future generations of scholars, professionals, politicians, and civil society leaders to contribute to building open and democratic societies that respect human rights and adhere to the rule of law."[72]

The nod to democracy and human rights is classic Soros. With that framing, any disagreement with his objectives is neatly blunted. And whereas he himself is antidemocratic and closed to differing viewpoints, his influence networks and political allies work diligently in his defense.

Soros served as Central European University's chairman of the board until 2007, when Bard College president Leo Botstein became his successor.[73]

The university ran into trouble, however, when the Hungarian government moved to curtail the left-wing school's adversarial influence aimed at undermining its host country and its prime minister, Viktor Orbán. Orbán, an oft-maligned conservative and antiglobalist, accused Soros and the university of subverting Hungarian sovereignty and breaking domestic law.[74]

European liberals, American progressives, and Soros himself blasted Orbán for heavy-handed tactics that shut down the university. In 2018, Central European University relocated its degree programs from Budapest to Vienna, Austria.[75]

Despite howls from mainstream media, US ambassador to Hungary David Cornstein said that he saw no hint that Orbán's government infringed on civil liberties or human rights.[76]

For decades, Soros spent lavishly to influence higher education. Most of the estimated $400 million he donated through his Open Society Foundations had gone to Central European University and Bard College, though he is also credited with funding thousands of targeted scholarships and directing over $1 million each to at least nineteen American colleges.

Recipients of Soros's largesse include elite universities such as Harvard and Georgetown, as well as state-university programs such as Ohio State's Kirwan Institute, dedicated to race and ethnicity, and the University of Connecticut's Human Rights Institute.[77]

In 2020, Soros laid bare his plan for global reeducation. Speaking at the WEF, he at once touted the Central European University and decried its limitations. "CEU is not strong enough by itself to become the educational institution the world needs. That requires a new kind of global educational network," he said.

While announcing a new $1 billion funding commitment in Davos, he explained that the nexus of Central European University and Bard College in the United States serves as a building block for a scalable international university system, which he claimed was already underway. "It will be called the Open Society University Network or OSUN for short," he said.

"To demonstrate our commitment to OSUN, we are contributing one billion dollars to it," Soros continued. "But we can't build a global network on our own; we will need partner institutions and supporters from all around the world to join us in this enterprise . . . I consider OSUN the most important and enduring project of my life and I should like to see it implemented while I am still around."[78]

The "Color Revolution" Playbook

George Soros has been associated with revolutions in one way or another for decades. News reports and open-source documents have tied Soros to the

Polish Solidarity movement in the 1980s, the Velvet Revolution in Czechoslo-
vakia in 1989, the Rose Revolution in Georgia in 2003, the Orange Revolution
in Ukraine in 2004, the Arab Spring in 2011, and another revolution in
Ukraine in 2014. Today, he is funding a revolutionary vanguard in America.[79]

Many of the so-called Color Revolutions have uncanny similarities. They
typically are not waged by a formal military force. Instead, Color Revolutions question a regime's legitimacy through mass protests, acts of civil dis-
obedience, and, more recently, through enticing favorable coverage in the
Western press with social media stunts.

The playbook was first used during the Cold War, when destabilizing
Soviet-bloc European governments was an imperative of US foreign policy.
And whenever Soros could insert himself, he was sure to bring his profit
motive. During a 1989 news interview cofeaturing none other than then
senator Joe Biden (D-DE), Soros advocated for the "radical reorganization of
the Polish economy," wherein he was the perfect consultant. All that was
needed was a massive taxpayer-funded "aid" program and the backing of
the US government.

"Do you think the US should back such a package of that magnitude this
weekend?" PBS anchor Robert MacNeil asked Senator Biden.[80]

"I think the United States has to back a package of that magnitude, and I
think the United States has to use its influence at the G7 meeting in order
to be able to not miss what is right now an historic opportunity," Biden declared. "You have a gentleman [Soros] on the program with me here who
knows more about [Polish] Solidarity than I'm going to ever know, but the
fact that seems to me is that Solidarity now has a stake in the outcome of the
Polish economy and the outcome of the political process."

"You're a student of the Polish economy as well as the Hungarian. What
do you say to that?" the PBS anchor asked Soros.

With a buy-low, sell-high grin and the public backing of a key US senator,
Soros replied, "In Poland, the political will is now there—and in a strange
way, the very bad condition of the Polish economy is an opportunity." Because the Polish economy was "spinning out of control" and "the [Polish]

standard of living is very low," Soros said, grinning wider still, "the resources that would be needed to turn it around were actually quite modest."[81]

Soros called the economic reorganization "a kind of macroeconomic debt-for-equity swap." That is a fancy way of saying taking control of a struggling nation's economy by shackling the nation's population with debt.[82]

The economic reorganization plan was instituted in 1990 and caused immediate hyperinflation. From the safety of Wall Street, Soros shrugged off the mass suffering while admitting the fallout was "very tough on the population, but people were willing to take a lot of pain in order to see real change."[83]

Soros had operated in both Russia and Ukraine before their post-Soviet separation. His Open Society Foundations and vast network of affiliated NGOs had infiltrated both countries during the Soviet era prior to 1990.[84]

In 1992, Russian president Boris Yeltsin signed off on a similar post–Soviet Union economic reorganization, which sent inflation skyrocketing 2,500 percent and led to a handful of connected oligarchs amassing unimaginable wealth by taking control of Russian state assets. Speaking to *The New Republic* in 1994 about his involvement in Russia's economic transition, Soros said, "Just write that the former Soviet Empire is now called the Soros Empire."

Soros was not shy about his engagement in the vulture capitalism that occurred amid popular confusion and insecurity that came with toppled governments. In fact, he was brazen about his destabilization and profit activities. In 1995, he told *The New Yorker* that fomenting civil unrest meant wearing "masks." "I would say one thing in one country and another thing in another country," he chuckled.[85] For example, in 2004, Soros initially denied any involvement in the toppling of Georgia's government after the country's Rose Revolution. But months later, he bragged to the *Los Angeles Times*, "I'm delighted by what happened in Georgia, and I take great pride in having contributed to it."[86]

For crisis profiteers such as George Soros, there are always opportunities in chaos.

7

Follow the Money

Behaviors are going to have to change. . . . You have to force behaviors [to change,] and at BlackRock we are forcing behaviors [to change].[1]

—*Larry Fink, CEO and founder of BlackRock, November 2017*

I n the summer of 2020, as Klaus Schwab was making the rounds across various corporate media outlets, one of the more critical imperatives described in his *Great Reset* book went largely unnoticed. Schwab and his Davos cronies—including the heads of some of the largest financial institutions in the world, such as BlackRock—began pushing a new system of financial control by eliminating cash and instituting a centralized digital currency system.

"The world must act jointly and swiftly to revamp all aspects of our societies and economies, from education to social contracts and working conditions," Schwab wrote in a WEF blog post. "We must build entirely new foundations for our economic and social systems," he added.[2]

Schwab's imperative appeared, on its face, to be a reference to his stakeholder capitalism system, but there were still many lingering questions. Questions such as: How might this new stakeholder system work? How would Schwab's stakeholder capitalism differ from free-market capitalism? Was there a connection between Schwab's stakeholder capitalism and WEF's push for this new thing called a "digital currency," and, if so, how would a centralized digital currency network affect other national currencies?

Most countries around the world have central banks that issue physical currency (i.e., cash). That cash is stored in private banks that allow for account holders to make electronic payments and electronic transfers. A central bank digital currency (CBDC) works much like electronic payments with physical currencies. The difference, however, is that if a central bank transitions to a CBDC and stops issuing physical currency, that society essentially becomes "cashless."[3]

A cashless society presents several problems and concerns that will be discussed throughout this chapter—the biggest threats that CBDCs and "going cashless" pose to freedom is that purchasers' privacy evaporates, surveillance (and social engineering) by authoritarians can surge, and the ability to financially "cancel" (or "de-bank") an entity or individual can become widespread.[4]

The current global financial system, which is built upon an exchange network of national currencies backed by their respective governments, seems to work well. Why would one central entity need to control currency? The reason, as with many other Controligarch schemes, is that a centralized digital currency also is put forward as the solution to many nonfinancial problems—from climate change to cyberattacks to the rise of so-called disinformation.

Approximately six months after Schwab revealed the Great Reset and the mandate to "digitalize" everything, the WEF released a short, cryptic, and ominous video titled "A Cyber-attack with COVID-like Characteristics?" The purpose of the video appeared to be a call to action for all the Davos Men and Women to create a new digital financial system that could be controlled with omnipotence and precision. Stakeholder capitalism needed a financial backbone, and CBDCs could provide that backbone.[5]

In the video, the WEF narrator warned that a digital virus (perhaps targeting the financial system) could spread further and faster than any biological virus—perhaps ten times faster than COVID-19—and the number of infected devices would multiply rapidly. In this scenario, the entire world—

from humans to hospitals to metro lines to banks—would be infected with a cyber virus within a matter of days. From such a theoretical crisis came another theoretical opportunity.

The only way to slow the spread of a COVID-like cyber virus would be to lock down the entire internet—and, thus, the entire global financial system. To flatten this curve, every device would have to be disconnected, which would cause untold sums in economic damages and, in the case of infected critical infrastructure like transportation and medicine, could potentially result in injuries or death.

Would the WEF's proposed digital cure be worse than the digital disease?

"COVID-19 was known as an anticipated risk," the WEF narrator stated plainly, and "so is the digital equivalent." Digital apocalypse might be imminent, the WEF narrator said in closing, so everyone should start preparing. "The time is now."[6]

It seemed counterintuitive: If a digital apocalypse might be imminent, why would digitalizing currency be a solution? The answer, it seemed, was that by digitalizing and centralizing financial systems, the people, and banks in control of this new system would be better prepared to stave off the hypothetical digital apocalypse.[7]

The "cyber pandemic" video has since been hidden on WEF's YouTube channel—its visibility is set to "unlisted," which means that you cannot find it by searching for it—but the problems (and solutions) appear to be adapted from a previous Schwab prophecy when, a year earlier and prior to COVID in 2019, the WEF sponsored a virtual wargame, with a variety of cybersecurity experts, dubbed "Cyber Polygon."[8]

The WEF's 2020 page about Cyber Polygon has also been removed, but a Wayback Machine archive of the page reveals that the WEF's partners in the Cyber Polygon initiative were Interpol, IBM, the World Wide Web's coordinator (called ICANN), a Russian bank (now-sanctioned SberBank), a Russian developer of cybersecurity solutions, and one of the oldest and largest banks in the world (Banco Santander).[9]

Cyber Polygon's website shows that the financial sector was well represented (along with a surprising number of Russian conglomerates). As the keynote speaker at the second Cyber Polygon forum, Schwab warned that a digital pandemic poses one of the greatest challenges to humanity since World War II.[10]

"Masks are not sufficient; we need vaccines to immunize ourselves," Schwab said in a video address to Cyber Polygon as he made a seamless pivot to cyberattacks: "We have to move from simple protection to immunization," Schwab continued, concluding, "We need to build IT infrastructures that have digital antibodies built in, inherently, to protect themselves."[11]

The so-called cyber pandemic threats flew under the radar in most of the Great Reset media coverage, but they were no less alarming. Schwab's digitalization agenda signaled the beginning of a tectonic shift in global financial policy—the rise of CBDCs and the push toward a global cashless society kicked into hyperdrive. Just as energy and agriculture officials mentioned in previous chapters had marched to the WEF drumbeat, Cyber Polygon's attendees—banking, finance, and Big Tech executives—sprang into action upon Schwab's command.[12]

The "Cyber Pandemic" Wargame

Not long after Schwab and his forum began signaling the cyber pandemic threats, top banking officials from ten countries participated in yet another cyber wargame called "Collective Strength" in December 2021. This exercise occurred as the Omicron variant was bringing COVID-19 infection rates to new heights. And few outside the world of high finance were likely focused on anything beyond their own exposures—both health and financial—to the coronavirus pandemic, let alone a cyber pandemic.[13]

The WEF prepared not only for health pandemics (like the Event 201 coronavirus simulation) but also for financial ones. Coincidentally, its solutions to both health and cyber pandemics ceded more power to the Controligarchs at the expense of the citizens.

The purpose of the Collective Strength simulation was to predict the next financial contagion (such as the ones that Schwab and the WEF had been warning about) and determine how the financial markets, central banks, and governments in some of the world's richest countries might respond. The ten-day exercise was originally scheduled to take place in the United Arab Emirates, but it was relocated to the Finance Ministry in Jerusalem because of an Omicron surge in the Arab country.

Treasury officials, finance ministers, and other banking experts from the United States, Switzerland, Israel, Italy, Germany, and other nations practiced hypothetical scenarios in which sophisticated hackers or malevolent state actors attacked the global financial infrastructure.

One scenario envisioned cyberattacks against the foreign currency exchange system. Another could-be digital breach led to massive troves of sensitive financial data leaked on the "dark web." Perhaps the most unsettling scenario these high-level officials were preparing for was, according to Reuters, "chaos in global [financial] markets" and a "run on banks" caused by a faceless villain that, in recent years, had become democracy's biggest foe: so-called fake news.

"The banks are appealing for emergency liquidity assistance in a multitude of currencies to put a halt to the chaos as counterparties withdraw their funds and limit access to liquidity, leaving the banks in disarray and ruin," warned the Collective Strength narrator (who remained nameless). In the exercise, fake news subscribers caused a run on banks that contributed to the collapse of the global financial system.

"Attackers are ten steps ahead of the defender," said one participating financial cyber manager. Proactive measures would be needed to deal with these threats. Schwab and his WEF members had already been preparing for these scenarios. For WEF members, the Collective Strength solutions were familiar: more control for cyber pandemic planners and corresponding crackdowns on the financial freedoms of those blissfully unaware of such cyber wargames.[14]

More than a decade after "too big to fail" entered the global lexicon, the financial officials and big bankers—almost all of whom are WEF members or sponsors and the types to attend Cyber Polygon and Collective Strength—decided to make themselves a whole lot bigger and less likely to fail.

The global central banks like the Federal Reserve bank (or the "Fed") are effectively owned and controlled by well-known financial titans such as BlackRock, JPMorgan Chase, Citigroup, and Bank of America. These big institutions—"member banks" as they are called—effectively decide how money is created and retracted via complex policies dealing with currency issuance and interest rates. All of these entities and even some lesser-known behemoths like the Vanguard Group and State Street Corporation—which along with BlackRock manage a staggering $22 trillion—have the power to affect or control the financial well-being of almost everyone.

Competition is all but illusory among those sacred banks deemed too big to fail—their arrangement is more like a gentleman's game of golf than the gladiator fights that small businesses such as restaurants and building contractors wage every day. Many of the too-big-to-fail banks have histories dating back decades or even centuries and they have long been committed to protecting their power, even if it means implementing new financial systems.

The most essential and alarming solution to address the simulated cyber-threats is the unilateral authority to de-bank enemies of the WEF and its supranational members (including the central banks). Citizens' abilities to withdraw their own money from the system's banks must be thwarted. To do this, banks must be given more power in the short term, and in the longer term, centralized digital currencies must be implemented worldwide.[15]

Central Bank Digital Currency vs. Decentralized Cryptocurrency

The WEF's Cyber Polygon exercises and the subsequent Collective Strength wargame revealed the battle lines in the financial Controligarchs' coming war over the future of digital currency. The WEF favors a *centralized* digital currency, while many people favor a *decentralized* digital currency.[16]

Centralized digital currencies have a command-and-control structure: the central banks, such as the Fed, which is led by its chairman. Decentralized digital currencies—typically known as cryptocurrencies, such as Bitcoin—do not. This type of currency is only governed by the digital ledger, which its users maintain. A centralized digital currency eliminates privacy; a decentralized one guarantees privacy.

This ledger is encrypted and distributed across the entire network of users—called the blockchain—and if a bad actor such as a hacker took out one or ten (or one million) users' computers, the ledger would be preserved. There remains some debate over how many users would need to be wiped out to crash the system, but it would have to be at least 51 percent of the estimated one billion cryptocurrency users worldwide (as of 2022). For this reason, decentralized cryptocurrencies are largely regarded as ironclad, and some experts describe the blockchain itself as "unhackable."

The WEF has acknowledged that decentralized cryptocurrencies have the benefit of "[generating] a lot of public interest" in digital currencies, generally, but they also "pose unprecedented challenges for financial and tax authorities, capital market regulators and the business community." In other words, cryptocurrencies are useful to the global banking establishment only insofar as they drive enthusiasm for the concept of digital currency. However, decentralized cryptos are hard to track, regulate, and control, so ultimately the WEF sees them as a threat.[17]

The Controligarchs' war on decentralized cryptocurrencies hit a breakthrough when the world's most famous crypto exchange, FTX, imploded in November 2022. FTX had been a marketplace to purchase cryptocurrencies like Bitcoin, and its collapse had a domino effect across the entire industry, crippling or even bankrupting numerous decentralized finance companies overnight.

The FTX implosion was caused not by the decentralized nature of its offerings but rather by mismanagement. Nonetheless, the FTX collapse led to mass skepticism over the stability of decentralized cryptocurrencies and provided a convenient opportunity for opponents of crypto to call for stricter regulation over the industry, including from Biden treasury secretary Janet Yellen.[18]

BlackRock CEO Laurence "Larry" Fink, whose firm invested $24 million in FTX, appeared unfazed by the spectacular downfall. At a *New York Times* DealBook event, Fink casually suggested that the FTX debacle meant that most crypto-related companies were headed for bankruptcy—they "are not going to be around," Fink said. It was a shocking suggestion with massive implications for the hundreds of billions of dollars in cryptocurrencies held by retail investors. The FTX collapse wiped out the holdings of nearly ten million investors almost overnight.[19]

FTX's founder, a thirty-year-old billionaire named Sam Bankman-Fried, has close connections to lawmakers and financial regulators. These include Maxine Waters (D-CA), then chairwoman of the House Financial Services Committee, and SEC chairman Gary Gensler, who runs the agency responsible for regulating cryptocurrencies.[20]

Bankman-Fried's parents are both high-profile attorneys with deep ties to Democrat powerbrokers. His father, Joseph Bankman, helped Senator Elizabeth Warren (D-MA) draft tax policy legislation in 2016, and his mother, Barbara Fried, cofounded a Silicon Valley–based Democratic dark money group called Mind the Gap. Bankman-Fried's aunt, Linda Fried, is on the WEF's Global Agenda Council on Ageing and has strong US political connections, including as an elected member of the Council on Foreign Relations.[21]

For his part, Sam Bankman-Fried was the second-largest donor to Democrats (after George Soros) during the 2022 midterm election cycle. Bankman-Fried and his fellow executives funneled more than $70 million to legislators, including the very legislators on high-profile committees that should be investigating him.[22] For example, rather than investigate Bankman-Fried, the House Financial Services Committee chairwoman praised the FTX founder. Months earlier, a widely circulated image showed Waters appearing chummy with Bankman-Fried at an FTX conference.[23]

Unlike George Soros, the FTX executives also donated at least $20 million to political entities run by top Republicans such as Representative Kevin McCarthy (R-CA) and Senator Mitch McConnell (R-KY). Bankman-Fried had been dumping investors' money by the billions into his shady side business called Alameda Research, which prosecutors allege was a criminal and fraudulent diversion of FTX clients' funds—a potential major crime. Bankman-Fried has claimed that he "didn't knowingly commingle funds" or that he "wasn't trying to commingle funds."[24]

While most independent observers called Bankman-Fried's FTX disaster an egregious fraud and a Ponzi scheme—perhaps worse than Bernie Madoff's notorious scam—Bankman-Fried's Controligarch allies sought to make the story go away. Instead of bashing FTX, BlackRock's CEO glossed over Bankman-Fried's alleged crimes—more than a dozen counts ranging from fraud to money laundering to bribing foreign officials—and mainstream media outlets such as *The New York Times* downplayed the debacle. The newspaper allowed Bankman-Fried the opportunity to whitewash his mistakes on its DealBook platform. Bankman-Fried (who has pleaded not guilty) faces more than one hundred years in prison if convicted and sentenced to the maximum penalties. The FTX trial is set for late 2023.[25]

But how did Bankman-Fried get away with it for so long? As all Controligarchs do: by establishing himself as a world-class do-gooder.

Bankman-Fried advocated a philosophy called "effective altruism." Effective altruism is an approach to philanthropy that seeks to do "the most good for the most people" and is something that Bill Gates, Elon Musk, Warren Buffett, and Mark Zuckerberg have all been affiliated with. But it has become quite clear that this form of so-called altruism helps these philanthropic opportunists the most, and Bankman-Fried admitted that his ethical posture was "mostly a front."

Preaching about ethics and "doing good" is a "dumb game we woke westerners play where we say all the right shiboleths [sic] and so everyone likes us," and supporting regulation of his industry was "pretty much just PR," he admitted in a November 2022 interview as his FTX empire was crumbling around him.[26]

The FTX fiasco dealt a major blow to decentralized digital currencies and was a boon for the WEF's preferred form: CBDCs. This WEF-favored centralized digital currency model is much different than the decentralized model that Bankman-Fried tarnished, perhaps irreparably. Under the centralized model (CBDCs), central banks would have total control over every aspect of the digital currency and therefore the economy—much as they do now, but far more absolute. They could turn the money supply on or off to an entire city, to an individual business, or even to an individual person.

The WEF's push to leverage access to banks and the global financial system in order to control behaviors reveals shocking potential for authoritarian abuse. The full possibilities for this level of financial power have become more apparent since the COVID pandemic began.

At a national level, a federal government can de-bank any business or individual deemed a threat to the established regime. In February 2022, the "Freedom Convoy" trucker protests in Canada revealed the raw authoritarian power that the Trudeau government had to not only unilaterally freeze or suspend the bank accounts of dissident businesses and individuals but also suspend the insurance coverage on the vehicles.[27]

At the international level, WEF members can de-bank an entire country. Starting in March 2022, the global banking system proved that the consortium of international central bankers can almost completely cut out a defiant nation like Russia from the system by blacklisting it from the Swift wire-transfer network.[28]

Nongovernment actors are also using their financial power to control behaviors. One of the world's largest online fundraising services, GoFundMe, has shut down at least five fundraising campaigns for apparently political reasons—especially campaigns against COVID-19 mandates. GoFundMe's top Silicon Valley investors, Accel and Greylock Partners, are both WEF partners and agenda contributors.[29]

In another instance of multinational financial companies using authoritarian tactics, the world's largest credit card and payment processors Visa, Mastercard, and American Express (all major WEF partners and agenda contributors) announced plans in September 2022 to closely track firearm purchases, at the urging of gun-control advocates. The move—reportedly paused in March 2023 after fierce pushback from gun-rights advocates— seemed to track with a politically motivated desire to create a nationwide database of gun owners.[30]

In recent years, digital payment processor PayPal acknowledged that it routinely flagged, restricted, or closed the accounts of individuals and businesses at the behest of left-wing activist organizations such as the Southern Poverty Law Center and the Anti-Defamation League.[31]

In October 2022, PayPal quietly implemented a policy to slap $2,500 fines on any users who spread "misinformation," further highlighting the power of financial conglomerates to control individuals' speech if they possess the wrong political beliefs. PayPal's stock price plummeted following the public backlash that led users to close their PayPal accounts. In addition, the company's former president strongly criticized the policy in a tweet. Amid this pressure, PayPal walked back the controversial policy and, to save face, said that it was sent in error.[32]

Later that month, leaked documents from the Department of Homeland Security showed that one of the world's largest banks, JPMorgan Chase, was working with government officials and Big Tech companies to target political enemies that they accused of spreading false information. This low-profile initiative sought to "curb speech" and "misinformation" and, to this day, remains largely unknown to the American public.[33]

BlackRock Pushes Digital Currency and Digital ID

Of all the big banks, BlackRock has become the biggest. But few people know what this institution actually does. Those who have heard of BlackRock know it as an asset manager with a variety of funds diversified across the stock market, which pension and retirement account managers invest in. On paper, BlackRock is a rather boring company. But its unparalleled holdings, which surpassed $10 *trillion* in assets under management in early 2022, make it the largest asset manager in the world, much bigger than Goldman Sachs.[34]

But behind the scenes, BlackRock is so much more than an ordinary asset manager. It has been called "the fourth branch of government" and "almost a shadow government." It is also the "most powerful institution in the financial system," according to German investigative journalist Heike Buchter. And it has deep ties to the WEF, playing a central role in the latter's push for digital ID and currency.[35]

BlackRock has enjoyed an unusually cozy relationship with the Federal Reserve for many years. The megabank employs former central bankers who, in 2019, proposed taking the Fed's monetary powers to a whole new level. In addition to the more than $10 trillion in assets that BlackRock directly controls, it also manages at least $20 trillion through its Aladdin risk-monitoring platform.[36]

BlackRock CEO Larry Fink is an enigma. For more than a decade, he has been one of the world's most influential people, but his meteoric rise is largely undocumented.

Born in 1952, Fink was raised in Van Nuys, California, by his mother, who was a professor, and his father, who owned a shoe shop.[37]

Fink received his BA in political science and his MBA in real estate in the mid-1970s—both from UCLA. In 1976, fresh out of business school, Fink got his first banking job working for First Boston Corporation, a Rockefeller-backed investment firm based in New York. At First Boston, Fink became one of the industry's first traders in mortgage-backed securities and later became the cohead of the First Boston division responsible for trading and distributing government bonds, mortgage-backed securities, and corporate securities.[38]

In 1988, Swiss bankers at Credit Suisse purchased First Boston, and that same year, Fink founded BlackRock Incorporated as a subsidiary of the Blackstone Group (another massive asset manager). Within a year, *The Wall Street Journal* identified Fink (in his mid-thirties) as one of the potential "business leaders of tomorrow."[39]

Fink has outsized influence at the WEF and has served in several leader-ship and governance roles, including as a member of the WEF's Board of Trustees, as a member of the WEF's International Business Council, and as a WEF agenda contributor. Fink does not "identify as powerful," so his as-cent to become the head of the world's most powerful financial corporation remains somewhat of a mystery.[40]

Two weeks into the pandemic, the Federal Reserve tapped BlackRock to head its coronavirus response financial program, which the company benefited from. Today, BlackRock shares a close relationship with the Biden administration and pushes policies congruent with the administration's goals.[41]

Fink and his central-banker buddies would be instrumental in another oligarch-backed control scheme: digital ID.[42]

Digital ID: Tracking Your Every Move

Crucial to the Great Reset was Schwab's ambition—shared by Gates and the Rockefellers, among others—to "digitalize" everything. That would include currencies and identities. When implemented together, digital currency and digital ID would create a global, interoperable system that allows WEF-allied central banks—the ruling class—to track, trace, surveil, and ultimately control how people spend their money.

Digital currency and digital ID are closely related; the former necessi-tates the latter—that is, to have a digital currency (or a cashless society), every transaction must be conducted between digitally identifiable and trackable persons and entities. But most people, especially Americans, do not want their entire identity digitalized.[43]

Digital ID is a major component of the move to a cashless society using central bank digital currencies. Much like digitalizing currency, digitaliz-ing identification systems such as driver's licenses and passports creates a centralized method for tracking the movements of every person on the planet. These technologies could potentially be used to turn off a person's access to the goods and services in society, a level of control without precedent in human history. So it should come as no surprise that entities such as the United Nations and the World Economic Forum along with oligarchs such as the Rockefellers, George Soros, and Bill Gates, have been working very hard (and have supplied at least $200 million) to create a global digital ID system.[44]

The digital ID initiative falls under the UN's Sustainable Development Goal number sixteen, which the benevolent globalist elites assure is to promote "peaceful and inclusive societies" for sustainable development, provide "access to justice for all," and build "effective, accountable and inclusive institutions at all levels."[45]

To achieve peace, inclusivity, and justice, according to the UN's Agenda 2030, is as simple as providing a "legal identity for all." The UN's plan for this digital ID utopia involves the use of biometric identity verification, which means that a digital ID will be directly tied to a person's biology—their DNA, fingerprints, faceprint, or retinal scan.[46]

The WHO and the UN's Population Fund (a longtime Rockefeller Foundation partner on population reduction projects) are the leading supranational organizations working on digital ID. In the private sector, the Rockefeller Foundation, the Gates Foundation and Microsoft, George Soros's Open Society Foundations, Mark Zuckerberg and Facebook, the Omidyar Network, BlackRock, Bloomberg, and Google have been building a digital ID system since 2015. The name of this Controligarch system is ID2020.[47]

The pandemic presented a major opportunity for the ID2020 effort via the new concept of mandatory vaccine passports. Vaccine passports appear to have been an interrelated goal with digital ID all along—years before the COVID-19 pandemic—as evidenced by one of ID2020's major partners: the Gates-founded (and -funded) Global Alliance for Vaccines and Immunization (Gavi). One year before the pandemic, the Gates Foundation spent at least $4.5 million studying digital ID and digital currency infrastructure.[48]

Just months before the COVID-19 outbreak, in September 2019, Gavi and the government of Bangladesh announced a digital vaccine identification program at the annual ID2020 summit in New York. One month later, the Gates Foundation and the WEF held the Event 201 coronavirus pandemic exercise after which Gavi and CEPI were listed as recommended collaborators for a future pandemic response.[49]

The fact that several Gates- and WEF-funded efforts to bring about digital ID alongside vaccine passports does not indicate some sinister conspiracy, but it does indicate that their efforts predated Schwab's Great Reset "opportunity" brought about by the COVID pandemic—a gift that keeps on giving.

While the vaccine passport agenda has lost steam as the virus has waned, at least one executive has admitted that there is a push for passports to become permanent. The founder and CEO of a biometric digital ID company called iProov confirmed to *Forbes* that vaccine passports are the method for implementing digital ID. "The evolution of vaccine certificates will actually drive the whole field of digital identity in the future," he said, adding, "So, therefore, this is not just about COVID, this is about something even bigger."[50]

As countries around the world began mandating synthetic mRNA injections, they also began requiring various forms of verification. Europe and Israel used something called a "green pass." While the United States did not implement a nationwide system, various states implemented their own versions of Europe's green pass. New York had the "Excelsior Pass," and Hawaii had the "Safe Travels Hawaii" pass.[51]

The mRNA mandates and the digital ID systems became self-reinforcing and were sold to citizens as tools for "safety" and "convenience." People were strongly encouraged that they must get the vaccine for safety and the corresponding vaccine passport digital ID for convenience. Resistance to either the vaccine or the digital passport was beyond inconvenient—and in countries such as Australia, New Zealand, and Canada, any pushback effectively turned dissenters into second-class citizens.

Canada did the world a favor when it revealed the relationship between digital ID and digital currency. Canadians rose in protest of the vaccine mandates and digital identification, which were some of the most restrictive in the world. The Canadian Freedom Convoy was an organized effort to protest these new mandates. The Trudeau government saw the danger of letting the truckers and other dissidents rise up, and it cracked down with an iron fist.

And when Canadian authorities froze the financial assets of the convoy protestors in Ottawa, they also froze the assets of convoy supporters who may not have even attended the protests. More shocking, the Trudeau government did this by invoking never before used emergency powers.

The Canadian finance minister, WEF acolyte Chrystia Freeland, took immediate steps to cut off the truckers and other protestors from the digital finance system. Financial companies like GoFundMe put up little (if any) resistance to government demands to shut down protestors' accounts. The government closed the dissidents' bank accounts, financial corporations paralyzed their fundraising apparatus, and the mainstream media named and shamed the dissidents' donors. The protests ended when the Trudeau government mandated that they do so. The Canadian uprising against vaccines and digital ID was crushed by digital currency and its WEF-aligned advocates.

Throughout the pandemic, other protests around the world sought to dismantle the vaccine passport regimes and digital ID went underground for a time as COVID-19 was thought to be defeated. But 2022 began with a new COVID-19 variant, and an updated mRNA jab hinted that fresh mandates may be just around the corner.

Even as the COVID-19 pandemic began to fade in the latter half of 2022 (and the vaccine mandate pushers suggested "pandemic amnesty" for their past authoritarian impulses), government officials along with the WEF announced a new digital ID pilot program that would be mandated as a vaccine passport.

In November 2022, world leaders from the top twenty countries assembled in Bali, Indonesia, for the G20 summit. There, the global leaders revealed that digital ID via a mandatory vaccine passport would be implemented before the "next pandemic." The WEF has long considered a vaccine passport as a de facto form of digital ID. "These [vaccine] passports by nature serve as a form of digital identity," according to a February 2022 WEF report on how to advance digital solutions, including the implementation of digital ID.[52]

The health minister of Indonesia was insistent: "Let's have a digital health certificate acknowledged by WHO—if you have been vaccinated or tested properly—then you can move around."[53]

At the same G20 summit, Canada's Justin Trudeau committed $80 million for global health systems, most of which was allotted for pandemic response. That same month, the government of New Zealand tapped a Microsoft partner, JNCTN, to begin rolling out a digital ID program.[54]

JNCTN, a Kiwi digital identity and credential management company, had been the government contractor managing and tracking digital credentials such as the proof of vaccinations for Prime Minister Jacinda Ardern's controversial military-run Managed Isolation and Quarantine (MIQ) program. Microsoft and JNCTN would begin by implementing the new digital ID regime for MIQ workers across the country, but they also expected to expand the program to include New Zealand job seekers.[55]

Earlier that year, in February 2022, the WHO tapped a subsidiary of Germany's Deutsche Telekom (a longtime partner of WEF, Microsoft, and other Controligarch entities) to build a global system for vaccine passports.[56]

In the United States, attempts to implement digital ID and CBDCs have, until very recently, met strong resistance. Americans' deep concerns over their privacy with respect to government snooping—particularly their digital privacy—have historically been a major obstacle to going cashless. Until recently, these pro-privacy preferences indicated that cash (and all the anonymity it provides) would remain a dominant feature of American life for the foreseeable future.[57]

And while Americans' trust in their government has been plummeting for many years, their wariness toward an increasingly cashless economy has dwindled because of perceived convenience. The pandemic led to increased adoption, voluntarily or otherwise, of "cashless" transactions in favor of more sanitary "contactless" payments. Likewise, digital ID systems have crept into numerous states, including California, New York, and Hawaii, under the guise of pandemic safety.

The potential downsides of centralized digital currencies and digital ID systems are vastly underreported by mainstream media. And no wonder: as we will see in the next chapter, most of the press is Controligarch owned and operated.

8

Mainstream
Mind Control

[The president] could have undermined the [media] messaging so
much that he can actually control exactly what people think, and
that is our job.[1]

—*Mika Brzezinski, MSNBC cohost, February 2017*

One spring day in April 2022, former president Barack Obama was in
Palo Alto, California, to deliver an important keynote lecture on his
billion-dollar foundation's latest crusade. Obama was at Stanford University
to deliver a tirade against not racism or climate change but rather an even
more faceless villain, "disinformation," which he declared "a threat to our
democracy."[2]

The Stanford University students in the audience roared with approval as
Obama strutted onto the stage. The forty-fourth president, now in his early
sixties, was beginning to show his age. His crown was more salt than pep-
per, and his face bore the wrinkles that any man's would after serving two
contentious terms as leader of the free world (only to be succeeded by a mor-
tal enemy, hell-bent on dismantling the Obama legacy).[3]

But Obama's characteristic swagger was still unmistakable. He wore a
crisp white button-down, open-collar shirt and a black sport coat—he was
cool and confident. He beamed, his eyes glinting, as he soaked in the ap-
plause for a few moments before he gestured toward the crowd to calm
down—"Everybody have a seat, thank you," he said in his casual drawl.[4]

Obama began his lecture by lambasting Russian president Vladimir Putin and his "brutal invasion of Ukraine." He quickly pivoted to blasting his domestic political opponents, stating, "Democratic backsliding isn't restricted to distant lands," and "Right here in the United States of America, we just saw a sitting president deny the clear results of an election and help incite a violent insurrection at the nation's capital."[5]

Obama waxed eloquent on the dangers of so-called disinformation (and its less menacing cousin, "misinformation") for more than an hour. The lecture was riddled with platitudes as he invoked the buzzword du jour "democracy" more than twenty times. Ironically, Obama disseminated plenty of his own misinformation throughout the sermon as he accused his political opponents of "violent insurrection" and claimed that his opponents desired to disenfranchise voters by "making it easier to overturn the will of the people in states where [his opponents] hold power."[6]

Obama lamented that misinformation was now so dangerous that it was killing people, because "despite the fact that we've now, essentially clinically tested the vaccine on billions of people worldwide, around 1 in 5 Americans is still willing to put themselves at risk and put their families at risk rather than get vaccinated." Obama and the global health experts like Bill Gates still have not explained how an unvaccinated individual puts others at risk.[7]

The crux of the problem, Obama implied, was that information had become harder to control. In the good old days, according to Obama, a news consumer could count the number of information propagators on one hand:

> If you were watching TV here in the United States between about 1960 and 1990 . . . chances are you were watching one of the big three networks. And this had its own problems, particularly the ways in which programming often excluded voices and perspectives of women and people of color and other folks outside of the mainstream. But it did fortify a sense of shared culture and when it came to the news, at least,

citizens across the political spectrum tended to operate using a shared set of facts, what they saw, what they heard from Walter Cronkite or David Brinkley or others.[8]

Today, there are limitless propagators—both good and bad—of information. And while traditional media outlets still generate "some of the most outrageous content on the Web," Obama conceded, he blamed social-media companies for accelerating what he called the "decline of newspapers and other traditional news sources" (though Obama credited some legacy media companies such as left-wing darling National Public Radio [NPR] with still "maintaining the highest standards of journalistic integrity").[9]

About halfway through his speech, Obama said the quiet part out loud: the First Amendment is all but obsolete in today's corporate-controlled information era. "[The First Amendment] doesn't apply to private companies like Facebook or Twitter, any more than it applies to editorial decisions made by *The New York Times* or Fox News," and "it never has," Obama said. If the private media outlets and platforms could eliminate free speech irrespective of the First Amendment, the government would not need to censor, Obama argued. But in reality mounting evidence indicated that the Biden administration had been secretly leaning on media corporations to push propaganda, receive more "favorable" news coverage, and censor unapproved narratives.[10]

Obama then emphasized private companies' obligation to perform "content moderation" (a new Orwellian euphemism for mass censorship) and use their algorithms and other tools to "slow the spread" of bad content. But while tackling the supply side of disinformation was important to Obama, so was addressing the demand side: "It starts with breaking through our information bubbles."[11]

How did Obama suggest breaking through information bubbles? He cited a study where researchers paid regular Fox News viewers to watch CNN exclusively for one month. The former president revealed that the results were promising:

And what the researchers found was that, at the end of the month, people's views on certain issues, like whether voting by mail should be
allowed or whether electing Joe Biden would lead to more violence
against police, on some of these issues, their views are changed by five,
eight, ten points.[12]

The problem with Obama's "solutions" is that they address a fake problem, casting politically contrary speech as "disinformation." Further, his
solutions are all top-down instead of bottom-up. Obama, and people like
him, often push for information to be tightly controlled by elite institutions
through strict regulation.

Throughout his speech, Obama touted Controligarch-funded outfits committed to activism, the training of journalists, and controlling information,
including a Soros-funded NGO called the K-Monitor Association and the
MIT Center for Constructive Communication (which receives funding from
the Bezos and Gates foundations, Comcast, Google, and a bevy of World Economic Forum partners and sponsors).[13]

Obama also touted the News Literacy Project, which is funded by billionaire foundations, multinational corporations, WEF partners, and mainstream
media titans such as Comcast and *The Washington Post* (along with News
Corp, Bloomberg News, *The New York Times*, and many others).[14]

The News Literacy Project has created digital tools that public schools
use to train students on how to recognize misinformation and disinformation, conspiracy theories, and online hoaxes. In 2017, the tax-exempt organization cofounded another information gatekeeper called the News Integrity
Initiative. Controligarchs such as Mark Zuckerberg and partisan Craigslist's
founder Craig Newmark, among others, provided funding for the News Integrity Initiative.[15]

Lest there be any doubt over the clear political objectives of these
billionaire-backed "grass roots" news integrity and literacy initiatives, the
press release stated their partisan impetus:

In the aftermath of the bitterly divisive 2016 presidential campaign, which featured daily assaults on truth and partisan attacks on the news media, the world learned hard lessons about the prevalence and power of online hoaxes and conspiracy theories. For us, the need to extend news literacy to the general population suddenly took on far greater urgency, since the bedrock of a healthy democracy is an informed and engaged electorate.[16]

Obama's top-down solutions, like increased censorship via "content moderation" and selective fact-checking, were ideas that Obama's billionaire friends such as George Soros and Laurene Powell Jobs supported. Soros and Powell Jobs had poured at least $1.71 billion into various efforts to control the mainstream narrative dating back more than a decade.[17]

Powell Jobs is the widow of Apple tycoon Steve Jobs and has become a major financier of left-wing causes since her husband passed away in 2011. Her largesse has earned her the nickname "the New Soros" by media critic Alexander Marlow. In fact, the billionaire heiress "had the former president's ear" and hosted Obama at her headquarters just prior to his April 2022 speech, helping to launch his foundation's crusade against disinformation.[18]

Inside Philanthropy named Powell Jobs the "least transparent megagiver" in 2019 because of her murky Emerson Collective investment vehicle. The Emerson Collective is a nonprofit and for-profit hybrid entity with opaque finances. It is a major partner of the Obama Foundation and committed $56 million to an Obama education initiative called My Brother's Keeper in the mid-2010s.[19]

Obama kicked off his crusade against so-called disinformation following meetings with the billionaire heiress, who had been waging her own information war by investing more than $100 million in a variety of major media companies, including *The Atlantic* (purchasing a majority stake in 2017), *Axios, Mother Jones,* the now-defunct Ozy Media (Powell Jobs distanced herself after Ozy Media was revealed as a massive fraud), and *ProPublica,* among other major magazines, podcast producers, start-ups, and media companies.[20]

In addition to her influence over legacy media and national outlets, Powell Jobs has funded a network of "local" and "grass roots" news sites that push left-wing propaganda (a tactic also known as "astroturfing," which was coined and mastered by Democratic political strategists).[21]

The fake-news network is called the *Courier Newsroom*, which was owned by an entity called ACRONYM that, in turn, was reportedly bankrolled by Powell Jobs. ACRONYM was instrumental in the 2020 election cycle by funding a controversial vote tabulation app ominously called Shadow, which came under fire for causing chaos in the Iowa caucus. During the 2020 campaign, ACRONYM launched a $100 million attack-ad spree—one of the largest digital operations that cycle—against Trump. *Courier*'s ads were "not considered political by Facebook."[22]

Soon, an FEC complaint was filed against the company for its lack of transparency (Biden's FEC waited until March 2022 before dismissing the complaint). In October 2021, the *Courier* "news" network was transferred to a new shadowy entity: Good Information. The price of the transaction was undisclosed, and the Powell Jobs PR agents pushed back on claims that she was an investor in the Good Information venture.[23]

Good Information—thus, *Courier*—is backed by Good Club member George Soros, along with tech billionaire (and previous ACRONYM funder) Reid Hoffman—both men were major Obama and Biden donors. The *Courier Newsroom* is so controversial that even *The Washington Post* and *Politico* published criticism that questioned the network's ethics and transparency, calling it a "clandestine political operation" at best, and "hyperlocal partisan propaganda" at worst.[24]

But the irony of tech billionaires funding astroturf propaganda operations (while claiming to be grassroots purveyors of truth) did not end with Obama's lecture on disinformation. In fact, Obama seems to have his own record of spreading disinformation. For example, Obama's most famous whopper—"If you like your health care plan, you can keep it"—was named the "Lie of the Year" by PolitiFact.

Another keynote speaker at the event was Ben Rhodes, Obama's former national-security advisor. In 2016, Rhodes admitted that the controversial 2015 Iran nuclear deal was the result of an "echo chamber" that the administration had created. He claimed that he "largely manufactured" the details of the deal, which were then validated by Obama allies in the mainstream media.[25]

The Stanford event and the Obama Foundation's new crusade were just the latest examples of raising the alarm over disinformation in a trend of projection by ruling-class propagandists. After all, Obama and his major donors (such as Soros and Powell Jobs) and the mainstream press were the ones who pushed the Trump-Russia collusion hoax and foisted it upon the world for years before it was thoroughly debunked.[26]

The number of misinformation and disinformation (or simply, propaganda) operations perpetrated by the very people warning about the threats to our democracy are myriad.

The pandemic misinformation (or disinformation) coming from people such as Anthony Fauci and Bill Gates could fill a separate volume, but one of the highlights included the repeated falsehood that the mRNA jabs prevent both spread and infection. The Clintons, Obama, and virtually every other political elite tweeted essentially the same message after they inevitably caught COVID. The script read something along the lines of "I am experiencing mild symptoms and am so glad that I was double vaccinated and boosted."

And when the 2022 midterm elections were once again marred by irregularities, CNN was quick to remind its viewers not to go reading information elsewhere:

> Trust your local officials, trust us here [at CNN], trust a news source that you know and trust to be honest about this—they're doing their jobs, they're doing it right.[27]

Trust the experts, trust the science, and trust CNN. The News Literacy Project likewise ran partisan interference against questions over election irregularities.[28]

The most troubling aspect of propaganda is not that it exists, but that it works. Governments have long understood this and have used propaganda to control information and manipulate public opinion accordingly. Why? Because legitimate power is derived from the support of the people. The more information that is controlled, the more people can be influenced, the more support is amassed, and the more powerful the propagandists become. And when rulers and regimes lose that support, revolutions often follow.

Consider the modern CCP. This ruling class has no intention of relinquishing power, despite monumental failures and shocking abuses of human rights. So, the CCP lies to its subjects—the Chinese people—through incessant mass-media messaging and denies the abuses to the rest of the world. All of this adds up to the CCP being terrified of losing its grip on power and information. This is because a populist revolt of even a tiny fraction of China's 1.4 billion citizens would be "an existential threat."[29]

It is no coincidence that the more authoritarian a society, the more tightly controlled and manipulated the mass-communication systems become. And it should come as no surprise that the Controligarchs have poured unfathomable sums—easily totaling more than $67.4 billion—into efforts to control information and promote themselves over the years.[30]

For example, Bill Gates and his various entities have spent at least $45.9 billion on media-related deals. Gates's earliest media projects include the 1990s-era Microsoft Network and the Microsoft-NBC joint venture, MSNBC, which sold to Comcast for $300 million in 2012. More recently, Microsoft spent more than $26 billion to acquire the networking and social media website LinkedIn, which Gates has used as a platform to promote himself and his ideas.[31]

Additionally, Gates and his foundation have funneled over $300 million into news initiatives and mainstream media "partnerships" with a multitude of foreign and domestic media outlets.[32]

Other billionaires also have significant media interests: Michael Bloomberg has Bloomberg News, Oprah has the Oprah Winfrey Network, George Soros has major financial relationships with dozens of media outlets ranging from NPR to the Pulitzer Prize–winning *ProPublica* organization, Ted Turner largely built his empire with the Turner Broadcasting System and CNN, and the Rockefellers have had deep connections to major media companies for several decades.[33]

Other billionaires have purchased large or even controlling stakes in mainstream media outlets, as Jeff Bezos did with *The Washington Post* in 2013 and Mexican oligarch Carlos Slim did with *The New York Times* in 2015.[34]

While major media outlets have long been dominated by the wealthy—such as press baron William Randolph Hearst, Arthur Ochs Sulzberger with *The New York Times*, Otis Chandler with the *Los Angeles Times*, and Robert McCormick's *Chicago Tribune*, to name a few—people trusted the legacy press. Now the modern media landscape is different—namely, in that fewer and fewer citizens rely on Big Media.

Controligarch-run media outlets, where the citizenry gets its news, have cratered public trust in the objectivity of "the news" and are perhaps the largest threats facing free societies around the world.[35]

But these outlets' reputational downfall notwithstanding, the corporate press continues to push destructive narratives.

Propaganda Drives the War Machine

America's Founding Fathers understood that a free press was crucial for a free society. Thus, they enshrined the First Amendment right to free speech and a free press in the Constitution. Most Americans believe that honest, independent individuals should *pressure* government officials for factual information and hold them accountable. The press has been called the "fourth estate," meaning a necessary check-and-balance system for the three government estates: the legislative, executive, and judicial branches.[36]

Adherence to these foundational ideals determines what direction society will follow and how free (or controlled) it will be. Public trust in the
corporate media is at a record low, which raises the question, Is the mainstream media a free press or a propaganda and misinformation machine?

Most people would agree that politicians (of every stripe) skillfully spread
innuendo and falsehoods against their political opponents to advance their
personal ambitions. Likewise, corporations have sold lethal and egregious
lies to consumers ranging from cigarettes are "healthy" to opioid painkillers
are "not highly addictive." The purpose of propaganda is often linked to
power, money, or both.[37]

The failure to expose political and corporate misinformation extends
beyond mere bias. It is a dereliction of duty by a dysfunctional press. Further, when the press itself engages in propaganda—especially corporate-
sponsored, progovernment, antidissent propaganda—the melding of political,
corporate, and media interests crystallizes authoritarianism.[38]

The US corporate media model is not the same as the state-sponsored
media in China or in the former Soviet Union. There are certainly more diverse viewpoints expressed. But in some ways, the billionaire-backed US
media model—in which just six multinational corporations own the majority of the major media outlets—is more insidious. The reach and scope
of its control over public opinion is massive—extending beyond borders—
but unlike state-owned media, there is a semblance of independence (and
thus legitimacy). And historically, the US corporate press has even emulated
state-owned media by working hand in glove with the government to achieve
state objectives, while the public remains largely unaware until long after
those objectives have been achieved.[39]

Pushing the public to support war is a common and recurring theme. In
the 1890s, newspaper barons William Randolph Hearst and Joseph Pulitzer
helped the US government galvanize the public into supporting the Spanish-
American War. Historians consider this conflict the nation's first "media
war," because of extreme bias, hyperbole, and outright falsehoods plastered

across daily newspapers with the aim of manipulating America into war with Spain. Powerful forces within the government wanted war and the spoils that would come with victory (i.e., Cuba's independence as well as US sovereignty over Guam, Puerto Rico, the Philippines, and Hawaii). In the meantime, Hearst and Pulitzer had vested interests in hyping the conflict to sell newspapers, increase their national profiles and garner government favors.[40]

And willfully dishonest reporters, for whom the term "yellow journalism" was invented, also pursued vested interests. Rather than report the unvarnished truth, they spun false and misleading narratives that fueled the government-media war agenda. Their incentives were clear: write what their publishers wanted and build their personal reporting brands.

A PBS account on the origins of yellow journalism put it this way: "Hearst's star reporters wrote stories designed to tug at the heartstrings of Americans. Horrific tales described the situation in Cuba—female prisoners, executions, valiant rebels fighting, and starving women and children figured in many of the stories that filled the newspapers."[41]

Of course, there was just one problem: the stories were not true.

Most wars since the Spanish-American War have gained (and lost) popular support because of media coverage—which was later revealed as propaganda—including the World Wars I and II, the Vietnam War, the Iraq War, and the global war on terror.[42]

New York Times reporters Michael Gordon and Judith Miller (citing unnamed "American officials") and many other mainstream reporters pushed the latter Bush administration's unsubstantiated narrative that Saddam Hussein was harboring Al Qaeda terrorists and hiding weapons of mass destruction (WMDs)—essential justifications for the invasion of Iraq.[43]

Miller remained adamant that her job was not to be an independent analyst, but rather to "tell readers of *The New York Times* what the government thought about Iraq's arsenal" (in other words, to push government propaganda). A 2021 Brown University study found that the global war on t had cost American taxpayers $8 trillion since the September 11, 2001, attacks on US soil and led to the death of nearly one million people worldwide.[44]

More than a century after Hearst's and Pulitzer's Spanish-American War coverage and two decades after the WMD debacle, the Information Age has created a vastly superior (and still growing) reach of digital media and highly targeted social media. Is there any wonder that the government and corporate news monopolies have led the world to the brink of yet another world war?

In 2022, the mainstream Western press—particularly Rupert Murdoch's media properties—promoted a hoax called the "Ghost of Kyiv." The story was that a legendary Ukrainian fighter pilot shot down at least forty Russian planes in the first months of the war between those nations. Songs were written about his bravery. But he did not exist.[45]

Another feel-good tale from corporate media was about the Ukrainian "heroes of Snake Island," who remained defiant to their valiant deaths at the hands of a merciless Russian warship. "Russian warship, go fuck yourself!" was their widely reported rallying cry shortly before they were attacked and killed. In truth, they had surrendered and were found "alive and well."[46]

Were these corporate media propaganda campaigns an effort to ratchet up Western support for the war in Ukraine? If so, they were effective, if by no other metric than the number of "Ghost of Kyiv," "Take a Stand Snake Island," and "Fight Like [a] Ukrainian" T-shirts and other merchandise created and sold. But the biggest Western care package came in the form of cash and weapons from American taxpayers: $196 billion (and counting) in less than a year.[47]

᠁ᴄouraging a global conflict with a nuclear-armed state, such as Russia,

᠁ᴄ Abraham Lincoln famously said, American destruction

᠁that danger "must spring up amongst us." Thus,

᠁igned to confuse, divide, and steer the public is

᠁the American way of life than global conflict is. In

᠁ɪrch media is a major threat to freedom and must be

dealt with if Americans are to enjoy the free exchange of ideas and opinions that is their birthright.[48]

The permanent political class in Washington, DC—the administrative state that has no intention of relinquishing control—has combined forces with the Controligarchs. Together, they wield policy and propaganda to persuade much of the public that the bureaucrats' and billionaires' enemies are middle-class America's enemies.

This unholy alliance of state and media power has had devastating real-life consequences for millions of innocent Americans. For example, the permanent political class and the media oligarchs have spent considerable time, money, and effort trying to paint roughly half of the American people as racists or Russian agents or insurrectionists—a "basket of deplorables," some might say.

These smears led to immense civil liberties abuses that have only gotten worse in recent years. In less extreme cases, American citizens have been censored, "shadow banned," and excommunicated by friends and family; in more extreme cases, they have been harassed by law enforcement and even thrown in jail. In particular, the level of media propaganda that resulted in civil rights violations reached previously unimaginable heights during the COVID-19 pandemic.

Censors Lied, People Died

In August 2022, less than three years after the pandemic began, former *New York Times* journalist Alex Berenson reported that the Biden administration was working directly with Twitter to eliminate dissent. And pandemic censorship aligned with the views and interests of Pfizer, Moderna, and other Big Pharma companies.[49]

COVID origin? Censored. Mask ineffectiveness? Censored. Hydroxychloroquine? Censored. Ivermectin? Censored. Vaccine side effects? Censored. Preventative treatments? Censored. Most of the thought policing came from Big Tech's social media monopolies—namely, Twitter, Facebook,

Instagram, Google, and YouTube. People noticed that videos were taken down, posts were slapped with warning labels or outright deleted, and users were suspended en masse.[50]

As it turned out, the pharmaceutical companies were coordinating with the tech giants. Big Pharma operatives were specifically concerned about their patents and an activist movement that sought to make the vaccines free to all. They contacted Twitter employees requesting an intervention. Twitter then shielded Big Pharma accounts, including Pfizer's and Moderna's, from negative posts and stifled a viral campaign promoting a #PeoplesVaccine, which would effectively remove the patent.[51]

Many in the media, government, and health industries made a total about-face after the death of George Floyd in spring 2020. With law-abiding citizens obediently locked down and small businesses shuttered across the country, suddenly many talking heads claimed it was medically sound to support giant protest gatherings.

"We should always evaluate the risks and benefits of efforts to control the virus," Jennifer Nuzzo, a Johns Hopkins epidemiologist, tweeted in June 2020 along with the following: "In this moment the public health risks of not protesting to demand an end to systemic racism greatly exceed the harms of the virus."[52]

"While I have voiced concerns that protests risk creating more outbreaks, the status quo wasn't going to stop #covid19 either," wrote Abraar Karan, a Brigham and Women's Hospital physician, on Twitter a couple of days earlier.[53]

With a blind eye to violence amid nationwide riots, corporate news narratives included headlines such as, "Blaming Protesters for COVID-19 Spread Ignores the Bigger Threats to Health" and "Public Health Experts Say the Pandemic Is Exactly Why Protests Must Continue."[54]

Tom Frieden, director of the CDC under President Obama, penned an authoritative pro-lockdown op-ed in *The Washington Post* at the outset of the pandemic, only to support the close-contact political protests as the election neared.[55]

And when Biden was declared the 2020 election winner, his massive victory parties seemed to indicate that the social distancing criticisms rigorously applied to Trump's campaign rallies had magically vanished. The hypocrisy and double standards were hard to ignore.

What was going on? Why did Big Pharma and social media oligarchs all seem to be on the same page?

Where propaganda is the front-facing side of controlling the public through manipulated information, censorship is about eliminating or obfuscating ideas that threaten to undermine official narratives. This is achieved by criminalizing alleged "hate speech," which appears to be speech that censors do not like; classifying absurd amounts of government documents that do not warrant the designation and ensuring that these never see the light of day; "deplatforming" journalists who dare to report on topics outside the approved discourse, such as Berenson and undercover video maker James O'Keefe (and many others); and accusing people of misinformation or disinformation for political gain, among other tactics.

What made Berenson's situation so important is that he obtained answers, albeit long after the election. He was a leading source of mainstream dissident information, either for those who had suspicions about the administration's COVID policies and media blackouts or for those who were curious about his alternative reporting. He amassed hundreds of thousands of followers in the process until one day, in August 2021, he was gone. Deplatformed.

Berenson sued Twitter in December 2021, and where others had failed, he got the goods. A smoking-gun exchange definitively proved that the Biden White House was working with the social media giant to censor individuals and information in what appeared to be a gross violation of the spirit, if not the letter, of the First Amendment.[56]

Berenson was further vindicated after Elon Musk took control of Twitter in late October 2022. Musk began releasing the "Twitter Files," which confirmed that the FBI and the Biden administration had indeed been pressuring the tech company to censor inconvenient information. Had the Constitution been violated? We may never know. Naturally, there was a near-complete media blackout surrounding the Twitter Files in the Controligarch press.

"They had one really tough question about why Alex Berenson hasn't been kicked off the platform," a Twitter employee wrote in an internal communication.[57]

"They really wanted to know about Alex Berenson. Andy Slavitt suggested they had seen data viz [visualization] that had showed he was the epicenter of disinfo that radiated outwards to the persuadable public," wrote another Twitter employee.[58]

Andy Slavitt was President Biden's White House COVID advisor during the period. Berenson claimed on his Substack account, "Unreported Truths," that in addition to government pressure, repressive journalists had also pressured the social media giant to silence him. But it was not until President Biden publicly accused Facebook of "killing people" in July 2021 for allowing "misinformation" that Berenson was censored.[59]

"A few hours after Biden's comment, Twitter suspended my account for the first time," Berenson said. A month later, he was permanently suspended. The irony of his removal is that he was banned for good-faith reporting, not for spreading disinformation. The offending August 2021 tweet that led to his suspension alleged that the COVID-19 vaccines did not stop infection or transmission—a fact that the health experts have since quietly admitted, though they likely knew it early on.[60]

"It doesn't stop infection. Or transmission. Don't think of it as a vaccine," Berenson wrote. "Think of it—at best—as a therapeutic with a limited window of efficacy and terrible side effect profile that must be dosed IN ADVANCE OF ILLNESS. And we want to mandate it? Insanity."[61]

Mainstream Media Consolidation = Corporate Mind Control

In 1983, fifty companies owned 90 percent of the US media. If that were to be spread evenly, that distribution would amount to one media company per state. The number of market players and the level of competition were vastly more diverse than in the decades that followed, especially compared with today's media landscape.

By 2012, just six companies controlled 90 percent of the US media, meaning that almost everything that Americans read, watched, or listened to ran through the corporate media giants of General Electric (GE), News Corp, Disney, Viacom, Time Warner, and CBS—and the 232 media executives who led them.[62]

Much has transpired in the intervening decade—namely, the explosion of digital media, streaming services, and cable news, as well as unprecedented ways of both distributing and consuming content. The internet boom was democratizing information, or so the mantra went. More than a decade into this historic transition, roughly the same six companies controlled mass media.

As of 2023, the six companies that control almost all the media are:

- AT&T (which acquired Time Warner in 2018 and rebranded it as WarnerMedia);

- Comcast (which partnered with GE in 2011 to purchase NBCUniversal before Comcast acquired GE's 49 percent ownership stake in NBCUniversal in 2013);

- Disney (which owns ABC and multiple news, media, and theme-park operations, as well as the massive ESPN Wide World of Sports Complex);

- News Corp (which owns Fox News, *The Wall Street Journal*, the *New York Post*, and other major media properties);

- Paramount Global (formerly ViacomCBS after the 2019 "remerger" of Viacom and CBS); and

- Sony (which owns several major film studios).

Each of these six companies is a publicly traded corporation, which means that none of them are wholly owned by our Controligarchs (though Black-

Rock, Vanguard, and State Street are typically their largest shareholders and many Controligarchs own media stocks). However, all six media conglomerates are WEF partners, and their executives certainly possess the Davos Spirit.[63]

It is breathtaking to consider that even through the hyperproliferation of mass media in the modern era, areas such as entertainment, news, and information are more tightly controlled and consolidated in corporate hands than ever. And that does not even include the vast reaches of the so-called FAANGs: Facebook, Apple, Amazon, Netflix, and Google, which are not considered traditional media companies but have perhaps more power to poison the information well.

These media empires are not just too big to fail, they are also too big to avoid or escape. Want to take your viewing dollars somewhere other than Disney because of the corporation's political leanings? Good luck. You would have to avoid the ABC broadcast network; ESPN; Pixar; Marvel; Lucasfilm; Disney+; ESPN+; Hulu; multiple other cable networks; magazines; publishing companies; music record labels; cruise lines; resorts; fourteen theme parks; lucrative "woke" corporate sports partnerships with the National Basketball Association, the Major League Baseball, the National Football League, the National Collegiate Athletic Association; and more. Even if you managed to steer clear, the few other media conglomerates offer similar vortexes with few viewpoint alternatives.[64]

Change the channel from slanted ABC News coverage or ESPN's bizarre daytime race-baiting sports programming, and one might land on a Warner Bros. Discovery property. The megamedia corporation—now majorly owned by AT&T—houses multiple cable networks, including HBO and Discovery Channel; Warner's film studios, which include DC Comics and New Line Cinema; a trove of international television programming; the Discovery+ streaming service; and HBO Max.[65]

Warner Bros. Discovery also owns CNN. The cable-news network— launched by media mogul Ted Turner in 1980—damaged its reputation in recent years by veering into extreme bias, outright propaganda, and disgraceful backroom dealings. The network has since tried to regain some of its credibility—and more importantly, halt the hemorrhaging of its viewers—by cleaning house.

Notably, CNN's former star anchor Chris Cuomo was fired in December 2021 after evidence emerged that he was advising New York governor Andrew Cuomo, his brother, on how to dodge sexual harassment accusations—which ultimately contributed to Andrew Cuomo's resignation.[66]

Chris Cuomo regularly interviewed his powerful brother, and the network covered the disgraced governor in glowing terms, all under the auspices of former CNN president Jeff Zucker. As part of the housecleaning, Zucker himself was forced to resign after an affair came to light during the Chris Cuomo investigation. Zucker's paramour, Allison Gollust, was CNN's marketing chief and had previously worked at NBC and as Andrew Cuomo's communications director.[67]

The ouster of CNN's top brass did little to help remedy public perception of the network. But no matter how swampy, misleading, and poorly rated CNN becomes, the network remains safely embedded into a giant media corporation where it is insulated from the consequences of failure and financial losses. This is because the real value of the network is not in journalism, but in its capacity to broadcast narratives and influence minds across the globe.

As of 2021, Comcast is the second-largest broadcasting and cable television company in the world by revenue. It is also the largest pay TV and home internet service provider in the United States and the largest pay TV provider in Europe. The colossal media and telecommunications conglomerate is vertically integrated from production to distribution, and its CEO Brian Roberts has golfed with Barack Obama.[68]

The media properties that fall under Comcast's umbrella span the globe and have numerous foreign-language spinoffs. As the parent company of NBCUniversal, Comcast's list of assets could run for pages. Notable domestic holdings include broadcast networks NBC, MSNBC, CNBC, USA Network, NBCSN, Bravo, E!, and Telemundo; the film studio Universal

Pictures; the streaming service Peacock; and the animation studios Dream-Works, Illumination, and Universal Animation Studios.[69]

Other Comcast-owned ventures include English- and Spanish-language TV-news affiliates in large-, medium-, and small-sized cities across the country; dozens of sports channels, networks, and stand-alone properties, such as the Golf Channel and NBC Olympics. NBCUniversal operates in every habitable continent: Africa, Asia, Australia, Europe, North America, and South America.[70]

NBCUniversal is headquartered at Rockefeller Center (30 Rockefeller Plaza) in Midtown Manhattan, which is the site of an earlier media transition that was spearheaded by one of the most consequential oligarch families in American history.

John D. Rockefeller Jr., son of the legendary and oft-reviled Standard Oil robber baron John D. Rockefeller, constructed what is commonly known today as "30 Rock" or "the Rock" between 1931 and 1933. With massive wealth at Rockefeller Jr.'s disposal, and all the connections that money could buy, he set out to dominate media in the Great Depression era—and, of course, beyond.

Radio was the main medium of the day, and Rockefeller built a city inside America's most powerful media market to headquarter his new empire; that is, Radio City in Midtown Manhattan (though at first it was popularly known as Rockefeller City). At the time, NBC was owned by the Radio Corporation of America (RCA), and Rockefeller landed NBC—America's oldest major broadcaster and the crown jewel of radio—as his principal tenant.[71]

Rockefeller Jr. courted additional tenants to fill out the sprawling complex, which included many foreign companies attracted to the Rockefeller name. Political perks soon followed. David Rockefeller, grandson of the Radio City founder, recalled in his 2002 memoir, "Congress agreed to special legislation that provided duty-free status for goods imported by firms taking space in the Center, and a number of foreign firms took long-term leases in some of the smaller buildings."[72]

Interestingly enough, RCA formed NBC in 1926, while RCA itself was co-owned by some of the biggest media players of recent years: General Electric, AT&T, and Westinghouse (which effectively merged with the CBS Corporation in the mid-1990s, was then acquired by Viacom in 1999, and ultimately reorganized into Paramount Global in 2022). In 1932, GE was forced to sell its RCA (and thus NBC) stake because of antitrust charges, only to reacquire it in 1986, or during the initial upswing of the mass information consolidation.[73]

And when Comcast bought out GE in 2013 by purchasing a controlling interest in NBCUniversal, Comcast secured its place at the top of the media food chain. For its part, the Rockefeller Center helped to launch point-to-mass radio, transitioned the nation to ubiquitous television programming, and now penetrates households and smartphones around the globe through digital broadcasting. Amazingly, the Rock consists of twenty-two acres of some of the most expensive land in the world and remains a thriving city within a city.

Media consolidation of such magnitude represents a threat to the republic, but perhaps even worse than the increasing lack of competition in the fourth estate is that foxes are guarding the henhouse.

The CIA, the FBI, and the TV Spies Who Lie

In recent years, former senior intelligence officials directly involved in alleged high-profile political and civil liberties abuses were featured uncritically in television news, even as elite media organizations claimed adherence to journalistic integrity. In early 2017, "Democracy Dies in Darkness," became *The Washington Post's* above-the-fold motto as it turned a blind eye to the overt integration of the intelligence community into the US media.

Officials such as John Brennan, the former director of the Central Intelligence Agency (CIA); James Clapper, the former director of National Intelligence; and Andrew McCabe, the former deputy director of the FBI—among others—made regular appearances on CNN, MSNBC, network news, and Sunday-morning news shows to air manipulated versions of events in which they and their agencies were involved, including election interference, political espionage, and leaking classified information during the Trump era.

Brennan, Clapper, McCabe, and ex-FBI director James Comey were among the figures being investigated by the Justice Department's inspector general (IG) Michael Horowitz, an Obama appointee, and Special Counsel John Durham, while their media hosts provided nationwide platforms to justify their activities and spin like-minded narratives. McCabe was even hired by CNN in 2019 to promote shared interests and distribute FBI talking points in what could only be considered misinformation, at best.[74]

In one instance, Jonathan Turley, a prominent legal analyst and professor at George Washington University Law School, sounded the alarm in 2020 for what he called "a new twist on echo journalism." Writing on his popular legal blog, Turley cited a CNN interview in which McCabe made "utterly absurd and untrue" statements about legal developments involving retired general Michael Flynn, whom McCabe himself allegedly snared in a so-called perjury trap in early 2017. Flynn then faced years of subsequent prosecutorial harassment and media character assassination because of McCabe's actions. Flynn even sold his home to pay for his legal bills.[75]

"Not only was McCabe not challenged on the statements, it was never mentioned that he was fired after being found by career investigators to have lied to them (the very charge against Flynn)," Turley wrote. "Despite the fact that his false statements were related to this very case, it was not deemed relevant to raise by CNN with CNN's senior analyst. McCabe however displayed the very bias and maliciousness documented by career investigators before he was fired." McCabe, of course, denies any wrongdoing.[76]

The "news" being offered was a complete scam that was delivered through a matrix of highly abusive politics, oligarchic platform control, and coordinated messaging—the type that currently dominates America's modern information landscape and is by no means limited to CNN.

As Turley noted, CNN allowed McCabe to push "utterly absurd and untrue" statements to its viewers without disclosing that he had been fired from the FBI for lying to internal investigators at the Department of Justice

(DOJ). Turley's analysis echoed IG Horowitz's previous findings. Horowitz had referred McCabe for criminal prosecution for multiple instances where McCabe "lacked candor," or lied, during an investigation into an unauthorized leak to the media. Horowitz wrote in a 2018 IG report that McCabe's actions were "designed to advance his personal interests at the expense of Department leadership" and "violated the FBI's and the Department's media policy and constituted misconduct."[77]

But CNN ignored all of that misconduct as it sought to benefit from McCabe's media profile. And as is so often the case, DOJ leadership declined to prosecute McCabe, despite the department's internal watchdog's own criminal referral. In fact, not only did he escape accountability but he also received enormous benefits at the taxpayers' expense. These included the restoration of his pension and more than $500,000 in legal bills paid. McCabe even had his personnel file scrubbed of all indicators of his termination for cause.[78]

Intelligence community involvement in the US media is not new. The FBI, the CIA, and other intel agencies have leaked information to the news media for decades. Usually, the motives boil down to an "I'll scratch your back if you scratch mine" approach that advances both sides' political agendas and personal gains.

"Deep Throat," the man who was the source for *Washington Post* journalists Bob Woodward and Carl Bernstein in the early 1970s during Watergate, is a prime example. Deep Throat's name was W. Mark Felt, and he, like Andrew McCabe, was the FBI's deputy director. *The Washington Post* and the mainstream media detested President Nixon, as did Felt. By leaking, Felt exacted revenge against Nixon for not appointing him to the FBI's newly opened directorship following the death of longtime FBI director J. Edgar Hoover.[79]

This tactic of presidential sabotage via leaks to the press would resurface in the 2016, 2020, and 2024 election cycles. Such leaks are just one of the "six ways from Sunday" that Senator Chuck Schumer warned that the intelligence community could get back at Trump. The Trump-hating media has been eager to publish and amplify the leaks.

While Americans may generally assume that intel officials leak to the media, they may not realize how incestuous the relationship actually is.

The Controligarchs and the Mockingbirds

During the course of the Watergate investigations in the mid-1970s, troubling revelations surfaced about executive branch and intelligence agency domestic surveillance programs. Shortly after, famed investigative journalist Seymour Hersh reported that the CIA had been violating its charter by spying on American citizens during the Vietnam War. Amid public outcry, Congress convened the Church Committee, named for Senator Frank Church (D-ID), the committee's chairman, and stunning discoveries of widespread news media involvement came to light.[80]

Although the Church Committee was careful to balance the institutional integrity of the CIA with the incredible abuses that it was tasked with addressing—always leaning on protecting "sources and methods" to obfuscate undesirable disclosures—Operation Mockingbird would eventually be revealed by none other than Watergate crusader Carl Bernstein.[81]

Put simply, Operation Mockingbird was a CIA program that secretly recruited leading American journalists and corporate media oligarchs. The practice went beyond the scope of the Watergate scandal and involved embedding intel assets within the media. The purpose was to manipulate the American public, and it had repercussions that arguably continue to this day.

The Church Committee held 126 full meetings and 40 subcommittee hearings, while interviewing roughly 800 witnesses and admitting 110,000 documents, though most of these activities and records were kept from public view. According to the official US Senate record, the committee published a report in 1976 that carefully highlighted a few selected cases of "unlawful or improper conduct," despite resistance from the institutional subjects of the investigations.[82]

"These hearings examined a CIA biological agents program, a White House domestic surveillance program, IRS intelligence activities, and the FBI's program to disrupt the civil rights and anti-Vietnam War movements," the Senate record states.

"Despite these numerous challenges, the Church Committee investigated and identified a wide range of intelligence abuses by federal agencies, including the CIA, FBI, IRS, and National Security Agency. In the course of their work, investigators identified programs that had never before been known to the American public, including NSA's Projects SHAMROCK and MINARET, programs which monitored wire communications to and from the United States and shared some of that data with other intelligence agencies," the Senate record continues.[83]

The Church Committee also confirmed that the intelligence community had cultivated relationships within the press. Without identifying names, the committee found approximately fifty journalists who had secret ties to the CIA. However, Bernstein expanded on the Church Committee's findings in his groundbreaking 1977 article "The CIA and the Media." Bernstein exposed Operation Mockingbird and attested that hundreds of journalists, publishers, and editors were carrying out CIA assignments.[84]

Bernstein cited Joseph Alsop, a leading syndicated columnist, as one of more than four hundred American journalists who had secretly worked for the CIA. "Some of these journalists' relationships with the Agency were tacit; some were explicit. There was cooperation, accommodation, and overlap.... Reporters shared their notebooks with the CIA. Editors shared their staffs," Bernstein wrote.

But it was not just reporters and editors. It was also their employers working together as a united front to influence media narratives.

"Among the executives who lent their cooperation to the Agency were William Paley of the Columbia Broadcasting System, Henry Luce of Time Inc., [and] Arthur Hays Sulzberger of *The New York Times*," Bernstein wrote. "Other organizations which cooperated with the CIA include the American

Broadcasting Company, the National Broadcasting Company, the Associated Press, United Press International, Reuters, Hearst Newspapers, Scripps-Howard, *Newsweek* magazine, the Mutual Broadcasting System, *The Miami Herald* and the old *Saturday Evening Post* and *New York Herald-Tribune*."[85]

As a result of the stunning abuses highlighted through the Watergate investigations, the Church Committee, and intrepid reporting—the sort that has been censored in recent years—Congress approved legislation to rein in the intelligence community.

The Senate approved Senate Resolution 400 in 1976, establishing the Senate Select Committee on Intelligence. The committee's mandate was, and is, to provide "vigilant legislative oversight over the intelligence activities of the United States to assure that such activities are in conformity with the Constitution and laws of the United States." Congress also approved, and President Jimmy Carter signed into law, the Foreign Intelligence Surveillance Act in 1978, "requiring the executive branch to request warrants for wiretapping and surveillance purposes from a newly formed FISA Court."[86]

In 2016, FISA played a key role in a disinformation operation that undermined a US presidential candidate (and later president). Obama's FBI and DOJ obtained FISA warrants targeting Trump and his advisors; they spied on his campaign, and then they selectively leaked bits and pieces of Team Trump's communications to the press. A 2018 DOJ IG report blasted the cozy and unprecedented relationships between Obama intelligence officials and corporate media reporters (but recommended no criminal charges).[87]

The mainstream press, particularly David Ignatius of the Bezos-owned *Washington Post*, David Corn of the Laurene Powell Jobs–funded *Mother Jones*, and Michael Isikoff of *Yahoo! News* (which Verizon agreed to purchase in 2016), peddled the narrative that the Obama administration in effect told them to publish: Donald Trump was an agent of Russia.[88]

This kind of propaganda peddling and media corruption is so staggering that it should have been criminal. Instead, many reporters earned Pulitzers.[89]

Deep State Disinformation
and Creeping Dystopia

But perhaps the most egregious disinformation operation in recent years is the Hunter Biden laptop cover-up. It exemplifies the widespread corruption in the intelligence community that spills over into the mainstream media.

When the *New York Post* obtained a copy of Hunter Biden's abandoned laptop from a computer repair shop just a few weeks before the 2020 election, "Deep State" operatives, the corporate media, and the Big Tech oligarchs sprang into action to defend Joe Biden and help make the story go away. More than fifty former US senior intelligence officials signed an open letter falsely stating that the laptop was a "Russian disinformation" operation.[90]

Mainstream outlets pushed the letter far and wide. Finally, social media oligarchs like Mark Zuckerberg at Facebook and the obscurantists at Twitter censored the *New York Post*'s article and banned its accounts. The result was a total media blackout of the Biden laptop story (other than regurgitated reports dismissing the laptop revelations with the all-too-familiar label of "Russian disinformation").

The widespread censorship of the Biden laptop story influenced the 2020 election. Multiple polls and surveys have indicated that citizens would have voted differently—half of the respondents in one survey—if they had been permitted to know the truth about the Biden family's foreign business dealings. And the unholy alliance is already making its presence felt ahead of the 2024 presidential election, too. Mainstream media rejoiced after receiving news of the FBI's raid on Trump's home ahead of the former president's unprecedented indictment.[91]

The US intelligence community's feeding information to the corporate media and Big Tech to stifle the Biden laptop story and influence the 2020 election is only just the beginning. Big Tech oligarchs' desire for domination extends far beyond controlling the flow of information.

9

The Dystopian Present

I have over 4,000 emails, pictures, addresses, SNS . . . People just submitted it. I don't know why. They "trust me." Dumb fucks.[1]

—*Mark Zuckerberg, Meta Platforms founder and CEO, 2004*

One late October day in 2021, one of the richest and most powerful men in the world, Mark Zuckerberg, hosted a virtual event where he revealed the future of his companies, which, he hoped, also happened to be the future of the known universe. It was a few days before Halloween, and Zuckerberg had treats to share with the world and even a few tricks up his sleeve. Zuckerberg's jovial demeanor indicated that he thought his announcement would be fun, but more than a few people found his vision for the future terrifying.[2]

The event was Facebook's annual "Connect" conference, where Zuckerberg and other personnel show off the newest features coming to the Facebook family of companies, which includes Threads (a Twitter-like platform launched in 2023), as well as the Instagram photo-sharing platform and the WhatsApp instant-messaging platform.

Zuckerberg, or "Zuck" as he is known, began the address while sitting in his living room. He was wearing all black—perhaps because he likes the color, or perhaps as an homage to Apple founder Steve Jobs's signature look, or perhaps because he wanted to look like a cartoon villain. After all, he had once boasted that his employees "lovingly" call him the "Eye of Sauron," after the evil force depicted as a blazing all-seeing eye in the *Lord of the Rings* saga.[3]

As Zuck meandered about his palatial abode, he walked virtual attendees through a quick history of online life, from his perspective. "Back when I started Facebook, that mostly meant text that we typed on computers," Zuck began. "Then we all got phones with cameras, and the internet became much more visual"—from desktop computers forty years ago to pocket computers, smartphones, today. "But this isn't the end of the line," the Facebook founder teased.[4]

Zuck spoke with his usual awkward cadence and a forced folksy sincerity that sounded robotic. In Zuck's future, which he called the metaverse, digital life would be even more immersive than the perpetual newsfeed scrolling of today. He called his vision an "embodied internet," where his users are in the experience and "not just looking at it."[5]

As the billionaire wandered around his mansion—it appeared to be a virtual rendering of his 1,500-acre Hawaiian estate on the scenic island of Kauai—he settled in front of the floor-to-ceiling panoramic windows looking out at the tropical horizon of his oceanfront view. It was here that Zuck decided to demonstrate an even cooler reality: Facebook Horizon.[6]

Facebook Horizon was Zuck's contribution to the metaverse, which is actually not a Zuck product. Rather, the metaverse is the purported future of the internet, and Facebook Horizon is Zuck's corner of it.

As he stared out at paradise, the virtual reality flickered on. A cartoon version (or avatar) of Zuck appeared in a skeleton onesie Halloween costume. He swiped through outfits for his avatar until he found his all-black cartoon villain look and zoomed off to a virtual space station where several of his virtual friends were playing virtual poker.[7]

As Zuck continued the metaverse tour, suddenly a piece of three-dimensional graffiti appeared. One of his friends in the real world was checking out a street art exhibit in SoHo and sent him a link. The real-life street art was designed in "augmented reality" (which means half in the real world, half in the metaverse). "This is stunning... awesome... amazing!" Zuck and his metaverse friends were impressed. "Wait, it's disappearing," said Zuck as the 3D graffiti started to fade away.[8]

"Hold on, I'll tip the artist, and they'll extend it," said the friend who was physically in SoHo at the virtual street art exhibit. It appeared that digital artwork could be infinitely monetized.[9]

There are limitless ways to spend money on intangible items and virtual upgrades in Zuck's virtual world. In addition to an infinite number of digital products that do not exist in the real world, there will also be real products for sale. One of the first virtual shops in the metaverse, for example, was a cannabis store.[10]

In addition to selling physical products such as marijuana, the metaverse would create whole new consumer product offerings—including physical and biotechnological upgrades for the human body.

Zuck had already filed a patent for bionic eyeballs so that metaverse users could one day bring their virtual reality with them everywhere and never have to leave. Bionic eyeball technology (technically called a "cortical visual prosthesis") was at least a decade old, and other attempts had left terrified users in the dark from time to time. But Zuck had other brand-new technologies that he was tinkering with, including a synthetic skin prototype called ReSkin or pneumatic haptic gloves, so that users could literally feel and grasp the metaverse.[11]

Innovators were even developing scent blasters that shoot chemical mist at a user's nose to allow them to "smell" the metaverse. In addition to basic scents like chocolate and strawberry (and even "beach"), there are more nuanced fragrances such as "fascinate," "annihilate," and "carouse."[12]

More than five hundred major corporations are also helping to build the metaverse.[13]

In May 2022, one of the world's largest beverage companies, Coca-Cola, released a new "pixel-flavored soda" that was "born in the metaverse." More companies are working on changing the flavor of your drink "with a swipe" and one company, called Taste the TV, devised a method to place flavoring strips over its television-shaped device. Users literally licked the screen to "taste the metaverse."[14]

Zuck has proven to be a master of capturing attention spans, and the metaverse could dominate all five of your senses for eternity, not to mention your wallet.

In his virtual event, Zuck revealed that unique virtual items and digital art could be bought, sold, and uniquely owned via a nonfungible token (NFT). NFTs had become the latest investment fad among so-called crypto bros and other millennial geeks who invest in things like meme stocks, of which GameStop and AMC Theaters were memorable examples.

The most popular NFTs had been colorful cartoons of drowsy-looking primates—called Bored Apes—which were inspired by the term for millennial meme stock investors. As the fad became a craze, one Bored Ape digital drawing sold for $3.4 million at a Sotheby's auction. As it turns out, this happened just a few days before Zuck's virtual event.[15]

Traditional investors were baffled by NFTs, given how easily digital art can be reproduced. Why would anyone pay for an NFT if someone else could just copy and paste or take a screenshot of it? Zuck had the answer: social media entrepreneurs could now sell exclusive virtual products (such as clothes, paintings, and even candles) for you to accessorize your metaverse avatar and decorate its digital dwelling. In theory, Facebook would not allow these to be "stolen" or reproduced.

"You could also drop an exclusive product in the metaverse where [it is] only available to your most ardent fans who paid a special access to get that product," Zuck's metaverse architect said excitedly. "That's dope," a digital candlemaker said. "Commerce is going to be a big part of the metaverse," the architect promised.[16]

Suddenly, they were transported to a "magical" place that the architect called "The Butterfly Effect." It was unclear if the irony of the name—which refers to the idea that tiny changes on one side of the world can result in catastrophic consequences on the other—was lost on the architect.

As technicolored butterflies floated in and out of digital picture frames, the digital candlemaker explained (seemingly via telepathy) what the metaverse meant to her: "I just feel like this is, like, endless possibilities of my imagination."[17]

The metaverse architect agreed with her. "I can't even begin to imagine how meaningful the metaverse will be, thanks to creators like you," he said.[18]

Some observers remarked that the whole thing felt scripted, cultlike, and "super weird."[19]

The Final Revolution

When most people envision a dystopian future, they often imagine some postapocalyptic world—cities reduced to ash heaps, perhaps with hordes of marauding zombies—completely unrecognizable from the current world. They typically do not think of a dystopia in the present. But Zuck and his fellow Controligarchs, whether they know it or not, are building a dystopia, digital brick by digital brick.

WEF thought leader Yuval Noah Harari's vision of the future, filled with useless humans, seems to mirror that of Aldous Huxley, whose fictional drug "Soma" in *Brave New World* made citizens love their servitude while placated by a relentless stream of entertainment and pornography. At a 1961 San Francisco symposium titled "Man and Civilization: Control of the Mind," Huxley elaborated on what he called "The Final Revolution":

> There will be in the next generation or so a pharmacological method of making people love their servitude and producing dictatorship without tears, so to speak. Producing a kind of painless concentration camp for entire societies so that people will in fact have their liberties taken away from them but will rather enjoy it, because they will be distracted from any desire to rebel by propaganda, or brainwashing, or brainwashing enhanced by pharmacological methods. And this seems to be the final revolution.[20]

Huxley did not necessarily look forward to these possibilities with delight. It is worth noting, however, that his family did much to normalize and advance the causes of technocracy, depopulation, eugenics, and the obliteration of religion in favor of "scientism." Aldous's grandfather, Thomas Huxley, coined the term "agnosticism" and was known as Charles Darwin's "bulldog" for his relentless support of Darwinian evolution as a means to end Christianity. The elder Huxley formed something called the X Club, which was like a nineteenth-century version of the Good Club: it advocated rule by a scientific elite and had strong Malthusian views on overpopulation and sought to curb it.[21]

Aldous's brother, Julian Huxley, was agnostic—or a "secular humanist," as he called the belief system—and highly influential in the international eugenics movement. Rockefeller's biographers described him as "a friend of Margaret Sanger and a population propagandist since 1926."[22]

"Unrestrained breeding, for man and animals alike, whether they are mice, lemmings, locusts, Italians, Hindoos, or Chinamen, is biologically a thoroughly evil thing," Julian Huxley wrote in a book with his grandfather's protégé, English writer H. G. Wells, and the latter's son, G. P. Wells.[23]

H. G. Wells gained fame as the author of *The War of the Worlds* (1898), but his lesser-known books—*The Open Conspiracy* (1928) and *The New World Order* (1940)—were among the earliest socialist manifestos that advocated for the abolition of nations, the formation of a "world commonwealth," and total control of the human population.[24]

H. G. Wells's writings inspired the UN's Universal Declaration of Human Rights, and while critics found Wells's manifestos antidemocratic and elitist, admirers say that Wells boosted the progressive "civil society" for modern-day groups such as Greenpeace and Amnesty International (both well-funded by the Controligarchs).[25]

In his book *New Bottles for New Wine* (1957), Julian Huxley coined the term "transhumanism," which is still used today as the all-encompassing term for the merger of man with machine. Another term that overlaps with "transhumanism" is "the Singularity." Ray Kurzweil, an AI visionary who worked for Google, advanced the term and projected that the Singularity—

the man-machine merger—would occur by 2045. Controligarch thinkers like Kurzweil dream of one day achieving the age-old quest for immortality, which he predicts could be attained as early as 2030. And considering Zuckerberg's virtual event (and his own life-extension ambitions), it appears that the metaverse ultimately endeavors to make accommodations for transhumanism and the Singularity.[26]

Many people think of techno-slavery as a nightmare version of the future, but it is not that far off. In fact, we are already living in a dystopian present. Simply put, there is perhaps no better description of the metaverse than a painless transhumanist concentration camp, as Aldous Huxley predicted nearly six decades ago.

A Transhuman Hellscape

Mark Zuckerberg's vision for the metaverse—to which he has devoted more than $36 billion—has drawn the attention of Klaus Schwab and the other Controligarchs of the WEF. There are no competitors (in the conventional sense) at the control level of the metaverse, only partners and stakeholders. Facebook (Meta), Microsoft, and Google, for example, not only are building competing virtual and augmented reality products but are also in business with one another.[27]

The WEF website has thousands of pages that mention the metaverse. With a newly formed 2022 WEF initiative titled "Defining and Building the Metaverse" and positive headlines such as "71% of Executives Say the Metaverse Will Be Good for Business. Here's Why," "Younger Generations Expect to Spend a Lot More Time in the Metaverse," and "Who Will Govern the Metaverse." Apparently, the WEF is positioning itself as the arbiter of "best practices" for this new digital world.[28]

The WEF considers the metaverse to be part of the Fourth Industrial Revolution, which Schwab has said will lead to "a fusion of our physical, our digital, and our biological identities."[29] It was a Davos keynote lecture in 1999 that first popularized the term the "Internet of Things"—things like smart cities, smart homes, smart appliances, and wearable tech, like smart watches—discussed in Chapter Three. Transhumanists such as Schwab and Harari and the Controligarchs building the metaverse have spoken of merging man with machine into an "Internet of Bodies."[30]

Indeed, the WEF has already stated its intention to draft metaverse "governance frameworks."[31]

The world's largest corporations followed Meta's lead and have also begun staking out their corners of the metaverse. Bill Gates, in particular, saw the COVID pandemic as a massive opportunity to catapult humanity into the virtual world.[32]

"The last two years have led to monumental leaps forward in how we use technology, accelerating changes that would've taken years—if not a decade or longer—otherwise," Gates wrote on his blog in December 2021, the height of the pandemic. "I'm really excited about the potential for experimentation," Gates went on, referring to what digitalization and the metaverse could do for worker productivity.[33]

Naturally, Microsoft—along with the FAANGs—would be playing a major role in constructing the metaverse.

In January 2022, Microsoft announced its plan to purchase one of the world's top video game developers, Activision Blizzard, for nearly $69 billion. Microsoft's goal with the Activision takeover was to add to its Xbox video game console empire and use the developer to assemble the "building blocks for the metaverse," according to Microsoft's press release. Video games, the WEF said, would be the key to mass metaverse adoption.[34]

If completed, the merger would make Microsoft the world's third-largest video game developer behind China's Tencent and PlayStation manufacturer Sony. The deal hit a speed bump in December 2022 when the FTC announced its intention to block the takeover. However, Microsoft intends to wage war against the FTC in order to complete the merger, and a former Justice Department deputy who had helped expose Gates's Embrace-Extend-Extinguish strategy during the Microsoft antitrust case in the 1990s called the FTC strategy "nutty."[35]

After announcing its intentions to use video games to build the metaverse, Microsoft revealed the "cornerstones for securing" the metaverse in March 2022. Managing digital identities would be a top concern. Gates was still working on the digital ID issue, as we learned in Chapter Seven, but the Microsoft outline indicated that the company was positioning itself to coordinate (and possibly manage) the privatized digital security forces in the metaverse.[36]

In early 2022, the company was also working to make its augmented reality glasses, called HoloLens, more affordable. The $3,500 Microsoft augmented reality (or "mixed reality") lenses would allow users to visit the metaverse without completely obfuscating the real world around them, unlike Zuckerberg's sub-$1,000 Oculus Quest virtual reality (VR) headset, which completely blacks out the wearer's vision, leading to a deluge of "VR Fail" videos of users breaking items in their homes and striking family members in the face.[37]

Google's "Project Iris" also endeavors to bring mixed-reality glasses to the market. Some Wall Street investors predicted that the dominance of Meta's Oculus VR headset would "erode" once Apple's secret mixed-reality project was unveiled. Even Disney has plans to make its corner of this new virtual world "the happiest place in the metaverse."[38]

Perhaps the greatest indicator of the Controligarchs' investment in the metaverse is that the big banks are fully behind it. BlackRock has launched multiple metaverse-focused investment funds to boost capital to developers (while profiting from the patents and intellectual property). "Step into the metaverse," BlackRock beckoned to investors on one of the multiple promotional pages on its website.[39]

Less than six months after Zuckerberg's Halloween Horizons tour, in February 2022, JPMorgan became the first Wall Street bank to stake its claim in the metaverse. JPMorgan opened the "Onyx Lounge" in Decentraland—a virtual world within the metaverse—and hung a framed digital portrait of the bank's CEO, Jamie Dimon, on its digital wall. On the first "floor" of the Onyx Lounge, a cartoon tiger wandered past the pixelated portrait of Dimon.

On the second "floor," visitors could experience crypto seminars from financial experts.[40]

In 2022, the bank predicted that the metaverse would "infiltrate" every sector in human life "in the coming years" and generate $1 trillion in annual revenues. JPMorgan analysts projected that digital real estate would be a growing sector within the metaverse, and they were not wrong. In February 2022, a wealthy metaverse visitor spent $450,000 for a single digital property next door to famous rapper Snoop Dogg's virtual mansion. That same month, a larger parcel sold for more than $2 million—for one piece of digital land.[41]

Around the same time, metaverse data analysts and investors revealed that more than $500 million changed hands for digital real estate in 2021 and projected that that amount would likely double in 2022. In fact, it almost tripled.[42]

Like JPMorgan, Bank of America has predicted that the metaverse will be a lucrative financial opportunity—particularly for digital currencies. Goldman Sachs forecasted that the metaverse will be even bigger than JPMorgan's trillion-dollar prediction: potentially $8 trillion in revenues and monetization, according to one Goldman analyst.[43]

A leaked 2014 Goldman Sachs internal memo had previously revealed that the massive bank had "dreams of oligopoly." In Goldman's dream, "too big to fail" became systemic. According to the memo:

> There is a natural pull toward consolidation among mature or maturing industries. An oligopolistic market structure can turn a cut-throat commodity industry into a highly profitable one. Oligopolistic markets are powerful because they simultaneously satisfy multiple critical components of sustainable competitive advantage—a smaller set of relevant peers faces lower competitive intensity, greater stickiness and pricing power with customers due to reduced choice, scale cost benefits including stronger leverage over suppliers, and higher barriers to new entrants all at once.[44]

The consolidation of the metaverse industry (the Microsoft-Activision merger, for example) inevitably leads to less intense competition and greater price-gouging power because of reduced consumer choices. In other words, having fewer market options will force consumers to pay more. In effect, it can put a paywall around your entire life.[45]

Market consolidation leads to fewer and fewer cell phone manufacturers dominating the market (Apple or Samsung?); fewer and fewer internet service providers (Comcast or Comcast?); fewer and fewer wireless carriers (AT&T or Verizon?); and even fewer and fewer airlines (American or Delta?). This means that your rates will go up, your internet speeds will go down unless you pay more, and your privacy options will decrease, as will your legroom and in-flight food and beverage options. And there is not much that you can do about it.

Other than useless scraps of intangible computer code called NFTs, in the metaverse you truly own nothing. But will you be happy?

The big banks will be happy. For Goldman Sachs, the Controligarch-dominated metaverse—with its relatively few architects and gatekeepers, such as Apple and Meta—could be a dream come true.[46]

Elon Musk has said that virtual worlds like the metaverse should be accessed directly, without the need for devices or peripherals such as VR or mixed-reality headsets. Musk's company, Neuralink, has been testing brand-new microchips that inject digital data straight into the human brain without the need for a cumbersome headset.

On November 30, 2022, Musk announced that a lab monkey with a Neuralink brain chip could telepathically "type" on a computer (Musk had already played a telepathic video game with another lab monkey in 2021). Musk pointed to the fact that the primate at the computer was not restrained as evidence that it enjoyed the brain chip—"they get the banana smoothie," he said—before laughing off concerns about animal welfare.[47]

But there were reasons to be concerned about the welfare of Musk's test subjects given that Neuralink-enabled lab monkeys were allegedly subjected to "extreme suffering." There was evidence that after having their skulls drilled into and the Neuralink electrodes implanted, some hapless monkeys experienced so much pain that at least one began gasping and vomiting relentlessly until it collapsed from exhaustion and had to be euthanized.

Another monkey was apparently found with some missing fingers and toes, possibly because it chewed them off after painful suffering or experiencing trauma. This animal was also euthanized. Neuralink "has killed about 1,500 animals, including more than 280 sheep, pigs, and monkeys, following experiments since 2018," according to a Reuters investigation published in December 2022.[48]

Despite these obvious red flags, Musk has imminent plans to begin Neuralink human trials after Biden's FDA gave his company the green light in May 2023. "We are excited to share that we have received the FDA's approval to launch our first-in-human clinical study!" Neuralink tweeted. Musk celebrated the news and continues to emphasize the purported treatment applications for neurological conditions and injuries such as paralysis.[49]

Would Musk's human test subjects also be treated to banana smoothies?

Musk has stated that Neuralink's "brain-machine interface" could one day "store your memories as a backup, and restore the memories" and claims to have uploaded his own brain to an online cloud. In December 2022, Bezos and Gates backed a $75 million funding round for a brain-computer interface start-up called Synchron, which has Neuralink-like ambitions.[50]

In 2021, conservative billionaire futurist Peter Thiel—an early Facebook investor and PayPal cofounder with Musk—invested $10 million in a company called Blackrock Neurotech and received an undisclosed number of shares. Blackrock Neurotech has claimed that its scientists have already successfully implanted dozens of humans with its brain-computer interface.[51]

The Controligarchs will not need pharmacological methods to control people in the future if they can persuade everyone to live a virtual existence and even microchip their own brains. And it seems that an increasing number of people will amble (or perhaps even sprint) into the virtual equivalent of Huxley's "painless concentration camp."

After selling his company to Facebook for $2 billion in 2014, the creator of the Oculus VR headset has sought to "make VR porn better with nerve implants." The bourgeoning VR-porn industry got a major boost—up to 30 percent—thanks to the pandemic. At least one Microsoft executive seems to be a VR porn fan, according to complaints made by horrified coworkers. More recently, the Oculus creator has "raise[d] the stakes to the maximum level" by rigging a VR headset prototype with explosives so that if a player dies in the game, they die in real life.[52]

Meanwhile, tech bloggers report excitedly on the prospect of sending and receiving telepathic text messages via Musk's Neuralink. And a stunning poll by Pew Research Center recently found that nearly six out of ten Americans would consider getting a computer chip implanted in their brains, provided that they could turn it off.

"This speaks to control," said Pew's deputy director of research of the poll results, which meant to him that Americans believed that "if I can control this technology, then I'm more open to it."[53]

With the ability to beam highly addictive VR porn and video games directly into human eyeballs already a reality and the ability to beam it directly into the human brain well on its way, tech addiction appears primed to get much, much worse.

Exploiting Tech Addiction

Since its beginning in the 2000s, Facebook's primary business model has relied on obliterating privacy and monetizing people's interactions. In a revealing exchange from the earliest days of Facebook, Zuckerberg privately admitted what he thought of his platform's users:

> ZUCK: Yeah so if you ever need info about anyone at Harvard. Just ask. I have over 4,000 emails, pictures, addresses, SNS.
>
> [REDACTED]: What? How'd you manage that one?
>
> ZUCK: People just submitted it. I don't know why. They "trust me." Dumb fucks.[54]

Is this the type of person who should be in control of the datasets that contain the expression of our deepest thoughts and desires?

And as it turned out, selling its users' privacy to the highest bidder was not even Facebook's biggest problem. Just weeks prior to the metaverse tour, former Facebook employee Frances Haugen blew the whistle on the destructive pattern of controlling users through addiction.[55]

Facebook's founding president, Sean Parker, described the addiction process in 2017. He called it a "social-validation feedback loop," in which every time a Facebook (or Instagram) user hears the phone chime with a notification, the brain emits a feel-good chemical called dopamine, and the user gets a rush or high. Dopamine is like the other pleasure chemicals called endorphins; it is a neurotransmitter that is released when endorphins reach the brain's reward centers, or opioid receptors. Dopamine is also the beating heart of addiction (whether it is drugs, food, gambling, sex, etc.).

The "little dopamine hit," as Parker described it, sucks Facebook (or Instagram) users back into the app to consume as much of their time and attention as possible. Everything from the colors within the app, to the sound of the notifications, to the addition of features such as the "Like" button are designed to keep users addicted.[56]

Just days after Parker made his comments, another ex-Facebook executive expressed his own regret over Facebook's addiction-based business model. In fact, former vice president Chamath Palihapitiya took Parker's concerns a step further:

> I think we have created tools that are ripping apart the social fabric of how society works.... The short-term, dopamine-driven feedback loops that we have created are destroying how society works. No civil discourse, no cooperation, misinformation, mistruth ... It is eroding the core foundations of how people behave by and between each other.[57]

In essence, social media platforms like Facebook and Instagram are like Huxley's "Soma" or that painless concentration camp that he imagined.

Zuckerberg's metaverse architect, Vishal Shah, began working as a developer for Instagram in 2015 (three years after Facebook acquired the photo-sharing app). Before becoming the metaverse architect, Shah was a top developer working on an "Instagram for kids" platform. In March 2021, Shah described the effort as "building a version of Instagram that allows people under the age of 13 to safely use Instagram for the first time." It also meant that billions of dollars could be generated by selling the eyeballs of young children to advertisers.[58] A 2019 study found that depression and suicidal tendencies are rising among teens, and they pointed to social media use as a possible culprit.[59]

Children's advocacy organizations were outraged by the project. "Facebook is going back to its old tricks, offering another product designed to get kids hooked when they are the most vulnerable," said the head of an organization called Common Sense. The Campaign for a Commercial-Free Childhood cited several studies to conclude the following:

> Research demonstrates that excessive use of digital devices and social media is linked to a number of risks for children and adolescents, including obesity, lower psychological wellbeing, increased risk of depression, and increases in suicide-related outcomes.[60]

The project was scrapped after widespread public outcry.[61]

Zuckerberg's coming-out party for Facebook Horizon in the metaverse coincided with a massive rebranding effort among his family of companies. The new umbrella corporation would be called Meta Platforms (replacing the Facebook umbrella).

The makeover was well-timed. Facebook was declining in popularity. Scientific studies indicated that depression and suicide were way up (particularly among teenage girls). Studies showed that these alarming trends were in part attributable to Facebook and Instagram's addictive business model.[62]

Meta Platforms (or simply "Meta" with a new ticker symbol $MVRS, later $META) was a convenient way for Zuckerberg to distance the company from the bad press.[63]

But does rebranding Facebook as a metaverse company assuage concerns over tech addiction, or does it make those concerns more pronounced?

Ghosts in the Machine

After the 2020 election, the Facebook founder came under more fire for perceived interference. Zuckerberg poured unprecedented sums—more than $400 million—into at least two benign-sounding outfits: the Center for Tech and Civic Life as well as the Center for Election Innovation and Research. These two entities used Zuckerberg's hundreds of millions to effectively run the election precincts in key battleground locations. Zuckerberg's money strategically funded controversial universal mail-in ballots, unmonitored ballot drop boxes, and other election procedures that were disproportionately favorable to Democrats.[64]

For obvious reasons, Democrats—who typically decry dark money in politics—were largely silent on the Facebook billionaire's massive spending on election infrastructure. And on the rare occasions when they did address the so-called 2020 "Zuckerbucks," the Democrats and many in the mainstream media provided air cover for Zuck, chalking up any criticism of his election activities to "conspiracy theories."

And when Zuckerberg confirmed on an August 2022 Joe Rogan podcast that Facebook had censored news stories that were unflattering to then candidate Joe Biden during the 2020 election, Zuckerberg laid the blame at the feet of the FBI.[65]

But as it turned out, Facebook was all too willing to take the word of intelligence community operatives. In fact, Facebook had been working on new "misinformation" control tools since the 2016 election. Facebook has hired more than one hundred intelligence officials—thirty-eight from the DHS, thirty-seven from the FBI, twenty-three from the National Security Agency (NSA), and seventeen from the CIA. Why? To curate how people perceived political realities.[66]

For example, Facebook's head of misinformation policy, Aaron Berman, spent more than fifteen years at the CIA before moving into the Big Tech sector. The former spook calls Facebook's content moderation strategy "Remove, Reduce, Inform." "Remove" and "reduce" mean either eliminating the content completely or dramatically throttling its reach. "Inform" means adding warning labels to content Facebook deems inaccurate.[67]

Berman touts Facebook's efforts to influence conversations about climate change, the Russia-Ukraine conflict, COVID origins, vaccines, and other pandemic-related content. He revealed that Facebook works with a "global network of more than eighty fact-checking organizations" to moderate content, and he has boasted of Facebook's attempts to "combat misinformation" in at least three national elections (those of the United States, the Philippines, and Brazil).[68]

In October 2022, Musk purchased Twitter, announcing his hope for "a common digital town square" and taking the company private. Free speech advocates cheered the move.[69]

True to his word, Musk rescinded some of Twitter's censorial policies and even restored accounts that the previous leadership had banned, like that of Donald Trump. Twitter cofounder Jack Dorsey, to his credit, acknowledged that banning the president of the United States "sets a precedent I feel is dangerous: the power an individual or corporation has over a part of the global public conversation."[70]

Musk's critics—mostly political-establishment operatives and left-leaning individuals—were apoplectic and treated his control over the global town square as an existential threat.

In December 2022, Musk began releasing what became known as the Twitter Files—the internal documents and communications that proved what many had long suspected: that Twitter censored crucial information about the Biden family that influenced the outcome of the 2020 US election.[71]

But the Twitter Files revealed so much more than just the company's content moderation abuses. They also revealed an unholy alliance: Big Tech

Controligarchs were colluding with the mainstream media and government intelligence and security services to control global narratives surrounding such critical topics as COVID, climate change, and international conflicts like the one in Ukraine.[72]

Much of the media coverage of the Twitter Files focused on the pressure that American intelligence services applied on the Big Tech companies to intervene in the 2020 election and to engage in politically motivated censorship and propaganda. But the reality is that the relationship between the Controligarch-run tech companies and the American national-security state is far more complicated.

Some believe that the Controligarchs in Silicon Valley are solely responsible for the propaganda and censorship that occur on their platforms—that the buck stops with them. Others believe that the American intelligence and security services—the Deep State—have foisted this information-control regime upon the private tech companies that would prefer to simply remain neutral. Zuckerberg would have you believe that it is the latter—that he is effectively just following orders.[73]

The truth is that it is not an "either-or," but a "both-and" situation. The Controligarchs in Silicon Valley and in Washington, DC, both seek to set political narratives because maintaining control over what people can say, hear, read, write, and even think is critical to a ruling class's perceived legitimacy. As progressive investigative journalist Glenn Greenwald puts it, the Controligarchs and the national-security state are "in bed together." And they have been for a long time.[74]

Like the earliest version of the internet, the Big Tech corporations—Alphabet (Google and YouTube), Amazon, Apple, Meta (Facebook, Instagram, and Threads), and Microsoft—have deep ties to the American national-security state. And those relationships—which are highly profitable for the Big Tech companies—are likely to get deeper with the imminent expansion of the Fourth Industrial Revolution, the digitalization of everything from currencies to identities, and the metaverse.

Democracy's Death by Fortification

The Twitter Files revealed that the Zuck-funded effort to influence—or "fortify," as Controligarch-friendly media termed it—the 2020 election and thereby oust Donald Trump from office began even before the WHO declared a global COVID pandemic.[75]

In January 2020, veteran media executive Vivian Schiller was tapped by a neoliberal think tank called the Aspen Institute to head up its digital division. Schiller was the perfect candidate to help build the bridge between Big Tech and Big Media. Just months before the 2020 election, Schiller would organize Aspen strategy sessions aimed at swinging the election in Joe Biden's favor.[76]

The Aspen Institute is a smaller-scale version of the WEF and puts on an annual confab in the swanky town of Aspen, Colorado, that has been called a "Davos-wannabe."[77]

The institute receives the bulk of its funding from billionaires, the US government, foreign governments such as Saudi Arabia and the United Arab Emirates, big banks such as BlackRock, and assorted Controligarchs.[78]

The Rockefeller Foundation, for example, has given more than $5 million to the Aspen Institute since 2015, and more than $2.15 million of that money came between the 2016 and the 2020 election cycles.[79]

The Gates Foundation is one of the largest funders of the Aspen Institute and has poured $123.8 million since 2002—nearly half of which ($61.4 million) came during the 2016 and 2020 election cycles.[80]

The eponymous foundation of Gates's former Harvard roommate and longtime Microsoft CEO, Steve Ballmer, also supports the Aspen Institute and has funneled more than $58.9 million into various control schemes and other left-wing political priorities (ranging from election-related efforts to crime and gun control to vaccines and COVID mandates).[81]

Media Controligarchs Craig Newmark and Pierre Omidyar, who bankroll many other misinformation-control initiatives, are also big Aspen Institute funders.[82] Like Powell, the Omidyar Network founder is a Soros- and

Obama-aligned Controligarch and has committed at least $550 million to controlling the narrative.[83]

The Bezos family has given "substantial funding" (undisclosed amounts) to the institute, as well, and Jeff Bezos's father serves as a trustee alongside powerful politicos such as Madeleine Albright and Condoleezza Rice and mainstream media talent such as Katie Couric.[84]

Facebook's deep ties to the Aspen Institute came to light in 2021 when *New York Times* writer David Brooks was forced to resign from the think tank because of a conflict-of-interest controversy. Brooks failed to inform the newspaper's readers that he had financial ties to a joint Facebook–Aspen Institute initiative called Weave: "The Social Fabric Project," which he promoted repeatedly in his columns. The Weave project received more than $500,000 from Facebook and Bezos's father in 2018.[85]

Schiller was the ultimate Controligarch media insider. She got her start working for Ted Turner's media empire, where she eventually became the head of CNN's documentary division. In 2002, she joined *The New York Times* and soon ran its digital division and worked with Big Tech companies such as Facebook and Twitter to boost the newspaper's reach. While serving as the News Literacy Project's first chairperson, Schiller became the president and CEO of NPR in 2009 and dramatically increased its digital presence.[86]

Schiller left NPR following a Project Veritas sting that revealed anticonservative bias, and she was swiftly hired by NBC News to run its digital division and oversee the acquisition of MSNBC's digital division from Microsoft and NBC, whose joint venture dated back to the earliest days of the internet. She left NBC for an executive role at Twitter, where she was tasked with expanding the platform's relationships with mainstream media organizations.[87]

Schiller left Twitter to be a private media consultant while serving as a member of the Council on Foreign Relations and as a director at the trust that owns *The Guardian* news outlet in the United Kingdom. It soon became clear that when the Aspen Institute hired Schiller in January 2020, she would be coordinating the efforts of Big Tech and Big Media to counter election "misinformation" with the help of the FBI and the DHS.[88]

In July 2020, the FBI proposed granting temporary security clearances to some Twitter employees so that they could receive top-secret briefings about foreign influence operations. The bureau claimed that a "hack and leak operation" of Biden–related material was imminent.[89]

In September 2020, the institute hosted a tabletop exercise called the Aspen Digital Hack-and-Dump Working Group. Schiller organized the exercise, which was attended by the Big Tech executives colluding with security service operatives.

This Hack-and-Dump Working Group was the election version of the Event 201 coronavirus pandemic wargame and the Collective Strength central bank cyberthreat wargame mentioned in previous chapters. Just like the Event 201 and other pandemic wargame scenarios, controlling the narrative was an essential aspect of the Aspen exercise.

With the imprimatur of the intelligence agencies' briefings, the Aspen Institute's prestige, and Schiller's deep experience and expertise, the September 2020 sessions prepared the media content moderators in attendance for an imminent release of Hunter Biden's documents and emails.[90]

One obvious reason that the organizers chose a "hack-and-dump" scenario is that social media policies prohibit the dissemination of hacked materials but not of legitimately obtained materials.[91]

Together, the multi-sector attendees manufactured and weaponized a fiction: a hostile foreign government had hacked Hunter Biden's laptop and, if leaked, the social and mainstream media companies must shut it down. The talking points had been finalized. They were all on the same page.

And then the month of the "hack" arrived: October 2020. The month of preelection surprises.

Back in the real world, the *New York Post* was preparing to release the first emails—which, crucially, were legitimately obtained—from Hunter Biden's laptop. But prior to this lawful release of information, the social media content moderators received another briefing. The FBI special agent overseeing Silicon Valley from the field office in San Francisco, Elvis Chan, contacted Twitter's Yoel Roth on October 14, 2020—just hours before the *New York Post* story dropped—to pressure the company to censor.[92]

And when the *New York Post* piece was published, the social media companies stuck with the plan developed in the Aspen strategy sessions. Twitter suspended the newspaper's account. It vaporized the story, disappearing it from the platform. It also suspended any account that mentioned the Hunter Biden laptop story, including that of Trump campaign spokeswoman Kayleigh McEnany—an unprecedented move. It even blocked users from sharing the story via direct message—a censorship tactic previously reserved only for preventing the sharing of child pornography.[93]

After the 2020 election, Vivian Schiller was promoted to head of the Aspen Institute's newly formed and Orwellian-sounding Commission on Information Disorder.[94]

This private-sector thought-police force assembled key Controligarch operatives from Meta, Microsoft, Google, Mozilla, several large foundations such as the Ford Foundation, academic institutions like Harvard and Johns Hopkins universities, and mainstream media outlets such as Jeff Bezos's *Washington Post*.[95]

With this commission, the Aspen Institute began laying the groundwork for their next information operations. And these commissions and alliances, among other tactics, are how unelected billionaires and bureaucrats continue to advance their global agenda to control information and obliterate free speech.

The Metaverse, Digital ID, and Human Livestock on the Blockchain

Where is all this headed?

A patent filed by Microsoft in early 2020 reveals how the company envisions the transhumanist revolution. The patent, numbered WO2020060606 (a coincidence that led Microsoft hawks to dub it the "666 patent"), endeavors to turn the human body into a cryptocurrency mining machine.

"Human body activity associated with a task provided to a user may be used in a mining process of a cryptocurrency system," reads the patent abstract. "Mining" is the term for generating cryptocurrency by lending computer-processing power to the crypto network, or blockchain, which acts as a secure ledger of all the transactions distributed across the network.[96]

Working-class folks with gumption could accomplish tasks such as "viewing an advertisement" while generating cryptocurrency on the blockchain. These tech-savvy entrepreneurs, with the help of either wearable tech like a smart watch, or a brain-computer interface like Musk's Neuralink or the Gates- and Bezos-backed Synchron or the Thiel-backed Blackrock Neurotech, could earn and spend their digital currency with their bodies "communicatively coupled to the [cloud] server," in the words of the 666 patent. A brave new world indeed.[97]

In addition to turning humans into crypto-mining livestock on the blockchain, Gates is funding research into a technology that could brand them using something called "biocompatible near-infrared quantum dots." Two years before the pandemic, the ID2020 project that Gates, Zuckerberg, and their fellow Controligarchs funded specifically identified vaccines as an "entry point" to push digital ID on the world.[98]

In December 2019, as COVID was just beginning to spread, *Scientific American* published a glowing piece about a revolutionary Gates-funded technology that could solve the "problem" of tracking children's vaccination status:

> Along with the vaccine, a child would be injected with a bit of dye that is invisible to the naked eye but easily seen with a special cell-phone filter, combined with an app that shines near-infrared light onto the skin. The dye would be expected to last up to five years, according to tests on pig and rat skin and human skin in a dish.[99]

"Eventually we will have some digital certificates to show who has recovered or been tested recently, or . . . who has received [the vaccine]," Gates wrote in a post just days into the pandemic.[100]

Gates and his affiliates have poured more than $10 billion into digital ID and vaccine technologies. In February 2023, Zuckerberg announced Facebook's own attempt to create a digital ID: "Meta Verified." Meanwhile, the Controligarchs have invested more than $4.5 billion in blockchain technologies—with Microsoft among the most prolific, having invested at least $477 million.[101]

So, what do vaccines and digital ID have to do with the blockchain?

The blockchain, according to the WEF, is going to "redistribute power in society" and will "serve as the operating system for the new economy." The WEF and its partners are working tirelessly to "identify gaps in governance that are impeding the adoption of this technology" and assure that they will prioritize the blockchain's "potential for financial inclusion" and "facilitate the use of the technology for social benefit."[102]

Translation: unless Klaus Schwab and the benevolent oligarchs in Davos are going to surrender their own wealth, they seem to believe that the blockchain can be used to further erode the middle class by "redistributing" Westerners' wealth to impoverished nations. Is it because they care about enriching indigenous persons in Malawi and marginalized groups in ghettos around the world? Or are they seeking to bring more bodies into the metaverse? Or are they aiming to turn more humans into crypto-mining cattle? Time will tell.

Using conservative figures, the Controligarchs have pumped staggering amounts—more than $50 billion—into increasingly terrifying and borderline hellish technologies. They are creating a dystopia, right before our eyes. Worse, they are doing so while aligned with America's greatest adversary: China.

Their end game, it seems, is to achieve total control by exporting American wealth and jobs to China while importing a form of Communism and corruption that spells doom for the rest of the world.

10

The End Game

> And if all others accepted the lie which the Party imposed—if all records told the same tale—then the lie passed into history and became truth. "Who controls the past," ran the Party slogan, "controls the future: who controls the present controls the past." . . . Whatever was true now was true from everlasting to everlasting. It was quite simple. All that was needed was an unending series of victories over your own memory. "Reality control," they called it: in Newspeak, "doublethink."[1]
>
> —*George Orwell,* Nineteen Eighty-Four, *1949*

O n a balmy Thursday evening, the first of September 2022, the city of Philadelphia once again played host to a critical moment in American history. This time, however, liberty was not on the agenda. Quite the opposite. This event demonstrated that a darkness had crept into America's most hallowed halls.[2]

The coronavirus was not China's only recent nefarious export to the rest of the world. China has also exported communist-style authoritarianism and corruption. Joe Biden's unimpeded ascent to the US presidency was perhaps the greatest evidence that Chinese influence over American institutions was on the rise. The Biden family had been compromised by Chinese intelligence long before Joe became America's commander in chief.

But the Controligarchs and even the US's national-security state seemed not to care about the security concerns that a compromised American president posed (in fact, they appeared to welcome him). And now, those chickens were coming home to roost. Biden was set to announce that America would become a lot more like the nation of his family's benefactors.

The setting was Independence Hall—the birthplace of the United States and the cradle of the American constitutional republic. The occasion was an official presidential address. The subject was "the continued battle for the soul of the nation." Its purpose? To declare war on Biden's and the Controligarchs' collective enemies: tens of millions of patriotic American citizens.[3]

The bell that sat where the iconic cracked Liberty Bell once sat over Independence Hall clanged eight times as the clock struck prime time. The teleprompters flickered on, and Joe Biden carefully descended the steps to the lectern alongside First Lady Jill Biden. The mood immediately shifted as Biden ambled into view. The white lights dimmed, and ominous bright blood-red lighting soaked the brick-wall backdrop. It was showtime.[4]

Two marines, standing at attention in their formal "dress blues," flanked Biden as he launched into an angry tirade against his enemies, whom he called "MAGA Republicans"—the same kind of people whom the previous Democratic presidential nominee, Hillary Clinton, had called "deplorables" and whom Barack Obama had dismissed as the kind that "cling to guns or religion."[5]

These perennial enemies of Obama, Clinton, and now Biden (and, often, the Controligarchs) include antivaccine "conspiracy theorists," treacherous "election deniers," gas-guzzling "climate deniers," and bigoted perpetrators of "hate speech," as well as the loyal American citizens slandered as "traitors," Putin's "puppets," and "agents of Russia" for merely questioning a seemingly endless stream of billion-dollar checks to the corrupt Zelenskyy regime.[6]

These are the kind of people who might also be described as pro-freedom and anti-Controligarch.

With ruthless zeal, Biden invoked fear-inducing words such as "violence," "extremism," and "insurrection," roughly three dozen times in the fervent address. He attached that violent rhetoric to his political opposition (roughly half the American people) more than thirty times—every minute or so. The signal that Biden sent to anyone watching or listening was unmistakable: his opposition does not deserve a voice. They must be "unpersoned," as Orwell put it. "Canceled."

It was a short speech—less than half an hour—and the entire rant had a dual purpose: to hijack the narrative ahead of the 2022 midterm elections (which many expected the Democrats to lose badly) and to cast Biden's opponents as a threat. In short, the speech was classic demagoguery: identify a "problem," get the public to react, and implement "solutions."

The message was clear: Biden's adversaries are dangerous, and dangerous people must be stopped by any means necessary.

Some reporters in the Biden-friendly mainstream media criticized the speech, particularly the use of marines as "props," but generally the corporate press covered the event positively. Some left-wing outlets did not believe that Biden was harsh enough.[7]

Independent- and right-leaning media commentators were outraged. They saw dictatorial themes reminiscent of Soviet dictator Joseph Stalin, CCP chairman Mao Zedong, and even Nazi leader Adolf Hitler, who used similar dark and militaristic imagery. They called Biden's "Red Sermon"—drenched in its sanguineous lighting—a declaration of war on half the country.[8]

Within twenty-four hours of the pugilistic address, Biden walked back his major claim. "I don't consider any Trump supporter to be a threat." It was a total reversal and a tacit admission that his Red Sermon was too extreme.[9]

But the signal had gone out; the damage was already done. Following Biden's address, lawmakers such as Senate Intelligence Committee chairman Mark Warner (D-VA) reemphasized past comparisons of so-called MAGA Republicans to the September 11 terrorists. On the 9/11 anniversary, Vice President Kamala Harris—who had previously compared the January 6 protest to the Pearl Harbor attack—reiterated Biden's incendiary rhetoric about domestic extremists.[10]

The Big Tech companies had already been deplatforming Biden's opponents for at least two years—even before the 2020 election. Within days of Biden's speech, these companies implemented more robust censorship regimes with fresh deplatforming of right-wing accounts under the guise of "content moderation."[11]

The Controligarch-owned mainstream media outlets, such as Laurene Powell Jobs's *Atlantic* and Jeff Bezos's *Washington Post*, vehemently supported increased content moderation (read: censorship). They reported favorably on Biden's speech, as well as on efforts to thwart pro-free-speech legislation.[12]

Think tanks and political activism organizations such as the Poynter Institute and the Center for American Progress—robustly funded by Controligarch entities such as Microsoft, Meta, Google, Amazon, the Omidyar Network, or Soros's Open Society Foundations—helped peddle fear over MAGA Republicans in the wake of Biden's address.[13]

Also, within days of the speech, the FBI raided the homes and offices of dozens of members of Biden's opposition who typically happened to be staunch opponents of the WEF and Klaus Schwab's Great Reset. These raids were likely facilitated by Big Tech companies, whose private customer data is available to the FBI—with (and sometimes without) a warrant.[14]

Opposition to Biden and the oligarchs who set his agenda, it seemed, could now be a criminal offense.[15]

The MAGA purge was well underway in time for the 2022 midterm elections, and Biden's speech was an admission that the White House supported the Controligarchs' ongoing efforts to stifle populist dissent. Following the midterms, one of the most popular MAGA Republican candidates, Arizona gubernatorial hopeful Kari Lake, claimed that her race had been stolen via a combination of irregularities at voting precincts and Big Tech interventions on behalf of her opponent.[16]

She learned, as Trump had, that there is minimal recourse for candidates who believe that their elections have been rigged or stolen.[17]

At best, Biden's speech had been a partisan campaign event that was classified as a presidential address, meaning that Biden's venom had effectively become the official policy of the entire US federal government. At worst, it was a harbinger of darker things to come.

Zero-COVID: Communism
through the Back Door

The leader of the free world's Red Sermon and the Controligarch-funded amplification of Biden's demonization of half the country were only the latest indicators that the Western world was slipping deeper into a quasi-communist system. Stakeholder capitalism, as this new system would apparently be called, was rolling out everywhere—without a single democratic vote.

Schwab's declaration of a Great Reset highlights what many Americans felt throughout the pandemic: something fishy was going on. The COVID response was not making any sense. The reactions and solutions coming down from the ruling class were not matching the problem: a flu-like virus that was, for many, not much worse than the common cold.[18]

So less than three years after the WHO declared a global pandemic, Biden's threatening address was more proof that Americans' concerns about the direction that the world was headed were not unfounded.[19]

Tectonic shifts in wealth and power dynamics were becoming apparent, and Schwab's "angrier world" prediction was coming true.[20]

But the protesting truckers in Canada and the farmers in the Netherlands were not the only ones getting angry that the global rulers were gaining powers at staggering speeds at the expense of the ruled. Citizens around the world were rising up because of oppressive pandemic lockdowns, the resultant deteriorating economic conditions, and rising costs due to inflation fueled by big COVID relief spending.[21]

Undeterred by mass international protests, Schwab and the Davos Men were moving fast to seize control over key industries and technologies.[22]

Indeed, a heist was in progress throughout the early 2020s. What was being stolen? The autonomy, personal freedom, businesses, wealth, education, and sanity of citizens. In essence, citizens were losing control over their very lives.

There was perhaps no other nation where the ruling class was amassing more control at the expense of its citizens than in the People's Republic of China. From the very first days of the pandemic, alarming videos emerged from the Communist country showing CCP thugs forcibly quarantining their massive population—snatching individuals, tossing them into tiny metal boxes with bars over the windows, and welding the doors shut on apartment complexes with residents inside.[23]

China had already implemented most of the control measures documented throughout this book that are creeping into the Western world. Enforcing mandatory COVID vaccinations seemed like a cakewalk for the CCP compared to its prior efforts to rip millions of babies from their mothers' wombs under the infanticidal one- and two-child policies.[24]

China was already well on its way to becoming a nation of serfs, climate-controlled renters, and forced mass-transit commuters. The Communists have a social-credit-score app and a centralized digital currency. Surveillance cameras with facial recognition are everywhere (as it happened, one of Hunter Biden's Chinese investment deals involved a facial recognition company that Beijing had used to target ethnic minorities). And the state-run media and tech companies are nothing more than tools for pro-CCP propaganda and censorship.[25]

From the very outset of the pandemic, Dr. Fauci, Bill Gates, and the other creators of global COVID policy admired China's authoritarian approach. They "did a lot of things right," according to Gates. Fauci's internal government emails revealed that Fauci had dispatched one of his deputies in February 2020 to learn about the virus and observe the CCP's pandemic response. The deputy informed Fauci that China's approach—a decidedly brutal one, according to most neutral observers—was worthy of consideration or even implementation. According to Fauci:

[My deputy] was very impressed about how, from a clinical public health standpoint, the Chinese were handling the isolation, the contact tracing, the building of facilities to take care of people, and that's what

I believed he meant when he said [they] were managing this in a very structured, organized way.[26]

A February 2020 email from Fauci's deputy stated that "China has demonstrated this infection can be controlled, albeit at great cost." When asked about the email and whether he believed that all of society must undergo extreme social distancing (i.e., lockdowns) as in China, Fauci confirmed that lockdowns would indeed need to "involve essentially the entire community."[27]

But as it turns out, Fauci and his deputy were wrong. Nearly three years after the world first learned about COVID, China's brutal approach and "Zero-COVID policy" had not gotten China any closer to controlling the rates of infection.[28]

By November 2022, Shanghai—China's most populous city with roughly twenty-five million residents—had become what some political observers described as "the largest prison camp in human history."[29]

Chilling videos surfaced of furious Shanghai citizens, who had been imprisoned in their homes, screaming out their windows, and in an arbitrary demonstration of the CCP's senseless cruelty, household pets were being rounded up and euthanized—it was a puppy massacre with no apparent public health benefits.[30]

The brutal Zero-COVID lockdowns were taking a heavy toll.[31]

And when thousands of Chinese workers took to the streets to protest the inhumane COVID policies and the deterioration of already terrible working conditions, the clenched fist of the Chinese Communists in power came down and pounded them. Throughout 2022, CCP tanks rolled into cities and towns across China. Citizens were not allowed to withdraw their money from the state-run banks. Protestors were rounded up by the thousands, arrested, and forced back into their homes or to unsanitary "quarantine camps."[32]

Human rights advocates around the world were horrified and issued a joint statement in December 2022—but not the Controligarchs. They had actively helped to cover up the CCP's atrocities in the past and were still willing to do so then.[33]

The world's richest corporation, Apple, had for years acquiesced to the CCP and tailored its products' privacy settings to appease the repressive regime (Apple's frenemy, Microsoft, had done likewise).[34]

Continuing this pattern, Apple leaped to the Communists' defense in November 2022 by quietly disabling a feature that had been critical to grassroots protestors trying to spread their message.[35]

Chinese dissidents had been using the iPhone's AirDrop function, which transmits data via Bluetooth rather than by the CCP-controlled wireless networks, in order to bypass the Communists' stranglehold on digital dissent by directly "dropping" antiregime messages to the phones of fellow passengers on the subway, for example. But Apple removed key AirDrop functions in a software update that only affected iPhone users in China.[36]

Apple's CEO Tim Cook has been a CCP apologist for a long time, and the company itself has been in cahoots with the Communists for even longer, reaping the massive financial benefits of Chinese slave-like labor at iPhone builder Foxconn's "sweatshops." Working conditions were so miserable that the company had to install "body-catching nets" on the buildings after numerous suicides.[37]

However, secretly removing the dissidents' communication tool to help the Communist regime thwart antilockdown protests in late 2022 was a new low for the company.

Controligarchs, such as the Good Club members and the Big Tech titans, with very few exceptions, are CCP apologists too. Zuckerberg has a strange infatuation with dictator Xi Jinping, keeping Xi's book on his desk and even going so far as to ask the CCP chairman to name his firstborn in Mandarin. Much of Bezos's Amazon fortune was made in China and even built upon the backs of slave laborers. And Musk has significant dealings with the CCP after opening a huge Tesla manufacturing plant in Shanghai.

Musk loves cheap Chinese labor. "They won't just be burning the midnight oil, they will be burning the 3 a.m. oil," he said of his Shanghai workforce. "They won't even leave the factory type of thing," Musk gushed before bashing the work ethic of American workers.[38]

Not only do the Controligarchs ignore or outright dismiss human rights abuses but, in some cases, they also praise the CCP's authoritarianism. Why? Many believe that the global elites' softness on China is due to their financial interests there, and that is certainly true. Good Club members such as Gates, Bloomberg, the Rockefellers, the Big Tech oligarchs, and many others do conduct substantial business there. But there is actually more to this than the riches gained from trading with China.[39]

The CCP is the Controligarchs' prototype for a global regime of total population control. The Rockefellers, their wealthy allies, their political grantees like Henry Kissinger and his protégé Klaus Schwab, and their ideological kin like Bill Gates, in effect, had a hand in this feat: creating a state-run capitalism powerhouse in a Communist country. This is not a secret; they boast about it.[40]

The Naked Communists

The Rockefellers have, for more than 150 years, seen China for what most Western capitalists see it as today: a gigantic business opportunity. John D. Rockefeller Sr. sold his first oil to China in 1863—decades before the founding of the CCP and more than a century before Mao's bloody Cultural Revolution. The Rockefeller Foundation opened a "flagship" location in China in 1921 and funded hundreds of institutions and thousands of Chinese scholars over the twentieth century.[41]

After World War II, the Rockefeller Foundation worked closely with Chinese state officials to access postwar funding available from the UN's Relief and Rehabilitation Administration, which the foundation effectively controlled under the aegis of a four-country committee (the United States, Great Britain, China, and the Soviet Union). With Rockefeller assistance, China scored at least $535 million in postwar commitments from the UN relief agency.[42]

Since that time, the Communists in China have collaborated with the United Nations to advance many of the goals embraced by Controligarchs such as the Rockefellers.[43]

In 1958, former FBI investigator W. Cleon Skousen published a book titled *The Naked Communist* that identified a list of "Current Communist Goals," which were immortalized in the US *Congressional Record* in 1963.[44]

Twenty of the Communists' forty-five goals are worth reprinting to demonstrate just how much the global movement has achieved:

1. Infiltrate and gain control of big business and unions.

2. Emphasize the need to raise children away from the negative influence of parents.

3. Discredit the family as an institution. Encourage promiscuity and easy divorce.

4. Present homosexuality, degeneracy, and promiscuity as "normal, natural, and healthy."

5. Infiltrate the churches and replace revealed religion with "social" religion.

6. Discredit the American founding fathers as selfish aristocrats [and racists].

7. Discredit the American Constitution by calling it inadequate and old-fashioned.

8. Capture one or both of the political parties in the United States.

9. Get control of the schools and teachers' associations. Soften the curriculum.

10. Gain control of all student newspapers.

11. Infiltrate the press.

12. Gain control of key positions in radio, TV, and pictures.

13. Eliminate all laws governing obscenity by calling them "censorship" and a violation of free speech and press.

14. Break down cultural standards of morality by promoting pornography and obscenity in the media.

15. Eliminate prayer or any phase of religious expression in the schools on the grounds that it violates the principle of "separation of church and state."

16. Belittle American culture and discourage the teaching of American history.

17. Discredit and eventually dismantle the FBI.

18. Transfer some of the powers of arrest from the police to social agencies. Treat all behavioral problems as mental health or social problems.

19. Repeal the Connally Reservation, allowing the World Court jurisdiction over nations and individuals alike.

20. Grant recognition of Red China and its admission to the UN.

How is it possible that a fringe movement that most Americans vehemently oppose achieved so much? These goals—particularly the ones relating to the elevation of "Red China" and the United Nations—reveal that the Communists and the Controligarchs were using different means to achieve the same ends. Their greatest shared objective was to pull off a global revolution, which they call the New World Order.

The United Nations—the unofficial governing body of the New World Order—has been a Controligarch-backed operation from the beginning. John D. Rockefeller Jr. donated the land for the UN's headquarters, right through the turn of the century, when CNN's Ted Turner spent $1 billion to create the depopulation-focused UN Foundation. The Rockefellers frequently hosted the UN's top brass for strategy sessions and dinner parties at the private Pocantico estate.[45]

Rockefeller confidant Henry Kissinger was the political operative who did the most to create a relationship with Communist China. Nelson Rockefeller and Kissinger first met in 1955 and quickly formed a lifelong relationship. Rockefeller appointed Kissinger director of his "Special Studies

Project," and he remained on Rockefeller's payroll until 1968, when he joined the Nixon administration and began the clandestine push to normalize relations with Communist China.[46]

After Kissinger made his secret trip to China in 1971 that led to Nixon's famous trip in 1972, *The New York Times* reported that Kissinger had received undisclosed "gifts" totaling at least $50,000—a scandalous amount at the time—from Rockefeller. This was revealed in October 1974, or less than two months into President Gerald Ford's administration. In fact, Nelson Rockefeller was vice president–designate to Ford at the time.[47]

Far from criticizing the Communists in China, Rockefeller and Kissinger elevated them. In a 1973 editorial published by *The New York Times*, David Rockefeller stated that "the social experiment in China under Chairman Mao's leadership is one of the most important and successful in human history." This was after Mao had killed untold millions of his own Chinese people.[48]

And Kissinger repeatedly praised Mao and the Chinese Communists, telling Nixon that "no other world leaders have the sweep and imagination of Mao and Chou [Zhou] nor the capacity and will to pursue a long-range policy." He would go on to establish Kissinger Associates, and he made millions advising Western businesses on how to cash in on trade with China.[49]

In the 1960s, Kissinger led a CIA-funded program at Harvard University that attracted a young German student named Klaus Schwab, and the two became lifelong friends.

Substantial evidence links Kissinger and other American Controligarchs to Schwab's 1971 founding of the European Management Symposium, which became the WEF. In fact, it was Kissinger who preceded Schwab and the WEF in getting into bed with the Chinese Communists.[50]

As detailed in Chapter Three, the WEF boasts of Schwab's efforts to open the Chinese economy, which began in 1979, when their gross domestic product was a mere $149.5 billion—a small fraction of the multitrillion-dollar US economy at that time.[51]

Controligarchs and power brokers such as Rockefeller, Kissinger, and

Schwab intentionally coupled the American (and global) economy to the Chinese economy and apparently have no regrets.

Why? Schwab's Young Global Leader in Canada, Justin Trudeau, once let slip one reason that he admires China: because its "basic dictatorship is allowing them to actually turn their economy around on a dime."[52]

In November 2022, Schwab echoed Trudeau's shocking sentiment and even went a step further in an interview with Chinese state-run television outlet CGTN. When asked about the recent G20 meeting (which was discussed in Chapter Seven regarding the aggressive push for digital IDs) and what direction the world was headed, Schwab replied, "We have to construct the world of tomorrow—it's a systemic transformation of the world."

Schwab was apparently referring to the Great Reset and offered a pathway for the transformation: "I respect China's achievements which are tremendous . . . I think it's a role model for many countries." Schwab then implied that adopting the Chinese model should be a "choice," before closing with a strong endorsement to the CCP interviewer: "The Chinese model is suddenly a very attractive model."[53]

The Chinese Communists presented one of their most prestigious awards to the WEF founder for his help turning their economy into a global juggernaut.

China's One-Child Policy Was a Controligarch Priority

On the issue of the CCP's human-rights abuses, the Controligarchs remain largely silent for the same reason that they are largely silent about the waves of illegal migrants flowing across the southern border: the Controligarchs benefit from cheap labor, and their allied supranational organizations such as the WEF, the UN, the WHO, and others benefit from the erosion of nationalism and American primacy.[54]

Furthermore, the "basic dictatorship" hybrid governance model of the CCP—part Communism and part capitalism—appears to be the system that the Controligarchs favor and are working to implement globally. Substantial evidence confirms their role in building this hybrid model dating back decades.

There is evidence that the Club of Rome's Malthusian imperatives influenced China's barbaric one-child program in the 1970s and 1980s. The Rockefellers' biographers wrote that in the first half of the twentieth century, "Communist countries were opposed to any programs of action in the population field" and that it took a number of years before Rockefeller efforts made "enough of an impact to stir Malthusian fears of a 'population explosion' in the public mind."[55]

The Rockefellers and Schwab were integral to the funding and promoting of the Club of Rome's *Limits to Growth* research. Malthusian Good Club member Ted Turner was fond of China's one-child policy, which resulted in forced sterilizations and the slaughter of countless Chinese babies through forced abortions.[56]

Turner worked to implement similar population control objectives in the West through his UN foundation and even suggested that the poor could sell their "fertility rights."[57]

For his part, Bill Gates tapped one of the key advisors to the CCP's "family planning" regime, a population control expert named Dr. Gordon Perkin, to be the first global health program director of the Gates Foundation. Like Bill Gates Sr., Perkin had worked for Planned Parenthood and was a major birth-control and abortion advocate concerned with overpopulation. It was Perkin who helped to steer the Gates Foundation's unprecedented efforts to tackle population growth and helped to create a global mass child vaccination program.[58]

Wall Street and the CCP

Controligarch financial firms such as Goldman Sachs (with its "dreams of oligopoly"), the Blackstone Group (which is gobbling up residential housing and turning America into a nation of renters), and BlackRock (with its powerful backing of the ESG social-credit-score system) are driving the United States toward a more plutocratic system. Coincidentally, these Wall Street monsters are all huge fans and beneficiaries—to the tune of tens of billions of dollars—of China's repressive regime.[59]

Goldman Sachs's John Thornton presided over Wall Street's cozying up to the CCP and was personal friends with a Shanghai mayor named Jiang Zemin in the 1980s—before Zemin became general secretary of the CCP and president of China. Thornton said that the rise of China is the "single most important thing to happen in our lifetime."[60]

Thornton has been awarded a medal of friendship by the CCP and was put on the payroll of the CCP-backed Tsinghua University, which is cofinanced by another Wall Street titan: Blackstone's Stephen Schwarzman, who has called Chairman Xi Jinping a "great guy."[61]

BlackRock's Larry Fink downplays the fact that, in his words, "some elements of [China's] society may have less rights" than others and has praised the CCP, saying that Beijing has "one of the best leadership teams in the world."[62]

George Soros, to his credit, has long been something of a China hawk—a rarity among Wall Street financier types. He has rebuked both the Party and its leader, Chairman Xi, on multiple occasions. Soros has criticized, in addition to the CCP, Western corporations that are in league with the CCP. For example, Soros lambasted BlackRock in 2021 for being on the "wrong side" of the West's "life and death" conflict with China and said that BlackRock's efforts "will damage the national security interests of the US and other democracies."[63]

But was Soros critical of China because of his strong moral convictions, or was it because the country had banned him from investing in its economy? Soros's similar history with Russia suggests that it may be the latter and that he has a pattern of selectively criticizing repressive countries depending on whether he is allowed to operate there or not.

Soros had, for example, invested and operated his shadowy network of NGOs in post-Soviet Russia for more than two decades—even after he helped cause a ruble crash in the late 1990s—until Putin banned him and his NGOs in 2013. It was only after Soros had been banned from Russia that he began funding a proxy war in Ukraine. The Soros-backed Orange Revolution led to the overthrow of Ukraine's Russia-friendly government, which ultimately resulted in the rise of the Volodymyr Zelenskyy regime and has put the world on the brink of a nuclear World War III.[64]

Soros and his foundations say nothing, of course, when the Zelenskyy government enacts antidemocratic policies such as criminalizing dissent, banning opposing parties, stifling religious freedom, and creating a state-run propaganda and censorship media monopoly.[65]

Soros had operated his NGOs in China since the mid-1980s. But when he tried to plunder Chinese interests, China sent him packing. In 1997, in the same way that he broke the Bank of England and crashed the ruble, Soros took down the Malaysian and Thai economies by shorting their currencies.[66]

The following year, Soros set his sights on crushing the Hong Kong dollar and attempted to short the currency. But Beijing spent billions on a stock-and-futures buying spree that propped up the currency and ended Soros's speculative binge in the region. Beijing beat Soros, who lost a potential killing and has been sour about it ever since.[67]

And for all Soros's recent criticism of China, he agrees with the rest of the Controligarchs that China will be essential to the creation of a New World Order and the removal of the US dollar as the world's reserve currency. In a 2009 interview with the *Financial Times*'s Chrystia Freeland (Schwab's Young Global Leader and WEF acolyte who now serves as Trudeau's finance minister), Soros commented on the Obama-Biden administration's overtures to China:

> I think this would be time [to strike a deal with China] because you really need to bring China into the creation of a new world order, a financial world order. They are kind of reluctant members of the [International Monetary Fund] . . . So I think you need a new world order that

China has to be part of the process of creating it and they have to buy
in. They have to own it the same way as, let's say, the United States
owns the Washington consensus, the current order, and I think this
would be a more stable one where you would have coordinated policies.[68]

Soros went on to dismiss concerns that replacing the US dollar as the
world's reserve currency might weaken the economy, stating that it was "not
necessarily in our interests to have the dollar as the sole world currency,"
and he effectively admitted that China would help to end the world's dependence on the US in a "healthy, if painful, adjustment that the world has
to go through."[69]

Notably, BlackRock declared in its *2023 Global Outlook* report that the
New World Order had finally been achieved. "We've entered into a new
world order," begins the report attributed to longtime Biden operative
Thomas Donilon, who now chairs the BlackRock Investment Institute. The
"fraught global environment"—which has been exacerbated by BlackRock
and its cronies at the WEF—will lead to a "new regime of greater . . . market
volatility" and "persistently higher inflation." Indeed, BlackRock predicts a
global recession with more volatility than ever before.[70]

BlackRock's New World Order declaration meant that the effects of the
pandemic had become permanent, and the Great Reset was, at this point,
unavoidable. Trillions of dollars had been transferred from the middle
classes around the world into the pockets of the Controligarchs. The minds
and bodies of the masses were controlled. Their food and shelter were controlled. There could be no escape.[71]

Scattered protests have popped up from time to time, but these seemed to
be easily quashed and forgotten (or did not receive widespread media coverage). And when WEF-aligned leaders in countries were ousted (sometimes via violent protest), other WEF-approved leaders soon found their
way back into power. Schwab's advisor Yuval Noah Harari was correct when
he warned that peasant uprisings were a thing of the past.[72]

The Controligarchs have fully penetrated the top governments around the world, including pretty much every government in the West. Even Russia's and China's leaders were aligned with the oligarchs (despite the occasional saber rattling).[73]

Over the years, citizens have feared that dystopia was just a few decades away. Now dystopia had finally arrived. Children are being openly brainwashed with sexual and racial propaganda. Students are being chemically castrated; teenage girls (the ones who are not suicidal from too much Instagram and TikTok usage) are getting double mastectomies and changing their genders.[74]

Capitalists and Communists Make Sinister Bedfellows

In December 2022, a group of Girl Scouts and their mothers traveled to Radio City Music Hall at Rockefeller Center in Manhattan for the annual Christmas Spectacular show featuring the Rockettes, a famous dance troupe whose benefactor, John D. Rockefeller Jr., once claimed was a reminder that "the only way we can find success in any walk of life is in working for the group and not for personal aggrandizement."[75]

One scout's mother was denied entry to the complex and was forced to wait outside after security guards were alerted by a facial recognition system that had identified her and her employer. Was she employed by a drug cartel or some other criminal outfit? No, the mother worked for a law firm in a different state that happened to be involved in litigation against the Radio City Music Hall's landlord.[76]

To recap: an American Girl Scout's mother had her biometric data harvested and analyzed and then she was banned from entering a public building—all for simply doing her job. It suddenly felt as if China's social-credit-score system and surveillance state tactics were being rolled out in the United States at an alarming rate.

The evidence that the capitalist Controligarchs are in bed with the Chinese

Communists was everywhere. It was not merely that they had both covered up the coronavirus origins—that was to be expected. It was that the entire Western establishment—from Big Tech to Big Academia to Big Finance to Big Media to, especially, Big Pharma and even its personification, Dr. Anthony Fauci, who claimed to embody science itself—endorsed the CCP's cover-up. Everyone from Klaus Schwab to billionaires such as Bill Gates was praising the authoritarian lockdowns happening in China. They seemed to love the tyrannical CCP system.

And then the lockdowns spread—from China's neighbors in Australia and New Zealand to its top trading partner in Europe (Italy) to the rest of Europe and, much closer to home, Canada. Eventually, lockdowns and mandates came to the United States (mostly in Democrat-run states).

The common denominator among the most oppressive decision-makers was not their allegiance to the CCP, however. It was membership in Schwab's Young Global Leaders program and allegiance to the WEF (which, as it happened, had taught the CCP how to merge capitalism with Communism decades prior).

As it turned out, the pandemic response had clear winners and losers. The undeniable winners were the Controligarchs, who simultaneously grabbed more than $1 trillion over the course of the pandemic (while locked-down middle-class workers and small-business owners lost approximately the same amount).

One of the biggest winners was Joe Biden. COVID mandates upended the 2020 presidential election process. The pandemic lockdowns resulted in widespread election rule changes (implemented without ratification of state legislatures as prescribed by the US Constitution).[77]

Massive ballot harvesting, ballot drop boxes (funded by oligarchs such as Mark Zuckerberg), new social media rules to crush so-called misinformation and disinformation relating to the pandemic, and, most eg   [?]11
tens of millions of unsolicited mail-in ballots meant that this v
tial election unlike any other.[78]

President Trump complained about the election rule

Tech censorship in real time, but all anyone heard about was the number of senior citizens he had killed with his failed pandemic response. If he wanted to hold a rally (a staple of his campaigns), he was called a mass murderer.[79]

Meanwhile, the twice-failed presidential candidate, Joe Biden, was able to spend almost the entire campaign in his sterile basement. He did not need to leave, and no one really expected him to. Once Biden was elected, it became clear: the real winners of the pandemic election were his handlers and benefactors—the nameless and faceless leviathan running his cabinet, writing his speeches, and drafting his dictates and executive orders—and the Controligarchs. It was clear that Biden was purely a figurehead.

The End Game: A Republic on the Brink of Extinction

As Biden was preparing to deliver his Red Sermon, a lawsuit filed jointly by the attorneys general in Missouri and Louisiana revealed that the Controligarch billionaires and bureaucrats had essentially obliterated free speech in America using Orwellian concepts such as "malinformation," misinformation, and disinformation.[80]

The setting for Biden's angry address was intentional. Independence Hall was where the Founding Fathers embarked on the greatest journey in world history on July 4, 1776. The great American experiment had been the most audacious disavowal of rule by controlling oligarchs to date.[81]

Outside Independence Hall, during Biden's speech, a protester with a bullhorn could be heard heckling and shouting, "Fuck Joe Biden!" Perhaps at that very corner outside the landmark, more than two centuries prior, an early Pennsylvanian colonist asked legendary founder Benjamin Franklin whether this new country would be monarchy or a republic. "A republic, if you can keep it," Franklin ominously replied.[82]

Nearly two centuries later, another famous patriotic American leader echoed Franklin's warning. "Freedom is a fragile thing," Ronald Reagan said, ıd it is "never more than one generation away from extinction." Reagan's

fear may yet be fulfilled within his children's lifetime—roughly two generations after his prescient speech.[83]

Freedom in America has held strong through five generations of Rockefeller dominance, four generations of Federal Reserve–driven booms and
busts, three generations of UN global governance, and two generations of
WEF corporatism.

But now, as the world hurtles closer to the year 2030, one generation of
Controligarchs, technocrats, and transhumanists in partnership with the
CCP has brought their collective end game—the extinction of freedom—
closer to fruition than at any point in modern history.

Epilogue

Today, the top 0.05 percent of Americans (fewer than two hundred thousand citizens) own more than does the bottom 90 percent—about three hundred million citizens that make up the dwindling middle class and the swelling lower class.

The Controligarchs are accelerating the managed decline of this country and of the entire world. With the help of the corporate media (which they own), the Controligarchs coerced us into lockdowns, mandated what are still considered experimental injections with unknown long-term effects, plundered our businesses, and robbed our children of nearly two years of socialization and education. These are crimes against humanity.

Many people still believe that COVID-19 is the cause of the economic suffering that continues to plague us to this day, bringing tragedies that range from overwhelmed small businesses to joblessness to crippling inflation to high gas prices to supply-chain shortages and more. But this virus that escaped from Wuhan, China—and which we now know may be no more lethal than seasonal influenza—did not itself do any of that. The Great Reset did.

Using the COVID-19 crisis as a pretext for plans that were long in the works, the billionaires and their bureaucrats shut down economies worldwide, hobbled the oil and gas industries, printed record amounts of new money, and tightened their control across virtually every sector of our lives.

The pandemic was a new form of warfare—one that George Orwell knew all too well. In *Nineteen Eighty-Four*, Orwell wrote:

> The economy of many countries was allowed to stagnate, land went out of cultivation, capital equipment was not added to, great blocks of the population were prevented from working and kept half alive by State charity.

"The essential act of war is destruction," Orwell concluded. But not the destruction of human life; rather, the destruction of infrastructure and other things that humans build (and must then rebuild). It is a way of destroying—"shattering to pieces, or pouring into the stratosphere, or sinking in the depths of the sea"—the products of human labor that can "make the masses too comfortable, and hence, in the long run, too intelligent."[1]

In other words, war—be it against a rogue nation or a tiny virus—is a way to control the masses.

The United States of America's founders fought and died to create a nation free from monarchy, oligarchy, and tyranny. Their descendants today find themselves called to a new fight for freedom. But today's war for independence is different from the founders' struggle.

So, how do we take back control? It is easier said than done. The Controligarchs have created products that make life easier, more convenient, and even downright fun. But we have become addicted (literally, in the case of dopamine-driven social media), and we must fight the addiction immediately.

At a time of extreme polarization in America, most people—regardless of political persuasion—still agree on two fundamental values:

1. Corruption is wrong, no matter who is guilty of it.

2. No one should be above the law.

We will need the help of our elected representatives—the few who remain outside the control of the billionaires and bureaucrats—to uphold these critical values. Our lawmakers *must* throw sand in the gears of the Controligarchy and enact legislation that works for the well-being of all Americans, not just the elite.

Here are seven legislative fixes that Congress must enact before it is too late:

1. End all funding to the Controligarchs' supranational elite organizations, such as the World Health Organization, the International Monetary Fund, the World Bank, and the United Nations.

2. Eliminate all taxpayer assistance to public-private partnerships that benefit Controligarch-funded organizations.

3. Promote the pro-America agenda, and redirect foreign aid toward domestic reforms.

4. Enact pro-family policies that advance the middle class, and reform primary, secondary, and higher education.

5. Ban (or strictly regulate) mind-melting apps for children, especially the CCP-linked TikTok, which has been called "digital fentanyl."

6. Reform both the tax code and the IRS now! The tax code, its loopholes, and the write-offs have run amok and are directly responsible for the Controligarchs' continued rise while bleeding the middle class dry.

7. Lift the heavy hand of government off the throats of small businesses.

But the most important unit of government is the smallest: ourselves. We must first guard ourselves, then guard our families, and be cognizant of what we are putting into our minds, bodies, and souls.

Here are seven steps that we can take today:

1. Exercise, eat healthily, and keep our heads clear of physical and digital drugs.

2. Practice pro–middle-class and pro-family policies.

3. Take a more active role in our children's upbringing and education.

4. Stop funding our enemies, and jealously guard our data and our wallets.

5. Cancel as many subscriptions to Controligarch services as we can.

6. Monitor and decrease both our own and our family's screen time.

7. Buy everything we possibly can locally.

Those on the political left decry the Controligarchs' mountain of riches and demand that they be redistributed more equitably. Others on the political right point to the Controligarchs' corruption and cronyism and insist that if only government were smaller, free-market capitalism would be able to sort out these problems. And both sides make valid points. But the Controligarchs are not the only ones to blame for the problems we face.

We the people also bear some responsibility. We have forgotten Benjamin Franklin's timeless warning—that we have "a republic, if you can keep it."

In his farewell address, George Washington warned us about the rise of domestic factions and foreign entanglements. The Controligarchs have tied us up in both.

Today, we must unify against the Controligarchs, resist their globalist agenda, and urge our elected officials to do likewise. The future of our freedom depends on it.

Note to Readers

This book makes some startling claims about a group of billionaires and bureaucrats I call the Controligarchs. In the interest of fair journalistic inquiry, I reached out to each of the principal characters for any comment or perspective they wished to add. As of this writing, none has chosen to respond.

Further information can be found at www.ControligarchsBook.com /media.

Acknowledgments

Investigating and writing such a complex book on such powerful characters requires a talented team with gravitas and guts to bring it to a successful completion. This book is the culmination of thousands of hours and hard work by a diligent and diverse group of patriotic people.

Peter Schweizer is at the top of my list of people to thank. Peter took a chance on me and hired me as an intern while I was still in college more than a decade ago. I have worked with him ever since and I will be forever grateful for his mentorship, leadership, and sage counsel. Peter is an American hero and a national treasure. I am proud to be fighting beside him in the trenches on the battlefield of ideas.

As founder and president of the Government Accountability Institute (GAI), Schweizer deserves credit for having the wisdom to bring many talented warriors aboard the GAI battleship. One of those is Peter J. Boyer, a true living legend and the most elegant writer that I know. Mr. Boyer showed me how to write a good story, and I hope that one day I become half the writer that he is. Ditto for the wizard of words, Wynton Hall. Getting the "green pen" treatment from Wynton is something that too few writers are blessed to receive.

I would like to give special mention to GAI's fact-checker and my friend, Tarik Noriega, without whom this book would have never made it across the finish line.

Additionally, I was blessed to have the assistance of the following GAI team members on this project: GAI's star publicists Sandy Schulz and Faith Bruner; our phenomenal editors Joe Duffus and Steve Post; fellow research director Jedd McFatter; Price Sukhia, Steven Richards, Peter Aagaard, and Katie Crain; and finally, GAI's general counsel Stuart Christmas, whose sharp legal mind gave me the confidence that everything we have put into this book is honest, true, and defensible.

I have benefited beyond measure from my agent, Jonathan Bronitsky, and the entire team at ATHOS. I thank them for their continued efforts on behalf of me and other great American patriots and authors. This is my first book with editor Helen Healey-Cunningham. Thank you, Helen, for your keen insights and helpful suggestions. You made the long editing process relatively painless, and I am sincerely grateful for you.

I would like to thank the entire team at Penguin Random House and Sentinel, especially Adrian Zackheim and Bria Sandford, for all their hard work, their guidance, and their wisdom, and especially for having the courage to publish an investigative book that focuses on the richest and most powerful individuals in the world.

Finally, the most thanks go to my family—to my patient, beautiful, and brilliant wife, Jillian, and our precious baby girl, Rosemary—along with the rest of my beloved family: Gretchen, my mom, and James Sr., my dad, and all my siblings—Meredith (and Sean and Levi), Julia (and Kevin), Sally (and Wilhelm and Crispin), Teddy (and Kristin), and Faith. Your support over the years has meant the world to me.

The author alone is responsible for the contents of this book.

Notes

Introduction

1. "The World's Real-Time Billionaires," *Forbes*, accessed June 1, 2023, https://www.forbes .com/real-time-billionaires/#4ca4c9153d78.
2. Tom Braithwaite, "Prospering in the Pandemic: The Top 100 Companies," *Financial Times*, June 19, 2020, https://www.ft.com/content/844ed28c-8074-4856-bde0-20f3bf4 cd8f0.

Chapter One: The Good Club

1. David Rockefeller, *Memoirs* (New York: Random House, 2002), 405.
2. Paul Harris, "They're Called the Good Club—and They Want to Save the World," *Guardian*, May 30, 2009, https://www.theguardian.com/world/2009/may/31/new-york-billionaire -philanthropists.
3. Niall O'Dowd, "Secret Meeting of World's Richest People Held in New York," *IrishCentral*, May 18, 2009, https://www.irishcentral.com/news/secret-meeting-of-worlds-richest-people -held-in-new-york-45304702-237642871.
4. "Bill and Melinda Gates, Warren Buffett Ask Nation's Super-Rich to Give Half Their Wealth to Charity," Candid, *Philanthropy News Digest*, June 17, 2010, https://philanthro pynewsdigest.org/news/bill-and-melinda-gates-warren-buffett-ask-nation-s-super -rich-to-give-half-their-wealth-to-charity.
5. John Harlow, "Billionaire Club in Bid to Curb Overpopulation," *Sunday Times*, May 24, 2009, on Internet Archive, https://web.archive.org/web/20110223015213/http://www.times online.co.uk/tol/news/world/us_and_americas/article6350303.ece.
6. Ibid.

7. Teresa Iacobelli and Barbara Shubinski, "Rockefeller Philanthropy and Population-Related Fields," RE:Source, Rockefeller Archive Center, January 5, 2022, https://resource.rockarch.org/story/rockefeller-philanthropy-and-population-related-fields.

8. Frederick S. Jaffe, "Activities Relevant to the Study of Population Policy for the United States," Technical Assistance Division of Planned Parenthood-World Population, March 11, 1969, 7–9.

9. "Abortion Care Network," Rockefeller Foundation, accessed February 15, 2022, https://www.rockefellerfoundation.org/grant/abortion-care-network-2022; Kelsey Piper, "How Billionaire Philanthropy Provides Reproductive Health Care When Politicians Won't," *Vox*, September 17, 2019, https://www.vox.com/future-perfect/2019/9/17/20754970/billionaire-philanthropy-reproductive-health-care-politics; Rachel Sandler, "MacKenzie Scott, Michael Bloomberg among the Biggest Billionaire Donors to Abortion-Rights Groups," *Forbes*, May 12, 2022, https://www.forbes.com/sites/rachelsandler/2022/05/12/mackenzie-scott-michael-bloomberg-among-the-biggest-billionaire-donors-to-abortion-rights-groups.

10. Bill Gates, "25 Years of Learning and Laughter," *GatesNotes* (blog), July 5, 2016, https://www.gatesnotes.com/About-Bill-Gates/25-Years-of-Learning-and-Laughter.

11. "Leaders of Gates, Rockefeller Foundations on Campus," *Rockefeller University* 12, no. 12 (December 15, 2000), on Internet Archive, https://web.archive.org/web/20010723032959/https://www.rockefeller.edu/pubinfo/news_notes/121500a.html; Karen Knudsen, "East-West Center Awarded $2.3 Million for Population and Health Research," Bill & Melinda Gates Foundation, press release, accessed October 27, 2022, https://www.gatesfoundation.org/ideas/media-center/press-releases/1999/02/the-eastwest-center.

12. "First Andrew Carnegie Medals Awarded to Seven Visionaries of Modern Philanthropy," Carnegie Corporation of New York, press release, December 10, 2001, https://www.carnegie.org/news/articles/first-andrew-carnegie-medals-awarded-to-seven-visionaries-of-modern-philanthropy; "The HIV/AIDS Pandemic Is #Solvable: Dr. Anthony Fauci," posted by The Rockefeller Foundation, December 1, 2019, YouTube video, https://www.youtube.com/watch?v=zjeuujJV2PA; Chaolin Huang, MD, et al., "Clinical Features of Patients Infected with 2019 Novel Coronavirus in Wuhan, China," *Lancet* 395, no. 10223 (February 15, 2020), https://www.thelancet.com/journals/lancet/article/PIIS0140-6736(20)30183-5.

13. Ronald Matte, "Scenario for the Future of Technology and International Development," Rockefeller Foundation, June 27, 2012, https://issuu.com/dueprocesstv/docs/scenario-for_the-future; "Event 201," Johns Hopkins Center for Health Security, accessed October 29, 2022, https://www.centerforhealthsecurity.org/our-work/exercises/event201.

14. "Digital Documentation of COVID-19 Certificates: Vaccination Status: Technical Specifications and Implementation Guidance," World Health Organization, guidance document, August 27, 2021, https://www.who.int/publications/i/item/WHO-2019-nCoV-Digital_certificates-vaccination-2021.1; "COVID-19 National Testing & Tracing Action Plan," Rockefeller Foundation, July 16, 2020, https://www.rockefellerfoundation.org/national-covid-19-testing-and-tracing-action-plan.

15. "Digital Documentation of COVID-19 Certificates"; "COVID-19 National Testing & Tracing Action Plan"; "Rockefeller Foundation and ACCESS Health International Launch a Report Uncovering the Role of Digital Technology in Tackling Covid-19," Access Health International, September 9, 2020, https://accessh.org/the-rockefeller-foundation-and-access-health-international-launch-a-report-uncovering-the-role-of-digital-technology-in-tackling-covid-19.

16. "Digital Documentation of COVID-19 Certificates."

17. "The Rockefeller Foundation Commits USD1 Billion to Catalyze a Green Recovery from Pandemic," Rockefeller Foundation, October 26, 2020, https://www.rockefellerfounda

tion.org/news/the-rockefeller-foundation-commits-usd1-billion-to-catalyze-a-green
-recovery-from-pandemic.

18. John Ensor Harr and Peter J. Johnson, *The Rockefeller Century* (New York: Scribner, 1988), 453–55, 458.

19. Robert Frank, "4 Secrets to Raising Wealthy Kids, According to the Billionaire Rockefeller Family," CNBC, updated March 28, 2018, https://www.cnbc.com/2018/03/26/david-rocke feller-jr-shares-4-secrets-to-wealth-and-family.html.

20. Ibid.

21. Paolo Lionni, *The Leipzig Connection* (Sheridan: Heron Books, 1993), 44.

22. Jules Abels, *The Rockefeller Billions: The Story of the World's Most Stupendous Fortune* (New York: Macmillan, 1965), 280; Lionni, *Leipzig Connection*, 45.

23. Peter Collier and David Horowitz, *The Rockefellers: An American Dynasty* (New York: New American Library, 1976), 38–60; Lionni, *Leipzig Connection*, 45–52.

24. Lionni, *Leipzig Connection*, 45–52.

25. Ibid.; Ron Chernow, *Titan: The Life of John D. Rockefeller, Sr.* (New York: Vintage, 2004), 774.

26. Lionni, *Leipzig Connection*, 45–52.

27. John D. Rockefeller, *Random Reminiscences of Men and Events* (Toronto: McClannand & Goodchild, 1909), 165; Lionni, *Leipzig Connection*, 49.

28. David M. Oshinsky, *Polio: An American Story* (New York: Oxford University Press, 2005), 14–18.

29. Ibid., 19–20.

30. Frank Fenner et al., "Development of the Global Smallpox Eradication Programme, 1958–1966," in *Smallpox and Its Eradication* (Geneva: World Health Organization, 1988), 373–79, https://biotech.law.lsu.edu/blaw/bt/smallpox/who/red-book/9241561106_chp9.pdf.

31. Barbara Shubinski and Teresa Iacobelli, "Public Health: How the Fight against Hookworm Helped Build a System," RE:Source, Rockefeller Archive Center, April 23, 2020, https://resource.rockarch.org/story/public-health-how-the-fight-against-hookworm -helped-build-a-system; Oshinsky, *Polio*, 14–20.

32. Fenner et al., *Smallpox and Its Eradication*, 389.

33. Oshinsky, *Polio*, 15–16, which cites the following sources: George W. Corner, *A History of the Rockefeller Institute, 1901–1953* (New York: Rockefeller Institute Press, 1964), 60–61; Chernow, *Titan*, 478; Joseph Frazier Wall, *Andrew Carnegie* (Oxford: Oxford University Press, 1970), 832.

34. Shubinski and Iacobelli, "Public Health"; "Health & Well-Being: Science, Medical Education and Public Health," Rockefeller Foundation, Centennial Series, March 28, 2015, https://www.slideshare.net/RockefellerFound/health-wellbeing-science-medical -education-and-public-health.

35. Fenner et al., *Smallpox and Its Eradication*, 373–75.

36. Oshinsky, *Polio*, 16–18.

37. Rodrigo Cesar da Silva Magalhães, "International Cooperation in Health in the Interwar Period: The Rockefeller Foundation's Worldwide Anti-Yellow Fever Campaign and Its Implementation in Brazil (1918–1939)," University of Maryland, 2012, https://rockarch.is suelab.org/resources/27869/27869.pdf; J. Gordon Frierson, "The Yellow Fever Vaccine: A History," *Yale Journal of Biology and Medicine* 83, no. 2 (June 2010), https://www.ncbi.nlm .nih.gov/pmc/articles/PMC2892770; Erling Norrby, "Yellow Fever and Max Theiler: The Only Nobel Prize for a Virus Vaccine," *Journal of Experimental Medicine* 204, no. 12 (November 26, 2007), https://www.ncbi.nlm.nih.gov/pmc/articles/PMC2118520.

38. Frierson, "Yellow Fever Vaccine."

39. Eric John Abrahamson, "Beyond Charity: A Century of Philanthropic Innovation," Rockefeller Foundation, accessed October 30, 2022, 160–61, https://www.rockefellerfoundation .org/wp-content/uploads/Beyond-Charity.pdf.pdf.

40. Frierson, "Yellow Fever Vaccine."

41. Associated Press, "World War II Hepatitis Outbreak Was Biggest in History," April 16, 1987, https://apnews.com/article/ce911d4f173f1c8ade810969005b9e57; Frierson, "Yellow Fever Vaccine."

42. "A Brief History of the Rockefeller Foundation's International Health Commission," University of Virginia, accessed October 31, 2022, http://exhibits.hsl.virginia.edu/hanson/a -brief-history-of-the-rockefeller-foundations-international-health-commission/#_ftn6.

43. "Yellow Fever Virus: Transmission," Centers for Disease Control and Prevention, accessed October 30, 2022, https://www.cdc.gov/yellowfever/transmission/index.html.

44. David Quammen, "And Then the Gorillas Started Coughing," *New York Times*, February 19, 2021, https://www.nytimes.com/2021/02/19/opinion/covid-symptoms-gorillas.html.

45. Fenner et al., *Smallpox and Its Eradication*, 374; Norman Howard-Jones, "The Scientific Background of the International Sanitary Conferences 1851–1938," World Health Organization, 1975, 97–98, http://apps.who.int/iris/bitstream/handle/10665/62873/14549 _eng.pdf.

46. Ryan W. Miller, "Millions of Genetically Modified Mosquitoes May Soon Be Buzzing in Florida and California, Here's Why," *USA Today*, March 8, 2022, https://www.usatoday .com/story/news/nation/2022/03/08/genetically-modified-mosquitoes-florida -california/9424548002; "Gates Foundation Awards $35 Million for Mosquito Research," *Philanthropy News Digest*, September 8, 2016, https://philanthropynewsdigest.org/news /gates-foundation-awards-35-million-for-mosquito-research; "Can Mutant Mosquitoes Be Used to Fight Zika and Dengue Fever?," *PBS NewsHour*, March 3, 2016, https://www .pbs.org/newshour/show/can-mutant-mosquitoes-be-used-to-fight-zika-and-dengue -fever-2.

47. F. M. Scherer, "Standard Oil as a Technological Innovator" (Faculty Research Working Paper Series, Harvard Kennedy School, January 2011), https://www.hks.harvard.edu /publications/standard-oil-technological-innovator.

48. Abrahamson, "Beyond Charity," 167–75.

49. Ibid.

50. Ibid., 24, 175–76.

51. "1902–2002: 100 Years of Pan-Americanism," Pan American Health Organization, accessed October 31, 2022, https://www.paho.org/en/who-we-are/history-paho/1902-2002 -100-years-pan-americanism.

52. Anne-Emanuelle Birn and Elizabeth Fee, "The Rockefeller Foundation and the International Health Agenda," *Lancet* 381, no. 9878 (May 11, 2013), https://www.thelancet.com /journals/lancet/article/PIIS0140-6736(13)61013-2.

53. Ibid.

54. Barry Goldberg, "The Long Road to the Yellow Fever Vaccine," RE:Source, Rockefeller Archive Center, November 2, 2019, https://resource.rockarch.org/story/the-long-road-to -the-yellow-fever-vaccine; Terry Wade and Anna Driver, "Rockefeller Family Fund Hits Exxon, Divests from Fossil Fuels," Reuters, March 23, 2016, https://www.reuters.com/art icle/us-rockefeller-exxon-mobil-investments/rockefeller-family-fund-hits-exxon -divests-from-fossil-fuels-idUSKCN0WP266; "Why the New 'Green Revolution' in Africa May Be Misguided," *Grist*, September 28, 2006, https://grist.org/article/gates.

55. Abrahamson, "Beyond Charity," 176.

56. Ibid.; Harr and Johnson, *Rockefeller Century*, 114, 454–58.

57. Dave Umhoefer, "Planned Parenthood Is the Biggest Abortion Provider in the Country," PolitiFact, May 15, 2017, https://www.politifact.com/factchecks/2017/may/15/glenn -grothman/glenn-grothman-says-planned-parenthood-leading-abo.

58. Harr and Johnson, *Rockefeller Century*, 454, 458.

59. "Birth Control or Race Control? Sanger and the Negro Project," Margaret Sanger Papers Project, Fall 2001, https://www.supremecourt.gov/opinions/URLs_Cited/OT2018/18-483 /18-483-1.pdf; "Eugenics and Birth Control," *American Experience*, PBS, https://www.pbs .org/wgbh/americanexperience/features/pill-eugenics-and-birth-control, accessed June 1, 2023; Ross Douthat, "160 Million and Counting," *New York Times*, June 26, 2011, http:// www.nytimes.com/2011/06/27/opinion/27douthat.html.

60. "Birth Control or Race Control?"

61. Harr and Johnson, *Rockefeller Century*, 191, 453–55, 458.

62. David Turner, "Foundations of Holocaust: American Eugenics and the Nazi Connection," *Jerusalem Post*, December 30, 2012, https://www.jpost.com/blogs/the-jewish-problem--- from-anti-judaism-to-anti-semitism/foundations-of-holocaust-american-eugenics-and -the-nazi-connection-364998.

63. Victor Grossman, "Bayer-Monsanto Merger Can't Erase Nazi Chemists' Past," *People's World*, September 22, 2016, https://www.peoplesworld.org/article/bayer-monsanto-merger -cant-erase-nazi-chemists-past; Ciara Torres-Spelliscy, "How Big Business Bailed Out the Nazis," Brennan Center for Justice, May 20, 2016, https://www.brennancenter.org/our -work/analysis-opinion/how-big-business-bailed-out-nazis.

64. *Trials of War Criminals before the Nuremberg Military Tribunals, Under Control Council Law No. 10* (Washington, DC: United States Government Printing Office, 1953), 1303.

65. William Brennan, "RU-486 Hoechsts Connection to the Jewish Holocaust," Life Issues Institute, March 1995, https://lifeissues.org/1995/03/ru-486-hoechsts-connection-jewish -holocaust; R. Alta Charo, "A Political History of RU-486," in *Biomedical Politics* (Washington, DC: Institute of Medicine, 1991), https://www.ncbi.nlm.nih.gov/books/NBK234199.

66. Harr and Johnson, *Rockefeller Century*, 454–62.

67. David J. Morrow, "Maker of Norplant Offers a Settlement In Suit over Effects," *New York Times*, August 27, 1999, https://www.nytimes.com/1999/08/27/us/maker-of-norplant -offers-a-settlement-in-suit-over-effects.html.

68. E. Thoss, "Introduction of RU 486 in the USA: Obstacles and Opportunities," *Planned Parenthood in Europe* 22, no. 3: 18–19, https://pubmed.ncbi.nlm.nih.gov/12288950; Birn and Fee, "Rockefeller Foundation."

69. Harr and Johnson, *Rockefeller Century*, 455, 458, 461–62.

70. Rachel Wimpee and Teresa Iacobelli, "Funding a Sexual Revolution: The Kinsey Reports," RE:Source, Rockefeller Archive Center, January 9, 2020, https://resource.rockarch.org /story/funding-a-sexual-revolution-the-kinsey-reports.

71. Ibid.

72. "US Sex Reassignment Surgery Market Size, Share & Trends Analysis Report by Gender Transition (Male to Female, Female to Male), and Segment Forecasts, 2022–2030," Grand View Research, https://www.grandviewresearch.com/industry-analysis/us-sex -reassignment-surgery-market, accessed June 1, 2023.

73. "Consequences of the Sexual Revolution," Uplifting Education, accessed November 6, 2022, https://www.upliftingeducation.net/consequences-of-the-sexual-revolution.

74. Harr and Johnson, *Rockefeller Century*, 459–62.

75. Judith Reisman, "The Origins of the Transgender Phenomenon: The Challenge and Opportunity for Training Lawyers, Judges and Policy Makers in the Historicity of Alfred Kinsey's Pansexual Worldview," Liberty University School of Law, November 2016, https://digitalcommons.liberty.edu/cgi/viewcontent.cgi?article=1073&context=lusol _fac_pubs.

76. Dianne N. Irving, "What Is 'Bioethics'?," accessed November 6, 2022, http://uffl.org /vol10/irving10.pdf; "The Hastings Center at Forty: A Look at Its Founding Four Issues," Hastings Center, accessed November 6, 2022, https://www.thehastingscenter.org/publi

cations-resources/special-reports-2/the-hastings-center-at-forty-a-look-at-its-founding
-four-issues.

77. Giovanna Breu, "Pro-Choice vs. Pro Life Is a Moral Dilemma, Says Daniel Callahan: We
Carry Both Traditions within Us," *People* 24, no. 7, on Internet Archive (August 12, 1985),
https://people.com/archive/pro-choice-vs-pro-life-is-a-moral-dilemma-says-daniel-cal
lahan-we-carry-both-traditions-within-us-vol-24-no-7.

78. L. Mastroianni Jr., P. J. Donaldson, and T. T. Kane, eds., *Developing New Contraceptives:
Obstacles and Opportunities* (Washington, DC: National Academic Press, 1990), https://
www.ncbi.nlm.nih.gov/books/NBK235214.

79. "President's Review & Annual Report, 1988," Rockefeller Foundation, 2003, https://www
.coreysdigs.com/wp-content/uploads/2019/06/Rockefeller-1988.pdf; G. P. Talwar and R.
Raghupathy, "Anti-fertility Vaccines," *Vaccine* 7, no. 2 (April 1989), https://doi.org/10.1016
/0264-410x(89)90043-1.

80. P. D. Griffin, "The WHO Task Force on Vaccines for Fertility Regulation. Its Formation,
Objectives and Research Activities," *Human Reproduction* 6, no. 1 (January 1991), 166–72,
https://academic.oup.com/humrep/article-abstract/6/1/166/875911; "Fertility Regulating
Vaccines," World Health Organization, August 17–18, 1992, https://apps.who.int/iris/bit
stream/handle/10665/61301/WHO_HRP_WHO_93.1.pdf.

81. Griffin, "The WHO Task Force."

82. Caitlin Flanagan, "Losing the *Rare* in 'Safe, Legal, and Rare,'" *Atlantic*, December 6, 2019,
https://www.theatlantic.com/ideas/archive/2019/12/the-brilliance-of-safe-legal-and
-rare/603151; Randi M. Albert, "Providing Incentives to the Industry to Develop New Contraceptives," LEDA at Harvard Law School, March 1995, https://dash.harvard.edu/bit
stream/handle/1/8965583/ralbert.html.

83. "Twentieth-Century Abortion Law Reform," Law Library—American Law and Legal
Information, accessed November 7, 2022, https://law.jrank.org/pages/447/Abortion
-Twentieth-century-abortion-law-reform.html; Tim Balk, "Harsh, Then a Haven: A Look
at New York's Abortion Rights History," *New York Daily News*, May 7, 2022, https://www
.nydailynews.com/news/politics/new-york-elections-government/ny-new-york
-history-of-abortion-roe-v-wade-20220507-uh74flvwcndrvg6lcffsyap73i-story.html.

84. Jay Maeder, "Repealing the Abortion Law, May 1972 Chapter 397," *New York Daily News*
(archive), July 10, 2001, https://archive.ph/20120710114424/http://articles.nydailynews
.com/2001-07-10/news/18369154_1_abortion-law-life-committee-repeal/4; Balk, "Harsh."

85. Nancy Berlinger, Bruce Jennings, and Susan M. Wolf, "The Hastings Center Guidelines for
Decisions on Life-Sustaining Treatment and Care near the End of Life," Hastings Center,
May 24, 2013, https://global.oup.com/academic/product/the-hastings-center-guidelines
-for-decisions-on-life-sustaining-treatment-and-care-near-the-end-of-life-9780
199974559.

86. Arthur Caplan and Cynthia B. Cohen, "Imperiled Newborns," *Hastings Center Report* 17,
no. 6 (December 1987): 5–32, https://doi.org/10.2307/3563441.

87. Alan Fine, "The Ethics of Fetal Tissue Transplants," *Hastings Center Report* 18, no. 3 (July
1988): 5–8, https://doi.org/10.2307/3562195.

88. David Maraniss, "First in His Class," *Washington Post*, accessed November 7, 2022, https://
www.washingtonpost.com/wp-srv/politics/special/clinton/stories/maranissbook.htm;
Connie Bruck, "Hillary the Pol," *New Yorker*, May 30, 1994, https://www.newyorker.com
/magazine/1994/05/30/hillary-the-pol.

89. Karen Tumulty and Marlene Cimons, "Clinton Lifts Restrictions on Abortion," *Los Angeles Times*, January 23, 1993, https://www.latimes.com/archives/la-xpm-1993-01-23-mn-1468
-story.html.

90. Albert, "Providing Incentives."

91. Melody Petersen, "Abortion Pill Distributor Energized by New Mission," *New York Times*, September 30, 2000, https://www.nytimes.com/2000/09/30/us/abortion-pill-distributor -energized-by-new-mission.html.

92. "Security Concerns for US Abortion Pill Company," CNN, September 28, 2000, https:// www.cnn.com/2000/HEALTH/women/09/28/abortion.pill.danco.reut/index.html.

93. "Abortion Pill Maker Revealed," CBS News, October 13, 2000, https://www.cbsnews.com /news/abortion-pill-maker-revealed.

94. Yale Kamisar, "Are Laws against Assisted Suicide Unconstitutional?," *Hastings Center Report* 23, no. 3 (May–June 1993): 32–41, https://deepblue.lib.umich.edu/bitstream/handle /2027.42/90532/3563366.pdf; John A. Robertson, "Rights, Symbolism, and Public Policy in Fetal Tissue Transplants," *Hastings Center Report* 18, no. 6 (December 1988): 5–12, https:// doi.org/10.2307/3563042.

95. "Actionable Ethics Oversight of Human-Animal Chimera Research," *Hastings Center Report*, accessed November 7, 2022, https://www.thehastingscenter.org/who-we-are/our -research/current-projects/actionable-ethics-oversight-human-animal-chimera -research.

96. Jocelyn Kaiser, "NIH Says Grantee Failed to Report Experiment in Wuhan That Created a Bat Virus That Made Mice Sicker," *Science*, October 21, 2021, https://www.science.org /content/article/nih-says-grantee-failed-report-experiment-wuhan-created-bat-virus -made-mice-sicker.

97. Cristina Richie, "In Search of Sterility," Hastings Center, November 1, 2013, https://www .thehastingscenter.org/in-search-of-sterility; "Undocumented Immigrants and Access to Health Care in New York," Hastings Center, October 14, 2015, https://undocumented.the hastingscenter.org/policy-impact-nyc; Bethany Blankley, "Biden Admin Authorizes Re-lease of 2 Billion Genetically Modified Mosquitos in Florida and California," *Capitolist*, March 10, 2022, https://thecapitolist.com/biden-admin-authorizes-release-of-2-billion -genetically-modified-mosquitos-in-florida-and-california; "CDC's Call to Open Schools Is 'Political and Unethical,'" Hastings Center, press release, accessed May 16, 2023, https:// www.thehastingscenter.org/a-national-plan-for-testing-and-tracing.

98. Fuguo Jiang and Jennifer A. Doudna, "CRISPR-Cas9 Structures and Mechanisms," *Annual Review of Biophysics* 46, no. 1 (March 2017): 505–29, https://doi.org/10.1146/annurev -biophys-062215-010822; Dennis Normile, "Chinese Scientist Who Produced Genetically Altered Babies Sentenced to 3 Years in Jail," *Science*, December 30, 2019, https://www .science.org/content/article/chinese-scientist-who-produced-genetically-altered-babies -sentenced-3-years-jail.

99. "CRISPR/Cas9 Methods," Research, Rockefeller University, updated March 9, 2015, https://www.rockefeller.edu/research/vosshall-laboratory/172291-crispr-cas9-methods.

100. Broad Institute, "The Rockefeller University and Broad Institute of MIT and Harvard Announce Update to CRISPR-Cas9 Portfolio Filed by Broad," press release, January 15, 2018, https://www.broadinstitute.org/news/rockefeller-university-and-broad-institute-mit -and-harvard-announce-update-crispr-cas9.

101. Kevin Loria, "Bill Gates and Others Just Invested $120 Million in a Revolutionary Medical Startup," *Business Insider*, August 10, 2015, https://www.businessinsider.com/bill-gates -and-others-invest-in-editas-for-crispr-gene-editing-2015-8; Ben Adams, "Facebook, Napster Billionaire Parker to Fund First-Ever CRISPR Trial," Fierce Biotech, June 22, 2016, https://www.fiercebiotech.com/biotech/facebook-napster-billionaire-parker-to-fund -first-ever-crispr-trial.

102. Jaffe, "Activities Relevant to the Study of Population Policy," 7–9.

103. Ibid.; "Population Planning: Sector Working Paper" (Washington, DC: World Bank, March 1972), 3–7; "Implications of Worldwide Population Growth for US Security and Overseas

Interests," *Kissinger Report*, December 10, 1974, 94–102, 110–14, https://pdf.usaid.gov/pdf_docs/Pcaab500.pdf.

104. William H. Frey, "US Population Growth Has Nearly Flatlined, New Census Data Shows," Brookings Institution, December 23, 2021, https://www.brookings.edu/research/u-s-population-growth-has-nearly-flatlined-new-census-data-shows.

105. Hasan Özbekhan, Erich Jantsch, and Alexander Christakis, "The Predicament of Mankind," Club of Rome, 1970, 9, https://web.archive.org/web/20140203125912/http://sunsite.utk.edu/FINS/loversofdemocracy/Predicament.PTI.pdf.

106. Ibid.

107. Alexander King and Bertrand Schneider, *The First Global Revolution* (New York: Pantheon, 1991), 75.

108. Benjamin Sarlin, "Behind the Billionaire Pact," *Daily Beast*, August 4, 2010, https://web.archive.org/web/20100809162345/http://www.thedailybeast.com/blogs-and-stories/2010-08-04/warren-buffett-bill-gates-and-the-billionaire-giving-pledge.

109. Benjamin Sarlin, "George Soros Responds to Gates/Buffett Pledge," *Daily Beast*, August 5, 2010, https://web.archive.org/web/20100819123245/https://www.thedailybeast.com/beltway-beast/george-soros-responds-to-billionaire-pledge.

110. Peter Kotecki, "The Billionaire 'Giving Pledge' Signed by Bill Gates and Elon Musk Could Soon Be Worth up to $600 Billion," *Business Insider*, July 18, 2018, https://www.businessinsider.com/bill-gates-elon-musk-giving-pledge-may-reach-600-billion-2018-7.

Chapter Two: The Gates of Hell

1. Walter Isaacson, "In Search of the Real Bill Gates," *Time*, January 13, 1997, http://content.time.com/time/printout/0,8816,1120657,00.html.

2. "A Great Day for Tennis, A Great Day for Charity," The Match in Africa, accessed March 15, 2022, https://www.match-in-africa.com.

3. Tracy Wang, "Bill Gates Doubles Up with Tennis Legend Roger Federer for Much-Anticipated Charity Match in South Africa," *Forbes*, February 4, 2020, https://www.forbes.com/sites/tracywang/2020/02/04/bill-gates-doubles-up-with-tennis-legend-roger-federer-for-much-anticipated-charity-match-in-south-africa.

4. "Bill & Melinda Gates Foundation Dedicates Additional Funding to the Novel Coronavirus Response," Bill & Melinda Gates Foundation, press release, February 5, 2020, https://www.gatesfoundation.org/Ideas/Media-Center/Press-Releases/2020/02/Bill-and-Melinda-Gates-Foundation-Dedicates-Additional-Funding-to-the-Novel-Coronavirus-Response.

5. United States v. Microsoft, 253 F.3d 34 (D.C. Cir. 2001), on Internet Archive, https://web.archive.org/web/20090916142802/http://www.usdoj.gov/atr/cases/f2600/v-a.pdf.

6. "Davos Launch for Coalition to Prevent Epidemics of Emerging Viruses," *Financial Times*, January 18, 2017, https://www.ft.com/content/5699ac84-dd87-11e6-86ac-f253db7791c6; Bill Gates, "What Our Leaders Can Do Now," *GatesNotes* (blog), April 2, 2020, https://www.gatesnotes.com/Health/What-our-leaders-can-do-now.

7. Bill Gates, *How to Prevent the Next Pandemic* (New York: Alfred A. Knopf, 2022), 3.

8. Michael Barbaro, "Can Bill Gates Vaccinate the World?," March 3, 2021, in *The Daily*, podcast, produced by Austin Mitchel, Rachelle Bonja, and Leslye Davis, MP3 audio, 33:34, https://www.nytimes.com/2021/03/03/podcasts/the-daily/coroanvirus-vaccine-bill-gates-covax.html; "William H. Gates Sr.," Leadership, Bill & Melinda Gates Foundation, March 30, 2022, https://www.gatesfoundation.org/about/leadership/william-h-gates-sr.

9. Barbaro, "Can Bill Gates Vaccinate the World?"

10. Ibid.; "Efforts of Gates, Clinton Foundations Increasingly Overlap," *Philanthropy News Digest*, July 22, 2006, https://philanthropynewsdigest.org/news/efforts-of-gates-clinton-foundations-increasingly-overlap.

11. "Efforts of Gates, Clinton Foundations Increasingly Overlap."

12. Gates, *How to Prevent the Next Pandemic*, 3; *The Working Dinner*, video series, hosted by Keith Klugman, presented by the Bill & Melinda Gates Foundation, February 2020, https://www.gatesfoundation.org/ideas/working-dinner.

13. Asa Fields and Mary Hudetz, "Coronavirus Spread at Life Care Center of Kirkland for Weeks, While Response Stalled," Times Watchdog, *Seattle Times*, March 18, 2020, https://www.seattletimes.com/seattle-news/times-watchdog/coronavirus-spread-in-a-kirkland-nursing-home-for-weeks-while-response-stalled.

14. Todd Bishop, "Bill Gates Warns That Coronavirus Impact Could Be 'Very, Very Dramatic,' Outlines Long-Term Solutions," *GeekWire*, February 14, 2020, https://www.geekwire.com/2020/bill-gates-warns-coronavirus-impact-dramatic-globally.

15. Bill Gates (@BillGates), Twitter, February 28, 2020, 10:50 a.m., https://twitter.com/BillGates/status/1233449330348085249.

16. Bishop, "Bill Gates Warns."

17. Andrew Edgecliffe-Johnson, "Bill Gates Donates Another $20Bn to His Charitable Foundation," *Financial Times*, July 13, 2022, https://www.ft.com/content/5e6808b1-3061-4af2-a54b-6c58cd6b8f74; Bill Gates, "The Next Outbreak? We're Not Ready," filmed in April 2015 in Vancouver, BC, TED video, 08:24, https://www.ted.com/talks/bill_gates_the_next_outbreak_we_re_not_ready.

18. Tim Schwab, "While the Poor Get Sick, Bill Gates Just Gets Richer," *Nation*, January 8, 2021, https://www.thenation.com/article/economy/bill-gates-investments-covid; Bill Gates, "The Best Investment I've Ever Made," *Wall Street Journal*, January 16, 2019, https://www.wsj.com/articles/bill-gates-the-best-investment-ive-ever-made-11547683309.

19. Jessica Bursztynsky, "Bill Gates Explains What We Need to Do to Stop the Coronavirus Pandemic and Reopen the Economy," CNBC, April 23, 2020, https://www.cnbc.com/2020/04/23/bill-gates-outlines-innovations-needed-to-stop-coronavirus-pandemic.html.

20. Lena H. Sun, "Bill Gates Calls on US to Lead Fight against a Pandemic That Could Kill 33 Million," *Washington Post*, April 27, 2018, https://www.washingtonpost.com/news/to-your-health/wp/2018/04/27/bill-gates-calls-on-u-s-to-lead-fight-against-a-pandemic-that-could-kill-millions; Rebecca G. Baker, "Bill Gates Asks NIH Scientists for Help in Saving Lives," *NIH Catalyst* 22, no. 1 (2014), updated April 27, 2022, https://irp.nih.gov/catalyst/22/1/bill-gates-asks-nih-scientists-for-help-in-saving-lives; David Brown, "Gates Foundation Giving $500 Million to Fight Disease," *Washington Post*, August 10, 2006, https://www.washingtonpost.com/archive/politics/2006/08/10/gates-foundation-giving-500-million-to-fight-disease/503602e2-dc7f-46b3-b44f-a96627a397dc.

21. Bill Gates, "Responding to COVID-19—A Once-in-a-Century Pandemic?," *New England Journal of Medicine* 382, no. 18 (April 2020): 1677–79, https://doi.org/10.1056/NEJMp2003762; "ICMJE Form for Disclosure of Potential Conflicts of Interest," International Committee of Medical Journal Editors, updated February 2021, https://www.nejm.org/doi/suppl/10.1056/NEJMp2003762/suppl_file/nejmp2003762_disclosures.pdf.

22. John E. Morely and B. Vellas, "COVID-19 and Older Adult," *Journal of Nutrition, Health, & Aging* 24, no. 4 (March 2020): 364–65, https://doi.org/10.1007%2Fs12603-020-1349-9.

23. "See Bill Gates' Chilling Pandemic Warnings—before the Coronavirus Outbreak Hit," MSNBC, 10:00, March 31, 2020, https://www.msnbc.com/msnbc/watch/see-bill-gates-chilling-pandemic-warnings-to-trump-before-the-coronavirus-outbreak-hit-814613

17980; Jay Greene, "The Billionaire Who Cried Pandemic," *Washington Post*, May 13, 2020, https://www.washingtonpost.com/technology/2020/05/02/bill-gates-coronavirus -science.

24. "Committed Grants," About, Bill & Melinda Gates Foundation, accessed April 3, 2022, https://www.gatesfoundation.org/about/committed-grants; Robert F. Kennedy, *The Real Anthony Fauci: Bill Gates, Big Pharma, and the Global War on Democracy and Public Health* (New York: Simon & Schuster, 2021), 53; Bill Gates, "The First Modern Pandemic," *Gates-Notes* (blog), April 23, 2020, https://www.gatesnotes.com/Pandemic-Innovation.

25. Anna Mikhailova, Christopher Hope, Michael Gillard, and Louisa Wells, "Exclusive: Government Scientist Neil Ferguson Resigns after Breaking Lockdown Rules to Meet His Married Lover," *Telegraph*, May 5, 2020, https://www.telegraph.co.uk/news/2020/05/05 /exclusive-government-scientist-neil-ferguson-resigns-breaking.

26. Gates, "The First Modern Pandemic."

27. "Transcript: Bill Gates Speaks to the FT about the Global Fight against Coronavirus," *Financial Times*, April 9, 2020, https://www.ft.com/content/13ddacc4-0ae4-4be1-95c5 -1a32ab15956a; Li Cohen, "Bill Gates Says Flying on a Private Jet Doesn't Make Him 'Part of the Problem' Because He Invests Billions into Fighting Climate Change," CBS News, February 10, 2023, https://www.cbsnews.com/news/bill-gates-private-jet-doesnt-make -him-hypocrite-because-he-invests-billions-into-climate-change.

28. Bill Gates, "A Conversation with Bill Gates: Population Growth," *GatesNotes* (blog), February 18, 2012, https://www.gatesnotes.com/about-bill-gates/a-conversation-with -bill-gates-population-growth.

29. Gabrielle Settles, "Bill Gates Didn't Say He Wanted to Use Vaccines to Reduce the Population," PolitiFact, October 11, 2021, https://www.politifact.com/factchecks/2021/oct/11 /blog-posting/bill-gates-didnt-say-he-wanted-use-vaccines-reduce.

30. *Inside Bill's Brain: Decoding Bill Gates*, episode 3, "Part 3," created and directed by Davis Guggenheim, aired September 20, 2019, Netflix, 02:48–03:56.

31. Emily Kirkpatrick, "Melinda Gates Says Bill Gates's Work with 'Abhorrent' Jeffrey Epstein Led to Divorce," *Vanity Fair*, March 3, 2022, https://www.vanityfair.com/style/2022/03 /melinda-gates-jeffrey-epstein-led-to-bill-gates-divorce-gayle-king-interview.

32. Lachlan Cartwright and Kate Briquelet, "Jeffrey Epstein Gave Bill Gates Advice on How to End 'Toxic' Marriage, Sources Say," *Daily Beast*, May 16, 2021, https://www.thedailybeast .com/jeffrey-epstein-gave-bill-gates-advice-on-how-to-end-toxic-marriage-sources-say; Emily Flitter and James B. Stewart, "Bill Gates Met with Jeffrey Epstein Many Times, Despite His Past," *New York Times*, October 12, 2019, https://www.nytimes.com/2019/10 /12/business/jeffrey-epstein-bill-gates.html.

33. Robert Kolker, "How Feng Zhang's Gene Editing Technique Will Change the World," *Bloomberg*, June 29, 2016, https://www.bloomberg.com/features/2016-how-crispr-will -change-the-world; "Nathan Wolfe," Disease Control Priorities, accessed March 31, 2022, http://dcp-3.org/author/nathan-wolfe.

34. Flitter and Stewart, "Bill Gates Met"; "Global Health Investment Fund I LLC Announcement of Collaborative Funding Agreement with Epistem Plc," JPMorgan Chase, July 22, 2014, https://www.jpmorganchase.com/news-stories/pr-ghif-agreement-epistem; "Jeffrey Epstein's Little Black Book Redacted," DocumentCloud, contributed by John Cook (Gawker .com), accessed December 30, 2022, https://www.documentcloud.org/documents/1508273 -jeffrey-epsteins-little-black-book-redacted.html; "About," Jeffrey Epstein VI Foundation, accessed December 30, 2022, http://www.jeffreyepstein.org/Jeffrey_Epstein.html.

35. Clark Mindock, "Jeffrey Epstein 'Wanted to Seed Human Race with His DNA' by Impregnating up to 20 Women at a Time, Report Says," *Independent*, August 1, 2019, https://www .independent.co.uk/news/world/americas/jeffrey-epstein-seed-human-race-dna-baby -ranch-new-mexico-eugenics-a9030411.html.

36. James B. Stewart, Matthew Goldstein, and Jessica Silver-Greenberg, "Jeffrey Epstein Hoped to Seed Human Race with His DNA," *New York Times*, July 31, 2019, https://www.nytimes.com/2019/07/31/business/jeffrey-epstein-eugenics.html; Luke Darby, "Private Jets, Parties and Eugenics: Jeffrey Epstein's Bizarre World of Scientists," *Guardian*, August 19, 2019, https://www.theguardian.com/us-news/2019/aug/18/private-jets-parties-and-eugenics-jeffrey-epsteins-bizarre-world-of-scientists; Gates, "Conversation with Bill Gates."

37. Bill Gates and Melinda Gates, "10 Tough Questions We Get Asked," Our 2018 Annual Letter, *GatesNotes* (blog), February 13, 2018, https://www.gatesnotes.com/2018-Annual-Letter.

38. Daniel Thomas, "Bill Gates Vows to Drop Off World's Rich List," *BBC News*, July 14, 2022, https://www.bbc.com/news/business-62162300.

39. Lisa Stiffler, "Bill Gates Sr. at 90: A Giant Impact on Technology, Philanthropy and the Seattle Region," *GeekWire*, November 25, 2015, https://www.geekwire.com/2015/life-and-times-of-bill-gates-sr-a-giant-impact-on-technology-philanthropy-and-the-seattle-region; Taylor Soper, "Early Amazon Investor Tom Alberg to Leave Board, 23 Years after Betting on Jeff Bezos' Little Startup," *GeekWire*, April 11, 2019, https://www.geekwire.com/2019/early-amazon-investor-tom-alberg-leave-board-23-years-betting-jeff-bezos-little-startup.

40. Doug Ford, "Inspiration from Those Who Knew Bill Gates Sr. Well," *Reporter*, updated August 29, 2018, https://www.thereporter.com/2015/10/02/doug-ford-inspiration-from-those-who-know-bill-gates-sr-well; Associated Press, "Bill Gates, Bremerton Native and Father of Microsoft Co-founder, Dies at 94," *Kitsap Sun*, updated September 16, 2020, https://www.kitsapsun.com/story/news/2020/09/15/bill-gates-sr-father-microsoft-co-founder-dies-94/5811116002.

41. *Encyclopedia Britannica Online*, s.v. "Bill Gates," last modified October 24, 2022, https://www.britannica.com/biography/Bill-Gates.

42. Bill Gates Sr. and Mary Ann Mackin, *Showing Up for Life: Thoughts on the Gifts of a Lifetime* (New York: Crown, 2009): 13–14.

43. Robert A. Guth, "Raising Bill Gates," *Wall Street Journal*, April 25, 2009, https://www.wsj.com/articles/SB124061372413054653.

44. Gates Sr. and Mackin, *Showing Up for Life*, 63; Biography.com, "Bill Gates," updated May 3, 2021, https://www.biography.com/business-leaders/bill-gates.

45. "In Tribute: W. Hunter Simpson (1926–2006)," About Us: Stories, Washington Research Foundation, accessed April 6, 2022, https://www.wrfseattle.org/story/in-tribute-w-hunter-simpson-1926-2006.

46. Stiffler, "Bill Gates Sr. at 90"; "K&L Gates Mourns Passing of Longtime Partner and Humanitarian William H. Gates, Sr.," K&L Gates, press release, September 15, 2020, https://www.klgates.com/KL-Gates-Mourns-Passing-of-Longtime-Partner-and-Humanitarian-William-H-Gates-Sr-9-15-2020.

47. Tom Griffin, "W. Hunter Simpson, 1926–2006," *University of Washington Magazine*, March 1, 2006, https://magazine.washington.edu/w-hunter-simpson-1926-2006.

48. Griffin, "W. Hunter Simpson."

49. Stiffler, "Bill Gates Sr. at 90."

50. "Royalties for Software Engineers Too," Support, IBM, accessed April 6, 2022, https://www.ibm.com/support/pages/royalties-software-engineers-too.

51. William "Bill" Gates, interview by David Allison, Division of Computers, Information, & Society at the National Museum of American History, Smithsonian Institution, September 1994, https://americanhistory.si.edu/comphist/gates.htm.

52. "UW Information Technology," About Us, University of Washington, accessed April 9, 2022, https://www.washington.edu/uwit/about-us/publications/history; Kathleen Elkins,

"Microsoft Co-founders Bill Gates and Paul Allen Got 'Busted' in High School for Exploiting a Bug in the Computer System," CNBC, July 2, 2019, https://www.cnbc.com/2019/07/02/microsoft-co-founders-bill-gates-and-paul-allen-met-in-high-school.html.

53. Elkins, "Microsoft Co-founders Bill Gates and Paul Allen."

54. Bill Gates, "Whether you're a recent grad or a college dropout, I'm sure your resume looks a lot better than mine did 48 years ago," LinkedIn, accessed March 26, 2022, https://www.linkedin.com/posts/williamhgates_whether-youre-a-recent-grad-or-a-college-activity-6948310563722579970-6qrH.

55. Zameena Mejia, "Microsoft Exists Because Paul Allen and Bill Gates Launched This High School Business First," CNBC, October 16, 2018, https://www.cnbc.com/2018/10/16/microsoft-exists-because-paul-allen-and-bill-gates-launched-this-high-school-business.html; Bill Gates, "Early Days as a Computer Programmer," *GatesNotes* (blog), October 27, 2011, https://www-new.gatesnotes.com/Early-Days-as-a-Computer-Programmer.

56. William "Bill" Gates, interview by David Allison; "When a Nerd Becomes Arrogant," *Chicago Tribune*, November 17, 1998, https://www.chicagotribune.com/news/ct-xpm-1998-11-18-9811180006-story.html.

57. "In Tribute: W. Hunter Simpson (1926–2006)," About Us: Stories, Washington Research Foundation.

58. Ibid.

59. Hannelore Sudermann, "License to Innovate," *University of Washington Magazine*, accessed April 9, 2022, https://magazine.washington.edu/feature/40-years-on-washington-research-foundation-keeps-making-bright-ideas-pay-off.

60. Tim Lewis, "Bill Gates: 'Vaccines Are a Miracle. It's Mind-Blowing Somebody Could Say the Opposite,'" *Guardian*, May 15, 2022, https://www.theguardian.com/culture/2022/may/15/bill-gates-vaccines-readers-questions-how-to-prevent-next-pandemic-interview.

61. Tom Abate, "Evolution of US Biotech Research/Several Scientific Clusters across the Nation Lead the Way on Breakthroughs and Discoveries—and Each Has Found Its Own Recipe for Success," *SFGate*, October 29, 2001, https://www.sfgate.com/business/article/Evolution-of-U-S-biotech-research-Several-2864767.php; Sudermann, "License to Innovate."

62. Kevin Bogardus, "Abramoff Divulges K Street Secrets," *The Hill*, November 2, 2011, https://thehill.com/business-a-lobbying/177491-abramoff-divulges-k-street-secrets.

63. John Greenwald, "The Colossus That Works," *Time*, July 11, 1983, https://content.time.com/time/subscriber/printout/0,8816,949693,00.html.

64. Ibid.; Denise Caruso, "Software Gambles: Company Strategies Boomerang," *InfoWorld* 6, no. 14 (1984): 82.

65. Greenwald, "Colossus That Works."

66. Tom Hormby, "The Apple vs. Microsoft GUI Lawsuit," Tech History, Low End Mac, August 25, 2006, https://lowendmac.com/2006/the-apple-vs-microsoft-gui-lawsuit.

67. "Today in 1988: Apple Sues Microsoft for Copyright Infringement," *Thomson Reuters* (blog), March 17, 2019, https://legal.thomsonreuters.com/blog/1988-apple-sues-microsoft; Hormby, "Apple vs. Microsoft GUI Lawsuit."

68. Hormby, "Apple vs. Microsoft GUI Lawsuit."

69. Ibid.; Emmie Martin, "Read Bill Gates' Answer to a Reddit Question about Whether He Copied Steve Jobs," *Business Insider*, March 13, 2017, https://www.businessinsider.com/bill-gates-answers-reddit-question-about-copying-steve-jobs-2017-3; "When Steve Met Bill: 'It Was a Kind of Weird Seduction Visit,'" *Fortune*, October 23, 2011, https://fortune.com/2011/10/24/when-steve-met-bill-it-was-a-kind-of-weird-seduction-visit.

70. "US v. Microsoft: Timeline," *Wired*, November 4, 2002, https://www.wired.com/2002/11/u-s-v-microsoft-timeline; John Burgess, "FTC Deadlocks Again in Microsoft Inves-

tigation," *Washington Post*, July 22, 1993, https://www.washingtonpost.com/archive
/business/1993/07/22/ftc-deadlocks-again-in-microsoft-investigation/dd8ce8ed-1d66
-4c32-b5af-6334f422e364.

71. Burgess, "FTC Deadlocks."

72. United States v. Microsoft, 253 F.3d 34 (D.C. Cir. 2001).

73. Ibid.; Joe Wilcox, "Microsoft Limits XML in Office 2003," *ZDNet News*, April 11, 2003,
https://web.archive.org/web/20050922005808/http:/news.zdnet.com/2100-3513_22
-996528.html; John Heilemann, "The Truth, the Whole Truth, and Nothing but the
Truth," *Wired*, November 1, 2000, https://www.wired.com/2000/11/microsoft-7.

74. United States v. Microsoft, 253 F.3d 34 (D.C. Cir. 2001), 219–21, 195–97; Heilemann,
"Truth, the Whole Truth."

75. United States v. Microsoft, 253 F.3d 34 (D.C. Cir. 2001); *Federal Register* 67, no. 157 (2002),
https://www.govinfo.gov/content/pkg/FR-2002-05-03/html/X02-180503.html; Reuters,
"In Brussels, Gates Takes a Pie in the Face," *New York Times*, February 5, 1998, https://
www.nytimes.com/1998/02/05/business/in-brussels-gates-takes-a-pie-in-the-face.html.

76. Dan Goodin, "Revisiting the Spectacular Failure That Was the Bill Gates Deposition," *Ars
Technica*, September 10, 2020, https://arstechnica.com/tech-policy/2020/09/revisiting
-the-spectacular-failure-that-was-the-bill-gates-deposition; "Microsoft's Teflon Bill,"
Bloomberg, November 29, 1998, https://www.bloomberg.com/news/articles/1998-11-29
/microsofts-teflon-bill; Adam Cohen, "A Tale of Two Bills," *Time*, January 25, 1999,
https://content.time.com/time/magazine/article/0,9171,18746,00.html; Adam Cohen,
"The Tale of the Gates Tapes," *Time*, November 16, 1998, https://content.time.com/time
/subscriber/article/0,33009,989570,00.html.

77. "Microsoft's Teflon Bill," *Bloomberg*.

78. "Verdict Stings Microsoft," Technology, CNN Money, April 3, 2000, https://money.cnn
.com/2000/04/03/technology/microsoft/#:~:text=Verdict%20stings%20Microsoft%20%
2D%20Apr.,3%2C%202000&text=NEW%20YORK%20(CNNfn)%20%2D%20In,operat-
ing%20systems%20to%20stifle%20competition; Alex Fitzpatrick, "A Judge Ordered Microsoft to Split. Here's Why It's Still a Single Company," *Time*, November 5, 2014, https://
time.com/3553242/microsoft-monopoly; "US v. Microsoft: Timeline," *Wired*.

79. *Inside Bill's Brain: Decoding Bill Gates*, episode 3, "Part 3."

80. "Microsoft Monopoly Caused Consumer Harm," Consumer Federation of America, accessed January 3, 2023, https://consumerfed.org/pdfs/antitrustpr.pdf.

81. "Reader's Guide to the Form 990-PF," Bill & Melinda Gates Foundation, 3, https://docs
.gatesfoundation.org/Documents/readersguide990-pf.pdf.

82. Thu-Huong Ha, "25 Years Ago Bill Gates's Mom Forced Him to Be Friends with Warren
Buffett," Quartz, July 5, 2016, https://qz.com/723902/25-years-ago-bill-gatess-mom-forced
-him-to-be-friends-with-warren-buffett.

83. "William H. Gates Sr.," Leadership, Bill & Melinda Gates Foundation; Gates Sr. and
Mackin, *Showing Up for Life*, 114.

84. "2001 Annual Report," Program for Appropriate Technology in Health, accessed January
3, 2023, https://media.path.org/documents/Annual_Report_2001_Final_screen.pdf; "2003
Annual Report," Program for Appropriate Technology in Health, accessed January 3,
2023, https://media.path.org/documents/RMER_annual_report_2003.pdf.

85. Gloria Galloway, "Ontario Doctor Gordon Perkin Became a Giant in Public Health," *Globe
and Mail*, September 15, 2020, https://www.theglobeandmail.com/world/article-ontario
-doctor-gordon-perkin-became-a-giant-in-public-health.

86. Andrew Mullen, "China's One-Child Policy: What Was It and What Impact Did It Have?,"
South China Morning Post, June 1, 2021, https://www.scmp.com/economy/china-economy
/article/3135510/chinas-one-child-policy-what-was-it-and-what-impact-did-it; Galloway,
"Ontario Doctor Gordon Perkin."

87. Tom Paulson, "Suzanne Cluett: 1942-2006: Her mission started with the Peace Corps," *Seattle Post-Intelligencer*, January 6, 2006, https://www.seattlepi.com/local/article/Suzanne-Cluett-1942-2006-Her-mission-started-1192114.php.

88. Robert D. McFadden, "Bill Gates Sr., Who Guided Billionaire Son's Philanthropy, Dies at 94," *New York Times*, September 15, 2020, https://www.nytimes.com/2020/09/15/business/bill-gates-sr-dead.html.

89. PATH, "The Birth of PATH," About PATH, accessed April 15, 2022, https://web.archive.org/web/20120507012048/www.path.org/about/birth-of-path.php; "Christopher Elias," Leadership, Bill & Melinda Gates Foundation, accessed April 14, 2022, https://www.gatesfoundation.org/about/leadership/christopher-elias.

90. "William H. Gates Sr.," Leadership, Bill & Melinda Gates Foundation; "Annual Report 1999," Bill & Melinda Gates Foundation, accessed May 8, 2023, chrome-extension://efaidnbmnnnibpcajpcglclefindmkaj/https://www.gatesfoundation.org/-/media/gfo/1annual-reports/1999gates-foundation-annual-report.pdf.

91. Diane Ravitch, "Bill Gates, the Nation's Superintendent of Schools," *Los Angeles Times*, July 30, 2006, https://www.latimes.com/archives/la-xpm-2006-jul-30-op-ravitch30-story.html; "Bill Gates," Profile, *Forbes*, accessed April 30, 2022, https://www.forbes.com/profile/bill-gates/?sh=7d6a7aac689f.

92. "Time Picks Bill and Melinda Gates, Bono as 'Persons of the Year,'" *Philanthropy News Digest*, December 20, 2005, https://philanthropynewsdigest.org/news/time-picks-bill-and-melinda-gates-bono-as-persons-of-the-year.

93. Craig Torres, "Convicted Felons Handle Gates Fortune," *Seattle Times*, March 7, 1993, https://archive.seattletimes.com/archive/?date=19930307&slug=1689167.

94. Ibid.; Christopher Byron, "An Ex-Con Friend of Gates Has His Own Dominion," Silicon Investor, June 7, 2000, https://www.siliconinvestor.com/readmsg.aspx?msgid=13853159; "Gates Foundation Awards up to $89 Million for Vaccine Development," *Philanthropy News Digest*, October 1, 2015, https://philanthropynewsdigest.org/news/gates-foundation-awards-up-to-89-million-for-vaccine-development; Bill Gates, "Vaccinate the World in Six Months," *GatesNotes* (blog), accessed April 30, 2022, https://www.gatesnotes.com/Health/Vaccinate-the-world-in-six-months.

95. "A World in Which Epidemics and Pandemics Are No Longer a Threat to Humanity," Our Mission, CEPI, accessed April 17, 2022, https://cepi.net/about/whyweexist; Reuters, "Epidemic Response Group to Invest up to $384 Mln in Novavax's Coronavirus Vaccine," May 11, 2020, https://www.reuters.com/article/health-coronavirus-vaccines-cepi/epidemic-response-group-to-invest-up-to-384-mln-in-novavaxs-coronavirus-vaccine-idINL4N2CT463; Novavax, "Novavax Reports Fourth Quarter and Full Year 2021 Financial Results and Operational Highlights," press release, February 28, 2022, https://ir.novavax.com/2022-02-28-Novavax-Reports-Fourth-Quarter-and-Full-Year-2021-Financial-Results-and-Operational-Highlights.

96. "Disease Surveillance Networks," Rockefeller Foundation Initiative, Rockefeller Foundation, 2013, accessed January 3, 2023, https://www.rockefellerfoundation.org/wp-content/uploads/Disease-Surveillance-Networks-Initiative.pdf; "EcoHealth Alliance Inc," Committed Grants, Bill & Melinda Gates Foundation, accessed January 3, 2023, https://www.gatesfoundation.org/about/committed-grants/2020/08/inv002838.

97. Michael J. Ainscough, "Next Generation Bioweapons: Genetic Engineering and BW," US Air Force Counterproliferation Center Future Warfare Series no. 14, 254–65, accessed April 17, 2022, https://media.defense.gov/2019/Apr/11/2002115480/-1/-1/0/14NEXTGENBIOWEAPONS.PDF; "International AIDS Vaccine Initiative Inc," Bill & Melinda Gates Foundation, accessed April 20, 2022, https://www.gatesfoundation.org/about/committed-grants/2016/10/opp1152832.

98. Jack Crowe, "Fauci Reportedly Relaunched NIH Gain-of-Function Research without Consulting White House," *National Review*, April 27, 2021, https://www.nationalreview.com/corner/fauci-reportedly-relaunched-nih-gain-of-function-research-without-consulting-white-house.

99. Jon Cohen, "Wuhan Coronavirus Hunter Shi Zhengli Speaks Out," *Science*, July 24, 2020, https://www.science.org/content/article/trump-owes-us-apology-chinese-scientist-center-covid-19-origin-theories-speaks-out.

100. Ebun Hargrave, "'Just a Coincidence?' Biden's Health Advisor Praises China's Research into COVID," *Express*, accessed March 27, 2022, https://www.express.co.uk/news/world/1586970/Anthony-Fauci-Covid-Lab-Leak-China-Virus-Pandemic-Coronavirus-Sars-Cov-2-Joe-Biden-VN; "Bill Gates Defends China's COVID-19 Response, Says It Did 'Lot of Things Right,'" *The Week*, April 27, 2020, https://www.theweek.in/news/world/2020/04/27/bill-gates-defends-chinas-covid-19-response-says-it-did-lot-of-things-right.html.

101. "$30 Million Research Effort to Develop New Tests for Deadly Infectious Diseases," Bill & Melinda Gates Foundation, accessed January 3, 2023, https://www.gatesfoundation.org/ideas/media-center/press-releases/2003/05/new-tests-for-deadly-infectious-diseases.

102. "Bill & Melinda Gates Foundation Funds Development of Pirbright's Livestock Antibody Hub Supporting Animal and Human Health," News, Pirbright Institute, November 15, 2019, https://www.pirbright.ac.uk/news/2019/11/bill-melinda-gates-foundation-funds-development-pirbright%E2%80%99s-livestock-antibody-hub.

103. Clive Cookson and Tim Bradshaw, "Davos Launch for Coalition to Prevent Epidemics of Emerging Viruses," *Financial Times*, January 18, 2017, https://www.ft.com/content/5699ac84-dd87-11e6-86ac-f253db7791c6.

104. "Investors Overview," CEPI, January 20, 2023, https://cepi.net/wp-content/uploads/2023/01/2023_01_20-CEPI-Investors-Overview.pdf; Wellcome, "Wellcome Trust Headquarters Opened," press release, December 3, 2004, https://wellcome.org/press-release/wellcome-trust-headquarters-opened.

105. Wellcome, "Wellcome Trust Headquarters Opened."

106. Daniel Roth, "Bill Gates on Getting to a New Normal," April 10, 2020, in *This Is Working with Daniel Roth*, podcast, MP3 audio, 24:16, https://podcasts.apple.com/us/podcast/bill-gates-on-getting-to-a-new-normal/id1475838548; Claire Anderson, "Coronavirus Vaccine Developed in Just THREE Hours—but Won't Be Administered for MONTHS," *Express*, February 13, 2020, https://www.express.co.uk/showbiz/tv-radio/1241948/coronavirus-cure-latest-update-news-vaccine-symptoms-infection-WHO-latest.

107. Roth, "Bill Gates on Getting to a New Normal," 05:50.

108. "This Is Working: Bill Gates Talks About Coronavirus, What Leaders Must Do, and More," LinkedIn News, accessed March 31, 2022, 22:15, https://www.linkedin.com/video/live/urn:li:ugcPost:6653713112593686528.

109. "Moderna's Work on a Potential Vaccine against COVID-19," Moderna, 2020, https://www.sec.gov/Archives/edgar/data/1682852/000119312520074867/d884510dex991.htm#:~:text=On%20January%2013%2C%202020%2C%20the,vaccine%20against%20the%20novel%20coronavirus.

110. Tal Zaks, "The Disease-Eradicating Potential of Gene Editing," filmed on December 8, 2017, in Boston, MA, TED video, 10:15, https://www.ted.com/talks/tal_zaks_the_disease_eradicating_potential_of_gene_editing.

111. Committee on Energy and Commerce, 115th Cong. (2018), witness disclosure requirement form of Rick Bright, Deputy Assistant Secretary for Preparedness and Response, https://docs.house.gov/meetings/IF/IF02/20180308/106967/HHRG-115-IF02-TTF-BrightR-20180308.pdf; "Universal Flu Vaccine," C-SPAN, October 29, 2019, https://www.c-span.org/video/?465845-1/universal-flu-vaccine.

112. "Gates Foundation Awards Grants for Polio, MR Delivery Patches," *Philanthropy News Digest*, March 8, 2017, https://philanthropynewsdigest.org/news/gates-foundation-awards-grants-for-polio-mr-delivery-patches.

113. Will Jeakle, "In Praise of Bill Gates: Entrepreneur, Normal Guy, Potential Savior of the World," *Forbes*, March 19, 2020, https://www.forbes.com/sites/williamjeakle/2020/03/19/in-praise-of-bill-gates-entrepreneur-normal-guy-potential-savior-of-the-world.

114. Bill Gates, "What You Need to Know about the COVID-19 Vaccine," *GatesNotes* (blog), April 30, 2020, https://www.gatesnotes.com/health/what-you-need-to-know-about-the-covid-19-vaccine.

115. "Elon Musk Speaking about mRNA, 'You Could Turn Someone into a Freaking Butterfly with the Right DNA Sequence," posted by twistedmetalplayer21, January 18, 2021, YouTube video, 00:39, https://www.youtube.com/watch?v=my8pmP0wgHI.

116. Tim Smedley, "Could mRNA Make Us Superhuman?," Change Agents, BBC News, November 22, 2021, https://www.bbc.com/future/article/20211122-could-mrna-make-us-superhuman.

117. "Playing God: 'We Are in the Midst of a Genetic Revolution,'" CBS News, updated November 8, 2017, https://www.cbsnews.com/news/playing-god-crispr-dna-genetic-ethics.

118. Amanda Morris, "Women Said Coronavirus Shots Affect Periods. New Study Shows They're Right," *Washington Post*, September 27, 2022, https://www.washingtonpost.com/wellness/2022/09/27/covid-vaccine-period-late; Ingraham Angle, "MIT Scientist's Warning for Parents about the COVID Vaccine," Fox News, January 13, 2022, 03:20, https://www.foxnews.com/video/6291706975001; Randi Hutter Epstein, "Luc Montagnier, Nobel-Winning Co-discoverer of HIV, Dies at 89," *New York Times*, February 10, 2022, https://www.nytimes.com/2022/02/10/science/luc-montagnier-dead.html; Marty Makary, "The Flimsy Evidence behind the CDC's Push to Vaccinate Children," *Wall Street Journal*, July 19, 2021, https://www.wsj.com/articles/cdc-covid-19-coronavirus-vaccine-side-effects-hospitalization-kids-11626706868.

119. Anderson Cooper, "Bill Gates Tells Anderson What Surprised Him about Covid Misinformation," CNN, 02:41, https://www.cnn.com/videos/health/2022/05/14/bill-gates-ac360-intv-covid-vaccine-sots-vpx.cnn; "Pfizer Did Not Know Whether Covid Vaccine Stopped Transmission before Rollout," posted by news.com.au, October 12, 2022, YouTube video, 00:45, https://www.youtube.com/watch?v=mnxlxzxoZx0.

120. Rose Berg and Victor Zonana, "Bill and Melinda Gates Make $25 Million Grant to International AIDS Vaccine Initiative," Bill & Melinda Gates Foundation, press release, accessed January 3, 2023, https://www.gatesfoundation.org/ideas/media-center/press-releases/1999/05/international-aids-vaccine-initiative.

121. "Pfizer Reports Record Full-Year 2022 Results and Provides Full-Year 2023 Financial Guidance," *Bloomberg*, January 31, 2023, https://www.bloomberg.com/press-releases/2023-01-31/pfizer-reports-record-full-year-2022-results-and-provides-full-year-2023-financial-guidance; Stephen Weiss, "Moderna Will Be the First Trillion Dollar Health-Care Company, Says Stephen Weiss," CNBC, 02:26, https://www.cnbc.com/video/2021/10/26/moderna-will-be-the-first-trillion-dollar-health-care-company-says-stephen-weiss.html.

Chapter Three: The Great Reset

1. "WEF Founder: Must Prepare for an Angrier World," CNBC, July 14, 2020, video, 00:16–05:42, https://www.cnbc.com/video/2020/07/14/wef-founder-must-prepare-for-an-angrier-world.html.

2. Ibid., 00:16–03:45.
3. Ibid., 01:31.
4. Ibid., 04:06 and 04:30; Klaus Schwab, "COVID-19 Pandemic Has Only Accelerated Trends Like Lack of Inclusion, WEF Founder Says," posted by CNBC International TV, July 14, 2020, YouTube video, 00:58–06:51, https://www.youtube.com/watch?v=HRLw6trwXco.
5. Klaus Schwab and Thierry Malleret, *Covid-19: The Great Reset* (Copenhagen: Forum Publishing Group, 2020).
6. Sandrine Dixson-Declève, Hans Joachim Schellnhuber, and Kat Raworth, "Could COVID-19 Give Rise to a Greener Global Future?," World Economic Forum, March 25, 2020, https://www.weforum.org/agenda/2020/03/a-green-reboot-after-the-pandemic.
7. Asma Khalid and Barbara Sprunt, "Biden Counters Trump's 'America First' with 'Build Back Better' Economic Plan," National Public Radio, July 9, 2020, https://www.npr.org/2020/07/09/889347429/biden-counters-trumps-america-first-with-build-back-better-economic-plan.
8. Adam Forrest, "Build Back Better: Who Said It First? Joe Biden or Boris Johnson?," *Independent*, November 5, 2020, https://www.independent.co.uk/news/uk/politics/biden-boris-johnson-build-back-better-b1613419.html; "Transcript: Boris Johnson on 'Face the Nation,' February 14, 2021," CNBC, February 14, 2021, https://www.cbsnews.com/news/transcript-boris-johnson-on-face-the-nation-february-14-2021.
9. "Britain: A 21st Century Partner for Global Growth," Young Global Leader United Kingdom Summit, December 4–6, 2011, Forum of Young Global Leaders, on Internet Archive, https://web.archive.org/web/20120912164651/http://www3.weforum.org/docs/WEF_YGL_LondonEvent_Programme_2011-12.pdf.
10. "A Global Coalition to Create New Vaccines for Emerging Infectious Diseases," CEPI, January 18, 2017, https://cepi.net/news_cepi/cepi-officially-launched.
11. Ida Auken, "Welcome to 2030. I Own Nothing, Have No Privacy, and Life Has Never Been Better," World Economic Forum, on Internet Archive, November 11, 2016, https://web.archive.org/web/20170220032503/https://www.weforum.org/agenda/2016/11/shopping-i-can-t-really-remember-what-that-is; World Economic Forum, "8 Predictions for the World in 2030," Facebook, video, 01:33, 00:00–00:10, https://www.facebook.com/watch/?v=10153920524981479; Sean Fleming, "Worms for Dinner? Europe Backs Insect-Based Food in a Bid to Promote Alternative Protein," World Economic Forum, May 6, 2021, https://www.weforum.org/agenda/2021/05/europe-insect-based-food-meat.
12. Mehul Desai, "The Benefits of a Cashless Society," World Economic Forum, January 7, 2020, https://www.weforum.org/agenda/2020/01/benefits-cashless-society-mobile-payments; Mariana Dahan, "How to Tackle Ebola with Digital Identities," World Economic Forum, July 17, 2015, https://www.weforum.org/agenda/2015/07/how-to-tackle-ebola-with-digital-identities; Arne Sorenson, "Is It Time for a Global Passport?," World Economic Forum, January 30, 2015, https://www.weforum.org/agenda/2015/01/is-it-time-for-a-global-passport; Armen Khatchatourov and Pierre-Antoine Chardel, "We Need to Reconsider Ethical and Philosophical Issues Surrounding Our Digital Identities," World Economic Forum, November 11, 2019, https://www.weforum.org/agenda/2019/11/the-ethical-challenges-of-digital-identity; Douglas Broom, "Most Adults Agree with Vaccine Passports for Travel, Survey Shows," World Economic Forum, April 28, 2021, https://www.weforum.org/agenda/2021/04/vaccine-passport-travel-covid-19.
13. Michael Elliott, "The Davos Man," *Time*, January 23, 2005, https://content.time.com/time/subscriber/printout/0,8816,1019830,00.html; Peter S. Goodman, "'He Has an Incredible Knack to Smell the Next Fad': How Klaus Schwab Built a Billionaire Circus at Davos," *Vanity Fair*, January 18, 2022, https://www.vanityfair.com/news/2022/01/how-klaus-schwab-built-a-billionaire-circus-at-davos; Roya Wolverson, "Is the Scene at Davos

Getting Old?," *Time*, January 25, 2013, https://business.time.com/2013/01/25/is-the-scene
-at-davos-getting-old; Ryan Heath, "Davos Is Dead," *Politico*, December 20, 2021, https://
www.politico.com/news/2021/12/20/davos-is-dead-525732.

14. Goodman, "He Has an Incredible Knack."

15. "Klaus Schwab," About, World Economic Forum, accessed April 24, 2022, https://www
.weforum.org/about/60ethe-schwab; "Klaus Schwab," Global Economy Prize 2018, Kiel
Institute, accessed April 24, 2022, https://www.ifw-kiel.de/institute/events/prizes-and
-awards/global-economy-prize/events/global-economy-prize-201860; M. C. Bitschi and
H. J. Winckelmann, "'Racial Improvement' in Ravensburg," *Urologe* 51, no. 6 (June 2012):
862–66, https://doi.org/10.1007/s00120-012-2849-y.

16. Tom Norton, "Fact Check: Was Davos Founder Klaus Schwab's Father Hitler's 'Confidant?'" *Newsweek*, May 26, 2022, https://www.newsweek.com/fact-check-was-davos
-founder-klaus-schwabs-father-hitlers-confidant-1710381.

17. "Whether Father Schwab Was a Nazi Is Not Certain, Nor What This Means for His Son,"
DPA Factchecking; Richard Bessel, *Nazism and War* (New York: Random House, 2006), 67.

18. Patrik Müller and Andreas Maurer, "Ein unmögliches Geschenk: Weshalb die Ein-
bürgerung von WEF-Gründer Klas Schwab scheitern wird," *Aargauer Zeitung*, August 20,
2019, https://www.aargauerzeitung.ch/schweiz/ein-unmogliches-geschenk-weshalb-die
-einburgerung-von-wef-grunder-klaus-schwab-scheitern-wird-ld.1144493; "Military Agency
Records RG 226," National Archives, accessed April 24, 2022, https://www.archives.gov
/research/holocaust/finding-aid/military/rg-226-3h.html.

19. Norton, "Fact Check."

20. Klaus Schwab, *Stakeholder Capitalism: A Global Economy That Works for Progress, People
and Planet* (New York: John Wiley & Sons, 2021), 253–58.

21. "Klaus Schwab," Global Economy Prize 2018, Kiel Institute.

22. Ibid.; "Davos 2017—A Conversation with Henry Kissinger on the World in 2017," posted by
World Economic Forum, January 20, 2017, YouTube video, 27:56, https://www.youtube
.com/watch?v=Apjzjsa8AIg; Robert D. McFadden, "Rockefeller Gave Kissinger $50,000,
Helped 2 Others," *New York Times*, October 6, 1974, https://www.nytimes.com/1974/10
/06/archives/rockefeller-gave-kissinger-50000-helped-2-others-he-denies-any.html.

23. "Klaus Schwab," Global Economy Prize 2018, Kiel Institute; Norton, "Fact Check."

24. Klaus Schwab and Hein Kroos, *Modern Company Management in Mechanical Engineering*
(Frankfurt: Verein Deutscher Maschinenbau-Anstalten, 1971), 5, https://www3.weforum
.org/docs/WEF_KSC_CompanyStrategy_Presentation_2014.pdf.

25. Ibid., 53–54.

26. Klaus Schwab, "Now Is the Time for a 'Great Reset,'" World Economic Forum, June 3,
2020, https://www.weforum.org/agenda/2020/06/now-is-the-time-for-a-great-reset.

27. Klaus Schwab, "Bank Bonuses and the Communitarian Spirit," *Wall Street Journal*,
January 14, 2010, https://www.wsj.com/articles/SB10001424052748704586504574654446
1600537756.

28. Peter Vanham and Johnny Harris, "After the Rise of the West and Asia, We Need a Better
Form of Capitalism," Industry Strategy Meeting 2021, World Economic Forum, January
28, 2021, https://www.weforum.org/agenda/2021/01/after-the-rise-of-the-west-and-asia
-we-need-a-better-form-of-capitalism; Isaac Stone Fish, "How Kissinger Became an Asset
of China," *Spectator*, March 26, 2022, https://www.spectator.co.uk/article/how-kissinger
-was-played-by-china.

29. Peter Vanham, "Klaus Schwab Releases 'Stakeholder Capitalism'; Making the Case for a
Global Economy That Works for Progress, People and Planet," News Releases, World
Economic Forum, January 29, 2021, https://www.weforum.org/press/2021/01/klaus
-schwab-releases-stakeholder-capitalism-making-the-case-for-a-global-economy-that

-works-for-progress-people-and-planet; Professor Klaus Schwab, Curriculum Vitae, World Economic Forum, accessed April 24, 2022, https://www3.weforum.org/docs/WEF_KSCFactsheet.pdf.

30. Gunter Pauli, "Gunter Pauli: 50 Years Club of Rome," posted by The Club of Rome, November 19, 2018, YouTube video, 24:46, https://www.youtube.com/watch?v=Rd3IB vomXus; *The World Economic Forum: A Partner in Shaping History* (Cologne: World Economic Forum, 2019), https://www3.weforum.org/docs/WEF_A_Partner_in_Shaping _History.pdf.

31. "Our Mission," About, World Economic Forum, accessed April 24, 2022, https://www.we forum.org/about/world-economic-forum.

32. Elliott, "Davos Man"; Goodman, "He Has an Incredible Knack"; "The (Evil?) Architect of the Great Reset," posted by Sorelle Amore Finance, June 9, 2022, YouTube video, 09:36, https://youtu.be/A6zy0D6YBfk?t=13.

33. Strobe Talbott, "America Abroad: The Birth of the Global Nation," *Time*, July 20, 1992, https://content.time.com/time/subscriber/article/0,33009,976015,00.html; Jessica Mathews, Ann Florini, and James B. Steinberg, "The Future of Global Governance," Brookings Institution/Carnegie Endowment for International Peace Briefing, moderated by Strobe Talbott, transcript by Federal News Service, Washington, DC, April 8, 2003, https://www .brookings.edu/wp-content/uploads/2012/04/20030408.pdf.

34. Goodman, "He Has an Incredible Knack."

35. Sharan Burrow, "It's Time for a New Social Contract," World Economic Forum, January 17, 2018, https://www.weforum.org/agenda/2018/01/time-new-social-contract-inequality -work-sharan-burrow.

36. Richard Wike, Katie Simmons, Bruce Stokes, and Janell Fetterolf, "How Do People View Democracy?," World Economic Forum, October 27, 2017, https://www.weforum.org /agenda/2017/10/this-is-how-people-view-democracy.

37. Barbara Shubinski, "'A Roomful of Brains': Early Advances in Computer Science and Artificial Intelligence," Rockefeller Archive Center, January 6, 2022, https://resource.rock arch.org/story/a-roomful-of-brains-early-advances-in-computer-science-and-artificial -intelligence.

38. Peter Passell, Marc Roberts, and Leonard Ross, "The Limits to Growth," *New York Times*, April 2, 1972, https://www.nytimes.com/1972/04/02/archives/the-limits-to-growth-a -report-for-the-club-of-romes-project-on-the.html; "Club of Rome Revisited," *Time*, April 26, 1976, https://content.time.com/time/subscriber/printout/0,8816,879689,00.html; Mark J. Perry, "40 Years Later, Time Has Not Been Kind to the Limits to Growth," American Enterprise Institute, June 26, 2013, https://www.aei.org/carpe-diem/40-years-later-time -has-not-been-kind-to-the-limits-to-growth; *World Economic Forum: A Partner in Shaping History*; "History of Spreadsheets," OfficeTuts, accessed April 24, 2022, https://excel .officetuts.net/training/history-of-spreadsheets.

39. Perry, "40 Years Later."

40. Hunter Lovins, Hans Joachim Schellnhuber, Kat Raworth, and Sandrine Dixson-Declève, "Club of Rome Calls for Green Reboot after Pandemic," *Technocracy*, May 11, 2020, https:// www.technocracy.news/club-of-rome-calls-for-green-reboot-after-pandemic; Gaya Herrington, "Data Check on the World Model That Forecast Global Collapse," Club of Rome, July 26, 2021, https://www.clubofrome.org/blog-post/herrington-world-model.

41. Herrington, "Data Check."

42. Passell, Roberts, and Ross, "Limits to Growth," 116.

43. Gaya Branderhorst, "Update to Limits to Growth: Comparing the World3 Model with Empirical Data" (master's thesis, Harvard Extension School, 2020), https://dash.harvard .edu/handle/1/37364868.

44. Walter Sullivan, "Scientists Fear Heavy Use of Coal May Bring Adverse Shift in Climate," *New York Times*, July 25, 1977, https://www.nytimes.com/1977/07/25/archives/scientists -fear-heavy-use-of-coal-may-bring-adverse-shift-in.html.

45. Alexander King, *The First Global Revolution* (New York: Pantheon, 1991), 75.

46. "Ozone Layer Recovery Is an Environmental Success Story," World Meteorological Organi- zation, September 15, 2021, https://public.wmo.int/en/media/news/ozone-layer-recovery -environmental-success-story; Corryn Wetzel, "The Great Pacific Garbage Patch Hosts Life in the Open Ocean," *Smithsonian*, December 6, 2021, https://www.smithsonianmag .com/smart-news/the-great-pacific-garbage-patch-hosts-life-in-the-open-ocean -180979168.

47. Donella Meadows, Jorgen Randers, and Dennis Meadows, *Limits to Growth: The 30-Year Update* (White River Junction, VT: Chelsea Green, 2004), xvi; "A Short History of a Ground-Breaking Publication: The Limits to Growth," Club of Rome, accessed April 24, 2022, https://www.clubofrome.org/wp-content/uploads/2022/02/CoR-LtG-ShortHis tory.pdf.

48. "The Limits to Growth Model: Still Prescient 50 Years Later," Earth4All: Deep-Dive Paper, Club of Rome, May 2022, accessed April 24, 2022, https://www.clubofrome.org /wp-content/uploads/2022/05/Earth4All_Deep_Dive_Herrington.pdf.

49. "Agenda 21," Division for Sustainable Development, UN Department of Economic and So- cial Affairs, accessed April 25, 2022, https://www.un.org/esa/dsd/agenda21; "Agenda 21," United Nations Conference on Environment and Development, 3, Rio de Janeiro, Brazil, June 3–14, 1992, United Nations Sustainable Development, https://sustainabledevelop ment.un.org/content/documents/Agenda21.pdf.

50. "Agenda 21," United Nations Conference on Environment and Development, 7–325.

51. Ibid., 156, 158–59.

52. Ibid., 168, 172, 176, 178–79, 182–83, 187, 195.

53. "Introduction, 2000–2015," UN Documentation: Development, Dag Hammarskjöld Li- brary, accessed April 24, 2022, https://research.un.org/en/docs/dev/2000-2015.

54. Joe Sommerlad, "What Is the 'New World Order' and Why Has Joe Biden Caused Uproar by Using the Phrase?," *Independent*, March 24, 2022, https://www.independent.co.uk /news/world/americas/us-politics/new-world-order-meaning-biden-b2043111.html.

55. "The SDGs in Action," Sustainable Development Goals, United Nations Development Pro- gramme, accessed April 24, 2022, https://www.undp.org/sustainable-development-goals.

56. Ibid.

57. Gerald O. Barney, *The Global 2000 Report to the President* (Washington, DC: US Govern- ment Printing Office, 1980), 43–45, https://www.cartercenter.org/resources/pdfs/pdf -archive/global2000reporttothepresident—enteringthe21stcentury-01011991.pdf.

58. Keith Bradsher, "The Story of China's Economic Rise Unfolds in Switzerland," *New York Times*, January 18, 2020, https://www.nytimes.com/2020/01/18/business/davos-china .html; *World Economic Forum: A Partner in Shaping History*, 42–47.

59. *World Economic Forum: A Partner in Shaping History*, 29.

60. Ibid., 40.

61. Ibid., 90.

62. Ibid., 147, 223; Carly Walsh and Lauren Said-Moorhouse, "China's President Xi Jinping Pushes Global Cooperation, Saying, 'Arrogant Isolation Will Always Fail,'" CNN, updated January 25, 2021, https://www.cnn.com/2021/01/25/business/xi-jinping-wef-multilat eralism-intl; "China's Xi Warns Davos World Economic Forum against 'New Cold War,'" France 24, last modified January 25, 2021, https://www.france24.com/en/live-news /20210125-china-s-xi-warns-davos-world-economic-forum-against-new-cold-war.

63. *World Economic Forum: A Partner in Shaping History*, 223, 227, 240, 249; "10 Foreigners Given Medals for Roles in Reform, Opening-Up," State Council Information Office,

People's Republic of China, updated December 19, 2018, http://english.scio.gov.cn/to pnews/2018-12/19/content_74291157.htm.

64. Schwab, "Now Is the Time"; André Du Plessis and Gabriel Galil, "Beyond Rainbows: Why Business Must Fight for LGBTI Rights Outside the Workplace," World Economic Forum, November 2, 2020, https://www.weforum.org/agenda/2020/11/private-sector-business -lgbti-equality.

65. Schwab, "Now Is the Time"; Lee Fang, "Green-Colored Glasses," *Intercept*, June 27, 2022, https://theintercept.com/2022/06/27/esg-funds-corporate-responsibility-dei.

66. Catherine Clifford, "These Are the World's Largest Banks That Are Increasing and De- creasing Their Fossil Fuel Financing," CNBC, April 22, 2021, https://www.cnbc.com /2021/04/22/which-banks-are-increasing-decreasing-fossil-fuel-financing-.html.

67. Fang, "Green-Colored Glasses."

68. Ibid.

69. Sheryl Estrada, "The Top Trends in ESG Disclosure from Fortune 100 Companies," *For- tune*, June 27, 2022, https://fortune.com/2022/06/27/top-trends-esg-disclosure-fortune -100-companies; "CNBC Transcript: Bank of America Chairman & CEO Brian Moynihan Speaks with CNBC's 'Squawk Box' Today," CNBC, May 23, 2022, https://www.cnbc.com /2022/05/23/cnbc-transcript-bank-of-america-chairman-ceo-brian-moynihan-speaks -with-cnbcs-squawk-box-today.html.

70. Alan Murray and David Meyer, "'ESG' Represents a Fundamental Shift in Business Strategy—but the Term Is Unclear, Unpopular, and Increasingly Polarizing," *Fortune*, July 21, 2022, https://fortune.com/2022/07/21/esg-fundamental-shift-unpopular-acronym; George Calhoun, "FTX and ESG: A Panorama of Failed Governance, Part I," *Forbes*, No- vember 21, 2022, https://www.forbes.com/sites/georgecalhoun/2022/11/21/ftx-and-esg-a -panorama-of-failed-governance-pt-1—the-internal-failures/?sh=1f0aa8012d9d

71. Bob Sanders, "NH Senate Panel Hears Bill Targeting 'Self-Appointed Financial Elites,'" *NH Business Review*, April 13, 2022, https://www.nhbr.com/nh-senate-panel-hears-bill -targeting-self-appointed-financial-elites.

72. Ellen Meyers, "Some States' Anti-ESG Push Garners Support in Congress," *Roll Call*, April 28, 2022, https://rollcall.com/2022/04/28/some-states-anti-esg-push-garners-support-in -congress.

73. Schwab, "Now Is the Time"; Klaus Schwab, *The Fourth Industrial Revolution* (Cologne: World Economic Forum, 2016), 7.

74. Schwab and Malleret, *Covid-19*, 67–68.

75. "Yuval Noah Harari," People, World Economic Forum, accessed April 25, 2022, https:// www.weforum.org/people/yuval-noah-harari; Yuval Harari, "Read Yuval Harari's Blis- tering Warning to Davos in Full," World Economic Forum, January 24, 2020, https:// www.weforum.org/agenda/2020/01/yuval-hararis-warning-davos-speech-future -predications; Yuval Noah Harari and Daniel Kahneman, "Death Is Optional," *Edge*, March 4, 2015, video, 41:54, https://www.edge.org/conversation/yuval_noah_harari -daniel_kahneman-death-is-optional.

76. "Yuval Noah Harari: Panel Discussion on Technology and the Future of Democracy," posted by Yuval Noah Harari, October 4, 2020, YouTube video, 32:40–33:00, https:// www.youtube.com/watch?v=JfyIW9wRvB4.

77. "Yuval Noah Harari: The 2021 *60 Minutes* Interview," posted by 60 Minutes, October 31, 2021, YouTube video, 09:15, https://www.youtube.com/watch?v=EIVTf-C6oQo&t; Harari and Kahneman, "Death Is Optional."

78. "Will the Future Be Human?—Yuval Noah Harari," posted by World Economic Forum, January 25, 2018, YouTube video, 03:25–03:43, https://youtu.be/hL9uk4hKyg4.

79. Yuval Noah Harari (@yuval-noah-harari), "Bill Gates has been a fan of Yuval Noah Hara- ri's work for several years," Instagram, August 25, 2018, https://www.instagram.com/p

/Bm5lGRsltpT; "Bill Gates, Mark Zuckerberg, and Barack Obama Are Fans. Meet Yuval Noah Harari," ABC News, September 4, 2018, https://www.abc.net.au/triplej/programs /hack/meet-yuval-harari-superstar-historian-to-mark-zuckerberg/10200906; Nick Romeo, "Yuval Harari's New Book Feeds the Tech Czar's God Complex," *Daily Beast*, updated May 23, 2017, https://www.thedailybeast.com/yuval-hararis-new-book-feeds-the-tech -czars-god-complex.

80. "Yuval Noah Harari: The 2021 *60 Minutes* Interview."

81. Ibid.

82. Ian Sample, "AI Will Create 'Useless Class' of Human, Predicts Bestselling Historian," *Guardian*, May 20, 2016, https://www.theguardian.com/technology/2016/may/20/silicon -assassins-condemn-humans-life-useless-artificial-intelligence.

83. Harari and Kahneman, "Death Is Optional."

84. Ibid.

85. "Yuval Noah Harari: The 2021 *60 Minutes* Interview."

86. Ibid.

87. "Yuval Noah Harari ve Daniel Kahneman Söyleşisi," posted by Kolektif Kitap, May 20, 2015, YouTube video, 29:54–31:16, https://www.youtube.com/watch?v=-3aPT8MuH_E.

88. Michael Auslin, "Yale Professor Named a Young Global Leader," YaleNews, February 1, 2006, https://news.yale.edu/2006/02/01/yale-professor-named-young-global-leader.

89. Klaus Schwab, "Klaus Schwab 2017 Young Global Leaders AUDIO Cleaned Up!" bacontrees, February 3, 2022, YouTube video, 00:00:44, https://www.youtube.com/watch?v= daE0jthD5F8.

90. "New Zealand to Use Vaccine Certificates as Delta Persists," Reuters, October 4, 2021, https://www.reuters.com/world/asia-pacific/new-zealand-use-vaccine-certificates -delta-persists-2021-10-05; Judith Levine, "Vaccine Passports Are Here to Stay. Why Worry?" *Intercept*, January 1, 2022, https://theintercept.com/2022/01/01/covid-vaccine -passports-surveillance; Sam Werthmuller, "From Entrepreneurs to Scientists: Meet the 2022 Class of Young Global Leaders," News Releases, World Economic Forum, April 20, 2022, https://www.weforum.org/press/2022/04/from-entrepreneurs-to-scientists-meet -the-2022-class-of-young-global-leaders; Lucy Craymer and Praveen Menon, "New Zealand's Parliament Protest Ends with Clashes, Arrests," Reuters, March 2, 2022, https:// www.reuters.com/world/asia-pacific/new-zealand-police-dismantle-tents-tow-vehicles -clear-anti-vaccine-protests-2022-03-01.

91. "Community," The Forum of Young Global Leaders, https://www.younggloballeaders.org /community.

92. Tulsi Gabbard (@TulsiGabbard), "@wef I'm honored to be selected as 2015 @YGLvoices— representing #Hawaii amongst leaders from around the world," Twitter, March 18, 2015, 7:24 a.m., https://twitter.com/TulsiGabbard/status/578185129471922177; "Pete Buttigieg," Community, The Forum of Young Global Leaders, accessed April 24, 2022, https:// www.younggloballeaders.org/community; Justin Chapman, "Brie Loskota Named a 2017 WEF Young Global Leader," Pacific Council on International Policy (website), March 17, 2017, https://www.pacificcouncil.org/newsroom/loskota-2017-ygl; "Daniel Crenshaw," Community, The Forum of Young Global Leaders, on Internet Archive, accessed April 25, 2022 (the screenshot of the site was captured November 18, 2020), https://web.archive .org/web/20201118110458/https://www.younggloballeaders.org/community?utf8=%E2 %9C%93&q=crenshaw&x=0&y=0&status=&class_year=&sector=&region=.

93. "List of 2015 Young Global Leader Honorees," The Forum of Young Global Leaders and World Economic Forum, accessed April 26, 2022, https://doczz.net/doc/6674846/full -list-of-2015-young-global-leaders; Gienna Shaw, "Trump White House Dismisses Vaccine Champion Surgeon General Vivek H. Murthy," Fierce Healthcare, April 24, 2017, https:// www.fiercehealthcare.com/healthcare/trump-replaces-surgeon-general-vivek

-h-murthy-opioid-addiction-guns-vaccines; "Meet the Key Members of Biden's Covid-19 Response Team," *New York Times*, accessed April 26, 2022, https://www.nytimes.com /2021/02/24/us/bidens-covid-19-response-team.html.

94. Tom Inglesby, "6 Ways Countries Can Prepare for the Next Infectious Disease Pandemic," World Economic Forum, July 18, 2018, https://www.weforum.org/agenda/2018/07/infec tious-disease-pandemic-clade-x-johns-hopkins; "Clade X: A Pandemic Exercise," John Hopkins Center for Health Security, May 15, 2018, https://www.centerforhealthsecurity .org/our-work/exercises/2018_clade_x_exercise/pdfs/Clade-X-exercise-presentation -slides.pdf; "Clade X Pandemic Exercise: Segment 4," posted by Johns Hopkins Center for Health Security, May 18, 2018, 48:32–48:59, https://www.youtube.com/watch?v=tqa7N Hq73xM&t=2910s.

95. "Event 201 Pandemic Tabletop Exercise," Johns Hopkins Center for Health Security, accessed May 9, 2023, https://centerforhealthsecurity.org/our-work/tabletop-exercises /event-201-pandemic-tabletop-exercise.

96. Ibid.

97. Derek Cheng, "Coronavirus: Jacinda Ardern Dismisses Nationwide Lockdown Specula- tion on Social Media," *New Zealand Herald*, March 18, 2020, https://www.nzherald .co.nz/nz/coronavirus-jacinda-ardern-dismisses-nationwide-lockdown-speculation -on-social-media/I2FTKPSA36LJIDNLBFIYECXDHM.

98. Zolan Kanno-Youngs and Cecilia Kang, "'They're Killing People': Biden Denounces Social Media for Virus Disinformation," *New York Times*, July 19, 2021, https://www.nytimes .com/2021/07/16/us/politics/biden-facebook-social-media-covid.html; Taylor Lorenz, "How the Biden Administration Let Right-Wing Attacks Derail Its Disinformation Ef- forts," *Washington Post*, May 18, 2022, https://www.washingtonpost.com/technology /2022/05/18/disinformation-board-dhs-nina-jankowicz.

99. Marcela García, "How the Disinformation Governance Board Fell Victim to Disinforma- tion," *Boston Globe*, updated May 20, 2022, https://www.bostonglobe.com/2022/05/20 /opinion/how-disinformation-governance-board-fell-victim-disinformation.

100. "Public-Private Cooperation for Pandemic Preparedness and Response," Event 201, Johns Hopkins Center for Health Security, https://centerforhealthsecurity.org/our-work /tabletop-exercises/event-201-pandemic-tabletop-exercise#recommendations.

101. "Pandemic Creates New Billionaire Every 30 Hours—Now a Million People Could Fall into Extreme Poverty at Same Rate in 2022," press release, Oxfam International, May 23, 2022, https://www.oxfam.org/en/press-releases/pandemic-creates-new-billionaire-every -30-hours-now-million-people-could-fall; "Profiting from Pain: The Urgency of Taxing the Rich amid a Surge in Billionaire Wealth and a Global Cost-of-Living Crisis," Oxfam Media Briefing, Oxfam, May 23, 2022, https://oi-files-d8-prod.s3.eu-west-2.amazonaws .com/s3fs-public/2022-05/Oxfam%20Media%20Brief%20-%20EN%20-%20Profiting %20From%20Pain%2C%20Davos%202022%20Part%202.pdf.

102. "The Coming Food Catastrophe," *Economist*, May 19, 2022, https://www.economist.com /leaders/2022/05/19/the-coming-food-catastrophe.

Chapter Four: The Power Grab

1. Viveca Novak, "Bum Rap for Rahm," FactCheck.org, January 13, 2021, https://www.fact check.org/2011/01/bum-rap-for-rahm.

2. "President Biden on Climate Change: 'This Is Code Red,'" posted by C-SPAN, September 7, 2021, YouTube video, 01:13, https://www.youtube.com/watch?v=pKoiM4eOmwA; "Re- marks by President Biden on the Administration's Response to Hurricane Ida," Speeches and Remarks, The White House, September 7, 2021, https://www.whitehouse.gov/brief

ing-room/speeches-remarks/2021/09/07/remarks-by-president-biden-on-the-adminis trations-response-to-hurricane-ida-2.

3. "President Biden on Climate Change"; "Remarks by President Biden on the Administration's Response to Hurricane Ida."

4. "Remarks by President Biden on the Administration's Response to Hurricane Ida."

5. Ibid.

6. Associated Press, "Biden Wants to Pass $4 Trillion Infrastructure Package 'Build Back Better' over the Summer," KTLA, March 29, 2021, https://ktla.com/news/nexstar-media -wire/nationworld/bidens-want-to-pass-4-trillion-infrastructure-package-build-back -better-over-the-summer.

7. Rajshree Agarwal, "Lessons from the 2009 American Recovery and Reinvestment Act for the American Jobs and Infrastructure Plan," Forbes, May 5, 2021, https://www.forbes .com/sites/rajshreeagarwal/2021/05/05/lessons-from-the-2009-american-recovery-and -reinvestment-act-for-the-american-jobs-and-infrastructure-plan; "Vice President Biden Announces Finalized $535 Million Loan Guarantee for Solyndra," Statements & Releases, The White House—Barack Obama, September 4, 2009, https://obamawhitehouse.archives .gov/the-press-office/vice-president-biden-announces-finalized-535-million-loan -guarantee-solyndra.

8. Michael Bathon, "Solyndra Lenders Ahead of Government Won't Get Full Recovery," Bloomberg, October 17, 2012, https://www.bloomberg.com/news/articles/2012-10-17 /solyndra-lenders-ahead-of-government-won-t-recover-fully.

9. John Mcardle, "Solyndra Spent Liberally to Woo Lawmakers Until the End, Records Show," New York Times, September 16, 2011, https://archive.nytimes.com/www.nytimes .com/gwire/2011/09/16/16greenwire-solyndra-spent-liberally-to-woo-lawmakers-unti -81006.html?pagewanted=all.

10. Carol D. Leonnig and Joe Stephens, "Venture Capitalists Play Key Role in Obama's Energy Department," Washington Post, February 14, 2012, https://www.washingtonpost.com /politics/venture-capitalists-play-key-role-in-obamas-energy-department/2011/12/30 /gIQA05raER_story.html.

11. Maegan Vazquez and Donald Judd, "Biden Signs Inflation Reduction Act into Law," CNN, updated August 16, 2022, https://www.cnn.com/2022/08/16/politics/biden-inflation -reduction-act-signing/index.html.

12. Jim Tankersley, "Biden Signs Expansive Health, Climate, and Tax Law," New York Times, August 16, 2022, https://www.nytimes.com/2022/08/16/business/biden-climate-tax-infl ation-reduction.html.

13. Mike Palicz, "List of Tax Hikes in Democrat Reconciliation Bill," Americans for Tax Reform, August 7, 2022, https://www.atr.org/list-of-tax-hikes-in-democrat-reconciliation -bill.

14. Katie Lobosco, "The IRS Is Set to Get Billions for Audit Enforcement. Here's What It Means for Taxpayers," CNN, updated August 11, 2022, https://www.cnn.com/2022/08/11 /politics/irs-inflation-act-funding-audit-enforcement/index.html.

15. "The IRS Is about to Go Beast Mode," Wall Street Journal, August 2, 2022, https://www .wsj.com/articles/the-irs-is-about-to-go-beast-mode-chuck-schumer-joe-manchin-audit -taxes-middle-class-joe-biden-11659477320.

16. Nick Mordowanec, "IRS Deletes Requirement That New Agents Be Willing to Use 'Deadly Force,'" Newsweek, August 12, 2022, https://www.newsweek.com/irs-deletes-requirement -that-new-agents-willing-use-deadly-force-1733352.

17. Burton W. Folsom, "John D. Rockefeller and the Oil Industry," Foundation for Economic Education, October 1, 1988, https://fee.org/articles/john-d-rockefeller-and-the-oil-ind ustry.

18. John Ensor Harr and Peter J. Johnson, *The Rockefeller Century* (New York: Scribner, 1988), 116.
19. Thomas Holst, "Peak Oil Theory Revisited," Kem C. Gardner Policy Institute, University of Utah, February 7, 2018, https://gardner.utah.edu/peak-oil-theory-revisited.
20. *Understanding the Peak Oil Theory: Hearing before the Subcommittee on Energy and Air Quality of the Committee on Energy and Commerce*, 109th Cong. (2005), https://www.gov info.gov/content/pkg/CHRG-109hhrg25627/html/CHRG-109hhrg25627.htm.
21. Steve Coll, *Private Empire: ExxonMobil and American Power* (New York: Penguin, 2012), 513; *Congressional Record* 154, part 8 (Washington, DC: US Government Publishing Office, 2008), 10412–15, https://www.govinfo.gov/content/pkg/CRECB-2008-pt8/html/CRECB -2008-pt8-Pg10412.htm.
22. "Impact Investing: An Introduction," Rockefeller Philanthropy Advisors, accessed May 16, 2022, https://www.rockpa.org/guide/impact-investing-introduction.
23. Suzanne Goldenberg, "Heirs to Rockefeller Oil Fortune Divest from Fossil Fuels over Climate Change," *Guardian*, September 22, 2014, https://www.theguardian.com/environ ment/2014/sep/22/rockefeller-heirs-divest-fossil-fuels-climate-change; "Impact Invest ments," Mission-Aligned Investing, Rockefeller Brothers Fund, accessed May 16, 2022, https://www.rbf.org/mission-aligned-investing/impact-investments.
24. "Bill Gates Raises $1B to Develop Clean Energy," Carbon Credits, September 24, 2021, https://carboncredits.com/bill-gates-raises-1b-to-develop-clean-energy; Jack Ellis, "Brief: Microsoft to Purchase up to $2M in Carbon Credits from Land O'Lakes," *AFN*, February 8, 2021, https://agfundernews.com/trucarbon-microsoft-to-purchase-2m-in-carbon-credits -from-land-olakes.
25. John Schwartz, "Exxon Mobil Accuses the Rockefellers of a Climate Conspiracy," *New York Times*, November 21, 2016, https://www.nytimes.com/2016/11/21/science/exxon -mobil-rockefellers-climate-change.html.
26. Mark J. Perry, "50 Years of Failed Doomsday Eco-pocalyptic Predictions; The So-Called 'Experts' Are 0–50," American Enterprise Institute, September 23, 2019, https://www.aei .org/carpe-diem/50-years-of-failed-doomsday-eco-pocalyptic-predictions-the-so-called -experts-are-0-50.
27. Andrew C. Revkin, "Hacked E-Mail Is New Fodder for Climate Dispute," *New York Times*, November 20, 2009, https://www.nytimes.com/2009/11/21/science/earth/21climate.html.
28. Jess Henig, "'Climategate': Hacked E-mails Show Climate Scientists in a Bad Light but Don't Change Scientific Consensus on Global Warming," FactCheck.org, updated December 22, 2009, https://www.factcheck.org/2009/12/climategate; Eli Kintisch, "IPCC/ Climategate Criticism Roundup," Science Insider, *Science*, February 15, 2010, https:// www.science.org/content/article/ipccclimategate-criticism-roundup.
29. "Breakthrough Energy Ventures," Crunchbase, accessed June 4, 2023, https://www .crunchbase.com/organization/breakthrough-energy-ventures/investor_financials; Matt Krantz, "Here's Who Owns Tesla Now That Elon Musk Is Selling Out," *Investor's Business Daily*, December 16, 2022, https://www.investors.com/etfs-and-funds/etfs/sp500-heres -who-owns-tesla-now-that-elon-musk-is-selling-out.
30. John Kartch, "Joe Biden: 'We Are Going to Get Rid of Fossil Fuels,'" Americans for Tax Reform, February 8, 2020, https://www.atr.org/joe-biden-we-are-going-get-rid-fossil -fuels.
31. Emma Mayer, "Californians Asked to Voluntarily Cut Electricity for Sixth Time Since Mid-June," *Newsweek*, July 28, 2021, https://www.newsweek.com/californians-asked -voluntarily-cut-electricity-sixth-time-since-mid-june-1613997.
32. Catherine Traywick, Mark Chediak, Naureen S. Malik, and Josh Saul, "The Two Hours That Nearly Destroyed Texas's Electric Grid," *Bloomberg*, updated February 21, 2021,

https://www.bloomberg.com/news/features/2021-02-20/texas-blackout-how-the
-electrical-grid-failed.

33. Judah Cohen and Matthew Barlow, "How Arctic Warming Could Be the Cause of Extreme
Cold-Weather Events," World Economic Forum, September 8, 2021, https://www.wefo
rum.org/agenda/2021/09/arctic-warming-trigger-extreme-cold-waves-texas-freeze
-study.

34. "Average Texas Electricity Prices Were Higher in February 2021 Due to a Severe Winter
Storm," Today in Energy, US Energy Information Administration, accessed May 16, 2022,
https://www.eia.gov/todayinenergy/detail.php?id=47876; Maria Halkias, "Griddy Customers Face $5,000 Electric Bills for 5 Freezing Days in Texas," *Dallas Morning News*,
February 19, 2021, https://www.dallasnews.com/business/2021/02/20/griddy-customers
-face-5000-bills-for-5-freezing-days-in-texas.

35. Doha Madani, "Six ERCOT Members Resign after Catastrophic Texas Blackouts during
Winter Storm," NBC, updated February 24, 2021, https://www.nbcnews.com/news/us
-news/four-ercot-board-members-resign-after-major-texas-blackouts-during-n1258656;
Ed Hirs, "The ERCOT Big Freeze of 2021 Exposed a National Security Weakness," *Dallas
Morning News*, February 15, 2022, https://www.dallasnews.com/opinion/commentary
/2022/02/15/the-ercot-big-freeze-of-2021-exposed-a-national-security-weakness.

36. Julia Fanzeres, "High Gas Prices Are Killing the Summer Road Trip," *Bloomberg*, June 28,
2022, https://www.bloomberg.com/news/articles/2022-06-28/fewer-americans-are-plan
ning-road-trips-as-gas-prices-soar.

37. Mark Moore and Samuel Chamberlain, "Buttigieg Begs for Electric Car Subsidies as
Americans Feel Pump Pain," *New York Post*, July 19, 2022, https://nypost.com/2022/07
/19/buttigieg-begs-for-electric-car-subsidies-as-americans-feel-pump-pain.

38. Emma Newburger, "Texas Grid Operator Tells Residents to Curb Power as Heat Hits
Record Highs," CNBC, July 11, 2022, https://www.cnbc.com/2022/07/11/ercot-tells
-texans-to-curb-power-use-as-extreme-heat-strains-the-grid.html; John Kartch (@john
kartch), "'Moderate' Joe Biden RT @tomselliott: @JoeBiden on fossil fuel execs: 'We
should put them in jail' for pollution," Twitter, December 29, 2019, 7:07 p.m., https://twit
ter.com/johnkartch/status/1211468882927423489.

39. Bill Gates, "Introducing the Green Premiums," *GatesNotes* (blog), September 29, 2020,
https://www.gatesnotes.com/Energy/Introducing-the-Green-Premiums.

40. Ibid.; Ian Schwartz, "Buttigieg: The More Painful the High Price of Gas Becomes, the
More Beneficial It Is to Have an Electric Car," *RealClearPolitics*, July 19, 2022, https://
www.realclearpolitics.com/video/2022/07/19/buttigieg_the_more_painful_the_high
_price_of_gas_becomes_the_more_beneficial_it_is_to_have_an_electric_car.html.

41. "For a Livable Climate: Net-Zero Commitments Must Be Backed by Credible Action," Climate Action, United Nations, accessed May 16, 2022, https://www.un.org/en/climat
echange/net-zero-coalition.

42. Akshat Rathi and Jennifer A. Dlouhy, "Bill Gates and the Secret Push to Save Biden's Climate Bill," *Bloomberg*, updated August 17, 2022, https://www.bloomberg.com/news/features
/2022-08-16/how-bill-gates-lobbied-to-save-the-climate-tax-bill-biden-just-signed.

43. Bill Gates, "My Message to the World at COP26," *GatesNotes* (blog), November 2, 2021,
https://www.gatesnotes.com/Energy/My-message-to-the-world-at-COP26.

44. Sofia Lotto Persio, "Billionaire Bill Gates Calls for Green Industrial Revolution to Stop Climate Change," *Forbes*, November 2, 2021, https://www.forbes.com/sites/sofialottopersio
/2021/11/02/billionaire-bill-gates-calls-for-green-industrial-revolution-to-stop-climate
-change.

45. Rathi and Dlouhy, "Bill Gates."

46. Ibid.
47. "Eight Awardees Announced as Part of $10 Million Data.org Inclusive Growth and Recovery Challenge," press release, Rockefeller Foundation, January 19, 2021, https://www.rockefellerfoundation.org/news/eight-awardees-announced-as-part-of-10-million-data-org-inclusive-growth-and-recovery-challenge.
48. "TerraPower Participates in Two Teams Awarded ARPA-E MEITNER Funding," Announcements, TerraPower, June 8, 2018, https://www.terrapower.com/terrapower-participates-in-two-teams-awarded-arpa-e-meitner-funding; "US Department of Energy Announces $160 Million in First Awards under Advanced Reactor Demonstration Program," Office of Nuclear Energy, October 13, 2020, https://www.energy.gov/ne/articles/us-department-energy-announces-160-million-first-awards-under-advanced-reactor.
49. Catherine Clifford, "Bill Gates' TerraPower Aims to Build Its First Advanced Nuclear Reactor in a Coal Town in Wyoming," CNBC, November 17, 2021, https://www.cnbc.com/2021/11/17/bill-gates-terrapower-builds-its-first-nuclear-reactor-in-a-coal-town.html.
50. Aimee Picchi, "Warren Buffett Resigns from Gates Foundation, Donates $4.1 Billion," CBS News, updated June 23, 2021, https://www.cbsnews.com/news/warren-buffett-resigns-gates-foundation; Aimee Picchi, "Richest 25 Americans Have a 'True Tax Rate' of Almost Nothing: Report," CBS News, updated June 9, 2021, https://www.cbsnews.com/news/income-tax-wealthy-bezos-buffett.
51. Chris Levesque, "Beyond Pledges: Bringing Advanced Nuclear from Research to Reality," TerraPower, November 17, 2022, https://www.terrapower.com/beyond-pledges-bringing-advanced-nuclear-from-research-to-reality; "Special Presidential Envoy for Climate Kerry and Ukraine Minister of Energy Galushchenko Announce Cooperation on a Clean Fuels from Small Modular Reactors Pilot, COP27 Climate Conference," US Department of State, press release, November 12, 2022, https://www.state.gov/special-presidential-envoy-for-climate-kerry-and-ukraine-minister-of-energy-galushchenko-announce-cooperation-on-a-clean-fuels-from-small-modular-reactors-pilot-cop27-climate-conference.
52. Jesse Eisinger, Jeff Ernsthausen, and Paul Kiel, "The Secret IRS Files: Trove of Never-Before-Seen Records Reveal How the Wealthiest Avoid Income Tax," ProPublica, June 8, 2021, https://www.propublica.org/article/the-secret-irs-files-trove-of-never-before-seen-records-reveal-how-the-wealthiest-avoid-income-tax.
53. "TerraPower Announces $750 Million Secured in Fundraise," Announcements, TerraPower, August 15, 2022, https://www.terrapower.com/fundraise; Ella Nilsen, "Clean Energy Package Would Be Biggest Legislative Climate Investment in US History," CNN, updated July 28, 2022, https://edition.cnn.com/2022/07/28/politics/climate-deal-joe-manchin/index.html.
54. United States Securities and Exchange Commission, "Republic Services, Inc." Schedule 13G, August 3, 2007, https://investor.republicservices.com/node/6381/html; City News Service, "Republic Services Sued for Charging Customers during Labor Strike," Fox 5 San Diego, updated January 27, 2022, https://fox5sandiego.com/news/business/republic-services-sued-for-charging-customers-during-labor-strike.
55. "Republic Services Reduces Waste with CNG Vehicles," Case Studies, Alternative Fuels Data Center, August 13, 2018, https://afdc.energy.gov/case/1425.
56. "National Clean Fleets Partnership," About, US Department of Energy, on Internet Archive, accessed May 16, 2022, https://web.archive.org/web/20110625054139/http://www1.eere.energy.gov/cleancities/national_partnership.html.
57. Paul Ausick, "Microsoft's Gates, Wind Icon Pickens Speak Out on Energy," InvestorPlace, August 25, 2010, https://investorplace.com/2010/08/microsofts-gates-wind-icon-pickens-speak-out-on-energy.

58. Nicole Raz, "Small-Business Owner Files Lawsuit against Republic Services," *Las Vegas Review-Journal*, March 5, 2018, https://www.reviewjournal.com/business/small-busi ness-owner-files-lawsuit-against-republic-services; Cole Rosengren, "Republic Services Sued by New Jersey County over Recycling Contamination Standards," Waste Dive, August 27, 2019, https://www.wastedive.com/news/republic-services-new-jersey-county -recycling-contamination-lawsuit/561704.

59. Keith Johnson, "Bill Gates Goes for Algae, Invests in Biofuel Maker Sapphire Energy," *Wall Street Journal*, September 17, 2008, https://www.wsj.com/articles/BL-EB-1900.

60. "Energy Department Announces up to $8 Million to Enable Breakthroughs in Algae -Based Biofuels," Office of Energy Efficiency and Renewable Energy, July 11, 2017, https:// www.energy.gov/eere/articles/energy-department-announces-8-million-enable -breakthroughs-algae-based-biofuels.

61. Eric Wesoff, "Hard Lessons from the Great Algae Biofuel Bubble," Greentech Media, April 19, 2017, https://www.greentechmedia.com/articles/read/lessons-from-the-great-algae -biofuel-bubble.

62. John Aidan Byrne, "The NYC Billionaires Who Got Richer during the COVID-19 Pandemic," *New York Post*, January 2, 2021, https://nypost.com/2021/01/02/the-nyc-billion aires-who-got-richer-amid-covid-19-pandemic.

63. Sebastien Malo, "Michael Bloomberg to Spend $500 Million to Close Coal Plants," Reuters, June 7, 2019, https://www.reuters.com/article/us-climate-change-coal-usa/michael -bloomberg-to-spend-500-million-to-close-coal-plants-idUSKCN1T82I5.

64. Lee Fang, "Bloomberg's Investment Portfolio Includes Bets on Private Equity, Fracking," *Intercept*, February 24, 2020, https://theintercept.com/2020/02/24/mike-bloomberg -investment-portfolio; Maggie Astor, "Michael Bloomberg Plans a $242 Million Investment in Clean Energy," *New York Times*, May 17, 2022, https://www.nytimes.com/2022 /05/17/climate/michael-bloomberg-climate-coal.html.

65. Umair Irfan, "Mike Bloomberg Says He Has the Best Record on Climate Change. Does He?," *Vox*, February 25, 2020, https://www.vox.com/2020/2/25/21145525/bloomberg -2020-debate-climate-change-beyond-coal.

66. Dave Levinthal, "How Mike Bloomberg Hid His Billions from You," Center for Public Integrity, March 4, 2020, https://publicintegrity.org/politics/mike-bloomberg-billions -disclosure-president.

67. Fang, "Bloomberg's Investment Portfolio."

68. Ibid.; Lisa Friedman, "Michael Bloomberg Promises $500 Million to Help End Coal," *New York Times*, June 7, 2019, https://www.nytimes.com/2019/06/06/climate/bloomberg -climate-pledge-coal.html.

69. James Lindsay, "Three Terms Communists Redefined to Subvert Society," Articles, New Discourses, September 1, 2022, https://newdiscourses.com/2022/09/three-terms-com munists-redefined-to-subvert-society; "Soros Justice Fellowships," Grants and Fellowships, Open Society Foundations, accessed May 31, 2022, https://www.opensocietyfoun dations.org/grants/soros-justice-fellowships.

70. George Soros, *The Alchemy of Finance* (Hoboken: John Wiley & Sons, 1994); George Soros, *Open Society: Reforming Global Capitalism* (New York: PublicAffairs, 2000); George Soros, *The Crash of 2008 and What it Means: The New Paradigm for Financial Markets* (New York: PublicAffairs, 2008).

71. Peter Schweizer, *Secret Empires: How the American Political Class Hides Corruption and Enriches Family and Friends* (New York: HarperCollins, 2018), 176–80; Thomas Landstreet, "Soros Doesn't Like Coal Stocks; He Likes Money," *Forbes*, August 28, 2015, https:// www.forbes.com/sites/thomaslandstreet/2015/08/28/soros-doesnt-like-coal-stocks -he-likes-money/?sh=457d9bae1f4d.

72. Mark Scott, "George Soros to Invest $1 Billion in Green Energy," *Bloomberg*, October 11, 2009, https://www.bloomberg.com/news/articles/2009-10-11/george-soros-to-invest-1-billion-in-green-energy.

73. Arathy S. Nair and Narottam Medhora, "SolarCity Raises $403 Million in George Soros Hedge Fund–Advised Deal," *Australian Financial Review*, updated September 13, 2016, https://www.afr.com/companies/energy/solarcity-raises-403-million-george-soros-hedge-fundadvised-deal-20160913-greu8b.

74. Eliza Haverstock, "Elon Musk, Nearing $300 Billion Fortune, Is the Richest Person in History," *Forbes*, October 26, 2021, https://www.forbes.com/sites/elizahaverstock/2021/10/26/elon-musk-nearing-300-billion-fortune-is-the-richest-person-in-history.

75. Schweizer, *Secret Empires*, 178.

76. Ibid.; Katherine Burton, "George Soros Commits $1 Billion to Start Global University to Fight Climate Change," *Financial Post*, January 23, 2020, https://financialpost.com/personal-finance/high-net-worth/george-soros-commits-1-billion-to-start-global-university-to-fight-climate-change.

77. Burton, "George Soros Commits $1 Billion"; Vibeka Mair, "George Soros Calls on Investors to Help Achieve Sustainable Development Goals," Responsible Investor, September 1, 2016, https://www.responsible-investor.com/george-soros-sdg.

78. Benzinga, "George Soros' Investment Firm Takes Position in Tesla, Bulks up on These Tech Stocks," *Business Insider*, August 13, 2022, https://markets.businessinsider.com/news/stocks/george-soros-investment-firm-takes-position-in-tesla-bulks-up-on-these-tech-stocks-in-q2-1031681088; "Tesla: The Biggest Winner from Joe Manchin's Inflation Reduction Act," Nasdaq, August 2, 2022, https://www.nasdaq.com/articles/tesla:-the-biggest-winner-from-joe-manchins-inflation-reduction-act.

79. Alexander Soros, "Great to see CA Governor Gavin Newsom in New York for the #Climate-Summit. He is doing a phenomenal job reducing carbon emissions in California!" Facebook, September 25, 2019, https://m.facebook.com/Alexandersorospublic/photos/great-to-see-ca-governor-gavin-newsom-in-new-york-for-the-climatesummit-he-is-do/1357005447795134; Matt Durot, "Here Are the Billionaires Backing California's Governor and His Opponent Caitlyn Jenner," *Forbes*, July 17, 2021, https://www.forbes.com/sites/mattdurot/2021/07/17/here-are-the-billionaires-backing-californias-governor-and-his-opponent-caitlyn-jenner/?sh=4824c2384d5f.

80. Coral Davenport, Lisa Friedman, and Brad Plumer, "California to Ban the Sale of New Gasoline Cars," *New York Times*, August 24, 2022, https://www.nytimes.com/2022/08/24/climate/california-gas-cars-emissions.html.

81. Khaleda Rahman, "Californians Told Not to Charge Electric Cars Days after Gas Car Sales Ban," *Newsweek*, August 31, 2022, https://www.newsweek.com/californians-told-not-charge-electric-cars-gas-car-sales-ban-1738398.

82. "Tesla Could Be One of the Big Winners in Biden's $2 Trillion Infrastructure Plan," *Barron's*, March 31, 2021, https://www.barrons.com/articles/tesla-could-be-one-of-the-big-winners-in-bidens-2-trillion-infrastructure-plan-51617194161.

83. Matt McFarland, "Elon Musk Didn't Want EV Tax Credits. Now Tesla Is Warming Up to Them," CNN, October 20, 2022, https://www.cnn.com/2022/10/20/business/tesla-tax-credit-evs/index.html.

84. McFarland, "Elon Musk Didn't Want EV Tax Credits."

85. Suzy Weiss, "Elon Musk's Die-Hard Fans Believe the Wacky Billionaire Can Do No Wrong," *New York Post*, July 8, 2020, https://nypost.com/2020/07/08/elon-musks-die-hard-fans-will-defend-him-to-the-death; "Who Has the Most Twitter Followers in 2022," *TweetBinder* (blog), Twitter, accessed May 16, 2022, https://www.tweetbinder.com/blog/top-twitter-accounts.

86. Samantha Masunaga, "A Quick Guide to Elon Musk's New Brain-Implant Company, Neuralink," *Los Angeles Times*, April 21, 2017, https://www.latimes.com/business/technology/la-fi-tn-elon-musk-neuralink-20170421-htmlstory.html; Max Chafkin, "Elon Musk Is Really Boring," *Bloomberg*, February 16, 2017, https://www.bloomberg.com/news/features/2017-02-16/elon-musk-is-really-boring; "Microsoft and OpenAI Extend Partnership," Microsoft (blog), January 23, 2023, https://blogs.microsoft.com/blog/2023/01/23/microsoftandopenaiextendpartnership.

87. Tami Brehse, "The 'Paypal Mafia' Formed in the Early 2000s, and Includes Everyone from Elon Musk to the Yelp Founders. Here's Where the Original Members Have Ended Up," *Business Insider*, on Internet Archive, November 24, 2019, https://web.archive.org/web/20220625091355/https://www.businessinsider.com/paypal-mafia-members-careers-elon-musk-peter-thiel-reid-hoffman-2019-11.

88. "Patent Pledge," Additional Resources, Tesla, accessed February 3, 2023, https://www.tesla.com/en_eu/legal/additional-resources.

89. Hillary Hoffower and Marguerite Ward, "Elon Musk Says Civilization Will Crumble If More People Don't Have More Children—and His Comments Shine a Light on a Heated Demographic Debate," *Business Insider*, December 7, 2021, https://www.businessinsider.com/elon-musk-pandemic-baby-bust-birth-rate-harmful-civilization-demographics-2021-12.

90. George Soros, "The AI Threat to Open Societies," Project Syndicate, January 24, 2019, https://www.project-syndicate.org/onpoint/the-ai-threat-to-open-societies-by-george-soros-2019-01.

91. John Thornhill, "The March of the Technocrats," *Financial Times*, February 19, 2018, https://www.ft.com/content/df695f10-154d-11e8-9376-4a6390addb44; Joseph C. Keating Jr. and Scott Haldeman, "Joshua N. Haldeman, DC: The Canadian Years, 1926–1950," *Journal of the Canadian Chiropractic Association* 39, no. 3 (1995): 172–86, https://www.ncbi.nlm.nih.gov/pmc/articles/PMC2485067/pdf/jcca00035-0046.pdf.

92. Keating Jr. and Haldeman, "Joshua N. Haldeman, DC."

93. John Authers, "Science Fiction and Grandfather's Views Shaped Musk, Historian Says," *BusinessLIVE*, November 1, 2021, https://www.businesslive.co.za/bd/world/2021-11-01-science-fiction-and-grandfathers-views-shaped-musk-historian-says.

94. "Technocracy Leader Charged at Regina," *Ottawa Journal*, October 14, 1940, https://www.newspapers.com/clip/14043096/dr-joshua-n-haldeman-regina; Thornhill, "The March of the Technocrats."

95. Neal E. Boudette, "Tesla Shines during the Pandemic as Other Automakers Struggle," *New York Times*, July 2, 2020, https://www.nytimes.com/2020/07/02/business/tesla-sales-second-quarter.html; "Elon Musk," Profile, *Forbes*, accessed on May 1, 2022, https://www.forbes.com/profile/elon-musk/?sh=22dc957a7999.

96. Brian Sozzi, "Biden's Electric Vehicle Ambitions May Send Tesla Stock Skyrocketing to $1,300: Analyst," *Yahoo! Finance*, April 5, 2021, https://news.yahoo.com/bidens-electric-vehicle-ambitions-may-send-tesla-stock-skyrocketing-to-1300-analyst-165650966.html.

97. Boudette, "Tesla Shines."

98. Eric Walz, "Tesla Plans to Start Work on a New Plant in China to Double Its Production Capacity," FutureCar, April 3, 2022, https://www.futurecar.com/5228/Tesla-Plans-to-Start-Work-on-a-New-Plant-in-China-to-Double-its-Production-Capacity; Peter Schweizer, *Red-Handed: How American Elites Get Rich Helping China Win* (New York: HarperCollins, 2022), 110–13.

99. Lachlan Markay, "Political Clout Pays Off Big for Elon Musk's SpaceX," *Washington Free Beacon*, August 27, 2014, https://freebeacon.com/politics/political-clout-pays-off-big-for-elon-musks-spacex.

100. Anna Palmer, Jake Sherman, and John Brenahan, "House of McCarthy," *Politico*, updated June 15, 2014, https://www.politico.com/story/2014/06/kevin-mccarthy-eric-cantor-107805.
101. Catherine Clifford, "Elon Musk: 'My Top Recommendation' for Reducing Greenhouse Gas Emissions Is a Carbon Tax," CNBC, February 12, 2021, https://www.cnbc.com/2021/02/12/elon-musk-reducing-greenhouse-gas-emissions-with-a-carbon-tax.html.
102. Brian Sozzi, "Tesla Stock Is 40% Undervalued after Inflation Reduction Act Signing, Analyst Argues," *Yahoo! Finance*, August 22, 2022, https://finance.yahoo.com/news/tesla-stock-inflation-reduction-act-significance-155640843.html.
103. Callie Patteson, "Buttigieg Slammed for Urging Electric Car Buying to Counter Gas Prices," *New York Post*, November 29, 2021, https://nypost.com/2021/11/29/buttigieg-slammed-for-urging-electric-car-buying-to-counter-gas-prices.
104. "Rick Scott Blasts Pete Buttigieg's 'Out of Touch' Push for Electric Vehicles: Americans 'Can't Afford It,'" Fox News, July 20, 2022, https://www.foxnews.com/media/rick-scott-blasts-pete-buttigieg-touch-push-electric-vehicles-americans-afford.
105. "Peter Paul Montgomery Buttigieg," Senate Commerce Committee Nominee Questionnaire, 117th Cong., accessed May 31, 2022, https://www.commerce.senate.gov/services/files/C9283286-F6C9-4572-8930-69CE2A8FCE18; Michela Tindera, "How Pete Buttigieg Earned More Than $800,000 in 2019 and 2020," *Forbes*, January 17, 2021, https://www.forbes.com/sites/michelatindera/2021/01/17/how-pete-buttigieg-earned-more-than-800000-in-2019-and-2020.
106. Phil LeBeau, "GM's Electric Volt: Is Hype Getting Out of Hand?," CNBC, updated September 13, 2013, https://www.cnbc.com/2008/08/15/gms-electric-volt-is-hype-getting-out-of-hand.html.
107. Ibid.; Associated Press, "Granholm Raves about Chevrolet Volt after Circling Capitol with Husband," *Michigan Local News*, September 14, 2010, https://www.mlive.com/auto/2010/09/granholm_raves_about_chevrolet.html.
108. "Chevrolet Volt Wins Gold Medal in 2011 Edison Awards," Chevrolet, April 6, 2011, https://media.chevrolet.com/media/us/en/chevrolet/home.detail.html/content/Pages/news/us/en/2011/Apr/0407_edison.html; Chris Isidore and Peter Valdes-Dapena, "Chevy Volt Wins Green Car of the Year for Second Time," CNN, November 19, 2015, https://money.cnn.com/2015/11/19/autos/chevy-volt-green-car-of-the-year/index.html.
109. Chuck Squatriglia, "It's Official: Chevrolet Volt Will Cost $41,000," *Wired*, July 27, 2010, https://www.wired.com/2010/07/its-official-chevrolet-volt-will-cost-41000; Lindsay Brooke, "For the Volt, How's Life after 40 (Miles)?," *New York Times*, November 19, 2009, https://www.nytimes.com/2009/11/22/automobiles/autoreviews/22-chevy-volt.html; "Feds Investigate Electric and Hybrid Vehicle Batteries after 5 Recalls," MoneyWatch, CBS News, April 5, 2022, https://www.cbsnews.com/news/national-highway-traffic-safety-investigation-vehicle-batteries-recalls.
110. "GM Recalls All Chevy Bolts due to Fire Risk, Says Owners Should Park Outside and Limit Charging," CBS News, August 23, 2021, https://www.cbsnews.com/news/chevy-bolt-recall-gm-fire-risk; Faiz Siddiqui, "GM Heralded This Plant as a Model for Its Electric Car Future. Then Its Batteries Started Exploding," *Washington Post*, January 7, 2022, https://www.washingtonpost.com/technology/2021/12/30/chevy-bolt-gm.
111. "President Biden Participates in a Virtual Tour of the Proterra Electric Battery Facility," posted by The White House, April 20, 2021, YouTube video, 22:48, https://www.youtube.com/watch?v=x-lCHaPSW7s; Michael Chamberlain, Correspondent, Letter to Teri L. Donaldson and Jocelyn Richards, Request for Investigation into Potential Ethics Violations by Secretary of Energy Jennifer Granholm, November 12, 2021, https://freebeacon.com/wp-content/uploads/2021/11/Granholm-Proterra-Ethics-Complaint.pdf.

112. Matthew Foldi, "Energy Secretary Granholm Violates Ethics Pledge to Boost Proterra, Watchdog Claims," *Washington Free Beacon*, November 12, 2021, https://freebeacon.com /biden-administration/energy-secretary-granholm-violates-ethics-pledge-to-boost -proterra-watchdog-claims.

113. "Client Profile: Proterra," OpenSecrets, 2021, accessed February 3, 2023, https://www .opensecrets.org/federal-lobbying/clients/summary?cycle=2021&id=D000065013; "Client Profile: Proterra," OpenSecrets, 2022, accessed February 3, 2023, https://www.opense crets.org/federal-lobbying/clients/summary?cycle=2022&id=D000065013; Ian Duncan, "Electric Buses Get Billions in Federal Aid. A Top Maker Just Went Bankrupt," *Washington Post*, August 12, 2023, https://www.washingtonpost.com/transportation/2023/08/12 /proterra-bankruptcy-electric-buses.

114. "Former CEO of Volkswagen AG Charged with Conspiracy and Wire Fraud in Diesel Emissions Scandal," Office of Public Affairs, United States Department of Justice, May 3, 2018, https://www.justice.gov/opa/pr/former-ceo-volkswagen-ag-charged-conspiracy-and -wire-fraud-diesel-emissions-scandal.

115. Dino Kurbegovic, "Rivian Stock Surges after Amazon Announces EV Roll Out across US," Finbold, July 22, 2022, https://finbold.com/rivian-stock-surges-after-amazon-announces -ev-roll-out-across-u-s; Steve Hanley, "Amazon Thumbs Its Nose at Sustainability, Orders 20,000 Conventional Mercedes Sprinter Vans," CleanTechnica, September 10, 2018, https://cleantechnica.com/2018/09/10/amazon-thumbs-its-nose-at-sustainability -orders-20000-conventional-mercedes-sprinter-vans.

116. Sissi Cao, "George Soros Is Buying Up Cheap Electric Vehicle Shares, but How Long Will He Own Them?," *Observer*, May 25, 2022, https://observer.com/2022/05/george-soros -invest-electric-vehicle-stock-rivian-nio-lucid.

117. John Dorfman, "Why George Soros Is Wrong about Rivian," *Forbes*, February 22, 2022, https://www.forbes.com/sites/johndorfman/2022/02/22/why-george-soros-is-wrong -about-rivian; Sissi Cao, "George Soros Is Buying Up Cheap Electric Vehicle Shares, but How Long Will He Own Them?" *Observer*, May 25, 2022, https://observer.com/2022/05 /george-soros-invest-electric-vehicle-stock-rivian-nio-lucid; Nathan Bomey, "The Next Tesla? Lucid Motors Plans Powerful Electric Car," *USA Today*, April 13, 2017, https://www .usatoday.com/story/money/cars/2017/04/13/lucid-motors-new-york-auto-show/100410446.

118. Luc Olinga, "Billionaire George Soros Continues to Sell Rivian," *TheStreet*, February 15, 2023, https://www.thestreet.com/technology/billionaire-george-soros-continues-to-sell -rivian; Cao, "George Soros Is Buying Up Cheap Electric Vehicle Shares, but How Long Will He Own Them?"

119. Eric Miller, "California Gov. Newsom's Spending Plan Includes $10B for EVs," *Transport Topics*, January 12, 2022, https://www.ttnews.com/articles/california-gov-newsoms -spending-plan-includes-10b-evs.

120. Rahman, "Californians Told Not to Charge Electric Cars Days after Gas Car Sales Ban."

121. Gavin Newsom (@GavinNewsom), "CA is experiencing an unprecedented heatwave. . . ." Twitter, September 6, 2022, https://twitter.com/GavinNewsom/status/15672465278775 17312; Natalie O'Neill and Marjorie Hernandez, "Not Cool! Gavin Newsom Slammed for AC 'Double Standard' amid Heatwave," *New York Post*, September 7, 2022, https://nypost .com/2022/09/07/gavin-newsom-slammed-for-ac-double-standard-amid-heatwave.

122. Matt Dougherty, "'Woke Up Sweating': Some Texans Shocked to Find Their Smart Thermostats Were Raised Remotely," KHOU 11, updated June 18, 2021, https://www.khou .com/article/news/local/texas/remote-thermostat-adjustment-texas-energy-shortage /285-5acf2bc5-54b7-4160-bffe-1f9a5ef4362a.

123. Andrew Miller, "Colorado Utility Company Locks 22,000 Thermostats in 90 Degree Weather due to 'Energy Emergency,'" Fox Business, September 2, 2022, https://www.foxbusi

ness.com/politics/colorado-utility-company-locks-22000-thermostats-in-90-degree
-weather-due-energy-emergency.

124. Ryan Curry, "NV Energy Offers Free Smart Thermostats; Can Control Your Home Temperature Remotely," KRNV, April 26, 2018, https://mynews4.com/news/local/nv-energy-offers-free-smart-thermostats-to-customers-but-will-increase-home-temperature; Jerod Macdonald-Evoy, "SRP Wants You to Have a Smart Thermostat. Here Are the Risks," *Arizona Mirror*, June 13, 2019, https://www.azmirror.com/2019/06/13/srp-wants-you-to-have-a-smart-thermostat-here-are-the-risks.

125. Macdonald-Evoy, "SRP Wants You."

126. Martina Igini, "Could the Bill Gates Smart City Lead the Way for Other Cities to Follow?," Earth.org, February 9, 2022, https://earth.org/bill-gates-smart-city.

127. "Bill Gates Bought Land in Arizona to Build Tech City," *BUILDER Online*, November 13, 2017, video, 01:50, https://www.builderonline.com/videos/kpnx-on-bill-gates-smart-city-plan-outside-phoenix_o.

128. Sophie Weiner, "Bill Gates Is Buying Land in Arizona to Build a 'Smart City,'" *Popular Mechanics*, November 12, 2017, https://www.popularmechanics.com/technology/a29005/bill-gates-smart-city; Matthew Keegan, "In China, Smart Cities or Surveillance Cities?," *US News & World Report*, January 31, 2020, https://www.usnews.com/news/cities/articles/2020-01-31/are-chinas-smart-cities-really-surveillance-cities.

129. Klaus Schwab, *The Fourth Industrial Revolution* (Cologne: World Economic Forum, 2016), 22.

130. Emily Crane, "Amazon Shuts Down Customer's Smart Home Devices After Delivery Driver's False Racism Claim," *New York Post*, June 15, 2023, https://nypost.com/2023/06/15/amazon-shuts-down-customers-smart-home-devices-over-false-racist-claim/; Annie Gaus, "What It's Like Working for Jeff Bezos and Amazon: Ring Exec," *TheStreet*, September 7, 2018, https://www.thestreet.com/technology/ring-ceo-explains-what-it-s-like-working-for-jeff-bezos-14705218.

Chapter Five: The War on Farmers

1. Bill Gates, *How to Avoid a Climate Disaster* (New York: Alfred A. Knopf, 2021), 115.

2. Vipal Monga, "Canada Urges Farmers to Cut Fertilizer Emissions, Prompting Backlash," *Wall Street Journal*, August 21, 2022, https://www.wsj.com/articles/canada-urges-farmers-to-cut-fertilizer-emissions-prompting-backlash-11661090581.

3. Ibid.

4. Isabeau van Halm, "The Dutch Nitrogen Crisis Shows What Happens When Policymakers Fail to Step Up," Energymonitor.ai, August 16, 2022, https://www.energymonitor.ai/policy/the-dutch-nitrogen-crisis-shows-what-happens-when-policymakers-fail-to-step-up.

5. Reuters, "Dutch Farmers Protest by Blocking Supermarket Distribution Centres," July 4, 2022, https://www.reuters.com/world/europe/dutch-farmers-protest-by-blocking-supermarket-distribution-centres-2022-07-04; Mike Corder, "Dutch PM Condemns Protests by Farmers at Minister's Home," AP News, June 29, 2022, https://apnews.com/article/netherlands-pollution-climate-and-environment-2e5901110047253d77b725362ad94134; Cagan Koc, "Dutch Farmers Bring Cows to Parliament to Protest Nitrogen Cuts," *Bloomberg*, June 28, 2022, https://www.bloomberg.com/news/articles/2022-06-28/dutch-farmers-bring-cows-to-parliament-to-protest-nitrogen-cuts.

6. Ciara Nugent, "Farmer Protests in the Netherlands Show Just How Messy the Climate Transition Will Be," *Time*, July 29, 2022, https://time.com/6201951/dutch-farmers-protests-climate-action.

7. Jen Skerritt, "Trudeau Spars with Farmers on Climate Plan Risking Grain Output," *Bloomberg*, July 27, 2022, https://www.bloomberg.com/news/articles/2022-07-27/trudeau-spars-with-farmers-on-climate-plan-cutting-fertilizer-grain-output.

8. Jack Power, "Irish Farmers 'Foisted' with Carbon Emissions Reductions, Protest Hears," *Irish Times*, November 21, 2021, https://www.irishtimes.com/news/ireland/irish-news/irish-farmers-foisted-with-carbon-emissions-reductions-protest-hears-1.4734762.

9. Rajiv J. Shah, "To Meet the SDGs by 2030, We Must Attract New Streams of Impact Capital," Rockefeller Foundation, March 12, 2019, https://www.rockefellerfoundation.org/blog/announcing-rockefeller-foundation-impact-investment-management-new-impact-investing-platform.

10. Ibid.

11. Alem Tedeneke, "World Economic Forum and UN Sign Strategic Partnership Framework," News Releases, World Economic Forum, June 13, 2019, https://www.WEForum.org/press/2019/06/world-economic-forum-and-un-sign-strategic-partnership-framework.

12. Zia Khan and John McArthur, "Rebuilding towards the Great Reset: Crisis, COVID-19, and the Sustainable Development Goals," Rockefeller Foundation, June 19, 2020, https://www.rockefellerfoundation.org/blog/rebuilding-towards-the-great-reset-crisis-covid-19-and-the-sustainable-development-goals.

13. "Building a Common Vision for Sustainable Food and Agriculture: Principles and Approaches," Food and Agriculture Organization of the United Nations, 2014, accessed July 1, 2022, https://www.fao.org/3/i3940e/i3940e.pdf.

14. Juergen Voegele, "Global Wheat Breeding Returns Billions in Benefits—but Stable Financing Remains Elusive," World Economic Forum, May 4, 2016, https://www.WEForum.org/agenda/2016/05/global-wheat-breeding-returns-billions-in-benefits-but-stable-financing-remains-elusive.

15. "How Patent Protection Can Secure the Future of Alt Meat," *Vegconomist*, February 7, 2022, https://vegconomist.com/politics-law/how-patent-protection-can-secure-the-future-of-alt-meat.

16. Albert J. Shmidl, Ammonium Sulfate Production, US Patent US2659659A, filed December 7, 1950, and issued November 17, 1953, https://patents.google.com/patent/US2659659A; Ellis Carleton, Cracking with Water Soluble Catalyst, US Patent US2288395A, filed August 12, 1938, and issued June 30, 1942, https://patents.google.com/patent/US2288395A.

17. Bart H. Meijer, "Chemical Maker DSM Sees Strong Demand for Methane-Reducing Cow Feed Additive," Reuters, September 30, 2019, https://www.reuters.com/article/us-climate-change-dsm/chemical-maker-dsm-sees-strong-demand-for-methane-reducing-cow-feed-additive-idUSKBN1WF1E8; Stephane Duval and Maik Kinderman, Use of Nitrooxy Organic Molecules in Feed for Reducing Methane Emission in Ruminants and/or to Improve Ruminant Performance, Worldwide Patent WO2012084629A1, filed December 20, 2011, 40, https://patents.google.com/patent/WO2012084629A1/en.

18. "Royal DSM," Partners, World Economic Forum, accessed July 1, 2022, https://www.WEForum.org/organizations/royal-dsm-nv.

19. Emma Cowan, "How Bayer Stands to Reinvent GMO with CRISPR and Monsanto Acquisition," *AFN*, September 19, 2016, https://agfundernews.com/how-bayer-stands-to-reinvent-gmo-with-crispr-and-monsanto-acquisition; Andrew Zaleski, "Why Bill Gates Is Betting on a Start-Up That Prints Synthetic DNA," CNBC, May 22, 2018, https://www.cnbc.com/2018/05/22/bill-gates-is-betting-on-this-synthetic-biology-start-up.html.

20. Peter Grant, "Media Mogul Turner Pays $11.6 Million for Florida Land," *Wall Street Journal*, February 9, 2000, https://www.wsj.com/articles/SB950049839692918373; Associated Press, "North Dakota AG Clears Farmland Purchase Tied to Bill Gates," *US News & World Report*, June 30, 2022, https://www.usnews.com/news/us/articles/2022-06-30/north-dakota-ag-clears-farmland-purchase-tied-to-bill-gates.

21. Bill Gates, "Future of Food," *GatesNotes* (blog), March 18, 2013, https://www.gatesnotes .com/About-Bill-Gates/Future-of-Food.

22. Justin Rowlatt, "IR8: The Miracle Rice Which Saved Millions of Lives," BBC News, December 1, 2016, https://www.bbc.com/news/world-asia-india-38156350; Claude Alvares, "The Great Gene Robbery," first published by *Illustrated Weekly of India*, March 23, 1986, accessed July 1, 2022, https://www.scribd.com/document/118909028/The-Great-Gene -Robbery-by-Claude-Alvares; Matthew Caire, "Sin Maíz, No Hay País: Corn in Mexico under Neoliberalism, 1940–2008" (master's thesis, Bowling Green State University, 2010), 45.

23. Caire, "Sin Maíz, No Hay País," 45.

24. "The Green Revolution: Norman Borlaug and the Race to Fight Global Hunger," *American Experience*, PBS, April 3, 2020, https://www.pbs.org/wgbh/americanexperience/features /green-revolution-norman-borlaug-race-to-fight-global-hunger; Viridiana Lázaro, "Mexico Banned GMOs. What Are the Next Steps?," Greenpeace, January 27, 2021, https:// www.greenpeace.org/international/story/46310/mexico-banned-gmos-next-steps; Barbara Shubinski, "The Rockefeller Foundation's Mexican Agriculture Program, 1943–1965," RE:Source, Rockefeller Archive Center, January 4, 2022, https://resource.rockarch.org /story/the-rockefeller-foundations-mexican-agriculture-program-1943-1965.

25. Doug McDonough, "Low Prices Prompt 1977 Farm Strike," *Plainview Herald*, December 12, 2009, https://www.myplainview.com/news/article/Low-prices-prompt-1977-farm-strike -8439933.php; Caire, "Sin Maíz, No Hay País"; Chris Bennett, "Tractorcade: How an Epic Convoy and Legendary Farmer Army Shook Washington, D.C.," *Farm Journal*, February 1, 2022, https://www.agweb.com/news/policy/politics/tractorcade-how-epic-convoy-and -legendary-farmer-army-shook-washington-dc.

26. Bennett, "Tractorcade"; McDonough, "Low Prices Prompt 1977 Farm Strike."

27. Caire, "Sin Maíz, No Hay País"; Andrew Moriarty, "Immigrant Farmworkers and America's Food Production: 5 Things to Know," FWD.us, September 14, 2022, https://www.fwd .us/news/immigrant-farmworkers-and-americas-food-production-5-things-to-know; "Farm Labor," USDA Economic Research Service, March 15, 2022, https://www.ers.usda .gov/topics/farm-economy/farm-labor.

28. Shubinski, "Rockefeller Foundation's Mexican Agriculture Program."

29. Michael Specter, "Seeds of Doubt," *New Yorker*, August 18, 2014, https://www.newyorker .com/magazine/2014/08/25/seeds-of-doubt.

30. Bill Gates, "Building Better Bananas," *GatesNotes* (blog), January 31, 2012, https://www .gatesnotes.com/development/building-better-bananas.

31. "Bill & Melinda Gates, Rockefeller Foundations Form Alliance to Help Spur 'Green Revolution' in Africa," Media Center, Bill & Melinda Gates Foundation, accessed July 1, 2022, https://www.gatesfoundation.org/ideas/media-center/press-releases/2006/09/founda tions-form-alliance-to-help-spur-green-revolution-in-africa.

32. "Alliance for a Green Revolution in Africa," Initiative, Rockefeller Foundation, accessed July 1, 2022, https://www.rockefellerfoundation.org/initiative/alliance-for-a-green-revo lution-in-africa; Ruchi Schroff, Carla Ramos Cortés, and Marion Bessol, "Bill Gates and His Fake Solutions to Climate Change," Navdanya International, accessed July 1, 2022, https://navdanyainternational.org/wp-content/uploads/2021/04/Bill-Gates-His-Fake -Solutions-to-Climate-Change.pdf.

33. "Our Partners," AGRA, accessed July 1, 2022, https://agra.org/our-partners/#private -sector-partners.

34. Schroff, Cortés, and Bessol, "Bill Gates and His Fake Solutions."

35. Erin Banco, Ashleigh Furlong, and Lennart Pfahler, "How Bill Gates and Partners Used Their Clout to Control the Global COVID Response—with Little Oversight," *Politico*, September 14, 2022, https://www.politico.com/news/2022/09/14/global-covid-pandemic -response-bill-gates-partners-00053969; Annalisa Merelli, "The WHO Has a Worrisome

Reliance on the Bill & Melinda Gates Foundation," Quartz, December 16, 2021, https://qz.com/2102889/the-who-is-too-dependent-on-gates-foundation-donations; Ben Riensche and Ajay Vir Jakhar, "Here's How We Can Use Agriculture to Fight Climate Change," World Economic Forum, September 20, 2019, https://www.weforum.org/agenda/2019/09/here-s-how-we-can-use-agriculture-to-fight-climate-change.

36. Tedeneke, "World Economic Forum and UN"; "Global Coalition Promises More Than $650 Million to Accelerate CGIAR Efforts to Help 300 Million Smallholder Farmers Adapt to Climate Change," CGIAR, September 23, 2019, https://www.cgiar.org/news-events/news/uncas-global-coalition-funds-cgiar.

37. "Global Coalition Promises More Than $650 Million."

38. "Bill & Melinda Gates Foundation Statement on Creation of Nonprofit Agricultural Research Institute," Media Center, Bill & Melinda Gates Foundation, January 21, 2020, https://www.gatesfoundation.org/ideas/media-center/press-releases/2020/01/gates-foundation-statement-on-creation-of-nonprofit-agricultural-research-institute.

39. "Overview and FAQ: Bill & Melinda Gates Agricultural Innovations," Bill & Melinda Gates Foundation, January 2020, accessed July 1, 2022, https://docs.gatesfoundation.org/Documents/GatesAgOne_OverviewandFAQ.pdf; "Joe Cornelius," Our Team, Feed the Future Innovation Lab for Crop Improvement, Cornell University, accessed July 1, 2022, https://ilci.cornell.edu/our-team/joe-cornelius.

40. "Qing Wang," Team Member, Gates Ag One, accessed July 1, 2022, https://www.gatesagone.org/news-updates/team-member/qing-wang.

41. "The Rockefeller Foundation Initiative: Disease Surveillance Networks," Rockefeller Foundation, 2013, accessed July 1, 2022, https://www.rockefellerfoundation.org/wp-content/uploads/Disease-Surveillance-Networks-Initiative.pdf; "Partners World Economic Forum," Research Program on Fish, CGIAR, accessed July 1, 2022, https://fish.cgiar.org/partner/world-economic-forum.

42. "Open Letter: 'One CGIAR' with Two Tiers of Influence?," IPES-Food, July 21, 2020, http://www.ipes-food.org/pages/OneGGIAR.

43. Chris Mooney, "Why the World Is Storing So Many Seeds in a 'Doomsday' Vault," Washington Post, April 15, 2016, https://www.washingtonpost.com/news/energy-environment/wp/2016/04/15/why-the-world-is-spending-half-a-billion-dollars-to-protect-humble-seeds.

44. Marie-Monique Robin, The World According to Monsanto: Pollution, Corruption, and the Control of Our Food Supply (New York: New Press, 2014), 309.

45. "Fertilizer: 2018 State of the Fertilizer Industry," Fertilizer Institute, accessed July 1, 2022, https://www.tfi.org/sites/default/files/tfi-stateoftheindustry-2018.pdf; Bill Gates, "Bill Gates: Here's My Plan to Improve Our World—and How You Can Help," Wired, November 12, 2013, https://www.wired.com/2013/11/bill-gates-wired-essay.

46. Gates, "Bill Gates."

47. John Vidal, "Why Is the Gates Foundation Investing in GM Giant Monsanto?," Poverty Matters Blog, Guardian, September 29, 2010, https://www.theguardian.com/global-development/poverty-matters/2010/sep/29/gates-foundation-gm-monsanto.

48. April Glaser, "McDonald's French Fries, Carrots, Onions: All of the Foods That Come from Bill Gates Farmland," NBC, updated June 9, 2021, https://www.nbcnews.com/tech/tech-news/mcdonald-s-french-fries-carrots-onions-all-foods-come-bill-n1270033.

49. Bill Gates and Rashida Jones, "Episode 04: Is It Too Late to Stop Climate Change?," December 7, 2020, in Bill Gates and Rashida Jones Ask Big Questions, podcast, MP3 audio, 50:22, https://www.gatesnotes.com/-/media/Files/Podcast/Bill%20Gates%20and%20Rashida%20Jones%20Ask%20Big%20Questions%20episode%2004%20transcript.pdf; Sarah Gordon, "Bill Gates and Monsanto Team Up to Fight World Hunger," Earth Eats (blog), Indiana Public Media, February 9, 2012, https://indianapublicmedia.org/eartheats/bill-gates-monsanto-team-world-hunger.php.

50. Ruth Bender, "How Bayer-Monsanto Became One of the Worst Corporate Deals—in 12 Charts," *Wall Street Journal*, August 28, 2019, https://www.wsj.com/articles/how-bayer-monsanto-became-one-of-the-worst-corporate-dealsin-12-charts-11567001577; Rex Weyler, "Monsanto: Busted," Greenpeace, May 3, 2019, https://www.greenpeace.org/international/story/21954/monsanto-busted.

51. Bayer, "Bayer and Ginkgo Bioworks Unveil Joint Venture, Joyn Bio, and Establish Operations in Boston and West Sacramento," Cision, March 20, 2018, https://www.prnewswire.com/news-releases/bayer-and-ginkgo-bioworks-unveil-joint-venture-joyn-bio-and-establish-operations-in-boston-and-west-sacramento-300616544.html.

52. Jason Kelly, "Ginkgo Expands Agricultural Biologicals Division, Closes Deal with Bayer," Ginkgo Bioworks, October 18, 2022, https://joynbio.com/about; John Cumbers, "Bill Gates–Backed Ginkgo Bioworks Has a New $40 Million Spinout Using Synthetic Biology to Clean Wastewater," *Forbes*, October 28, 2020, https://www.forbes.com/sites/johncumbers/2020/10/28/bill-gates-backed-ginkgo-bioworks-has-a-new-40-million-spin-out-using-synthetic-biology-to-clean-wastewater; "Urine as a Commercial Fertilizer? Bill & Melinda Gates Foundation," Bill & Melinda Gates Foundation, press release, accessed July 1, 2022, https://www.gatesfoundation.org/ideas/media-center/press-releases/2010/10/urine-as-a-commercial-fertilizer.

53. Bill Gates, "Reinvented Toilet Expo," Speeches, Bill & Melinda Gates Foundation, November 6, 2018, https://www.gatesfoundation.org/ideas/speeches/2018/11/reinvented-toilet-expo.

54. "The Fertilizer Institute: 2008 Annual Report," Fertilizer Institute, accessed July 1, 2022, https://www.tfi.org/sites/default/files/documents/2008_AnnualReport.pdf.

55. Fertilizer Institute Staff, "Increasing Interest in Fertilizers," *Fertilizer Focus* 37, no. 1 (January/February 2020), https://www.tfi.org/sites/default/files/fertilizer_focus_jan-feb_2020.pdf.

56. Evanto, "Final Report: Review of the African Green Revolution Forum 2010 Outcomes," Alliance for a Green Revolution in Africa, August 2012, accessed July 1, 2022, https://www.agrf.org/docs/AGRF-review-Final-Report_02-09-2012.pdf; "Accelerating Africa's Path to Prosperity: Growing Inclusive Economies and Jobs through Agriculture—Forum Report," African Green Revolution Forum 2017, accessed July 1, 2022, https://agrf.org/wp-content/uploads/2021/09/2017-AGRF-Report.pdf.

57. "Yara: The Fertiliser Giant Causing Climate Catastrophe," Corporate Watch, accessed May 12, 2023, https://corporatewatch.org/yara-the-fertiliser-giant-causing-climate-catastrophe/; "Yara International: This Fertilizer Giant Reeks of Corruption," Whistleblower Justice Network, accessed July 1, 2022, https://whistleblowerjustice.net/yara-international-this-fertilizer-giant-reeks-of-corruption; "Yara International," World Economic Forum, accessed May 12, 2023, https://www.weforum.org/organizations/yara-international-asa.

58. Office of the Spokesperson, "Launching the First Movers Coalition at the 2021 UN Climate Change Conference," US Department of State, November 4, 2021, https://www.state.gov/launching-the-first-movers-coalition-at-the-2021-un-climate-change-conference.

59. "Client Profile: YARA International 2016," OpenSecrets, accessed July 1, 2022, https://www.opensecrets.org/federal-lobbying/clients/summary?cycle=2016&id=D000091145; "ESG Investor Seminar," Yara International, December 7, 2020, https://www.yara.com/siteassets/investors/057-reports-and-presentations/capital-markets-day/2020-esg/esg-investor-seminar-2020-slides.pdf.

60. Zacks, "You'll Never Guess How Much Bayer and Monsanto Spend on Lobbying," Nasdaq, September 16, 2016, https://www.nasdaq.com/articles/youll-never-guess-how-much-bayer-and-monsanto-spend-lobbying-2016-09-16.

61. Keith Griffith, "Bill Gates Wins Legal Approval to Buy Huge Swath of North Dakota Farmland Worth $13.5M after Outcry from Residents Who Say They Are Being Exploited by the Ultra-Rich," *Daily Mail*, updated July 1, 2022, https://www.dailymail.co.uk/news/article

-10971639/Bill-Gates-wins-legal-approval-buy-huge-swath-North-Dakota-farmland
-worth-13-5M.html.

62. Ibid.

63. Glaser, "McDonald's French Fries, Carrots, Onions: All of the Foods That Come from Bill Gates Farmland."

64. Doug Ohlemeier, "UPDATED: Coggins and Stanley Farms Start Generation Farms," *Packer*, March 7, 2016, https://www.thepacker.com/news/industry/updated-coggins-and -stanley-farms-start-generation-farms.; Coral Beach, "Vidalia Growers Sell Operations to Bill Gates," *Packer*, on Internet Archive, October 17, 2014, https://web.archive.org/web /20150708232109/https://www.thepacker.com/fruit-vegetable-news/Vidalia-growers -sell-operations-to-Bill-Gates-279612682.html; "Bill Gates Is in Trouble over His Onions in Georgia," *Economic Times*, updated August 6, 2015, https://economictimes.indiatimes .com/news/international/business/bill-gates-is-in-trouble-over-his-onions-in-georgia /articleshow/48370968.cms.

65. Beach, "Vidalia Growers Sell Operations"; Ohlemeier, "Coggins and Stanley Farms Start Generation Farms"; Jack Ellis, "Bill Gates Tells Reddit Why He's Bought So Much Farmland," *AFN*, March 22, 2021, https://agfundernews.com/bill-gates-tells-reddit-why-hes -acquired-so-much-farmland.

66. Christopher Burbach, "Bill Gates' 20,000 Acres in Nebraska Help Make Him the Top Farmland Owner in the US," *Lincoln Journal Star*, updated September 21, 2021, https:// journalstar.com/agriculture/bill-gates-20-000-acres-in-nebraska-help-make-him-the -top-farmland-owner-in/article_ce5560f6-f14b-5a5a-86ae-f3fba47cf1f4.html; Kristen Mos brucker, "Bill and Melinda Gates Own 70,000 Acres of Louisiana Farmland; What Happens to It in Their Divorce?," *New Orleans Advocate*, May 4, 2021, https://www.nola .com/news/business/bill-and-melinda-gates-own-70-000-acres-of-louisiana-farmland -what-happens-to-it/article_68ff8874-acf1-11eb-b3b4-936cf2ca6ed5.html.

67. "100 Circle Farms," Meet Our Suppliers, McDonald's, accessed July 1, 2022, https://www .mcdonalds.com/us/en-us/about-our-food/meet-our-suppliers/100-circle-farms.html; Glaser, "McDonald's French Fries, Carrots, Onions: All of the Foods That Come from Bill Gates Farmland."

68. Lydia Mulvaney, "Bill Gates Invests in Clean Air-to-Nitrogen Fertilizer Startup," *Bloomberg*, April 30, 2020, https://www.bloomberg.com/news/articles/2020-04-30/bill -gates-invests-in-clean-air-to-nitrogen-fertilizer-startup; Jenny Splitter, "Pivot Bio Se cures $70M Investment for Nitrogen-Producing Microbes," *Forbes*, October 3, 2018, https://www.forbes.com/sites/jennysplitter/2018/10/03/pivot-bio-secures-70-million -investment-for-nitrogen-producing-microbes; Nick Estes, "Bill Gates Is the Biggest Private Owner of Farmland in the United States. Why?," *Guardian*, April 5, 2021, https:// www.theguardian.com/commentisfree/2021/apr/05/bill-gates-climate-crisis-farmland; Robin Wigglesworth, "Bill Gates Loves Trash," *Financial Times*, February 1, 2023, https:// www.ft.com/content/77e57e96-4eb6-4ab4-ba97-69d3a40269dc.

69. Bill Gates (@/thisisbillgates), "I'm Bill Gates, Co-chair of the Bill and Melinda Gates Foundation and Author of 'How to Avoid a Climate Disaster.' Ask Me Anything," Reddit, March 19, 2021, https://www.reddit.com/r/IAmA/comments/m8n4vt/comment/grid8pt.

70. Ibid.

71. Schroff, Cortés, and Bessol, "Bill Gates and His Fake Solutions."

72. Lynda Kiernan Global AgInvesting, "Bill Gates Purchases Washington Farmland," *Agri-View*, October 29, 2018, https://www.agupdate.com/agriview/briefs/crop/bill-gates-pur chases-washington-farmland/article_fa5be8e0-c575-5601-94dc-77541ed969b0.html; Darah Fuller, "Big Business Is Investing in Water Banks," Environment at 5280, February 13, 2022, https://environmentat5280.org/du-env-blog/big-business-is-investing-in-water-banks.

73. Christa Meland, "Bill Gates Gets OK to Up Stake in Ecolab to 25%," *Daily Developments* (blog), Twin Cities Business, on Internet Archive, May 8, 2012, https://web.archive.org /web/20160304093123/https://tcbmag.blogs.com/daily_developments/2012/05 /bill-gates-gets-ok-to-up-stake-in-ecolab-to-25.html; Ed Lin, "Bill Gates Buys $177 Million in Ecolab Stock," *Barron's*, March 12, 2018, https://www.barrons.com/articles/bill -gates-buys-177-million-in-ecolab-stock-1520874067.

74. "Impacting What Matters: 2021 Annual Report," Ecolab, accessed July 1, 2022, https:// www.ecolab.com/-/media/Ecolab/Ecolab-Home/Documents/DocumentLibrary/Re ports/Annual/2021-Ecolab-Annual-Report-pdf.pdf.

75. "Ecolab Bets on ESG," Ecolab, December 8, 2021, https://www.ecolab.com/news/2021/12 /ecolab-bets-on-esg; "2020 ESG Overview," Ecolab, accessed July 1, 2022, https://en-uk .ecolab.com/-/media/Widen/Sustainability/Corporate-Sustainability-Report/Ecolab -2020-ESG-Overview.pdf; Bill Dunbar, "EcoLab Pays $214K Penalty for Hazardous Waste, Pesticides Violations and 2019 Tacoma Tideflats Fire," US Environment Protection Agency, October 22, 2021, https://www.epa.gov/newsreleases/ecolab-pays-214k-penalty -hazardous-waste-pesticides-violations-and-2019-tacoma; "Client Profile: Ecolab Inc 2020," OpenSecrets, accessed July 1, 2022, https://www.opensecrets.org/federal-lobbying/cli ents/issues?cycle=2020&id=D000025625&spec=ENV&specific_issue=Environment+% 26; "Agriculture," Branches, Ecolab, accessed February 22, 2023, https://www.ecolab -engineering.de/en/branches/agriculture; "Ammonia and Fertilizer," Ecolab, accessed February 22, 2023, https://www.ecolab.com/about/industries-we-serve/chemical-pro cessing/ammonia-and-fertilizer; Wigglesworth, "Bill Gates Loves Trash."

76. Amber Vann, "Bill Gates Gobbling Up Florida Farmland," *Valdosta Daily Times*, October 22, 2014, https://www.valdostadailytimes.com/news/local_news/bill-gates-gobbling-up -florida-farmland/article_20e31caa-59f5-11e4-a96c-5717cc7b5da4.html; Dan Hilliard, "Gates' Investments Threaten Florida's Iconic Springs," *Gainesville Sun*, August 18, 2016, https://www.gainesville.com/story/opinion/columns/more-voices/2016/08/21/dan -hilliard-gates-investments-threaten-floridas-iconic-springs/25610719007.

77. Leading Harvest, "Leading Harvest Sets Universal Standard for Agriculture Sustainabil-ity," Cision PR Newswire, April 22, 2020, https://www.prnewswire.com/news-releases /leading-harvest-sets-universal-standard-for-agriculture-sustainability-301043571.html.

78. Eric O'Keefe, "Bill Gates Is about to Change the Way America Farms," *Successful Farming*, January 15, 2021, https://www.agriculture.com/farm-management/farm-land/bill-gates -is-about-to-change-the-way-amer-ca-farms; "Leading Harvest," Our Actions, Oak River Farms, accessed July 1, 2022, https://oakriverfarms.com/our-actions/#leading-harvest; "Our Standard," Leading Harvest, accessed July 1, 2022, https://www.leadingharvest.org /standard.

79. John Heilemann, "The Truth, the Whole Truth, and Nothing but the Truth," *Wired*, No-vember 1, 2000, https://www.wired.com/2000/11/microsoft-7; United States v. Microsoft Corp., 253 F.3d 34 (D.C. Cir. 2002), https://www.justice.gov/atr/competitive-processes -anticompetitive-practices-and-consumer-harm-software-industry-analysis.

80. Leading Harvest, accessed July 1, 2022, https://www.leadingharvest.org.

81. "Membership," Leading Harvest, accessed July 1, 2022, https://www.leadingharvest.org /membership; "Our Standard," Leading Harvest.

82. "Heifer International and IBM Work with Coffee and Cocoa Farmers in Honduras to In-crease Access to Data and Global Markets," IBM Newsroom, IBM, July 7, 2021, https:// newsroom.ibm.com/2021-07-07-Heifer-International-and-IBM-Work-with-Coffee-and -Cocoa-Farmers-in-Honduras-to-Increase-Access-to-Data-and-Global-Markets.

83. "Is Apeel Appealing?," Weston A. Price Foundation, October 27, 2018, https://www.westona price.org/health-topics/is-apeel-appealing; Jenny Du, email to Office of Food Additive Safety,

"Apeel Science GRAS Notice Submission for a Mixture of Monoacylglycerides Derived from Grape Seed," October 9, 2019, https://www.fda.gov/media/135999/download.

84. Gates, "Future of Food."

85. Andrew Martin and Andrew Pollack, "Monsanto Looks to Sell Dairy Hormone Business," *New York Times*, August 6, 2008, https://www.nytimes.com/2008/08/07/business/07bo vine.html.

86. "Publix Switches to Hormone-Free Private Label Milk," *Progressive Grocer*, April 30, 2007, https://progressivegrocer.com/publix-switches-hormone-free-private-label-milk; Mike Barris, "Lilly to Pay $300 Million for Dairy Hormone Business," *Wall Street Journal*, August 20, 2008, https://www.wsj.com/articles/SB121923768836656505.

87. Bethany McLean, "Profile in Persistence: In 1977 Steve Demos Had an Idea to Sell Soy-Based Foods to Health-Conscious Americans. Two Decades Later, It's Paying Off," CNN, May 1, 2001, https://money.cnn.com/magazines/fsb/fsb_archive/2001/05/01/302536/in dex.html.

88. "White Wave Acquired by Dean Foods," *Natural Products Insider*, May 8, 2002, https://www.naturalproductsinsider.com/specialty-nutrients/white-wave-acquired-dean -foods-0.

89. Jenny Eagle, "Danone $12.5bn WhiteWave Acquisition 'Comes as No Surprise' Say Industry Specialists," *DairyReporter*, updated July 7, 2016, https://www.dairyreporter.com /Article/2016/07/07/Danone-12.5bn-WhiteWave-acquisition-comes-as-no-surprise; Brooke DiPalma, "Danone's Silk Introduces 'Nextmilk' in a Plant-Based Play for Dairy Lovers," *Yahoo! Finance*, January 19, 2022, https://finance.yahoo.com/news/plant-based -milk-gets-an-upgrade-danones-silk-targets-dairy-lovers-150049930.html.

90. "Danone," Organizations, World Economic Forum, accessed February 22, 2023, https://www.weforum.org/organizations/danone; "Client Profile: Groupe Danone 2020," OpenSecrets, accessed February 22, 2023, https://www.opensecrets.org/federal-lobbying/cli ents/summary?cycle=2020&id=D000042446; WhiteWave Services Inc., Silk Nextmilk, US Trademark, serial no. 90529501, filed February 15, 2021, https://uspto.report/TM /90529501/APP20210218073338.

91. Rebecca Flint Marx, "The Omnivore's Disrupter," *New York*, January 31, 2014, https://ny mag.com/news/intelligencer/hampton-creek-eggs-2014-2; Allison Aubrey, "Why Bill Gates Is Investing in Chicken-less Eggs," National Public Radio, June 13, 2013, https://www.npr.org/sections/thesalt/2013/06/13/191029875/why-bill-gates-is-investing-in -chicken-less-eggs.

92. Monica Watrous, "What Happened to Hampton Creek?," Food Business News, April 4, 2018, https://www.foodbusinessnews.net/articles/11575-what-happened-to-hampton -creek.

93. Aditi Roy, "Bill Gates' Climate-Change Investment Firm Bets on Lab-Produced Breast Milk," CNBC, June 16, 2020, https://www.cnbc.com/2020/06/16/biomilq-raises-3point5 -million-from-bill-gates-investment-firm.html.

94. "IMGC Team—Michelle Egger," Our Team, IMGC International Milk Genomics Consortium, https://www.milkgenomics.org/team-member/michelle-egger; Roy, "Bill Gates' Climate-Change Investment Firm."

95. Nora Macaluso, "Gates' Investment in Startup Firm is Not Related to Baby Formula Shortage," FactCheck.org, May 18, 2022, https://www.factcheck.org/2022/05/gates-invest ment-in-startup-firm-is-not-related-to-baby-formula-shortage; Alexander Belderok, "The Rise of Alternative Proteins," Roland Berger, March 22, 2021, https://www.rolandberger .com/en/Insights/Publications/The-rise-of-alternative-proteins.html.

96. Kat Eschner, "Winston Churchill Imagined the Lab-Grown Hamburger," *Smithsonian*, December 1, 2017, https://www.smithsonianmag.com/smart-news/winston-churchill-ima gined-lab-grown-hamburger-180967349.

97. Chase Purdy, "The Idea for Lab-Grown Meat Was Born in a Prisoner-of-War Camp," *Quartz*, September 24, 2017, https://qz.com/1077183/the-idea-for-lab-grown-meat-was -born-in-a-prisoner-of-war-camp.

98. "World's First Lab-Grown Burger Is Eaten in London," BBC News, August 5, 2013, https:// www.bbc.com/news/science-environment-23576143.

99. Ibid.

100. Ariel Schwartz, "This Startup Is Making Real Meatballs in a Lab without Killing a Single Animal," *Business Insider*, November 15, 2016, https://www.businessinsider.com/mem phis-meats-lab-grown-meatballs-2016-11; "World's First Lab-Grown Burger," BBC News.

101. "Scaling Cell-Cultured Beef: Mosa Meat Completes US$85M Series B Investment Round," *FoodIngredientsFirst*, February 23, 2021, https://www.foodingredientsfirst.com/news /scaling-cell-cultured-beef-mosa-meat-completes-us85m-series-b-investment-round .html; Kate Kelland, "First Taste of Test-Tube Burger Declared 'Close to Meat,'" Reuters, August 6, 2013, https://www.reuters.com/article/us-science-meat-in-vitro-idUSBRE9740 PL20130806; "Annual Meeting of the New Champions 2015: Charting a New Course for Growth," World Economic Forum, September 2015, https://www3.weforum.org/docs /WEF_AMNC15_Report.pdf;"Leonardo DiCaprio & Mosa Meat," Mosa Meat, https://mo sameat.com/leonardodicaprio-mosa-meat.

102. Ricki Lewis, "Anatomy of an Impossible Burger," *PLOS*, May 16, 2019, https://dnascience .plos.org/2019/05/16/anatomy-of-an-impossible-burger; Robin Simsa, John Yuen, Andrew Stout, Natalie Rubio, Per Fogelstrand, and David L. Kaplan, "Extracellular Heme Pro- teins Influence Bovine Myosatellite Cell Proliferation and the Color of Cell-Based Meat," *Foods* 8, no. 10 (2019): 521, https://doi.org/10.3390/foods8100521; Jack Appiah Ofori and Yun-Hwa Peggy Hsieh, "The Use of Blood and Derived Products as Food Additives," *Food Additive*, 230–256, accessed at IntechOpen, https://doi.org/10.5772/32374; Lisa Lupo, "Sci- entists Find Myoglobin Improves Cultured Meat," *Quality Assurance & Food Safety*, De- cember 2, 2019, https://www.qualityassurancemag.com/article/scientists-find-myoglobin -improves-cultured-meat.

103. Jeff Bercovici, "Why Richard Branson and Bill Gates Are Betting Big on a Food Startup You've Never Heard Of," *Inc.*, October 26, 2017, https://www.inc.com/jeff-bercovici/mem phis-meats-richard-branson.html; Elle Perry, "Lab-Grown Memphis Meats Raise $17 Mil- lion in Seed Funding," *Memphis Business Journal*, August 23, 2017, https://www.bizjour nals.com/memphis/news/2017/08/23/lab-grown-memphis-meats-raise-17-million -in-seed.html.

104. Michael Pellman Rowland, "Memphis Meats Raises $161 Million in Funding, Aims to Bring Cell-Based Products to Consumers," *Forbes*, January 22, 2020, https://www.forbes .com/sites/michaelpellmanrowland/2020/01/22/memphis-meats-raises-161-million -series-b-funding-round-aims-to-bring-cell-based-products-to-consumers-for-the-first -time; Mitch, "Memphis Meats Rebrands as 'UPSIDE Foods' & Announces First Consumer Lab-Grown Chicken," LabGrownMeat.com, May 17, 2021, https://labgrownmeat.com /memphis-meats-rebrand-upside-foods; Nicholas Genovese, Danielle Nicole Desmet, and Eric Schulze, Methods for extending the replicative capacity of somatic cells during an ex vivo cultivation process, US Patent 20190024079A1, filed January 17, 2017, issued January 24, 2019, https://patents.google.com/patent/WO2017124100A1; "Patents Assigned to Memphis Meats, Inc.," Patents, Justia, accessed July 1, 2022, https://patents.justia.com /assignee/memphis-meats-inc.

105. Alex Bitter, "A Memphis Meats Cofounder Has Left the Lab-Grown Meat Company, Now Called Upside Foods, as Skepticism about the Entire Industry Grows," *Business Insider*, October 28, 2021, https://www.businessinsider.com/genovese-carswell-leave-lab-grown -meat-startup-upside-foods-2021-10.

106. Ibid.

107. "USDA and FDA Announce a Formal Agreement to Regulate Cell-Cultured Food Products from Cell Lines of Livestock and Poultry," US Department of Agriculture, press release, March 7, 2019, https://www.usda.gov/media/press-releases/2019/03/07/usda-and-fda -announce-formal-agreement-regulate-cell-cultured-food; "Global Cultured Meat Market Size Estimated to Reach USD 499.9 Million by 2030, With 16.2% CAGR: Statistics Report by Polaris Market Research," Cision PR Newswire, April 12, 2022, https://www .prnewswire.com/news-releases/global-cultured-meat-market-size-estimated-to-reach -usd-499-9-million-by-2030—with-16-2-cagr-statistics-report-by-polaris-market -research-301523708.html.

108. "Introducing the Technology Pioneers Cohort of 2018," World Economic Forum, accessed July 1, 2022, https://widgets.WEForum.org/techpioneers-2018/index.html; Lora Kolodny, "Modern Meadow Raises $10M to Grow Leather in Labs, Not from Livestock," *Wall Street Journal*, June 18, 2014, https://www.wsj.com/articles/BL-VCDB-14803.

109. Belderok, "Rise of Alternative Proteins."

110. Bill Gates, "Humans Are Using Up Earth's Biomass," *GatesNotes* (blog), March 26, 2013, https://www.gatesnotes.com/books/harvesting-the-biosphere; Bill Gates, "Talking Meat with Michael Pollan," *GatesNotes* (blog), March 18, 2013, https://www.gatesnotes.com /About-Bill-Gates/Future-of-Food-Michael-Pollan-Q-and-A; James Temple, "Bill Gates: Rich Nations Should Shift Entirely to Synthetic Beef," *MIT Technology Review*, February 14, 2021, https://www.technologyreview.com/2021/02/14/1018296/bill-gates-climate-change -beef-trees-microsoft.

111. Cameron Jenkins, "Bill Gates: Rich Nations Should Move to '100 Percent Synthetic Beef,'" *The Hill*, February 16, 2021, https://thehill.com/homenews/news/538991-bill-gates-rich -nations-should-move-to-100-percent-synthetic-beef.

112. Ibid.

113. United States Securities and Exchange Commission, Form S-1 (Amendment no. 1), Beyond Meat Inc. (Delaware: 2000); Jade Scipioni, "Beyond Meat CEO Hangs Posters with Critics' Negative Comments in His Office: 'You Have to Let It Fuel You,'" CNBC, updated May 20, 2021, https://www.cnbc.com/2021/04/27/beyond-meat-ceo-ethan-brown-on-letting-critics -energize-you.html.

114. Sissi Cao, "Bill Gates' Foundation Quietly Cashed Out Beyond Meat Stock before Its Epic Crash," *Observer*, December 3, 2019, https://observer.com/2019/12/bill-gates-foundation -sold-beyond-meat-stock-third-quarter-before-market-crash.

115. "Beyond Meat Share Price," Market Summary, Google Finance, accessed July 1, 2022, https://www.google.com/search?q=beyond+meat+share+price&oq=Beyond+meat+share+ price&aqs=chrome.0.0i131i433i512j0i512l9.3210j1j7.

116. Deena Shanker and Leslie Patton, "Taco Bell Abandoned Plan to Test Beyond Meat's Carne Asada," *Bloomberg*, December 10, 2021, https://www.bloomberg.com/news/articles/2021 -12-09/taco-bell-abandoned-plan-to-test-beyond-meat-s-carne-asada; Kathryn Hardi- son, "Beyond Meat Plans to Lay off 4% of Global Workforce," *Wall Street Journal*, August 4, 2022, https://www.wsj.com/articles/beyond-meat-plans-to-lay-off-4-of-global-work force-11659654564; Adam Kovac, "Fake Meat Fail? Beyond Meat Reels as Sales Slow and Stock Plummets, with an Analyst Saying It's 'Burning Through Cash' and May Go Bank- rupt as Partnerships with McDonald's and Taco Bell Don't Pan Out," *Daily Mail*, August 4, 2022, https://www.dailymail.co.uk/sciencetech/article-11081705/Fake-meat-fail-Meat -reels-sales-slow-stock-drops-partnerships-dont-pan-out.html.

117. Leslie Patton and Deena Shanker, "Faux Meat Falters at the Drive-Thru," *Bloomberg*, September 24, 2021, https://www.bloomberg.com/news/articles/2021-09-24/which-fast -food-has-fake-meat-not-many-serve-beyond-meat-impossible-foods; Leslie Patton and Deena Shanker, "Burger King Cuts Impossible Whopper Price on Slowing Sales," Bloomberg, January 22, 2020, https://www.bloomberg.com/news/articles/2020-01-22

/burger-king-cuts-impossible-whopper-price-as-sales-taper-off; Amelia Lucas, "An Impossible Foods Competitor is Going After One of Its Key Patents in an Ongoing Legal Battle," CNBC, April 20, 2022, https://www.cnbc.com/2022/04/20/impossible-foods-patent-at-risk-in-legal-battle-with-motif-foodworks.html.

118. Praveen Paramasivam, "Beyond Meat Sales Under Threat as Plant-Based Boom Withers," Reuters, August 3, 2022, https://www.reuters.com/business/retail-consumer/beyond-meat-sales-under-threat-plant-based-boom-withers-2022-08-03.

119. "Series C—Beyond Meat," Crunchbase, accessed July 1, 2022, https://www.crunchbase.com/funding_round/beyond-meat-series-c—def8ef4f; "Christopher Isaac 'Biz' Stone," Beyond Meat, accessed February 22, 2023, https://investors.beyondmeat.com/board-member/christopher-isaac-biz-stone; Clint Witchalls, "Can Faux Chicken—or Any Other Meat Substitute—Win Over Committed Carnivores," Independent, April 18, 2013, https://www.independent.co.uk/life-style/food-and-drink/features/can-faux-chicken-or-any-other-meat-substitute-win-over-committed-carnivores-8579182.html; "Beyond Meat Completes Series D Fundraising," Finsmes, July 29, 2014, https://www.finsmes.com/2014/07/beyond-meat-completes-series-d-financing.htm.

120. Series D—Beyond Meat," Crunchbase, accessed July 1, 2022, https://www.crunchbase.com/funding_round/beyond-meat-series-d—6834da1c; "Environmental, Social, and Governance Update July 2022," Lecture, Beyond Meat, https://investors.beyondmeat.com/static-files/6fcd4169-617f-4fe2-9b40-cdfd8de77be3; Lydia Mulvany, Deena Shanker, and Michael Hytha, "Beyond Meat Nearly Triples in First Day of Trading," Seattle Times, May 2, 2019, https://www.seattletimes.com/business/beyond-meat-doubles-in-market-debut-after-241-million-ipo.

121. "Method and Compositions for Consumables," Patents Assigned to Maraxi, Inc., Justia, July 12, 2013, https://patents.justia.com/assignee/maraxi-inc; "Series B—Impossible Foods," Crunchbase (website), July 17, 2013, accessed July 1, 2022, https://www.crunchbase.com/funding_round/impossible-foods-series-b—14784063; "Impossible Foods Closes a $75 Million Investment after Achieving Key Milestones," Business Wire, August 1, 2017, https://www.businesswire.com/news/home/20170801005659/en/Impossible-Foods-Closes-a-75-Million-Investment-After-Achieving-Key-Milestones.

122. "Impossible Foods Closes a $75 Million Investment," Business Wire; Rachel Fraser, Patrick O'Reilly Brown, Jessica Karr, Celeste Holz-Schietinger, and Elysia Cohn, Methods and compositions for affecting the flavor and aroma profile of consumables, US Patent 9700067B2, filed July 10, 2015, issued July 11, 2017, https://patents.google.com/patent/US9700067B2; Marija Vrljic, Sergey Solomatin, Rachel Fraser, Patrick O'Reilly Brown, Jessica Karr, Celeste Holz-Schietinger, Michael Eisen, and Ranjani Varadan, Methods and Compositions for Consumables, US Patent 10039306B2, filed July 10, 2015, issued August 7, 2018, https://patents.google.com/patent/US10039306B2.

123. Rebecca Spalding, "Ginkgo Bioworks Raises $350 Million Fund for Biotech Spinouts," Business Insider, October 9, 2019, https://www.businessinsider.com/gingko-bioworks-raises-350-million-fund-for-biotech-spinouts-2019-10; Tom Huddleston Jr., "This $1 Billion Start-up Backed by Bill Gates Prints New DNA—and Everyone from the DOD to Bayer Is On Board," CNBC, December 21, 2018, https://www.cnbc.com/2018/12/21/bill-gates-backed-start-up-ginkgo-bioworks-prints-synthetic-dna.html; Riley de León, "Bill Gates–Backed Ginkgo Bioworks Going Public via $15 Billion SPAC," CNBC, May 11, 2021, https://www.cnbc.com/2021/05/11/bill-gates-backed-ginkgo-bioworks-going-public-in-15-billion-spac-.html.

124. Catherine Shu, "Mark Zuckerberg and Bill Gates Join Forces to Invest in Clean Energy Technology," TechCrunch, November 29, 2015, https://techcrunch.com/2015/11/29/breakthrough-energy-coalition.

125. Amelia Lucas, "An Impossible Foods Competitor Is Going After One of Its Key Patents in an Ongoing Legal Battle," CNBC, April 20, 2022, https://www.nbcwashington.com/news

/business/money-report/impossible-foods-could-be-at-risk-of-losing-a-key-patent-in-legal-battle-with-motif-foodworks/3029793/; "Motif," Crunchbase, accessed July 1, 2022, https://www.crunchbase.com/organization/motif-ingredients; Motif FoodWorks, Inc. (@motiffoodworks), "Thank you to @BillGates for the mention in his recent interview with @guardian," Twitter, May 16, 2022, 11:31 a.m., https://twitter.com/motiffoodworks/status/1526253942610571264.

126. Louisa Burwood-Taylor, "Tiny Farms Raises Seed Round from a Zuckerberg as Cricket Farming Heats up—Exclusive," *AFN*, February 18, 2016, https://agfundernews.com/tiny-farms-raises-seed-round-from-a-zuckerberg-as-cricket-farming-heats-up5396.

127. Bob Woods, "Bezos, Gates Back Fake Meat and Dairy Made from Fungus as Next Big Alt-Protein," CNBC, updated July 6, 2021, https://www.cnbc.com/2021/07/03/bezos-gates-back-fungus-fake-meat-as-next-big-alt-protein-.html.

128. Kate Krader, "Fungus Born of Yellowstone Hot Spring Makes Menu at Le Bernardin," *Bloomberg*, July 19, 2022, https://www.bloomberg.com/news/articles/2022-07-19/natures-fynd-fy-a-fungus-from-a-hot-spring-is-now-served-at-le-bernardin.

129. Woods, "Bezos, Gates Back Fake Meat and Dairy."

130. Christopher Ingraham, "Maggots: A Taste of Food's Future," *Washington Post*, July 3, 2019, https://www.washingtonpost.com/business/2019/07/03/maggots-could-revolutionize-global-food-supply-heres-how.

131. Amanda Brown, "Canadian Food Companies Pushing Insect Ingredients into a Snack Near You," *Western Standard*, July 21, 2022, https://www.westernstandard.news/news/canadian-food-companies-pushing-insect-ingredients-into-a-snack-near-you/article_77a0763e-0904-11ed-ab25-c3d70dacc768.html. Arnold van Huis et al., "Edible Insects: Future Prospects for Food and Feed Security," Food and Agriculture Organization of the United Nations, 2013, https://www.fao.org/3/i3253e/i3253e.pdf.

132. Francesca Bacardi, "Anna Faris, Tituss Burgess, and James Corden Eat Gourmet Foods . . . Made with Bugs—Watch Now!" E! News, April 29, 2015, https://www.eonline.com/news/651482/anna-faris-tituss-burgess-and-james-corden-eat-gourmet-foods-made-with-bugs-watch-now.

133. "Nicole Kidman Eats Bugs: Secret Talent Theatre, Vanity Fair," posted by Vanity Fair, January 29, 2018, YouTube video, 01:51, https://www.youtube.com/watch?v=e3UqLAtdZO4.

134. Ibid., see comments section.

135. Tracey Furniss, "Angelina Jolie, Zac Efron, and Justin Timberlake Eat Bugs, and So Do 2 Billion Others—Which Celebrities Munch Crickets, Spiders and Locusts for Health and Protein?," *South China Morning Post*, July 20, 2020, https://www.scmp.com/magazines/style/celebrity/article/3093640/angelina-jolie-zac-efron-and-justin-timberlake-eat-bugs.

136. "Will You Be Eating Insects Soon?," posted by The Economist, January 25, 2022, YouTube video, 13:21, https://www.youtube.com/watch?v=O8-uCob-_XE; "Why You Will Be Eating Bugs Very Soon: James Rolin TEDxBozeman," posted by TEDx Talks, June 3, 2019, YouTube video, 07:01, https://www.youtube.com/watch?v=HTNMwAB9A_M; "Changing What We Eat Could Offset Years of Carbon Emissions | Ways to Change the World," posted by World Economic Forum, September 14, 2020, YouTube video, 01:48, https://www.youtube.com/watch?v=WCb8QkUOYvg; Sandee LaMotte, "The Food That Can Feed, and Maybe Save, the Planet: Bugs," CNN, October 25, 2019, https://www.cnn.com/2019/10/25/health/insects-feed-save-planet-wellness; Ingraham, "Maggots: A Taste of Food's Future."

137. Vivienne Walt, "With Backing from Hollywood, French Startup Ÿnsect Plans to Bring Edible Insects to America," *Fortune*, October 12, 2020, https://fortune.com/2020/10/12/robert-downey-jr-french-startup-ynsect-edible-insects.

138. The Late Show (@colbertlateshow), "@RobertDowneyJr Teaches us about insect protein," Twitter, February 7, 2021, 10:45 p.m., https://twitter.com/colbertlateshow/status/13586532 06713221123.

139. "Agtech Startup Ÿnsect Joins the World Economic Forum's Global Innovators Community," Ÿnsect, January 25, 2021, http://www.ynsect.com/en/agtech-startup-ynsect-joins -the-world-economic-forums-global-innovators-community; Antoine Hubert, "Why We Need to Give Insects the Role They Deserve in Our Food Systems," World Economic Forum, July 12, 2021, https://www.WEForum.org/agenda/2021/07/why-we-need-to-give -insects-the-role-they-deserve-in-our-food-systems.

140. "Agtech Startup Ÿnsect Joins the World Economic Forum's Global Innovators Community."

141. Andrea Lo, "Two Brothers Want to Revolutionize the Food Industry with Maggots," CNN, September 27, 2018, https://www.cnn.com/2018/09/27/business/agriprotein-fly-farming /index.html; Stefano Pozzebon, "This Bill Gates–Supported Startup Is about to Open the World's Largest Fly Farm in South Africa," *Business Insider*, February 16, 2015, https:// www.businessinsider.com/jason-drew-magmeal-farm-in-south-africa-2015-2.

142. "Black Soldier Fly (BSF) Larvae for Faecal Sludge Reduction—Research in South Africa (with the Company Agriprotein)," Forum, SuSanA, accessed July 1, 2022, https://forum .susana.org/147-production-of-insect-biomass-from-excreta-or-organic-waste/4430 -black-soldier-fly-bsf-larvae-for-faecal-sludge-reduction-research-in-south-africa-with -the-company-agriprotein; Pozzebon, "This Bill Gates–Supported Startup."

143. Brown, "Canadian Food Companies."

144. Ali Montag, "Here's What Dinner with Warren Buffet and Bill Gates Is Like, according to Their Omaha Waitress," CNBC, June 22, 2018, https://www.cnbc.com/2018/06/22/in side-dinner-with-warren-buffett-and-bill-gates-at-piccolo-in-omaha.html; Virginia Chamlee, "Grilling Tips from Mark Zuckerberg, Barbecue Nerd," *Eater*, October 10, 2016, https:// www.eater.com/2016/10/10/13227568/mark-zuckerberg-barbecue-nerd.

145. "The Strange Tale of Jeff Bezos and the Single Cow Burger," Brad Stone, accessed July 1, 2022, https://brad-stone.com/single-cow-burger.

146. "José Andrés Receives Surprise $100 Million Award from Jeff Bezos," Yahoo!, video, 00:37, https://www.yahoo.com/video/jos-andr-receives-surprise-100-170018551.html; "Las Vegas," Menus, The Bazaar by José Andrés, accessed July 1, 2022, https://www.thebazaar .com/las-vegas-menus.

147. Paramasivam, "Beyond Meat Sales Under Threat as Plant-Based Boom Withers."

Chapter Six: The Open Society Scheme

1. Rachel Ehrenfeld and Shawn Macomber, "George Soros: The 'God' Who Carries Around Some Dangerous Demons," *Los Angeles Times*, October 4, 2004, https://www.latimes .com/archives/la-xpm-2004-oct-04-oe-ehrenfeld4-story.html.

2. "Remarks Delivered at the 2022 World Economic Forum in Davos," George Soros, May 24, 2022, https://www.georgesoros.com/2022/05/24/remarks-delivered-at-the-2022-world -economic-forum-in-davos.

3. John Solomon and Seamus Bruner, *Fallout: Nuclear Bribes, Russian Spies, and the Washington Lies That Enriched the Clinton and Biden Dynasties* (New York: Post Hill Press, 2020), 176–85.

4. Jennifer Ablan, "Russia Bans George Soros Foundation as State Security 'Threat,'" Reuters, November 30, 2015, https://www.reuters.com/article/russia-soros/russia-bans-george -soros-foundation-as-state-security-threat-idUSL1N13P22Y20151130.

5. George Soros, "Opening the Balkans," Project Syndicate, July 5, 1999, https://www.pro ject-syndicate.org/commentary/opening-the-balkans; "Power Broker," *Forbes*, November 15, 1999, https://www.forbes.com/global/1999/1115/0223108a.html; George Soros, "How to Save Europe," Project Syndicate, May 29, 2018, https://www.project-syndicate.org/on point/how-to-save-europe-by-george-soros-2018-05.

6. Shaun Walker, "George Soros: 'Brexit Hurts Both Sides—My Money Was Used to Educate the British Public,'" *Guardian*, November 2, 2019, https://www.theguardian.com/busi ness/2019/nov/02/george-soros-brexit-hurts-both-sides-money-educate-british-public.

7. George Soros, "Toward a New World Order: The Future of NATO," GeorgeSoros.com, No- vember 1, 1993, https://www.georgesoros.com/1993/11/01/toward-a-new-world-order-the -future-of-nato; George Soros, "George Soros: How to Save the EU from the Euro Crisis— The Speech in Full," *Guardian*, April 9, 2013, https://www.theguardian.com/business /2013/apr/09/george-soros-save-eu-from-euro-crisis-speech.

8. Soros, "Toward a New World Order."

9. John Maszka, "Superpowers, Hyperpowers, and Uberpowers," *International Journal of Research in Humanities and Social Studies* 7, no. 10 (2020): 18–36, https://www.ijrhss.org /papers/v7-i10/3.pdf.

10. "Death to the New World Order," BBC News, October 5, 1998, http://news.bbc.co.uk/2/hi /special_report/1998/09/98/conspiracy_-_radio_5_live/185161.stm.

11. George Soros, "The Fight of Our Lives," Project Syndicate, May 24, 2022, https://www .project-syndicate.org/onpoint/davos-address-open-society-against-russia-china-by -george-soros-2022-05.

12. Brooke Singman, "Soros Calls China's Xi Jinping 'The Greatest Threat That Open Soci- eties Face Today,'" Fox Business, February 1, 2022, https://www.foxbusiness.com/pol itics/soros-china-xi-jinping-greatest-threat-open-societies-face.

13. Michael Steinberger, "George Soros Bet Big on Liberal Democracy. Now He Fears He Is Losing," *New York Times*, July 17, 2018, https://www.nytimes.com/2018/07/17/magazine /george-soros-democrat-open-society.html; Soros, "The Fight of Our Lives."

14. Soros, "The Fight of Our Lives."

15. "Racial Justice in the United States," Open Society Foundations, July 13, 2020, https:// www.opensocietyfoundations.org/newsroom/racial-justice-in-the-united-states.

16. "States of Change: Attitudes in Central and Eastern Europe 30 Years after the Fall of the Berlin Wall," Open Society Foundations, November 2019, accessed February 22, 2023, https://www.opensocietyfoundations.org/publications/states-of-change-attitudes-in -central-and-eastern-europe-30-years-after-the-fall-of-the-berlin-wall; Soros, "The Fight of Our Lives."

17. Ellen Chesler, "The Abortion Debate: Finding Common Ground," *Ideas for an Open Society* 1, no. 2 (May 2001): 1–8, https://www.opensocietyfoundations.org/uploads/3a5dec8e -d474-422d-805d-f0aa0a28f5ae/ideas_reproductive_health.pdf; "Soros Foundations Net- work Report 2007," Open Society Institute, 2008, accessed February 22, 2023, https:// www.opensocietyfoundations.org/uploads/3d4ebf2b-918b-4621-a226-dc7a886d8faf/a _complete_4.pdf.

18. "Who Are the Biggest Donors?," Elections Overview, OpenSecrets, accessed August 16, 2022, https://www.opensecrets.org/elections-overview/biggest-donors?cycle=2022; Ga- briel Benedetti, "Ranking the Most Influential Democratic Donors in the 2020 Race."

19. Soros, "Toward a New World Order."

20. James P. Pinkerton, "Strobe Talbott Leads toward One World," *Los Angeles Times*, June 8, 1999, https://www.latimes.com/archives/la-xpm-1999-jun-08-me-45260-story.html.

21. "A Global Alliance for Open Society," 2001 Report, Soros Foundations Network, accessed August 16, 2022, https://www.opensocietyfoundations.org/uploads/0025bb89-fc0b-4dd6 -b134-5d861e9095ef/a_complete_9.pdf.

22. Ibid.
23. "Partnerships: Donor Partnerships," Open Society Institute, accessed February 22, 2023, https://www.opensocietyfoundations.org/uploads/2519658d-a95b-44bd-b9d3-edec9039de24/partners_20090720_0.pdf.
24. "Democracy PAC II," Campaign Finance Data, Federal Election Commission, accessed August 16, 2022, https://www.fec.gov/data/committee/C00786624/?tab=about-committee.
25. "Soros Fund Management 2022," OpenSecrets, accessed February 22, 2023, https://www.opensecrets.org/orgs/soros-fund-management/summary?id=D000000306&topnumcycle=2022.
26. "PAC Profile: Colorofchange.org," PACs, OpenSecrets, accessed August 16, 2022, https://www.opensecrets.org/political-action-committees-pacs/C00428557/summary/2020; "PAC Profile: DNC Services Corp," PACs, OpenSecrets, accessed August 16, 2022, https://www.opensecrets.org/political-action-committees-pacs/C00010603/summary/2022; "PAC Profile: Justice & Public Safety," PACs, OpenSecrets, accessed August 16, 2022, https://www.opensecrets.org/political-action-committees-pacs/justice-public-safety/C00651505/summary/2020; "Democratic Senatorial Campaign Cmte Fundraising Overview," Political Parties, OpenSecrets, accessed August 16, 2022, https://www.opensecrets.org/parties/totals.php?cmte=DSCC&cycle=2020; "PAC Profile: Democracy PAC," PACs, OpenSecrets, accessed August 16, 2022, https://www.opensecrets.org/political-action-committees-pacs/democracy-pac/C00693382/summary/2020; "PAC Profile: Forward Majority Action," PACs, OpenSecrets, accessed August 16, 2022, https://www.opensecrets.org/political-action-committees-pacs/forward-majority-action/C00631549/summary/2020.
27. Elena Schneider, "Soros Pours $125M into Super PAC Ahead of Midterms," *Politico*, January 28, 2022, https://www.politico.com/news/2022/01/28/soros-pours-125m-into-super-pac-ahead-of-midterms-00002847.
28. Matt Palumbo, *The Man behind the Curtain: Inside the Secret Network of George Soros* (New York: Liberatio Protocol, 2022), 24.
29. Ibid., 31.
30. John Tagliabue, "Soros Is Found Guilty in France On Charges of Insider Trading," *New York Times*, December 21, 2002, https://www.nytimes.com/2002/12/21/business/soros-is-found-guilty-in-france-on-charges-of-insider-trading.html.
31. Kenneth P. Vogel, "Soros-Linked Group Hit with Huge Fine," *Politico*, August 29, 2007, https://www.politico.com/story/2007/08/soros-linked-group-hit-with-huge-fine-005555.
32. Ibid.; "FEC Collects $630,000 in Civil Penalties from Three 527 Organizations," Federal Election Commission, press release, December 13, 2006, https://www.fec.gov/updates/fec-collects-630000-in-civil-penalties-from-three-527-organizations.
33. John Heilemann, "Money Chooses Sides," *New York*, April 13, 2007, https://nymag.com/news/politics/30634.
34. Steinberger, "George Soros Bet Big."
35. Kenneth P. Vogel, "George Soros Rises Again," *Politico*, July 27, 2016, https://www.politico.com/story/2016/07/george-soros-democratic-convention-226267.
36. Gregory Zuckerman and Juliet Chung, "Billionaire George Soros Lost Nearly $1 Billion in Weeks after Trump Election," *Wall Street Journal*, updated January 13, 2017, https://www.wsj.com/articles/billionaire-george-soros-lost-nearly-1-billion-in-weeks-after-trump-election-1484227167.
37. Ibid.
38. Bess Levin, "George Soros Declares War on Trump as Ex-Soros Employee Prepares to (Maybe) Join His Cabinet," *Vanity Fair*, November 14, 2016, https://www.vanityfair.com/news/2016/11/george-soros-declares-war-on-trump.

39. Jerry Dunleavy, "FISA Court Mistakenly Says Fusion GPS Was Digging Up Dirt on Hillary Clinton, Not Trump," *Washington Examiner*, March 5, 2020, https://www.washingtonex aminer.com/news/fisa-court-mistakenly-says-fusion-gps-was-digging-up-dirt-on -hillary-clinton-not-trump.

40. Robert Barnes, "The Crusade of a Democratic Superlawyer with Multimillion-Dollar Backing," *Washington Post*, August 7, 2016, https://www.washingtonpost.com/politics /courts_law/the-crusade-of-a-democratic-super-lawyer-with-multimillion-dollar -backing/2016/08/07/2c1b408c-5a54-11e6-9767-f6c947fd0cb8_story.html.

41. Joe Schoffstall, "Clinton's Top Lawyer Joins Soros-Funded Super PAC to Fight Voting Laws," *Washington Free Beacon*, February 6, 2017, https://freebeacon.com/politics/hil larys-top-lawyer-joins-soros-funded-super-pac-fight-voting-laws; Dunleavy, "FISA Court Mistakenly Says."

42. Barnes, "Crusade of a Democratic Superlawyer."

43. David Smith, "Did Mueller's Testimony Kill the Trump Impeachment Debate," *Guardian*, July 26, 2019, https://www.theguardian.com/us-news/2019/jul/26/mueller-testimony -democrats-impeachment.

44. Aaron Klein, "Emails: Open Society Kept Alleged 'Whistleblower' Eric Ciaramella Updated on George Soros's Personal Ukraine Activities," *Breitbart*, November 17, 2019, https://www.breitbart.com/politics/2019/11/17/emails-open-society-kept-alleged -whistleblower-eric-ciaramella-updated-on-george-soross-personal-ukraine-activities.

45. Ibid.

46. Aaron Klein, "Soros-Backed Org Fuels Deceptive Timeline for Impeachment Case," *Breitbart*, December 24, 2019, https://www.breitbart.com/politics/2019/12/24/soros-backed -org-fuels-deceptive-timeline-for-impeachment-case.

47. Ibid.; Nicholas Fandos, "Trump Acquitted of Two Impeachment Charges in Near Party-Line Vote," *New York Times*, February 5, 2020, https://www.nytimes.com/2020/02/05/us /politics/trump-acquitted-impeachment.html.

48. Brian Schwartz and Thomas Franck, "George Soros Rips Trump and Xi, Says the 'Fate of the World' Is at Stake in 2020," CNBC, updated January 24, 2020, https://www.cnbc.com /2020/01/23/davos-2020-george-soros-says-china-leader-xi-is-trying-to-exploit -trumps-weaknesses.html; Eliza Collins, "George Soros: Donald Trump Is 'Doing the Work of ISIS,'" *Politico*, January 22, 2016, https://www.politico.eu/article/george-soros -donald-trump-is-doing-the-work-of-isis-terrorism-u-s-election.

49. Joe Schoffstall, "Soros Pours Record $50 Million into 2020 Election," *Washington Free Beacon*, July 27, 2020, https://freebeacon.com/elections/soros-pours-record-50-million -into-2020-election.

50. "What George Soros' Life Is Really Like," *Business Insider India*, June 28, 2019, https://www .businessinsider.in/miscellaneous/what-george-soros-life-is-really-like-how-the -former-hedge-fund-manager-built-his-8-3-billion-fortune-purchased-a-sprawling -network-of-new-york-homes-and-became-the-topic-of-international-conspiracy-theories /slidelist/69992394.cms; James Kirchick, "The Truth about George Soros," *Tablet*, November 18, 2018, https://www.tabletmag.com/sections/news/articles/the-truth-about -george-soros.

51. Kirchick, "The Truth about George Soros."

52. Palumbo, *Man behind the Curtain*, 9.

53. Ibid., 10.

54. Ibid., 11.

55. Ibid., 14.

56. "Who Is George Soros? Here Are 4 Things You Wanted to Know (But Were Afraid to Ask)," CBC Radio, updated October 14, 2018, https://www.cbc.ca/radio/thecurrent/the -current-for-may-15-2018-1.4662381/who-is-george-soros-here-are-4-things-you

-wanted-to-know-but-were-afraid-to-ask-1.4662405; Emily Flitter, "Henry Arnhold, Patriarch of a Storied Banking Family, Dies at 96," *New York Times*, October 24, 2018, https://www.nytimes.com/2018/08/29/business/henry-arnhold-dead.html; "The Latest on George Soros's Portfolio: He's Short Emerging Markets and Got Hurt by Gold in January," *Business Insider*, February 16, 2011, https://www.businessinsider.com/george-soros-is-short-emerging-markets-hurt-by-gold-in-january-2011-2.

57. Michael T. Kaufman, *Soros: The Life and Times of a Messianic Billionaire* (New York: Alfred A. Knopf, 2002), 157.

58. Anna Porter, *Buying a Better World: George Soros and Billionaire Philanthropy* (Toronto, ON: Dundurn, 2015), 23.

59. DealBook, "Soros' Insider-Trading Conviction Upheld," *New York Times*, June 14, 2006, https://archive.nytimes.com/dealbook.nytimes.com/2006/06/14/soros-insider-trading-conviction-upheld-in-paris; "Insider Trading Conviction of Soros Is Upheld—Business—*International Herald Tribune*," *New York Times*, June 14, 2006, https://www.nytimes.com/2006/06/14/business/worldbusiness/14iht-soros.1974397.html.

60. DealBook, "When Soros Decided to 'Go for the Jugular,'" *New York Times*, June 4, 2010, https://archive.nytimes.com/dealbook.nytimes.com/2010/06/04/when-soros-decided-to-go-for-the-jugular; Palumbo, *Man behind the Curtain*, 17.

61. Stefan Kanfer, "Connoisseur of Chaos: The Dystopian Vision of George Soros, Billionaire Funder of the Left," *City Journal*, Winter 2017, accessed February 22, 2023, https://www.city-journal.org/html/connoisseur-chaos-14954.html; Palumbo, *Man behind the Curtain*, 17.

62. Palumbo, *Man behind the Curtain*, 17.

63. Paul Krugman, *The Accidental Theorist: And Other Dispatches from the Dismal Science* (New York: W.W. Norton, 2010), 160–61.

64. Robert Frank, Gregory Zuckerman, and Steve Eder, "Soros Fund All in the Family," *Wall Street Journal*, updated July 27, 2011, https://www.wsj.com/articles/SB10001424053111903999904576469761599552864.

65. Igor Bosilkovski, "After Big Gift, George Soros' Fortune Shrinks, Knocking Him Down the Forbes List," *Forbes*, October 19, 2017, https://www.forbes.com/sites/igorbosilkovski/2017/10/19/after-big-gift-george-soros-fortune-more-than-halved-falls-40-spots-on-rich-list-ck; "How Transparent Are Think Tanks about Who Funds Them 2016?," Transparify, https://static1.squarespace.com/static/52e1f399e4b06a94c0cdaa41/t/5773022de6f2e1ecf70b26d1/1467154992324/Transparify+2016+Think+Tanks+Report.pdf.

66. Neil Maghami, "Whither the Soros Foundations—After Soros?," *Capital Research Center*, February 14, 2018, https://capitalresearch.org/article/whither-the-soros-foundations-after-soros-part-three.

67. Gregory Zuckerman, "George Soros Hands Control to His 37-Year-Old Son: 'I'm More Political,'" *Wall Street Journal*, June 11, 2023, https://www.wsj.com/articles/george-soros-heir-son-alexander-soros-e3c4ca13.

68. Palumbo, *Man behind the Curtain*, 99–124.

69. Alvin L. Bragg Jr., email message to All Staff, "Achieving Fairness and Safety," January 3, 2022, https://assets1.cbsnewsstatic.com/i/cbslocal/wp-content/uploads/sites/14578484/2022/01/Day-One-Letter-Policies-1.03.2022.pdf; "District Attorney Bragg Announces 34-Count Felony Indictment of Former President Donald J. Trump," press release, April 4, 2023, https://manhattanda.org/district-attorney-bragg-announces-34-count-felony-indictment-of-former-president-donald-j-trump.

70. Palumbo, *Man behind the Curtain*, 73.

71. Ibid., 74; Aisha Labi, "For President of Central European U., All Roads Have Led to Budapest," *Chronicle of Higher Education*, May 2, 2010, https://www.chronicle.com/article/for-president-of-central-european-u-all-roads-have-led-to-budapest; "Central European

University May Yet Be Saved in Hungary," Study International, October 5, 2017, https://www.studyinternational.com/news/central-european-university-may-yet-saved-hungary.

72. "History," About, Central European University, accessed August 16, 2022, https://www.ceu.edu/about/history.

73. "George Soros Steps Down as Chairman of CEU Board," Central European University, on Internet Archive, accessed February 22, 2023, https://web.archive.org/web/20071023204822/http://www.ceu.hu/news-event.jsp?nr=2467&content_type=1.

74. Robert Hackwill, "Everything You Need to Know about the Central European University Controversy," Euronews, updated June 4, 2017, https://www.euronews.com/2017/04/06/everything-you-need-to-know-about-the-central-european-university-controversy.

75. "The Central European University Is Moving to Vienna," Economist, December 5, 2018, https://www.economist.com/europe/2018/12/05/the-central-european-university-is-moving-to-vienna.

76. Griff White, "The Trump Administration Tried to Save a US University by Playing Nice with an Autocrat. It Failed," Washington Post, November 30, 2018, https://www.washingtonpost.com/world/europe/the-trump-administration-tried-to-save-a-us-university-by-playing-nice-with-an-autocrat-it-failed/2018/11/30/f028718a-e831-11e8-8449-1ff263609a31_story.html.

77. Palumbo, Man behind the Curtain, 79.

78. George Soros, "Remarks Delivered at the World Economic Forum," George Soros, January 23, 2020, https://www.georgesoros.com/2020/01/23/remarks-delivered-at-the-world-economic-forum-3.

79. Borzou Daragahi, "Georgian Unrolls the 'Velvet' Revolution," Los Angeles Times, September 3, 2008, https://www.latimes.com/archives/la-xpm-2008-sep-03-fg-velvet3-story.html; Natasha Mozgovaya, "Glenn Beck, George Soros and a Row about the Holocaust," Haaretz, November 12, 2010, https://www.haaretz.com/2010-11-12/ty-article/glenn-beck-george-soros-and-a-row-about-the-holocaust/0000017f-e8db-dc7e-adff-f8ff0e290000; Michael McFaul and Kathryn Stoner-Weiss, "The Myth of the Authoritarian Model," Foreign Affairs, January 1, 2008, https://www.foreignaffairs.com/articles/russia-fsu/2008-01-01/myth-authoritarian-model; George Soros, "Why Obama Has to Get Egypt Right," Washington Post, February 2, 2011, https://www.washingtonpost.com/opinions/why-obama-has-to-get-egypt-right/2011/02/02/e0e949da-2f1e-11e0-8d1b-ad31ce3d725e_story.html; Richard Miniter, "Are George Soros' Billions Compromising US Foreign Policy?," Forbes, September 9, 2011, https://www.forbes.com/sites/richardminiter/2011/09/09/should-george-soros-be-allowed-to-buy-u-s-foreign-policy.

80. "Embracing the East; Talking Drugs; Conversation," MacNeil/Lehrer NewsHour, July 12, 1989, https://advance-lexis-com.proxycu.wrlc.org/api/document?collection=news&id=urn:contentItem:3S36-6PS0-001S-C2WJ-00000-00&context=1516831.

81. Ibid.

82. George Soros, Underwriting Democracy: Encouraging Free Enterprise and Democratic Reform among the Soviets and in Eastern Europe (New York: PublicAffairs, 1990), https://www.georgesoros.com/wp-content/uploads/2017/10/underwriting_democracy-chap-1-2017_10_05.pdf.

83. Palumbo, Man behind the Curtain, 24.

84. "OSI Condemns Takeover of Moscow Foundation," Open Society Foundations, press release, on ArchiveToday, November 23, 2003, https://archive.fo/6lVz1; "The Open Society Foundations in Ukraine," Open Society Foundations, May 18, 2022, https://www.opensocietyfoundations.org/newsroom/the-open-society-foundations-in-ukraine.

85. Palumbo, Man behind the Curtain, 24–26.

86. Ibid., 8–9.

Chapter Seven: Follow the Money

1. Ken Chenault and Larry Fink, "DealBook 2017: The Economy, Consumers, and Redefining the Long Term," posted by New York Times Events, November 9, 2017, YouTube video, 27:51–28:03, https://www.youtube.com/watch?v=-cCs9Kh2Q08.

2. Schwab, "Now Is the Time"; Klaus Schwab, *The Fourth Industrial Revolution* (Cologne: World Economic Forum, 2016).

3. "Money and Payments: The US Dollar in the Age of Digital Transformation," Board of Governors of the Federal Reserve System, January 2022, accessed August 16, 2022, https://www.federalreserve.gov/publications/files/money-and-payments-20220120.pdf.

4. Arjun Bisen, "Will Digital Money Belong to Democrats or Despots?," Atlantic Council, August 20, 2021, https://www.atlanticcouncil.org/blogs/new-atlanticist/will-digital-money-belong-to-democrats-or-despots.

5. "A Cyber-Attack with COVID-like Characteristics?," posted by World Economic Forum, January 18, 2021, YouTube video, 01:41, https://www.youtube.com/watch?v=-OoZA1B3ooI.

6. Ibid.

7. Tim Maurer and Arthur Nelson, "International Strategy to Better Protect the Financial System against Cyber Threats," Carnegie Endowment for International Peace, in collaboration with World Economic Forum, accessed October 1, 2022, https://carnegieendowment.org/files/FinCyber_Executive_Summary.pdf; "Cyber Polygon 2021," Cyber Polygon, accessed October 1, 2022, https://cyberpolygon.com/results-2021.

8. Mark Hay, "COVID Truthers Have Found a New 'Pandemic' to Freak Out About," *Daily Beast*, updated May 1, 2022, https://www.thedailybeast.com/conspiracy-theorists-are-already-freaking-out-about-the-next-pandemic-as-part-of-the-so-called-great-reset.

9. "Cyber Polygon," Projects, World Economic Forum, accessed October 1, 2022, https://web.archive.org/web/20200624141615/https://www.weforum.org/projects/cyber-polygon.

10. "Partners and Participants," Cyber Polygon, accessed October 1, 2022, https://2021.cyberpolygon.com/participants-and-partners.

11. "Cyber Polygon 2021 Opening. Mikhail Mishustin, Klaus Martin Schwab, Herman Gref," posted by BI.ZONE, July 14, 2021, YouTube video, 23:24–24:36, https://www.youtube.com/watch?v=DnwtG1VDvh0.

12. "Digital Currency Governance Consortium White Paper Series," Reports, World Economic Forum, November 19, 2021, https://www.weforum.org/reports/digital-currency-governance-consortium-white-paper-series; Andrew Stanley, "The Ascent of CBDCs," International Monetary Fund, September 2022, accessed October 1, 2022, https://www.imf.org/en/Publications/fandd/issues/2022/09/Picture-this-The-ascent-of-CBDCs.

13. Steven Scheer, "EXCLUSIVE IMF, 10 Countries Simulate Cyberattack on Global Financial System," Reuters, December 9, 2021, https://www.reuters.com/markets/europe/exclusive-imf-10-countries-simulate-cyber-attack-global-financial-system-2021-12-09.

14. Ibid.

15. "Digital Currency Governance Consortium White Paper Series," Compendium Report, World Economic Forum, November 2021, accessed October 1, 2022, 75–76, https://www3.weforum.org/docs/WEF_Digital_Currency_Governance_Consortium_White_Paper_Series_2021.pdf.

16. "Cyber Polygon: International Online Training for Raising Global Cyber Resilience," Cyber Polygon Report, Cyber Polygon.

17. Ibid.; "Digital Currency Governance Consortium White Paper Series," Compendium Report, World Economic Forum.

18. Christopher Condon, "FTX Debacle Shows Need for Crypto Regulation, Yellen Says," *Bloomberg*, November 12, 2022, https://www.bloomberg.com/news/articles/2022-11-12/yellen-says-ftx-debacle-shows-need-for-crypto-regulation.

19. Kristopher J. Brooks, "Bankrupt FTX Trading Owes Creditors More Than $3 Billion," CBS News, November 21, 2022, https://www.cbsnews.com/news/ftx-bankruptcy-3-billion-crypto-sam-bankman-fried.

20. Grace Dean, "Caroline Ellison Said She Grew Up 'Exposed to a Lot of Economics.' Here's Everything We Know about Her MIT Economist Parents," *Business Insider*, December 26, 2022, https://www.businessinsider.com/who-are-caroline-ellisons-parents-alameda-research-fraud-ftx-sbf-2022-12.

21. "Senator Warren Introduces Bill to Simplify Tax Filing," Reports, Senator Elizabeth Warren, April 13, 2016, https://www.warren.senate.gov/oversight/reports/senator-warren-introduces-bill-to-simplify-tax-filing; "Meeting the Needs of Cognitive Decline," World Economic Forum, report, chrome-extension://efaidnbmnnnibpcajpcglclefindmkaj/https://www3.weforum.org/docs/WEF_Meeting_Needs_Cognitive_Decline_070916.pdf; "Linda P. Fried, MD, MPH: 2019 Alma Dea Morani Awardee," Women in Medicine Legacy Foundation, accessed February 3, 2023, https://www.wimlf.org/linda-p-fried-md-mph.

22. Marco Quiroz-Gutierrez, "Sam Bankman-Fried Says He Donated Just as Many Millions to Republicans as Democrats, but Didn't Publicize It Because Reporters Would 'Freak the F–k out,'" *Fortune*, November 29, 2022, https://fortune.com/crypto/2022/11/29/sam-bankman-fried-political-donations-democrats-republicans-dark-money.

23. Timothy Nerozzi, "Maxine Waters Praises FTX Founder Sam Bankman-Fried for 'Candid' Interviews After Billions Go Missing," Fox Business, December 4, 2022, https://www.foxbusiness.com/politics/maxine-waters-praises-ftx-founder-bankman-fried-candid-interviews-losing-people-billions.

24. Marco Quiroz Gutierrez, "Congress Will Be Taking a Closer Look at Sam Bankman-Fried's Political Spending Spree," *Fortune*, November 12, 2022, https://fortune.com/crypto/2022/11/21/congress-investigates-sam-bankman-fried-ftx-political-donations; Aaron Navarro, "Sam Bankman-Fried Donated over $40 Million in the 2022 Election Cycle. Where Did It Go?," CBS News, December 15, 2022, https://www.cbsnews.com/news/ftx-sam-bankman-fried-political-donations-2022; Tory Newmyer, "Bankman-Fried Says He Was Careless at FTX. Prosecutors Say It's Fraud," *Washington Post*, December 15, 2022, https://www.washingtonpost.com/business/2022/12/15/sbf-fraud-docs.

25. Will Daniel, "Former FTX Users Say the Failed Crypto Exchange Was a 'Ponzi Scheme.' Here's How Those Work, and What We Know about How Sam Bankman-Fried Operated," *Fortune*, December 3, 2022, https://fortune.com/2022/12/03/ftx-sam-bankman-fried-crypto-how-ponzi-schemes-work-sbf; Carolina Mandl, "BlackRock's Fink Says Crypto Technology Still Relevant despite FTX," Reuters, November 30, 2022, https://www.reuters.com/technology/blackrocks-fink-says-there-may-have-been-misbehaviors-ftx-2022-11-30; David Yaffe-Bellany and Matthew Goldstein, "Sam Bankman-Fried Pleads Not Guilty to Additional Set of Charges," *New York Times*, March 30, 2023, https://www.nytimes.com/2023/03/30/business/sam-bankman-fried-charges.html.

26. Kelsey Piper, "Sam Bankman-Fried Tries to Explain Himself," *Vox*, November 16, 2022, https://www.vox.com/future-perfect/23462333/sam-bankman-fried-ftx-crypto-currency-effective-altruism-crypto-bahamas-philanthropy.

27. Brian Plat and Jen Skerritt, "Banks Freeze Millions in Convoy Funds under Trudeau Edict," BNN *Bloomberg*, February 22, 2022, https://www.bnnbloomberg.ca/banks-freeze-millions-in-truck-convoy-funds-under-trudeau-edict-1.1727032.

28. Nicholas Comfort and Natalia Drozdiak, "Why Swift Ban Is Such a Potent Sanction on Russia," *Washington Post*, June 3, 2022, https://www.washingtonpost.com/business/why-swift-ban-is-such-a-potent-sanction-on-russia/2022/06/03/a6809b30-e340-11ec-ae64-6b23e5155b62_story.html.

29. Ryan King, "Five Times GoFundMe Shut Down Conservative Fundraisers," *Washington Examiner*, February 7, 2022, https://www.washingtonexaminer.com/news/five-times

-gofundme-shut-down-conservative-fundraisers; Michael Arrington, "Key Video from the World Economic Forum's Social Networking Powerhouse Panel," *TechCrunch*, January 27, 2010, https://techcrunch.com/2010/01/27/world-economic-forums-social-networking-powerhouse-panel.

30. "More Credit Card Companies Are Making It Easier to Track Gun Sales," National Public Radio, September 11, 2022, https://www.npr.org/2022/09/11/1122261276/visa-mastercard-american-express-gun-sales; Ken Sweet, "Visa, Mastercard Pause Decision to Track Gun Shop Purchases," Associated Press, March 9, 2023, https://apnews.com/article/master card-visa-guns-second-amendment-c2f5db1f0be066458ee0041a5816736e.

31. Peter Rudegeair, "PayPal CEO Grapples with Fringe Groups," *Wall Street Journal*, February 24, 2019, https://www.wsj.com/articles/paypal-ceo-grapples-with-fringe-groups-11551016800.

32. Christiaan Hetzner, "PayPal Tells Users It Will Fine Them $2,500 for Misinformation, Then Backtracks Immediately," *Fortune*, October 10, 2022, https://fortune.com/2022/10/10/paypal-users-fine-misinformation-aup-error-confusion.

33. Ken Klippenstein and Lee Fang, "Truth Cops: Leaked Documents Outline DHS's Plans to Police Disinformation," *Intercept*, October 31, 2022, https://theintercept.com/2022/10/31/social-media-disinformation-dhs.

34. Harriet Agnew and Robin Wigglesworth, "BlackRock Surges Part $10tn in Assets under Management," *Financial Times*, January 14, 2022, https://www.ft.com/content/7603e676-779b-4c13-8f46-a964594e3c2f.

35. Ellen Brown, "Meet BlackRock, the New Great Vampire Squid," *Common Dreams*, June 22, 2020, https://www.commondreams.org/views/2020/06/22/meet-blackrock-new-great-vampire-squid.

36. Brown, "Meet BlackRock"; Matthew Goldstein, "The Fed Asks for BlackRock's Help in an Echo of 2008," *New York Times*, March 25, 2020, https://www.nytimes.com/2020/03/25/business/blackrock-federal-reserve.html.

37. "Larry Fink," Profile, *Forbes*, accessed October 1, 2022, https://www.forbes.com/profile/larry-fink/?sh=1edf95a520f4; Alan Deutschman, Peter Newcomb, Richard Siklos, Duff McDonald, and Jessica Flint, "The Vanity Fair 100," *Vanity Fair*, September 1, 2010, https://www.vanityfair.com/news/2010/10/the-vf-100-201010.

38. "Laurence D. Fink (MBA '76)," UCLA Anderson School of Management, on Internet Archive, accessed October 1, 2022, https://web.archive.org/web/20120524164722/http://www.anderson.ucla.edu/x20552.xml; "Rockefeller's Entourage," North American Congress on Latin America, September 25, 2007, https://nacla.org/article/rockefeller%27s-entourage.

39. Erik Schatzker, "Larry Fink Q&A: 'I Don't Identify as Powerful,'" *Bloomberg*, April 18, 2017, https://www.bloomberg.com/features/2017-blackrock-larry-fink-interview.

40. Ibid.; "World Economic Forum Appoints New Members to Board of Trustees," News Releases, World Economic Forum, accessed October 1, 2022, https://www.weforum.org/press/2019/08/world-economic-forum-appoints-new-members-to-board-of-trustees; "Leadership and Governance," About, World Economic Forum, accessed October 1, 2022, https://www.weforum.org/about/leadership-and-governance; "Laurence D. Fink," World Economic Forum, accessed October 1, 2022, https://www.weforum.org/agenda/authors/larry-fink.

41. Matthew Goldstein, "Fed Releases Details of BlackRock Deal for Virus Response," *New York Times*, March 27, 2020, https://www.nytimes.com/2020/03/27/business/coronavirus-blackrock-federal-reserve.html.

42. World Economic Forum, in collaboration with Deloitte, "A Blueprint for Digital Identity: The Role of Financial Institutions in Building Digital Identity," presentation as part of the Future of Financial Services Series, August 2016, accessed February 8, 2023, https://www3.weforum.org/docs/WEF_A_Blueprint_for_Digital_Identity.pdf.

43. Jeffrey M. Jones, "Americans Using Cash Less Often; Foresee Cashless Society," Gallup, August 25, 2022, https://news.gallup.com/poll/397718/americans-using-cash-less-often -foresee-cashless-society.aspx.

44. "Digital Transformation," Initiative, Rockefeller Foundation, accessed October 1, 2022, https://www.rockefellerfoundation.org/initiative/digital-transformation; Chris Burt, "Gates Foundation Commits $200M to Digital ID and Other Public Infrastructure," Biometric Update, September 27, 2022, https://www.biometricupdate.com/202209/gates-foundation -commits-200m-to-digital-id-and-other-public-infrastructure.

45. "Goal 16: Promote Just, Peaceful and Inclusive Societies," Sustainable Development, United Nations, accessed February 8, 2023, https://www.un.org/sustainabledevelopment /peace-justice.

46. "UN Legal Identity Agenda Task Force," United Nations Legal Identity Agenda, accessed October 1, 2022, https://unstats.un.org/legal-identity-agenda/UNLIATF; Christine Gerlier, "Private Sector Engagement Roundtable, 18–19 May 2021: Future of Technology and Institutional Governance in Identity Management," United Nations Development Programme Event Report, edited by David Wooff and Erin Barrett, accessed February 8, 2023, https:// unstats.un.org/legal-identity-agenda/meetings/2021/UNLIA-FutureTech/docs/report.pdf.

47. ID2020, "ID2020 Holds Inaugural Summit at the United Nations," Medium, May 20, 2016, https://medium.com/id2020/id2020-holds-inaugural-summit-at-the-united-nations -7112014add5e; Charlotte Arnaud, "Opportunities in the New Digital Age," UNHCR (blog), UN Refugee Agency, October 26, 2017, https://www.unhcr.org/blogs/opportunities-in -the-new-digital-age; ID2020, "Facebook Joins ID2020 Alliance," LinkedIn, August 26, 2021, https://www.linkedin.com/pulse/facebook-joins-id2020-alliance-identity2020.

48. "The ID2020 Alliance Is Setting the Course for Digital ID," ID2020, accessed February 8, 2023, https://id2020.org/overview; "The Institute of Development Studies," Bill & Melinda Gates Foundation, accessed February 8, 2023, https://www.gatesfoundation.org /about/committed-grants/2019/11/opp1213601.

49. Christ Burt, "ID2020 and Partners Launch Program to Provide Digital ID with Vaccines," Biometric Update, September 20, 2019, https://www.biometricupdate.com/201909 /id2020-and-partners-launch-program-to-provide-digital-id-with-vaccines; Johns Hopkins Center for Health Security, World Economic Forum, and Bill & Melinda Gates Foundation, "Public-Private Cooperation for Pandemic Preparedness and Response: A Call to Action," Event 201, Johns Hopkins Center for Health Security, accessed October 1, 2022, https://www.centerforhealthsecurity.org/our-work/exercises/event201/event201 -resources/200117-PublicPrivatePandemicCalltoAction.pdf.

50. Ollie A. Williams, "Inside the Race to Create a Covid Passport and Change Travel as We Know It," Forbes, February 21, 2021, https://www.forbes.com/sites/oliverwilliams1/2021 /02/21/inside-the-race-to-create-a-covid-passport-and-change-travel-as-we-know-it.

51. "Green Pass: All You Need to Know about Italy's Digital Covid Cert," Wanted in Rome, December 2, 2021, https://www.wantedinrome.com/news/green-pass-all-you-need-to -know-about-italys-digital-covid-cert.html; "Excelsior Pass Plus," New York State, accessed February 3, 2023, https://epass.ny.gov/home; SafeTravels Hawaii, accessed February 3, 2023, https://safetravelshawaii.com.

52. Anne Josephine Flanagan and Sheila Warren, "Advancing Digital Agency: The Power of Data Intermediaries," Insight Report February 2022, World Economic Forum, accessed October 1, 2022, https://www3.weforum.org/docs/WEF_Advancing_towards_Digital _Agency_2022.pdf.

53. "B20 Summit Indonesia 2022 | Day 1," posted by ASEAN BAC INDONESIA 2023, November 12, 2022, YouTube video, 1:22:47–1:23:59, https://www.youtube.com/live/IXve TRjU1Yc?feature=share&t=4974.

54. Dylan Robertson, "Trudeau Pledges Cash for Infrastructure and Making Vaccines in Developing Countries," CTV News, November 15, 2022, https://www.ctvnews.ca/canada/trudeau-pledges-cash-for-infrastructure-and-making-vaccines-in-developing-countries-1.6153213; Gaurav Sharma, "As MIQ Ends, JNCTN Seeks Potential in Digital Credentialing," IT Brief New Zealand, November 15, 2022, https://itbrief.co.nz/story/as-miq-ends-jnctn-seeks-potential-in-digital-credentialing.
55. Sharma, "As MIQ Ends."
56. McKinsey & Company and World Economic Forum, "Capturing Opportunities in Energy Efficiency," accessed October 1, 2022, https://www3.weforum.org/docs/AM11/WEF_AM11_IT_EnergyEfficiencyOpportunities_2011.pdf; "WHO Facilitates 194 Member States to Introduce Digital Vaccination Certificates," T-Systems, February 23, 2022, https://web.archive.org/web/20220410003752/https://www.t-systems.com/de/en/news room/news/checking-covid-19-certificates-498326.
57. Chris Weller, "America Has the Technology to Go Cashless, but Nobody Trusts It Enough to Use It," Business Insider, November 17, 2016, https://www.businessinsider.com/america-too-paranoid-go-cashless-2016-10.

Chapter Eight: Mainstream Mind Control

1. "Anger, Dissatisfaction at Federal Government, Poll Shows," Morning Joe, MSNBC, February 22, 2017, video, 02:20–02:30, https://www.msnbc.com/morning-joe/watch/anger-dissatisfaction-at-federal-government-poll-shows-882295875866.
2. Barack Obama, "Disinformation Is a Threat to Our Democracy," Medium, April 21, 2022, https://barackobama.medium.com/my-remarks-on-disinformation-at-stanford-7d7af7ba28af; "A Year of Hope. A Year of Action," Obama Foundation, accessed February 8, 2023, https://www.obama.org/year-in-review-2021.
3. "Challenges to Democracy in the Digital Information Realm," posted by FSIStanford, April 21, 2022, YouTube video, 00:08:50–01:13:10, https://youtu.be/YrMMiDXspYo?t=530.
4. Ibid., 08:50–09:15.
5. Ibid., 11:16–13:10.
6. Obama, "Disinformation Is a Threat to Our Democracy"; Melissa De Witte, Taylor Kubota, and Ker Than, "'Regulation Has to be Part of the Answer' to Combating Online Disinformation, Barack Obama Said at Stanford Event," Stanford News, April 21, 2022, https://news.stanford.edu/2022/04/21/disinformation-weakening-democracy-barack-obama-said.
7. "Challenges to Democracy in the Digital Information Realm," 28:11–28:56.
8. Obama, "Disinformation Is a Threat to Our Democracy."
9. Ibid.
10. Ryan Lovelace, "Biden Team Worked with Social Media Companies to Censor Content, Records Show," Washington Times, September 1, 2022, https://www.washingtontimes.com/news/2022/sep/1/biden-team-worked-social-media-companies-censorshi.
11. Obama, "Disinformation Is a Threat."
12. Ibid.
13. Stacie Slotnick, "Research Contracts and Special Funds," MIT Media Lab, October 2018, https://www.media.mit.edu/posts/research-contracts-and-special-funds; Stacie Slotnick, "Member Companies," MIT Media Lab, November 4, 2021, https://www.media.mit.edu/posts/member-companies; Stacie Slotnick, "Endowment and Naming Grant Donors," MIT Media Lab, August 6, 2018, https://www.media.mit.edu/posts/endowment-and-naming-grant-donors.

14. "Supporters," News Literacy Project, updated December 12, 2022, https://newslit.org/about/supporters.
15. Alan C. Miller, "NLP to Be Founding Participant in News Integrity Initiative," News Literacy Project, April 3, 2017, https://newslit.org/updates/nlp-to-be-founding-participant-in-news-integrity-initiative; "Mission," News Literacy Project, accessed February 8, 2023, https://newslit.org/about/mission.
16. Miller, "NLP to Be Founding Participant."
17. Michael Calderone, "Laurene Powell Jobs Solidifies Control of *The Atlantic* as Bradley Relinquishes Duties," *Politico*, November 20, 2019, https://www.politico.com/news/2019/11/20/laurene-jobs-the-atlantic-072210; Robert P. Baird, "Benevolent Haze," *Columbia Journalism Review*, January 21, 2021, https://www.cjr.org/special_report/emerson-collective-media.php.
18. Alexander Marlow, "The 'New Soros': Marlow Media Exposé Reveals Immense Secret Power of Tech Heiress Laurene Powell Jobs," *Breitbart*, May 19, 2021, https://www.breitbart.com/the-media/2021/05/19/the-new-soros-marlow-media-expose-reveals-immense-secret-power-of-tech-heiress-laurene-powell-jobs; Theodore Schleifer, "Can Laurene Powell Jobs Save the World?," Puck, October 14, 2021, https://puck.news/can-laurene-powell-jobs-save-the-world.
19. "Philanthropy Awards, 2019," *Inside Philanthropy*, December 31, 2019, https://www.insidephilanthropy.com/home/2019/philanthropy-awards; Baird, "Benevolent Haze."
20. Sarah Ellison, "Exclusive: Mike Allen and Jim Vandehei Reveal Their Plan for Media Domination," Hive, *Vanity Fair*, on Internet Archive, November 30, 2016, https://web.archive.org/web/20170508112452/https://www.vanityfair.com/news/2016/11/mike-allen-and-jim-vandehei-reveal-their-plan-for-media-domination-axios; *Mercury News*, "Laurene Powell Jobs Buying *The Atlantic* Magazine," *Denver Post*, July 28, 2017, https://www.denverpost.com/2017/07/28/laurene-powell-jobs-buying-the-atlantic-magazine.
21. Jonathan Stein, "Astroturf Axelrod?," *Mother Jones*, March 26, 2008, https://www.motherjones.com/politics/2008/03/astroturf-axelrod.
22. Sara Fischer, "Exclusive: Billionaires Back New Media Firm to Combat Disinformation," *Axios*, October 26, 2021, https://www.axios.com/2021/10/26/soros-hoffman-disinformation-tara-mcgowan; Sara Fischer, "Exclusive: ACRONYM Co-founder Tara McGowan on Iowa Caucus App," *Axios*, February 5, 2020, https://www.axios.com/2020/02/06/2020-election-acronym-iowa-caucus-app; Anna Massoglia, "'Dark Money' Networks Hide Political Agendas Behind Fake News Sites," OpenSecrets, May 22, 2020, https://www.opensecrets.org/news/2020/05/dark-money-networks-fake-news-sites.
23. Fischer, "Exclusive: Billionaires Back New Media Firm to Combat Disinformation."
24. Alex Thompson, "Newsroom or PAC? Liberal Group Muddies Online Information Wars," *Politico*, July 14, 2020, https://www.politico.com/news/2020/07/14/newsroom-pac-liberal-info-wars-356800; Gabby Deutch, "A Website Wanted to Restore Trust in the Media. It's Actually a Political Operation," *Washington Post*, February 6, 2020, https://www.washingtonpost.com/opinions/2020/02/06/is-it-local-journalism-or-just-local-propaganda.
25. David Samuels, "The Aspiring Novelist Who Became Obama's Foreign-Policy Guru," *New York Times*, May 5, 2016, https://www.nytimes.com/2016/05/08/magazine/the-aspiring-novelist-who-became-obamas-foreign-policy-guru.html.
26. Amy Chozick, "Donations by Media Companies Tilt Heavily to Obama," *New York Times*, August 22, 2012, https://archive.nytimes.com/mediadecoder.blogs.nytimes.com/2012/08/22/donations-by-media-companies-tilt-heavily-to-obama; Gillian B. White, "Emerson Collective Acquires Majority Stake in *The Atlantic*," *Atlantic*, July 28, 2017, https://www.theatlantic.com/business/archive/2017/07/emerson-collective-atlantic-coalition

/535215; Franklin Foer, "Russiagate Was Not a Hoax," *Atlantic*, August 19, 2020, https://www.theatlantic.com/ideas/archive/2020/08/russiagate-wasnt-a-hoax/615373.

27. Alaina Demopoulos, "Sexy Khakis and Giant Graphics: How US TV Pundits Spent Election Night," *Guardian*, November 9, 2022, https://www.theguardian.com/us-news/2022/nov/08/us-midterms-news-coverage-cnn-fox-msnbc.

28. "Election Misinformation Rundown," RumorGuard, November 2, 2022, https://www.rumorguard.org/post/election-misinformation-rundown; The News Literacy Project (@News LitProject), "It's #ElectionDay! Here are a few resources to help you be informed, not misled online," Twitter, November 8, 2022, 6:03 a.m., https://twitter.com/NewsLitProject/status/1589966745544101888.

29. Jerome A. Cohen, "Communist China's Painful Human Rights Story," Council on Foreign Relations, September 26, 2019, https://www.cfr.org/article/communist-chinas-painful-human-rights-story.

30. Paul Farhi, *Washington Post to Be Sold to Jeff Bezos, the Founder of Amazon," Washington Post*, August 5, 2013, https://www.washingtonpost.com/national/washington-post-to-be-sold-to-jeff-bezos/2013/08/05/ca537c9e-fe0c-11e2-9711-3708310f6f4d_story.html; David Teather, "How I Lost $8bn, by Ted Turner," *Guardian*, February 6, 2003, https://www.theguardian.com/business/2003/feb/06/usnews.media; Peter Bright, "Microsoft Buys Skype for $8.5 Billion. Why, Exactly?," *Wired*, May 10, 2011, https://www.wired.com/2011/05/microsoft-buys-skype-2; David Lazarus, "Microsoft Buys WebTV," *Wired*, April 7, 1997, https://www.wired.com/1997/04/microsoft-buys-webtv.

31. Jessi Hempel, "Now We Know Why Microsoft Bought LinkedIn," *Wired*, March 14, 2017, https://www.wired.com/2017/03/now-we-know-why-microsoft-bought-linkedin; "Bill Gates Used LinkedIn to Share His 'Impressive' Resume from When He Was 18 Years Old," *Marca*, November 7, 2022, https://www.marca.com/en/lifestyle/celebrities/2022/07/12/62cc9d3746163f00778b4603.html.

32. Roy Schestowitz, "Why BBC Is Microsoft Media (Video)," TechRights, June 25, 2008, http://techrights.org/2008/06/25/msbbc-grilled-video; Alan MacLeod, "Documents Show Bill Gates Has Given $319 Million to Media Outlets to Promote His Global Agenda," *The Grayzone*, November 21, 2021, https://thegrayzone.com/2021/11/21/bill-gates-million-media-outlets-global-agenda.

33. Dan Gainor, "Why Don't We Every Hear about Soros' Ties to over 30 Major News Organizations?," Fox News, May 7, 2015, https://www.foxnews.com/opinion/why-dont-we-hear-about-soros-ties-to-over-30-major-news-organizations; Keach Hagey, "Soros Gives $1 Million to Media Matters," *Politico*, October 20, 2010, https://www.politico.com/blogs/onmedia/1010/Soros_gives_1_million_to_Media_Matters.html; Brian Chapetta, "Soros Reloads on Big Tech with Amazon, Google and New Tesla Bet," *Bloomberg*, August 12, 2022, https://www.bloomberg.com/news/articles/2022-08-12/soros-reloads-on-big-tech-with-amazon-google-and-new-tesla-bet; Geraldine Fabrikant, "Rockefeller Broadcast Unit Is Sold," *New York Times*, February 6, 1986, https://www.nytimes.com/1986/02/06/business/rockefeller-broadcast-unit-is-sold.html; Nancy Rivera Brooks, "Rockefeller Group May Sell Part of Empire," *Los Angeles Times*, September 12, 1989, https://www.latimes.com/archives/la-xpm-1989-09-12-fi-2020-story.html; Laura Miller, "War of the Worlds: Rockefeller Philanthropies, Disinformation, and Media Literacy in the 1930s," RE:source, Rockefeller Archive Center, December 2, 2021, https://resource.rockarch.org/story/war-of-the-worlds-rockefeller-philanthropies-disinformation-and-media-literacy-in-the-1930s.

34. Ravi Somaiya, "Carlos Slim More Than Doubles His Stake in *Times* Company," *New York Times*, January 14, 2015, https://www.nytimes.com/2015/01/15/business/carlos-slim-more-than-doubles-his-stake-in-times-company.html.

35. Megan Brenan, "Americans' Trust in Media Remains Near Record Low," Gallup, October 18, 2022, https://news.gallup.com/poll/403166/americans-trust-media-remains-near-record-low.aspx.

36. American Press Institute, "Chapter 2, Holding Power Accountable: The Press and the Public," *How the Press and Public Can Find Common Purpose*, December 18, 2019, https://www.americanpressinstitute.org/publications/reports/survey-research/holding-power-accountable-the-press-and-the-public.

37. Associated Press, "Finally, Science Shows That Politicians Are Lying Liars Who Lie," *New York Post*, April 17, 2016, https://nypost.com/2016/04/17/finally-science-shows-that-politicians-are-lying-liars-who-lie; Barry Meier, "Origins of an Epidemic: Purdue Pharma Knew Its Opioids Were Widely Abused," *New York Times*, May 29, 2018, https://www.nytimes.com/2018/05/29/health/purdue-opioids-oxycontin.html; Adam Smith, "These Are the Adverts That Told People Smoking Was Good for Them," *Metro*, September 12, 2018, https://metro.co.uk/2018/09/12/these-are-the-insane-adverts-that-told-people-smoking-was-good-for-them-7936951.

38. John Hudson, "US Repeals Propaganda Ban, Spreads Government-Made News to Americans," *Foreign Policy*, July 14, 2013, https://foreignpolicy.com/2013/07/14/u-s-repeals-propaganda-ban-spreads-government-made-news-to-americans; Klippenstein and Fang, "Truth Cops."

39. Becky Little, "Inside America's Shocking WWII Propaganda Machine," *National Geographic*, December 19, 2016, https://www.nationalgeographic.com/history/article/world-war-2-propaganda-history-books; Dmitry Chernobrov and Emma L. Briant, "Competing Propagandas: How the United States and Russia Represent Mutual Propaganda Activities," *Politics* 42, no. 3 (August 2022): 393–409, https://doi.org/10.1177/0263395720966171.

40. Lesley Kennedy, "Did Yellow Journalism Fuel the Outbreak of the Spanish-American War?," History, August 21, 2019, https://www.history.com/news/spanish-american-war-yellow-journalism-hearst-pulitzer.

41. "Yellow Journalism," *Crucible of Empire*, PBS, accessed November 1, 2022, https://www.pbs.org/crucible/frames/_journalism.html.

42. Roy Greenslade, "First World War: How State and Press Kept Truth off the Front Page," *Guardian*, July 27, 2014, https://www.theguardian.com/media/2014/jul/27/first-world-war-state-press-reporting; Elizabeth Becker, "The Secrets and Lies of the Vietnam War, Exposed in One Epic Document," *New York Times*, June 9, 2021, https://www.nytimes.com/2021/06/09/us/pentagon-papers-vietnam-war.html; Daniel Bessner and Derek Davison, "The Afghanistan War Was Founded on Lies. Some People Are Still Telling Them," The Soapbox, *New Republic*, August 16, 2021, https://newrepublic.com/article/163291/afghanistan-war-founded-lies-people-still-telling-them.

43. Michael R. Gordon and Judith Miller, "Threats and Responses: The Iraqis; US Says Hussein Intensifies Quest for A-Bomb Parts," *New York Times*, September 8, 2002, https://www.nytimes.com/2002/09/08/world/threats-responses-iraqis-us-says-hussein-intensifies-quest-for-bomb-parts.html.

44. Michael Massing, "Now They Tell Us," *New York Review of Books*, February 26, 2004, https://www.nybooks.com/articles/2004/02/26/now-they-tell-us; Jill Kimball, "Costs of the 20-Year War on Terror: $8 Trillion and 900,000 Deaths," News, Brown University, September 1, 2021, https://www.brown.edu/news/2021-09-01/costsofwar.

45. Laurence Peter, "How Ukraine's 'Ghost of Kyiv' Legendary Pilot Was Born," BBC News, May 1, 2022, https://www.bbc.com/news/world-europe-61285833; "Ghosts of Kyiv: A Song for Ukraine," posted by Saher Galt, February 26, 2022, YouTube video, 02:12, https://www.youtube.com/watch?v=r7Ic4UIgslk; "Cryovile—the Ghost of Kyiv," posted by Cryovile, February 26, 2022, YouTube video, 04:07, https://www.youtube.com/watch?v=m5L2KlsbUSg.

46. Jamie Ross, "Ukraine's 'Go Fuck Yourself' Heroes Who Defended Snake Island Still Alive, Its Navy Says," *Daily Beast*, February 28, 2022, https://www.thedailybeast.com/ukraines -go-fck-yourself-heroes-who-defended-snake-island-are-still-alive-its-navy-says; Marta Pascual Juanola, "Ukraine's Snake Island Heroes 'Alive and Well' after Surrendering to the Russians," *Sydney Morning Herald*, March 1, 2022, https://www.smh.com.au/world /europe/ukraine-s-snake-island-heroes-alive-and-well-after-surrendering-to-the -russians-20220301-p5a0l9.html.

47. Lawrence Richard, "US Leads the Rest of the World with $196 Billion Given to Ukraine amid War with Russia," Fox News, February 12, 2023, https://www.foxnews.com/politics /us-leads-rest-of-the-world-196-billion-ukraine-war-russia.

48. "Lyceum Address," Speeches and Writings, Abraham Lincoln Online, accessed February 8, 2023, https://www.abrahamlincolnonline.org/lincoln/speeches/lyceum.htm.

49. Joseph A. Wulfsohn, "White House Asked Twitter Why Alex Berenson Wasn't Banned from the Platform, Lawsuit Reveals," Fox News, August 12, 2022, https://www.foxnews .com/media/white-house-asked-twitter-why-alex-berenson-wasnt-banned-from -platform-lawsuit-reveals.

50. Katie Spence, "Twitter Suppressed Early COVID-19 Treatment Information and Vaccine Safety Concerns: Cardiologist," *Epoch Times*, December 16, 2022, https://www.theepoch times.com/mkt_app/twitter-suppressed-early-covid-19-treatment-information-and -vaccine-safety-concerns-cardiologist_4929265.html; Jordan Boyd, "Amazon Censors Alex Berenson's Booklet Pointing Out Face Mask Ineffectiveness," *Federalist*, November 25, 2020, https://thefederalist.com/2020/11/25/amazon-censors-booklet-pointing-out -face-mask-ineffectiveness.

51. Lee Fang, "COVID-19 Drugmakers Pressured Twitter to Censor Activists Pushing for Generic Vaccine," *Intercept*, January 16, 2023, https://theintercept.com/2023/01/16/twit ter-covid-vaccine-pharma.

52. Dan Diamond, "Suddenly, Public Health Officials Say Social Justice Matters More Than Social Distance," *Politico*, June 4, 2020, https://www.politico.com/news/magazine/2020 /06/04/public-health-protests-301534.

53. Ibid.

54. Shannon Palus, "Public Health Experts Say the Pandemic Is Exactly Why Protests Must Continue," *Slate*, June 2, 2020, https://slate.com/technology/2020/06/protests-coronavi rus-pandemic-public-health-racism.html.

55. System Update, "The Abrupt, Radical Reversal in How Public Health Experts Now Speak about the Coronavirus and Mass Gatherings," *Intercept*, June 11, 2020, https://theinter cept.com/2020/06/11/the-abrupt-radical-reversal-in-how-public-health-experts-now -speak-about-the-coronavirus-and-mass-gatherings.

56. Wulfsohn, "White House Asked Twitter."

57. Ibid.

58. Ibid.

59. Ibid.

60. Ibid.; "CDC Director Admits Vaccines Don't Prevent Transmission," posted by TheDC Shorts, January 10, 2022, YouTube video, 04:04, https://www.youtube.com/watch?v= Z5PWsMkhGDE.

61. Wulfsohn, "White House Asked Twitter."

62. Ashley Lutz, "These 6 Corporations Control 90% of the Media in America," *Business Insider*, June 14, 2012, https://www.businessinsider.com/these-6-corporations-control-90 -of-the-media-in-america-2012-6.

63. Adam Levy, "The Big 6 Media Companies," *Motley Fool*, updated June 10, 2022, https:// www.fool.com/investing/stock-market/market-sectors/communication/media-stocks /big-6.

64. Ibid.

65. "AT&T and Discovery Close WarnerMedia Transaction," AT&T, April 8, 2022, https://about.att.com/story/2022/close-warnermedia-transaction.html.

66. Jess O'Neill, "Chris Cuomo Fired after CNN Learned of Alleged Sex Attack during Office 'Lunch': Report," *New York Post*, February 16, 2022, https://nypost.com/2022/02/16/chris-cuomo-fired-after-cnn-learned-of-alleged-sex-attack-during-office-lunch-report.

67. Thomas Kaplan, "Cuomo Picks Communications Chief with NBC Ties," *New York Times*, October 9, 2012, https://www.nytimes.com/2012/10/10/nyregion/cuomo-names-allison-gollust-as-communications-director.html.

68. Levy, "Big 6 Media Companies"; "Brian L. Roberts, Chairman and Chief Executive Officer," Leadership Overview, Comcast, accessed November 1, 2022, https://corporate.comcast.com/news-information/leadership-overview/brian-l-roberts; Dylan Byers, "Obama Golfs with Comcast CEO," *Politico*, August 14, 2013, https://www.politico.com/blogs/media/2013/08/obama-golfs-with-comcast-ceo-170524.

69. "Brands," NBCUniversal, accessed February 8, 2023, https://www.nbcuniversal.com/brands.

70. Ibid.; "About," NBCUniversal, accessed February 8, 2023, https://www.nbcuniversal.com/about.

71. "Radio City to Bear the Name of Rockefeller; Formal Title Will Be Chosen in a Few Days," *New York Times*, December 21, 1931, https://timesmachine.nytimes.com/timesmachine/1931/12/21/98091856.pdf; John Ensor Harr and Peter J. Johnson, *The Rockefeller Century* (New York: Scribner, 1988), 326–27; "David Sarnoff (1891–1971)," posted by historycomestolife, April 3, 2011, YouTube video, 02:58, https://www.youtube.com/watch?v=Ukk6_OF0UPU.

72. David Rockefeller, "To Be a Rockefeller," *Vanity Fair*, August 14, 2008, https://www.vanityfair.com/news/2002/10/rockefeller_excerpt200210.

73. "To Inaugurate Radio Service," clipping from *Pittsburgh Press*, September 13, 1926, on Newspapers.com, accessed February 22, 2023, https://www.newspapers.com/clip/119255125/to-inaugurate-radio-service; "Broadcasting Monopoly Seen in WEAF Sale," clipping from *Messenger-Inquirer*, July 22, 1926, on Newspapers.com, accessed February 22, 2023, https://www.newspapers.com/clip/119283053/broadcasting-monopoly-seen-in-kjz-sic; Jonathan Berr, "Here Is Everything You Need to Know about the Viacom-CBS Merger," *Forbes*, November 26, 2019, https://www.forbes.com/sites/jonathanberr/2019/11/26/here-is-everything-you-need-to-know-about-the-viacom-cbs-merger.

74. Tucker Higgins, "Former Top FBI Official Andrew McCabe, Who Sparred with Trump, Is Joining CNN as a Contributor," CNBC, August 23, 2019, https://www.cnbc.com/2019/08/23/former-top-fbi-official-andrew-mccabe-is-joining-cnn-as-a-contributor.html.

75. "Andrew McCabe's Bizarre CNN Interview," *Jonathan Turley* (blog), May 8, 2020, https://jonathanturley.org/2020/05/08/our-utter-incompetence-actually-helps-us-mccabes-bizarre-cnn-interview; Andrew C. McCarthy, "The FBI Set Flynn Up to Preserve the Trump-Russia Probe," *National Review*, May 2, 2020, https://www.nationalreview.com/2020/05/fbi-set-up-michael-flynn-to-preserve-trump-russia-probe; Aaron Blake, "Russia Investigation Critics Have Found Their Supposed 'Perjury Trap,'" *Washington Post*, December 12, 2018, https://www.washingtonpost.com/politics/2018/12/12/russia-investigation-critics-have-finally-found-their-supposed-perjury-trap.

76. "Andrew McCabe's Bizarre CNN Interview," *Jonathan Turley* (blog).

77. Office of the Inspector General, "A Report of Investigation of Certain Allegations Relating to Former FBI Deputy Director Andrew McCabe," US Department of Justice, February 2018, accessed November 1, 2022, https://oig.justice.gov/reports/2018/o20180413.pdf.

78. Kevin R. Brock, "Andrew McCabe's Settlement with the Department of Justice Is a Signal to John Durham," *The Hill*, October 19, 2021, https://thehill.com/opinion/criminal-justice/577356-andrew-mccabes-settlement-with-the-department-of-justice-is-a-signal.

79. Bob Woodward, "How Mark Felt Became 'Deep Throat,'" *Washington Post*, June 20, 2005, https://www.washingtonpost.com/politics/how-mark-felt-became-deep-throat/2012/06/04/gJQAlpARIV_story.html.

80. "Senate Select Committee to Study Governmental Operations with Respect to Intelligence Activities," Art & History, US Senate, accessed November 1, 2022, https://www.senate.gov/about/powers-procedures/investigations/church-committee.htm.

81. "Senate Select Committee to Study Governmental Operations," Art & History, US Senate; Carl Bernstein, "The CIA and the Media," *Rolling Stone*, October 20, 1977; Frank Chung, "Conspiracy Theories That Turned Out to Be True," *Chronicle*, December 30, 2019, https://www.thechronicle.com.au/news/conspiracy-theories-that-turned-out-to-be-true/news-story/767607d322591ac3ccae3656568a2b80.

82. "Senate Select Committee to Study Governmental Operations," Art & History, US Senate.

83. Ibid.

84. David P. Hadley, "Introduction," in *The Rising Clamor: The American Press, the Central Intelligence Agency, and the Cold War* (Lexington: University Press of Kentucky, 2019), 3–4, 10; Bernstein, "CIA and the Media."

85. Bernstein, "CIA and the Media."

86. "Congressional Record—Senate," May 19, 1976, vol. 122, part 12, 14673–75, https://www.senate.gov/about/resources/pdf/church-committee-sres400-ssci.pdf.

87. "A Review of Various Actions by the Federal Bureau of Investigation and Department of Justice in Advance of the 2016 Election," Office of the Inspector General, June 2018, accessed February 22, 2023, https://www.justice.gov/file/1071991/download.

88. "Verizon to Acquire Yahoo's Operating Business," Verizon, July 25, 2016, https://www.verizon.com/about/news/verizon-acquire-yahoos-operating-business; David Ignatius, "Is Donald Trump an American Putin?" *Washington Post*, August 15, 2015. https://www.washingtonpost.com/opinions/is-donald-trump-an-american-putin/2015/08/18/46c3dd38-45db-11e5-8ab4-c73967a143d3_story.html; Alexander Bisley, "David Corn on Why Russian Interference Is a Bigger Deal Than Watergate," *Macleans*, April 4 2018, https://macleans.ca/politics/washington/david-corn-why-russian-interference-is-a-bigger-deal-than-watergate.

89. Zach Schonfeld, "Trump Sues Pulitzer Board for Defamation in Defending Winning Russia Collusion Stories," *The Hill*, December 14, 2022, https://thehill.com/homenews/media/3775079-trump-sues-pulitzer-board-for-defamation-in-defending-winning-russia-collusion-stories.

90. Natasha Bertrand, "Hunter Biden Story Is Russian Disinfo, Dozens of Former Intel Officials Say," *Politico*, October 19, 2020, https://www.politico.com/news/2020/10/19/hunter-biden-story-russian-disinfo-430276; Emma-Jo Morris and Gabrielle Fonrouge, "Smoking-Gun Email Reveals How Hunter Biden Introduced Ukrainian Businessman to VP Dad," *New York Post*, October 14, 2020, https://nypost.com/2020/10/14/email-reveals-how-hunter-biden-introduced-ukrainian-biz-man-to-dad.

91. Ed Kilgore, "Now Trump Wants a New 2020 Election: He's Blaming His Loss on an FBI Conspiracy, and His Supporters May Believe Him," *Intelligencer*, August 29, 2022, https://nymag.com/intelligencer/2022/08/trump-demands-a-new-2020-election-right-now.html; James Reinl, "Exclusive: If Only We'd Known: Three Quarters of Survey Respondents Say Voters Lacked 'Critical' Information about Hunter Biden's Laptop during the 2020 Elections, and Half Would Have Voted Differently," *Daily Mail*, updated December 19, 2022, https://www.dailymail.co.uk/news/article-11529381/Hunter-Bidens-laptop-Voters-lacked-critical-information-2020-election-survey-shows.html; Fox News Staff, "Compagno Rips Mainstream Media for 'Toxic Celebration' of FBI's Raid on Trump's Mar-a-Lago," Fox News, August 15, 2022, https://www.foxnews.com/media/compagno-rips-mainstream-media-toxic-celebration-fbis-raid-trumps-mar-a-lago.

Chapter Nine: The Dystopian Present

1. Laura Raphael, "Mark Zuckerberg Called People Who Handed Over Their Data Dumb F****," *Esquire*, March 20, 2018, https://www.esquire.com/uk/latest-news/a19490586/mark-zuckerberg-called-people-who-handed-over-their-data-dumb-f.
2. "The Metaverse and How We'll Build It Together—Connect 2021," posted by Meta, October 28, 2021, YouTube video, 1:17:26, https://www.youtube.com/watch?v=Uvufun6xer8.
3. Rebecca Davis O'Brien, "*The Social Network*'s Woman Problem," *Daily Beast*, on Internet Archive, September 8, 2010, https://web.archive.org/web/20101016073355/http://www.thedailybeast.com/blogs-and-stories/2010-09-08/mark-zuckerberg-at-harvard-the-truth-behind-the-social-network/full; Andrew Paul, "Mark Zuckerberg Thinks Employees 'Lovingly' Call Him 'Eye of Sauron,'" *Input*, April 6, 2022, https://www.inputmag.com/culture/mark-zuckerberg-employees-call-him-eye-sauron.
4. "Metaverse and How We'll Build It Together," 00:45.
5. Ibid., 01:09.
6. Ibid., 05:22 and 10:50.
7. Ibid., 04:22.
8. Ibid., 05:02.
9. Ibid., 05:22.
10. Ann-Marie Alcántara, "Cannabis Companies Try the Metaverse as a New Marketing Plan," *Wall Street Journal*, June 2, 2022, https://www.wsj.com/articles/cannabis-companies-try-the-metaverse-as-a-new-marketing-platform-11654164001.
11. Bipasha Mandal, "Meta Received the Patent for Mechanical Bionic Eye," *Techgenyz*, January 17, 2022, https://www.techgenyz.com/2022/01/17/meta-mechanical-bionic-eye; Thomas Lauritzen, Jessy D. Dorn, Robert J. Greenberg, Jordan Matthew Neysmith, Neil Hamilton Talbot, David Daomin Zhou, Cortical Visual Prosthesis, US patent 20140222103A1, filed February 4, 2014, issued April 5, 2016, https://patents.google.com/patent/US20140222103A1.
12. Zara Stone, "Inside the Smell-O-Verse: Meet the Companies Trying to Bring Scent to the Metaverse," *Fast Company*, May 19, 2022, https://www.fastcompany.com/90744828/inside-the-smell-a-verse-meet-the-companies-trying-to-bring-smell-to-the-metaverse.
13. Dean Takahashi, "Newzoo: More Than 500 Companies Are Building the Metaverse," GamesBeat Summit, June 28, 2022, https://venturebeat.com/games/newzoo-more-than-500-companies-are-building-the-metaverse.
14. Katie Caviness, "Taste the 'Metaverse' in Coca-Cola's New Pixel-Flavored Soda," KATV, May 9, 2022, https://katv.com/news/offbeat/taste-the-metaverse-in-coca-colas-pixel-flavored-soda-soft-drink-beverage-what-is-the-metaverse-starlight-zero-sugar-byte-new-flavors-of-coke-fortnite-creative; "Now You Can Taste Food in the Metaverse by Licking Your TV Screen," *Disruptive.Asia*, December 23, 2021, https://disruptive.asia/taste-food-licking-your-tv-screen.
15. Samantha Hissong, "How Four NFT Novices Created a Billion-Dollar Ecosystem of Cartoon Apes," *Rolling Stone*, November 1, 2021, https://www.rollingstone.com/culture/culture-news/bayc-bored-ape-yacht-club-nft-interview-1250461.
16. "Metaverse and How We'll Build It Together," 43:05.
17. Ibid., 43:26.
18. Ibid., 43:50.
19. "Iceland Roasts Mark Zuckerberg's Metaverse in Tourism Video; Touts 'Open-World Experience Where Everything Is Real,'" *Deadline*, November 12, 2021, https://deadline.com/2021/11/facebook-metaverse-meta-mark-zuckerberg-iceland-1234873459.
20. Aldous Huxley, "The Ultimate Revolution," 1961, Tavistock Group, California Medical School, audio recording, 44:10, https://archive.org/details/AldousHuxley—TheUltimateRevolution—ABlueprintToEnslaveTheMasses.

21. Paul Weindling, "Julian Huxley and the Continuity of Eugenics in Twentieth-Century Britain," *Journal of Modern European History* 10, no. 4 (2012): 480–99, https://www.ncbi .nlm.nih.gov/pmc/articles/PMC4366572; Manvir Singh, "How the Huxleys Electrified Evolution," *New Yorker*, November 21, 2022, https://www.newyorker.com/magazine /2022/11/28/how-the-huxleys-electrified-evolution.

22. Julian Huxley and H. G. Wells, *The Science of Life* (London: Cassell, 1939); Weindling, "Julian Huxley"; John Ensor Harr and Peter J. Johnson, *The Rockefeller Century* (New York: Scribner, 1988), 460; Alden Whitman, "Julian Huxley, Scientist and Writer, Dies," *New York Times*, February 16, 1975, https://www.nytimes.com/1975/02/16/archives/julian -huxley-scientist-and-writer-dies-julian-huxley-scientist-and.html.

23. Huxley and Wells, *Science of Life*, 606.

24. H. G. Wells, *The New World Order* (London: Secker & Warburg, 1940), Project Gutenberg Australia, first posted September 2004, http://gutenberg.net.au/ebooks04/0400671h .html; Eve Glasberg, "H. G. Wells Sparked Modernism and the Literary Imagination," Columbia News, Columbia University, October 23, 2019, https://news.columbia.edu/news /book-h-g-wells-sarah-cole.

25. Ali Smith, "Celebrating HG Wells's Role in the Creation of the UN Declaration of Human Rights," *Guardian*, November 20, 2015, https://www.theguardian.com/books/2015/nov /20/ali-smith-celebrates-hg-wells-role-creation-un-declaration-of-human-rights.

26. Julian Huxley, *New Bottles for New Wine* (London: Chatto & Windus, 1957), 13, https:// archive.org/details/NewBottlesForNewWine/page/n15/mode/2up; Adriana Diaz, "Immortality Is Attainable by 2030: Google Scientist," *New York Post*, March 29, 2023, https:// nypost.com/2023/03/29/immortality-is-attainable-by-2030-google-scientist/; Adam Clark Estes, "Immortality, Sponsored by Mark Zuckerberg," *Vice*, February 20, 2013, https:// www.vice.com/en/article/xyy3gq/immortality-sponsored-by-mark-zuckerberg.

27. Alex Hammer, "How Mark Zuckerberg Pumped $36 Billion Into His Failing Metaverse— and Lost $30 Billion of It," *Daily Mail*, October 29, 2022, https://www.dailymail.co.uk /news/article-11369273/How-Mark-Zuckerberg-pumped-36-BILLION-failing -Metaverse-lost-30-billion-it.html; Charlie Bell, "The Metaverse Is Coming. Here Are the Cornerstones for Securing It," Microsoft (blog), Microsoft, March 28, 2022, https://blogs .microsoft.com/blog/2022/03/28/the-metaverse-is-coming-here-are-the-cornerstones -for-securing-it; Kali Hays, "Meta Competed Fiercely with Google and Microsoft for Years. Now It's Working with Former Rivals as CEO Mark Zuckerberg Pushes for an 'Open' Metaverse," *Business Insider*, October 11, 2022, https://www.businessinsider.com /facebook-youtube-vr-app-quest-headset-microsoft-metaverse-2022-10.

28. Cathy Li, "Who Will Govern the Metaverse?," World Economic Forum, May 25, 2022, https://www.weforum.org/agenda/2022/05/metaverse-governance; Emma Charlton, "71% of Executives Say the Metaverse Will Be Good for Business. Here's Why," World Economic Forum, April 5, 2022, https://www.weforum.org/agenda/2022/04/metaverse -will-be-good-for-business; Adario Strange, "Younger Generations Expect to Spend a Lot More Time in the Metaverse," World Economic Forum, August 19, 2022, https://www .weforum.org/agenda/2022/08/metaverse-technology-virtual-future-people; Rabindra Ratan and Dar Meshi, "Why You Can't Have the Metaverse without the Blockchain," World Economic Forum, January 20, 2022, https://www.weforum.org/agenda/2022/01 /metaverse-crypto-blockchain-virtual-world/; Victoria Masterson, "Feel the Metaverse With Your Bare Hands—Using Ultrasonic Wave," Worled Economic Forum, May 11, 2022, https://www.weforum.org/agenda/2022/05/metaverse-vr-ultrasonic-tech-emerge.

29. Stefan Bramilla Hall and Moritz Baier-Lentz, "3 Technologies That Will Shape the Future of the Metaverse—and the Human Experience," World Economic Forum, February 7, 2022, https://www.weforum.org/agenda/2022/02/future-of-the-metaverse-vr-ar-and-brain -computer; Ratan and Meshi, "Why You Can't Have the Metaverse without the Blockchain."

30. Xiao Liu, "Tracking How Our Bodies Work Could Change Our Lives," World Economic Forum, June 4, 2020, https://www.weforum.org/agenda/2020/06/internet-of-bodies-covid19-recovery-governance-health-data.

31. "Governance Track," World Economic Forum, https://initiatives.weforum.org/defining-and-building-the-metaverse/govern..

32. "Strategic Partners," World Economic Forum, accessed December 1, 2022, https://www.weforum.org/communities/strategic-partnership-b5337725-fac7-4f8a-9a4f-c89072b96a0d; "Our Partners," World Economic Forum, accessed December 1, 2022, https://www.weforum.org/partners/#search.

33. Bill Gates, "Reasons for Optimism after a Difficult Year," *GatesNotes* (blog), December 7, 2021, https://www.gatesnotes.com/About-Bill-Gates/Year-in-Review-2021.

34. Microsoft News Center, "Microsoft to Acquire Activision Blizzard to Bring the Joy and Community of Gaming to Everyone, across Every Device," Microsoft, January 18, 2022, https://news.microsoft.com/2022/01/18/microsoft-to-acquire-activision-blizzard-to-bring-the-joy-and-community-of-gaming-to-everyone-across-every-device; John Letzing, "What Microsoft's Acquisition of Activision Blizzard Means for the Metaverse," World Economic Forum, January 19, 2022, https://www.weforum.org/agenda/2022/01/microsoft-buy-activision-blizzard-metaverse.

35. Oli Welsh, "Microsoft CEO Argues That Buying Activision Blizzard Will Help Him Build the Metaverse," *Polygon*, February 4, 2022, https://www.polygon.com/22917625/microsoft-activision-blizzard-metaverse-satya-nadella; "FTC Seeks to Block Microsoft Corp.'s Acquisition of Activision Blizzard, Inc.," Federal Trade Commission, press release, https://www.ftc.gov/news-events/news/press-releases/2022/12/ftc-seeks-block-microsoft-corps-acquisition-activision-blizzard-inc; Sarah E. Needleman, "Microsoft Prepares to Go to Battle with FTC over Activision Deal," *Wall Street Journal*, updated December 17, 2022, https://www.wsj.com/articles/microsoft-prepares-to-go-to-battle-with-ftc-over-activision-deal-11671283792; United States v. Microsoft, 253 F.3d 34 (D.C. Cir. 2001), Department of Justice, accessed December 12, 2022, https://www.justice.gov/atr/us-v-microsoft-proposed-findings-fact-1.

36. Bell, "Metaverse Is Coming."

37. Jack Kelly, "The Metaverse Set Off a Battle between Tech Giants Google, Apple, Microsoft, and Meta to Build Virtual and Augmented Reality Headsets," *Forbes*, January 21, 2022, https://www.forbes.com/sites/jackkelly/2022/01/21/the-metaverse-set-off-a-battle-between-tech-giants-google-apple-microsoft-and-meta-to-build-virtual-and-augmented-reality-headsets.

38. Dawn Chmielewski, "Disney Wants to Become the Happiest Place in the Metaverse," Reuters, November 10, 2021, https://www.reuters.com/technology/disney-wants-become-happiest-place-metaverse-2021-11-11.

39. Reld Menge, "The Metaverse: Investing in the Future Now," BlackRock, February 14, 2022, https://www.blackrock.com/us/individual/insights/metaverse-investing-in-the-future; "Step into the Metaverse," BlackRock, May 3, 2022, https://www.blackrock.com/uk/solutions/step-into-the-metaverse.

40. Zacks Equity Research, "JPMorgan (JPM) Enters Metaverse, Unveils Virtual Onyx Lounge," Nasdaq, February 16, 2022, https://www.nasdaq.com/articles/jpmorgan-jpm-enters-metaverse-unveils-virtual-onyx-lounge.

41. "Opportunities in the Metaverse: How Businesses Can Explore the Metaverse and Navigate the Hype vs. Reality," JPMorgan, accessed December 1, 2022, https://www.jpmorgan.com/content/dam/jpm/treasury-services/documents/opportunities-in-the-metaverse.pdf; Carmela Chirinos, "Someone Just Paid $450,000 to Be Snoop Dogg's Neighbor in the Metaverse. Here's How You Can Live by a Celebrity Too," *Fortune*, February 2, 2022,

https://fortune.com/2022/02/02/how-to-buy-metaverse-real-estate-snoop-dogg
-celebrity-neighbor.

42. Robert Frank, "Metaverse Real Estate Sales Top $500 Million Metametric Solutions, and
    Are Projected to Double This Year," CNBC, February 1, 2022, https://www.cnbc.com
    /2022/02/01/metaverse-real-estate-sales-top-500-million-metametric-solutions-says
    .html; "2022 Annual Metaverse Virtual Real Estate Report," Parcel, January 10, 2023,
    https://parcel.so/learn/2022-annual-metaverse-virtual-real-estate-report.

43. Harry Robertson, "The Metaverse Is a Massive Opportunity for Crypto That Calls for New
    Platforms and Tokens, Bank of America Strategist Says," *Business Insider*, November
    30, 2021, https://markets.businessinsider.com/news/currencies/metaverse-crypto-crypto
    currencies-blockchain-technology-decentraland-bank-of-america-2021-11; Kevin Helms,
    "Goldman Sachs Sees the Metaverse as $8 Trillion Opportunity," Bitcoin.com, January 24,
    2022, https://news.bitcoin.com/goldman-sachs-metaverse-8-trillion-opportunity.

44. "Goldman's Dreams of Oligopoly," *Financial Times*, October 12, 2016, https://www.ft.com
    /content/f9b9ddb2-cde1-3a29-bd2b-61884f138fb7; Justin Elliott, "The American Way,"
    ProPublica, October 11, 2016, https://www.propublica.org/article/airline-consolidation
    -democratic-lobbying-antitrust.

45. Jason Parham, "Everything Is Becoming Paywalled Content—Even You," *Wired*, March 3,
    2020, https://www.wired.com/story/everyone-is-a-subscription.

46. Will Canny, "Goldman Says Apple, Meta Lead in Developing Metaverse Technology,"
    CoinDesk, April 21, 2022, https://www.coindesk.com/business/2022/04/21/goldman
    -says-apple-meta-lead-in-developing-metaverse-technology.

47. Grace Kay, "Elon Musk's Brain-Chip Startup Shares Video It Says Shows a Monkey Tele-
    pathically 'Typing,'" *Business Insider*, December 1, 2022, https://www.businessinsider
    .com/elon-musk-neuralink-brain-chip-startup-monkey-typing-video-2022-12; Sam Shead,
    "Elon Musk Says His Start-Up Neuralink Has Wired Up a Monkey to Play Video Games
    Using Its Mind," CNBC, updated February 2, 2021, https://www.cnbc.com/2021/02/01
    /elon-musk-neuralink-wires-up-monkey-to-play-video-games-using-mind.html.

48. Theo Wayt, "Elon Musk's Neuralink Allegedly Subjected Monkeys to 'Extreme Suffer-
    ing,'" *New York Post*, February 10, 2022, https://nypost.com/2022/02/10/elon-musks
    -neuralink-allegedly-subjected-monkeys-to-extreme-suffering; Rachael Levy, "Exclu-
    sive: Musk's Neuralink Faces Federal Probe, Employee Backlash over Animal Tests," Reu-
    ters,December6,2022,https://www.reuters.com/technology/musks-neuralink-faces-federal
    -probe-employee-backlash-over-animal-tests-2022-12-05.

49. Jeremy Kahn, Jonathan Vanian, and Mahnoor Khan, "Elon Musk Claims Neuralink's
    Brain Implants Will 'Save' Memories Like Photos and Help Paraplegics Walk Again.
    Here's a Reality Check," *Fortune*, July 7, 2022, https://fortune.com/2022/07/07/elon-musk
    -neuralink-brain-implant-claims; Daniel Gilbert and Faiz Siddiqui, "Elon Musk's Neura-
    link Says It Has FDA Approval for Human Trials. What to Know," *Washington Post*, May
    25, 2023, https://www.washingtonpost.com/business/2023/05/25/elon-musk-neuralink
    -fda-approval.

50. Megan Sauer, "Elon Musk Says Humans Could Eventually Download Their Brains into
    Robots—and Grimes Thinks Jeff Bezos Would Do It," CNBC, updated April 9, 2022,
    https://www.cnbc.com/2022/04/08/elon-musk-humans-could-eventually-download
    -their-brains-into-robots.html; Sarah McBride, "Bezos and Gates Back Synchron in Drive
    for Brain Implant Breakthrough," *Bloomberg*, December 15, 2022, https://www.bloomberg
    .com/news/articles/2022-12-15/bezos-and-gates-back-synchron-in-drive-for-brain
    -implant-breakthrough; "Elon Musk Confirms He Already Uploaded His Brain to a Cloud,
    He Spoke to Himself," *Marca*, July 29, 2022, https://www.marca.com/en/lifestyle/celebri
    ties/2022/07/29/62e4032a268e3e9c338b45bb.html.

51. Sam Shead, "Peter Thiel Is Backing a Rival to Elon Musk's Brain Implant Company," CNBC, May 19, 2021, https://www.cnbc.com/2021/05/19/peter-thiel-is-backing-a-rival-to-elon-musks-neuralink-.html.

52. Lindsay Dodgson, "More and More People Are Turning to VR Porn during Self-Isolation for Comfort from Depression, Anxiety, and Frustration," *Business Insider*, April 5, 2020, https://www.insider.com/adult-entertainment-industry-seeing-rise-in-vr-porn-isolation-2020-3; Theo Wayt, "Microsoft Executive Watched 'VR Porn' in Front of Subordinates: Report," *New York Post*, May 26, 2022, https://nypost.com/2022/05/26/microsoft-executive-watched-vr-porn-in-front-of-subordinates-report; "Palmer Luckey Wants to Make VR Porn Better with Nerve Implants," *EconoTimes*, September 29, 2017, https://www.econotimes.com/Palmer-Luckey-Wants-To-Make-VR-Porn-Better-With-Nerve-Implants-920763; Matthew Gault, "Palmer Luckey Made a VR Headset That Kills the User If They Die in the Game," *Vice*, November 7, 2022, https://www.vice.com/en/article/dy7kbq/palmer-luckey-made-a-vr-headset-that-kills-the-user-if-they-die-in-the-game.

53. Jonathan Vanian, "Most People Say They're Cool with Having Chips Implanted in Their Brains, but Only If They Can Turn Them Off," *Fortune*, March 17, 2022, https://fortune.com/2022/03/17/brain-chips-pew-survey-elon-musk-neuralink.

54. Nicholas Carlson, "Well, These New Zuckerberg IMs Won't Help Facebook's Privacy Problems," *Business Insider*, May 13, 2010, https://www.businessinsider.com/well-these-new-zuckerberg-ims-wont-help-facebooks-privacy-problems-2010-5; Raphael, "Mark Zuckerberg."

55. Ja'han Jones, "Facebook Knows You're Addicted, and They Plan to Keep It That Way," MSNBC, October 5, 2021, https://www.msnbc.com/msnbc/facebook-whistleblower-frances-haugen-testimony-rcna2618; Kevin Roose, "The Metaverse Is Mark Zuckerberg's Escape Hatch," *New York Times*, October 29, 2021, https://www.nytimes.com/2021/10/29/technology/meta-facebook-zuckerberg.html.

56. Olivia Solon, "Ex-Facebook President Sean Parker: Site Made to Exploit Human 'Vulnerability,'" *Guardian*, November 9, 2017, https://www.theguardian.com/technology/2017/nov/09/facebook-sean-parker-vulnerability-brain-psychology.

57. Julia Carrie Wong, "Former Facebook Executive: Social Media Is Ripping Society Apart," *Guardian*, December 12, 2017, https://www.theguardian.com/technology/2017/dec/11/facebook-former-executive-ripping-society-apart.

58. "Vishal Shah," Profile, LinkedIn, accessed December 1, 2022, https://www.linkedin.com/in/vishalnshah; Ryan Mac and Craig Silverman, "Facebook Is Building an Instagram for Kids under the Age of 13," *BuzzFeed News*, March 18, 2021, https://www.buzzfeednews.com/article/ryanmac/facebook-instagram-for-children-under-13.

59. Ashley Welch, "Depression, Anxiety, Suicide Increase in Teens and Young Adults, Study Finds," CBS News, March 14, 2019, https://www.cbsnews.com/news/suicide-depression-anxiety-mental-health-issues-increase-teens-young-adults; Evelyn M. Rusli, "Facebook Buys Instagram for $1 Billion," *New York Times*, April 9, 2012, https://archive.nytimes.com/dealbook.nytimes.com/2012/04/09/facebook-buys-instagram-for-1-billion.

60. David Monahan, "Health Advocates Ask Facebook to Scrap Planned Instagram for Kids," Fairplay, press release, April 15, 2021, https://fairplayforkids.org/apr_15_2021_scrap_instagram_forkids.

61. Jonathan Vanian and Jeremy Kahn, "Meet the Meta Executive Tasked with Bringing Mark Zuckerberg's High-Stakes Metaverse Vision to Life," *Fortune*, June 13, 2022, https://fortune.com/2022/06/13/what-will-the-metaverse-look-like-meta-platforms-vishal-shah; Jessica Bursztynsky, "Facebook Says It's Pausing Effort to Build Instagram for Kids," CNBC, September 27, 2021, https://www.cnbc.com/2021/09/27/facebook-pausing-effort-to-build-instagram-for-kids.html.

62. Roose, "Metaverse"; Georgia Wells, Jeff Horwitz, and Deppa Seetharaman, "Facebook Knows Instagram Is Toxic for Teen Girls, Company Documents Show," *Wall Street Journal*, September 14, 2021, https://www.wsj.com/articles/facebook-knows-instagram -is-toxic-for-teen-girls-company-documents-show-11631620739.

63. Roose, "Metaverse."

64. William Doyle, "Mark Zuckerberg Spent $419M on Nonprofits Ahead of 2020 Election— and Got Out the Dem Vote," *New York Post*, October 13, 2021, https://nypost.com/2021/10 /13/mark-zuckerberg-spent-419m-on-nonprofits-ahead-of-2020-election-and-got-out -the-dem-vote.

65. Bruce Golding, "Zuckerberg Says Facebook Censored *The Post*'s Hunter Biden Stories Because FBI Warned of Russian Misinfo 'Dump,'" *New York Post*, August 26, 2022, https://ny post.com/2022/08/26/zuckerberg-blames-fbi-for-censoring-the-posts-hunter-biden-scoop.

66. Mike Isaac, "Facebook Mounts Effort to Limit Tide of Fake News," *New York Times*, December 15, 2016, https://www.nytimes.com/2016/12/15/technology/facebook-fake-news .html.

67. Caitlin Doornbos and Jon Levine, "Facebook, Twitter Stocked with Ex-FBI, CIA Officials in Key Posts," *New York Post*, December 22, 2022, https://nypost.com/2022/12/22/face book-twitter-stocked-with-ex-fbi-cia-officials.

68. "The Role of Social Media Companies—Dr. Anne Merritt, Aaron Berman, and Brian Clarke," Stanford Department of Emergency Medicine, September 16, 2021, YouTube video, 01:30–03:26, https://www.youtube.com/watch?v=hB_YNbnt8x4&t=90s..

69. Jana Katsuyama, "Elon Musk Takes Over Twitter, Saying It Will Be 'Digital Town Square' Not a 'Free-For-All,'" KTVU, October 27, 2022, https://www.ktvu.com/news/elon-musk -takes-over-twitter-saying-it-will-be-digital-town-square-not-a-free-for-all.

70. Ryan Mac and Kellen Browning, "Elon Musk Reinstates Trump's Twitter Account," *New York Times*, November 19, 2022, https://www.nytimes.com/2022/11/19/technology/trump -twitter-musk.html.

71. Matt Taibbi (@mtaibbi), "Thread: Twitter Files Supplemental," Twitter, December 6, 2022, 2:38 p.m., https://twitter.com/mtaibbi/status/1600243405841666048; Bari Weiss (@bariweiss), "Thread: The Twitter Files Part Two. Twitter's Secret Blacklists," Twitter, December 8, 2022, 5:15 p.m., https://twitter.com/bariweiss/status/1601007575633305600; Matt Taibbi (@mtaibbi), "1. Thread: The Twitter Files. The Removal of Donald Trump Part One: October 2020—January 6th," Twitter, December 9, 2022, 4:04 p.m., https://twit ter.com/mtaibbi/status/1601352083617505281; Michael Shellenberger (@ShellenbergerMD), "1. Twitter Files, Part 4. The Removal of Donald Trump: January 7. As the pressure builds, Twitter executives build the case for a permanent ban," Twitter, December 10, 2022, 4:28 p.m., https://twitter.com/ShellenbergerMD/status/1601720455005511680; Bari Weiss (@bariweiss), "Thread: The Twitter Files Part Five. The Removal of Trump from Twitter," Twitter, December 12, 2022, 11:06 a.m., https://twitter.com/bariweiss/status /1602364197194432515; Matt Taibbi (@mtaibbi), "1. Thread: The Twitter Files, Part Six. Twitter, The FBI Subsidiary," Twitter, December 16, 2022, 2:00 p.m., https://twitter.com /mtaibbi/status/1603857534737072128; Michael Shellenberger (@ShellenbergerMD), "1. Twitter Files: Part 7. The FBI & the Hunter Biden Laptop," Twitter, December 19, 2022, 9:09 a.m., https://twitter.com/ShellenbergerMD/status/1604871630613753856; Lee Fang (@lhfang), "1. Twitter Files Part 8. *How Twitter Quietly Aided the Pentagon's Covert Online PsyOp Campaign*," Twitter, December 20, 2022, 1:02 p.m., https://twitter.com/lh fang/status/1605292454261182464.

72. Weiss (@bariweiss), "Thread: The Twitter Files Part Two. Twitter's Secret Blacklists"; Brian Flood, "Twitter Files Part 8: Platform 'Directly Assisted' US Military's Influence Operations," Fox News, December 20, 2022, https://www.foxnews.com/media/twitter -files-part-8-platform-directly-assisted-u-s-militarys-influence-operations.

73. Golding, "Zuckerberg Says Facebook Censored *The Post*'s Hunter Biden Stories."

74. Tucker Carlson, "Glenn Greenwald: The National Security State Is in Bed with Big Tech," Fox News, December 2, 2022, video, 03:58–05:05, https://www.foxnews.com/video /6316507548112; CIA, "Letter to James Bitoni from Stansfield Turner," June 14, 1979, on Internet Archive, accessed December 1, 2022, https://archive.org/details/CIA-RDP05S 00620R000100050006-0.

75. Molly Ball, "The Secret History of the Shadow Campaign That Saved the 2020 Election," *Time*, February 4, 2021, https://time.com/5936036/secret-2020-election-campaign.

76. Bruce Golding, "What Is the Mysterious Aspen Institute and Why Did It Hold a Hunter Biden 'Exercise'?," *New York Post*, December 19, 2022, https://nypost.com/2022/12/19 /what-is-mysterious-aspen-institute-and-why-did-it-hold-hunter-biden-exercise.

77. "Annual Conference," Aspen Institute, accessed February 22, 2023, https://www.aspenin stitutece.org/program/annual-conference; "Can the World Economic Forum Keep Its Mojo?," *Economist*, January 18, 2020, https://www.economist.com/business/2020/01/18 /can-the-world-economic-forum-keep-its-mojo.

78. "Financial Supporters," Aspen Institute, accessed December 1, 2022, https://www.aspen institute.org/programs/business-and-society-program/financial-supporters; Golding, "Mys-terious Aspen Institute"; "Aspen Leaders Forum," Aspen Institute, accessed February 22, 2023, https://www.aspeninstitute.org/programs/business-and-society-program/aspen -leaders-forum.

79. "Our Grants," About Us, Rockefeller Foundation, accessed December 1, 2022, https:// www.rockefellerfoundation.org/grants.

80. "Aspen Institute," Committed Grants, Bill & Melinda Gates Foundation, accessed December 1, 2022, https://www.gatesfoundation.org/about/committed-grants?q=aspen%20institute.

81. Glenn Gamboa, "Ballmer Crafts New Funding Strategy to Confront Gun Violence," AP Wire, March 9, 2022, https://apnews.com/article/covid-health-business-united-states -violence-872139d05edb0f710514894e45f0288b; Grace Turner, "Washington's Ballmer Group Donates $5.9 to Detroit Schools to Create Online Student Progress Portal," *DBusi-ness*, December 17, 2019, https://www.dbusiness.com/daily-news/washingtons-ballmer -group-donates-5-9m-to-detroit-schools-to-create-online-student-progress-portal; Reid Goldsmith, "Steve Ballmer Group Donates over $25 Million to Seattle, Los Angeles, and SE Michigan," *ClutchPoints*, March 27, 2020, https://clutchpoints.com/clippers-news -steve-ballmer-group-donates-over-25-million-to-seattle-los-angeles-and-se-michigan.

82. "Final Report November 2021: Commission on Information Disorder," Aspen Digital, As-pen Institute, accessed December 1, 2022, https://www.aspeninstitute.org/wp-content /uploads/2021/11/Aspen-Institute_Commission-on-Information-Disorder_Final-Report .pdf; "Financial Supporters," Aspen Institute.

83. "Who Pays for PolitiFact?," PolitiFact, updated January 2022, accessed November 1, 2022, https://www.politifact.com/who-pays-for-politifact; "Poynter's Top Funding Sources," Poynter, updated October 2022, https://www.poynter.org/major-funders; "Financials," Democracy Fund, accessed November 1, 2022, https://democracyfund.org/who-we-are /financials; Andrew Rice, "The Pierre Omidyar Insurgency," *New York*, November 2, 2014, https://nymag.com/intelligencer/2014/10/pierre-omidyar-first-look-media.html.

84. Golding, "Mysterious Aspen Institute"; US Department of Treasury, Internal Revenue Service Form 990, Aspen Institute, accessed December 12, 2022, https://www.aspeninsti tute.org/wp-content/uploads/2021/11/ASPEN-2020-12-Tax-990-Public-Disclosure -Copy.pdf.

85. Paul Farhi, "*New York Times* Columnist Brooks Resigns from Think Tank amid Conflict-of-Interest Controversy," *Washington Post*, March 6, 2021, https://www.washingtonpost .com/lifestyle/media/david-brooks-resigns-from-aspen-institute/2021/03/06/ae67ccfa

-7eb1-11eb-a976-c028a4215c78_story.html; Craig Silverman and Ryan Mac, "Facebook Helped Fund David Brooks's Second Job. Nobody Told the Readers of the *New York Times*," *BuzzFeed News*, March 3, 2021, https://www.buzzfeednews.com/article/craigsilverman /david-brooks-nyt-weave-facebook-bezos; "2018 Transparency Report: Gifts, Grants and Program Support ($25K and Over)," Aspen Institute, accessed February 22, 2023, https:// www.aspeninstitute.org/wp-content/uploads/2019/07/2018-Transparency-Report.pdf.

86. "Vivian Schiller Appointed President and CEO of NPR," Updates, News Literacy Project, November 20, 2008, https://newslit.org/updates/vivian-schiller-appointed-president-and -ceo-of-npr; "*Times* Names Web Site Executive," *New York Times*, April 25, 2006, https:// www.nytimes.com/2006/04/25/business/media/times-names-web-site-executive.html; "Vivian Schiller," Our People, Aspen Institute, accessed February 22, 2023, https://www .aspeninstitute.org/people/Vivian-schiller; "Vivian Schiller," Profile, LinkedIn, accessed February 22, 2023, https://www.linkedin.com/in/vivianschiller.

87. Brian Stelter, "Microsoft and NBC Complete Web Divorce," *New York Times*, July 15, 2012, https://www.nytimes.com/2012/07/16/business/media/msnbccom-renamed -nbcnewscom-as-microsoft-and-nbc-divorce.html; "Vivian Schiller," Profile, LinkedIn; Tony Maglio, "Vivian Schiller Steps Down as Twitter's Head of News as Part of Ongoing Reorganization," *TheWrap*, October 9, 2014, https://www.thewrap.com/vivian-schiller -twitter-head-of-news-katie-stanton.

88. "Vivian Schiller," Our People, Aspen Institute; "Vivian Schiller," Profile, LinkedIn.

89. Joseph Clark, "'Twitter Files' Show FBI Offered Executives Top Secret Info to Guide 2020 Election Censorship," *Washington Times*, December 19, 2022, https://www.washington times.com/news/2022/dec/19/twitter-files-show-fbi-offered-executives-top-secr.

90. Golding, "Mysterious Aspen Institute."

91. Steven Musil, "Twitter Revises Policy on Posting Hacked Materials after Hunter Biden Story," CNET, October 16, 2020, https://www.cnet.com/tech/services-and-software /twitter-revises-policy-on-posting-hacked-materials-after-hunter-biden-story.

92. Jesse O'Neill, "FBI Pressured Twitter, Sent Trove of Docs Hours before Post Broke Hunter Laptop Story," *New York Post*, December 19, 2022, https://nypost.com/2022/12/19/fbi -reached-out-to-twitter-before-post-broke-hunter-biden-laptop-story.

93. Matt Taibbi (@mtaibbi) "1. Thread: The Twitter Files."

94. "Towards a Stronger Information Ecosystem: Commission on Information Disorder Report & Recommendations," Aspen Institute, November 15, 2021, https://www.aspeninsti tute.org/videos/towards-a-stronger-information-ecosystem-commission-on-infor mation-disorder-report-recommendations.

95. Ibid.

96. "1. WO2020060606—Cryptocurrency System Using Body Activity Data," PatentScope, March 26, 2020, https://patentscope.wipo.int/search/en/detail.jsf?docId=WO2020060606.

97. Ibid.

98. Kevin J. McHugh et al., "Biocompatible Near-Infrared Quantum Dots Delivered to the Skin by Microneedle Patches Record Vaccination," *Science Translational Medicine* 11, no. 523 (December 2019), https://doi.org/10.1126/scitranslmed.aay7162; ID2020, "Immuniza tion: An Entry Point for Digital Identity," Medium, March 28, 2018, https://medium.com /id2020/immunization-an-entry-point-for-digital-identity-ea37d9c3b77e.

99. Karen Weintraub, "Invisible Ink Could Reveal Whether Kids Have Been Vaccinated," *Scientific American*, December 18, 2019, https://www.scientificamerican.com/article/invis ible-ink-could-reveal-whether-kids-have-been-vaccinated.

100. Devin Coldewey, "Bill Gates Addresses Coronavirus Fears and Hopes in AMA," *TechCrunch*, March 18, 2020, https://techcrunch.com/2020/03/18/bill-gates-addresses -coronavirus-fears-and-hopes-in-ama.

101. Matthew J. Belvedere, "Bill Gates: My 'Best Investment' Turned $10 Billion into $200 Billion Worth of Economic Benefit," CNBC, January 23, 2019, https://www.cnbc.com/2019 /01/23/bill-gates-turns-10-billion-into-200-billion-worth-of-economic-benefit.html; Ryan Browne, "Microsoft Dives into Web3 with Investment in Ethereum Co-founder's Start-Up ConsenSys," CNBC, updated March 21, 2022, https://www.cnbc.com/2022/ 03/15/consensys-doubles-valuation-to-7-billion-with-microsoft-backing.html; "Alphabet, BlackRock, Morgan Stanley among Top 5 Investors in Blockchain Firms," *Mint*, August 17, 2022, https://www.livemint.com/market/cryptocurrency/alphabet-blackrock-morgan-stan ley-among-top-5-investors-in-blockchain-firms-11660750378052.html; "Testing Meta Verified to Help Creators Establish Their Presence," Meta, February 19, 2023, https://about .fb.com/news/2023/02/testing-meta-verified-to-help-creators.

102. Sheila Warren, "How Are the Forum and Partners Shaping the Future of Blockchain and Distributed Ledger Technologies?," posted by World Economic Forum, March 27, 2020, YouTube video, 02:44, https://www.youtube.com/watch?v=fXgkgTa0y6Y.

Chapter Ten: The End Game

1. George Orwell, *Nineteen Eighty-Four* (London: Secker & Warburg, 1949), 28–29.

2. "Weather in Philadelphia, September 1," World Weather, accessed December 12, 2022, https://world-weather.info/forecast/usa/philadelphia_1/01-september.

3. "Remarks by President Biden on the Continued Battle for the Soul of the Nation," Speeches and Remarks, The White House, September 1, 2022, https://www.whitehouse.gov/brief ing-room/speeches-remarks/2022/09/01/remarks-by-president-bidenon-the-continued -battle-for-the-soul-of-the-nation.

4. Joe Biden, "Biden Warns of Dangers to Democracy in Prime-Time Address—9/1 (Full Live Stream)," posted by *Washington Post*, September 1, 2022, YouTube video, 1:00:57, https:// youtu.be/2LGYTj1slik.

5. Ed Rogers, "The Consequences of Clinton's 'Deplorables' and Obama's 'Clingers,'" *Denver Post*, September 13, 2016, https://www.denverpost.com/2016/09/13/the-consequences-of -clintons-deplorables-and-obamas-clingers.

6. "Remarks by President Biden on Fighting the COVID-19 Pandemic," Speeches and Remarks, The White House, September 9, 2021, https://www.whitehouse.gov/briefing-room /speeches-remarks/2021/09/09/remarks-by-president-biden-on-fighting-the -covid-19-pandemic-3; "Remarks by President Biden at Virtual Democratic National Committee Event," Speeches and Remarks, The White House, August 3, 2022, https://www .whitehouse.gov/briefing-room/speeches-remarks/2022/08/03/remarks-by-president -biden-at-virtual-democratic-national-committee-event; "Remarks by President Biden on the Continued Battle for the Soul of the Nation," Speeches and Remarks, The White House; "Tucker Carlson: Life, Death, Power, the CIA & the End of Journalism," *Tulsi Gabbard Show*, December 13, 2022, YouTube video, 39:10–47:00, https://www.youtube.com/watch? v=SKEWD4-nwyA.

7. "Biden Gives 'Soul of the Nation' Prime-Time Address Ahead of Midterm Elections," MSNBC, updated September 1, 2022, https://www.msnbc.com/white-house/presidential -address/live-blog/biden-speech-midterm-elections-rcna45777; Chas Danner, "A Guide to the Intense Debate over Biden's Bid Democracy Speech," *Intelligencer*, updated September 6, 2022, https://nymag.com/intelligencer/2022/09/a-guide-to-the-intense-debate-over -bidens-democracy-speech.html; David Frum, "The Justification for Biden's Speech," *Atlantic*, September 2, 2022, https://www.theatlantic.com/ideas/archive/2022/09/joe-bidens -speech-trump-republicans/671326.

8. William Vaillancourt, "Fox Hosts Fume over 'Blood-Red Nazi' Lightning in Biden Speech," *Daily Beast*, September 1, 2022, https://www.thedailybeast.com/fox-news-hosts-fume-over-blood-red-nazi-lighting-in-joe-biden-speech.

9. Tristan Justice, "In Speech Walkback, Biden Now Admits He's the Real Threat to Democracy," *Federalist*, September 2, 2022, https://thefederalist.com/2022/09/02/in-speech-walkback-biden-now-admits-hes-the-real-threat-to-democracy.

10. Sarah Al-Arshani, "Senate Intelligence Chair Says It's 'Stunning' That over 20 Years after Sept. 11, Attacks on the Symbol of Democracy Are 'Not Coming from Terrorists' but from 'Insurgents' at the Capitol on Jan. 6," *Business Insider*, September 11, 2022, https://www.businessinsider.com/senate-intelligence-chair-911-january-6-symbol-attack-democracy-2022-9; Alec Schemmel, "Kamala Harris Likens Jan 6 to Pearl Harbor and 9/11 in Anniversary Speech," KATV, January 6, 2022, https://katv.com/news/nation-world/kamala-harris-likens-jan-6-to-pearl-harbor-and-911-in-anniversary-speech.

11. Sheila Dang, "Twitter to Expand Its Community Fact-Checking Experiment, Birdwatch," Reuters, September 7, 2022, https://www.reuters.com/technology/twitter-expand-its-community-fact-checking-experiment-birdwatch-2022-09-07; Jody Serrano, "How Will Twitter's Birdwatch Community Debunking Actually Work? A VP Answers Our Questions," *Gizmodo*, September 9, 2022, https://gizmodo.com/twitter-vp-birdwatch-community-debunk-qanon-fact-check-1849514292.

12. Frum, "Justification for Biden's Speech"; Charlie Warzel, "Is This the Beginning of the End of the Internet?," *Atlantic*, September 28, 2022, https://www.theatlantic.com/ideas/archive/2022/09/netchoice-paxton-first-amendment-social-media-content-moderation/671574; "Members," Computer and Communications Industry Association, accessed December 12, 2022, https://www.ccianet.org/about/members; "Our Mission," About Us, NetChoice, accessed December 12, 2022, https://netchoice.org/about; Shoshana Wodinsky, "Here's Who Funds the Tech Think Tanks Asking Congress to Reconsider This Whole Antitrust Thing," *Gizmodo*, June 21, 2021, https://gizmodo.com/heres-who-funds-the-tech-think-tanks-asking-congress-to-1847142650.

13. "MAGA Republicans," Topic, Center for American Progress Action Fund, accessed February 22, 2023, https://www.americanprogressaction.org/topic/maga-republicans/; "Our Supporters," Center for American Progress Action Fund, accessed February 22, 2023, https://www.americanprogress.org/c3-our-supporters; Jon Greenberg, "What Is a MAGA Republican?," Poynter Institute, September 23, 2022, https://www.poynter.org/fact-checking/2022/what-is-a-maga-republican; "Poynter's Top Funding Sources," Poynter Institute, updated October 2022, https://www.poynter.org/major-funders.

14. Rachel Bovard, "Biden's 'MAGA Republican' Screed Gives Gatekeepers the Green Light to Purge Political Foes," *Federalist*, September 8, 2022, https://thefederalist.com/2022/09/08/bidens-maga-republican-screed-gives-gatekeepers-the-greenlight-to-purge-political-foes; Elizabeth Goitein, "How the FBI Violated the Privacy Rights of Tens of Thousands of Americans," Brennan Center for Justice, October 22, 2019, https://www.brennancenter.org/our-work/analysis-opinion/how-fbi-violated-privacy-rights-tens-thousands-americans.

15. Bovard, "Biden's 'MAGA Republican' Screed."

16. "Kari Lake to Claim in Court Arizona Governor's Race Was Stolen from Her," CBS News, December 21, 2022, https://www.cbsnews.com/news/kari-lakes-stolen-election-claims-trial; Kari Lake v. Katie Hobbs, Stephen Richer, Scott Jarrett, and the Maricopa County Board of Supervisors, 39 (Ariz. Supr. Ct. 2022), https://savearizonafund.com/lawsuit.

17. Tony Hall, "A Closer Look at Voter Fraud, San Francisco Style!" *Epoch Times*, updated August 4, 2021, https://www.theepochtimes.com/a-closer-look-at-voter-fraud-san-francisco-style_3929085.html.

18. Bret Stephens, "The Mask Mandates Did Nothing. Will Any Lessons Be Learned?," *New York Times*, February 21, 2023, https://www.nytimes.com/2023/02/21/opinion/do-mask-mandates-work.html.

19. Nicholas Giordano, "Biden's Sinister 'Soul of the Nation' Speech Wasn't His First Attempt to Target Political Opponents," *Federalist*, September 2, 2022, https://thefederalist.com/2022/09/02/bidens-sinister-soul-of-the-nation-speech-wasnt-his-first-attempt-to-target-political-opponents.

20. "WEF Founder: Must Prepare for an Angrier World," CNBC, July 14, 2020, MP3 audio, 05:51, https://www.cnbc.com/video/2020/07/14/wef-founder-must-prepare-for-an-angrier-world.html.

21. Kelvin Chan, "Inflation Protests across Europe Threaten Political Turmoil," ABC News, October 23, 2022, https://abcnews.go.com/Business/wireStory/inflation-protests-europe-threaten-political-turmoil-91905279; Reuters, "Thousands Protest in Germany Demanding Solidarity in Energy Relief," October 22, 2022, https://www.reuters.com/world/europe/thousands-protest-germany-demanding-solidarity-energy-relief-2022-10-22; Reuters, "COVID Protest Convoy Arrives in Brussels," February 14, 2022, https://www.reuters.com/world/europe/covid-protest-convoy-arrives-brussels-2022-02-14.

22. "Pandemic Creates New Billionaire Every 30 Hours—Now a Million People Could Fall into Extreme Poverty at the Same Rate in 2022," Oxfam, May 23, 2022, https://www.oxfam.org/en/press-releases/pandemic-creates-new-billionaire-every-30-hours-now-million-people-could-fall.

23. Minyvonne Burke, Suzanne Ciechalski, and Dawn Liu, "Video Appears to Show People in China Forcibly Taken for Quarantine over Coronavirus," NBC, February 8, 2020, https://www.nbcnews.com/news/world/video-appears-show-people-china-forcibly-taken-quarantine-over-coronavirus-n1133096; "Coronavirus: Welding Doors Shut," CBC, accessed December 12, 2022, https://www.cbc.ca/player/play/1703503427818.

24. Yaqiu Wang, "China's Use of Force and Coercion to Drive Up Its COVID-19 Vaccination Rate Is Not the Answer," Human Rights Watch, September 28, 2021, https://www.hrw.org/news/2021/09/28/chinas-use-force-and-coercion-drive-its-covid-19-vaccination-rate-not-answer; Simon Denyer, "Horrors of One-Child Policy Leave Deep Scars in Chinese Society," *Washington Post*, October 30, 2015, https://www.washingtonpost.com/world/asia_pacific/horrors-of-one-child-policy-leave-deep-scars-in-chinese-society/2015/10/30/6bd28e0c-7e7b-11e5-bfb6-65300a5ff562_story.html.

25. Thomas Hale and Cheng Leng, "'What's the Point of Buying?' China's Property Woes Push Young to Rent," *Financial Times*, December 8, 2022, https://www.ft.com/content/f737dd05-26ed-452f-8acf-b16139fcea3d; Celia Hatton, "Chinese Freeze before Gov't Turns on the Heat," CBS News, October 21, 2010, https://www.cbsnews.com/news/chinese-freeze-before-govt-turns-on-the-heat; Lee Fang, "Chinese Fund Backed by Hunter Biden Invested in Major Chinese Surveillance Firm," *Intercept*, May 3, 2019, https://theintercept.com/2019/05/03/biden-son-china-business; Nicole Kobie, "The Complicated Truth about China's Complicated Social Credit System," *Wired*, July 6, 2019, https://www.wired.co.uk/article/china-social-credit-system-explained; Alfred Ng, "How China Uses Facial Recognition to Control Human Behavior," CNET, August 11, 2020, https://www.cnet.com/news/politics/in-china-facial-recognition-public-shaming-and-control-go-hand-in-hand; David Bandurski, "China and Russia Are Joining Forces to Spread Disinformation," Brookings Institution, March 11, 2022, https://www.brookings.edu/techstream/china-and-russia-are-joining-forces-to-spread-disinformation.

26. Jack Salo, "Bill Gates Says China 'Did a Lot of Things Right' with Coronavirus Response," *New York Post*, April 27, 2020, https://nypost.com/2020/04/27/bill-gates-defends-chinas-response-to-coronavirus; Brianna Herlihy, "Fauci Deputy Was 'Very Impressed' with China's COVID Lockdown Methods, Despite 'Great Cost,'" Fox News, December 5, 2022,

https://www.foxnews.com/politics/fauci-deputy-impressed-chinas-covid-lockdown-methods-despite-cost.

27. Herlihy, "Fauci Deputy Was 'Very Impressed' with China's COVID Lockdown Methods."

28. Siladitya Ray, "How China's Zero-COVID Policy Failed to Prevent Record Infections and Triggered Rare Protests," *Forbes*, November 28, 2022, https://www.forbes.com/sites/siladityaray/2022/11/28/how-chinas-zero-covid-policy-failed-to-prevent-record-infections-and-triggered-rare-protests.

29. Tucker Carlson, "Tucker Carlson: Shanghai Is the Largest Prison Camp in Human History," Fox News, November 28, 2022, https://www.foxnews.com/opinion/tucker-carlson-shanghai-largest-prison-camp-human-history.

30. Sinéad Baker, "Chinese City Orders All Indoor Pets Belonging to COVID-19 Patients in One Neighborhood to Be Killed," *Business Insider*, March 30, 2022, https://www.businessinsider.com/china-langfang-district-says-kill-covid-patients-pets-2022-3.

31. Austin Ramzy, "China Eases Zero-COVID Rules as Economic Toll and Frustrations Mount," *Wall Street Journal*, updated November 11, 2022, https://www.wsj.com/articles/china-eases-some-covid-19-rules-even-as-cases-pass-10-000-11668150369.

32. Tom Norton, "Did China Deploy Tanks against Protestors? What We Do Know, What We Don't," *Newsweek*, July 21, 2022, https://www.newsweek.com/did-china-deploy-tanks-against-protesters-what-we-do-know-what-we-dont-1726908; Emma Graham-Harrison and Helen Davidson, "China COVID Protests: Authorities Call for Crackdown on 'Hostile Forces,'" *Guardian*, November 29, 2022, https://www.theguardian.com/world/2022/nov/29/china-targets-older-people-in-covid-19-vaccination-drive.

33. Terril Yue Jones, "What the Tiananmen Protest Can Tell Us about China's Zero-COVID Unrest," *Politico*, December 6, 2022, https://www.politico.com/news/magazine/2022/12/06/tiananmen-protest-china-zero-covid-00072430; Cindy Zhan, "Has Big Tech Been Censoring China Sensitive Topics?," *Epoch Times*, updated November 30, 2022, https://www.theepochtimes.com/has-big-tech-been-censoring-china-sensitive-topics_4226989.html.

34. Schweizer, *Red-Handed*, 86–95; Arjun Kharpal and Kif Leswing, "Apple's New Privacy Feature, Designed to Mask Users' Internet Browsing, Won't Be Available in China," CNBC, updated June 8, 2021, https://www.cnbc.com/2021/06/08/apple-wwdc-new-private-relay-feature-will-not-be-available-in-china.html.

35. Karen Gilchrist, "Apple Limited a Crucial AirDrop Function in China Just Weeks before Protests," CNBC, November 30, 2022, https://www.cnbc.com/2022/11/30/apple-limited-a-crucial-airdrop-function-in-china-just-weeks-before-protests.html.

36. Yuan Li, "A Lonely Protest in Beijing Inspires Young Chinese to Find Their Voice," *New York Times*, October 24, 2022, https://www.nytimes.com/2022/10/24/business/xi-jinping-protests.html.

37. Brian Merchant, "Life and Death in Apple's Forbidden City," *Guardian*, June 18, 2017, https://www.theguardian.com/technology/2017/jun/18/foxconn-life-death-forbidden-city-longhua-suicide-apple-iphone-brian-merchant-one-device-extract.

38. Wilfred Chan, "Elon Musk Praises Chinese Workers for 'Burning the 3am Oil'—Here's What That Really Looks Like," *Guardian*, May 12, 2022, https://www.theguardian.com/technology/2022/may/12/elon-musk-praises-chinese-workers-for-extreme-work-culture.

39. Schweizer, *Red-Handed*, 83–122; 137–49.

40. David Rockefeller, *Memoirs* (New York: Random House, 2002), 242–47; *World Economic Forum: A Partner in Shaping History*; "About Microsoft's Presence in China," Microsoft, accessed February 22, 2023, https://news.microsoft.com/about-microsofts-presence-in-china.

41. Mary Brown Bullock, "The Oil Prince's Legacy, Rockefeller Philanthropy in China," Asia Foundation, October 12, 2011, https://asiafoundation.org/2011/10/12/the-oil-princes-legacy-rockefeller-philanthropy-in-china.

42. Jiayi Tao, "Envisioning the Future of the Rockefeller Foundation in Wartime and Post-War China, 1943–1946," Rockefeller Archive Center, August 18, 2020, https://rockarch.is suelab.org/resource/envisioning-the-future-of-the-rockefeller-foundation-in-wartime -and-post-war-china-1943-1946.html.

43. Seth Borenstein, Ellen Knickmeyer, and Frank Jordans, "China, US Pledge to Increase Co-operation at U.N. Climate Talks," AP News, November 11, 2021, https://apnews.com/article /climate-science-united-nations-glasgow-europe-1203ed9bfccfc13869d81d90fb368857.

44. "Willard Skousen Part 7 of 7," FBI Records: The Vault, Federal Bureau of Investigation, accessed February 22, 2023, https://vault.fbi.gov/willard-skousen/willard-skousen-part -7-of-7; Tom Licata, "45 Communist Goals from 58 Years Ago," Ethan Allen Institute, July 2, 2021, https://www.ethanallen.org/45_communist_goals_from_58_years_ago.

45. Rockefeller, *Memoirs*, 162, 223; "Ted Turner's United Nations Foundation Delivers $1 Billion to UN Causes," United Nations, October 11, 2006, https://press.un.org/en/2006 /dev2594.doc.htm.

46. Ann Rockefeller Roberts, "Excerpts from Eulogies at Memorial for Rockefeller," *New York Times*, February 3, 1979, https://www.nytimes.com/1979/02/03/archives/excerpts-from -eulogies-at-memorial-for-rockefeller-an-eternal.html.

47. "The Beijing-Washington Back-Channel and Henry Kissinger's Secret Trip to China September 1970–July 1971," *National Security Archive Electronic Briefing Book* no. 66 (February 27, 2002), edited by William Burr, https://nsarchive2.gwu.edu/NSAEBB/NSAE BB66; Robert D. McFadden, "Rockefeller Gave Kissinger $50,000, Helped 2 Others," *New York Times*, October 6, 1974, https://www.nytimes.com/1974/10/06/archives/rockefeller -gave-kissinger-50000-helped-2-others-he-denies-any.html.

48. David Rockefeller, "From a China Traveler," *New York Times*, August 10, 1973, https:// www.nytimes.com/1973/08/10/archives/from-a-china-traveler.html.

49. Schweizer, *Red-Handed*, 152–58.

50. Johnny Vedmore, "Dr. Klaus Schwab or: How the CFR Taught Me to Stop Worrying and Love the Bomb," Unlimited Hangout, March 10, 2022, https://unlimitedhangout.com /2022/03/investigative-reports/dr-klaus-schwab-or-how-the-cfr-taught-me-to-stop -worrying-and-love-the-bomb.

51. "Opening the Door to China: 1979," World Economic Forum, accessed February 22, 2023, https://widgets.weforum.org/history/1979.html.

52. *A Partner in Shaping History: The First 40 Years, 1971–2010* (Geneva: World Economic Forum, 2009), https://www3.weforum.org/docs/WEF_First40Years_Book_2010.pdf.

53. Disclose.tv (@disclosetv), "NEW—Klaus Schwab says China is a 'role model for many countries,'" Twitter, November 23, 2022, 7:24 a.m., https://twitter.com/disclosetv/status /1595423002606600193.

54. Schweizer, *Red-Handed*, 83–120.

55. Susan Greenhalgh, "Missile Science, Population Science: The Origins of China's One-Child Policy," *China Quarterly* 182 (2005): 253–76, https://doi.org/10.1017/S030574 1005000184; John Ensor Harr and Peter J. Johnson, *The Rockefeller Century* (New York: Scribner, 1988), 460.

56. Robert Golub and Joe Townsend, "Malthus, Multinationals and the Club of Rome," *Social Studies of Science 7*, no. 2 (May 1977): 201–22, https://www.jstor.org/stable/284875; "How China's One-Child Policy Led to Forced Abortions, 30 Million Bachelors," *Fresh Air*, National Public Radio, February 1, 2016, https://www.npr.org/2016/02/01/465124337/how -chinas-one-child-policy-led-to-forced-abortions-30-million-bachelors; *Forced Abortion and Sterilization in China: The View from the Inside, Hearing on H.R. before the Subcommittee on International Operations and Human Rights*, 105th Cong. (1998), June 10, 1998, http://commdocs.house.gov/committees/intlrel/hfa49740.000/hfa49740_0f.htm.

57. Paul Farhi, "Nothing Left but Billions," *Washington Post*, April 4, 2001, https://www
.washingtonpost.com/archive/lifestyle/2001/04/04/nothing-left-but-billions/99fa4b04
-27bf-45f3-8585-2d1aa5ddabee; Ujala Sehgal, "Ted Turner Urges World Leaders to Adopt
China's One Child Policy on Global Scale," *Business Insider*, December 7, 2010, https://
www.businessinsider.com/ted-turner-urges-world-leaders-to-adopt-chinas-one-child
-policy-on-global-scale-2010-12.

58. Heidi Morefield, "Making PATH: The Ford Foundation and Appropriate Technology for
International Health," Rockefeller Archive Center, April 10, 2018, https://rockarch.is
suelab.org/resource/making-path-the-ford-foundation-and-appropriate-technology-for
-international-health.html.

59. Matt Turner and Jordan Parker Erb, "Blackstone's $280 Billion Real-Estate Team Is Buy-
ing Up Everything from Warehouses to Campus Housing to Biotech Lab Space. Here's a
Look at Its Power Players," *Yahoo! Finance*, April 24, 2022, https://finance.yahoo.com
/news/blackstones-280-billion-real-estate-122000286.html; Matthew Goldstein and Mau-
reen Farrell, "BlackRock's Pitch for Socially Conscious Investing Antagonizes All Sides,"
New York Times, December 23, 2022, https://www.nytimes.com/2022/12/23/business
/blackrock-esg-investing.html.

60. Schweizer, *Red-Handed*, 130–44.

61. Ibid., 130.

62. Ibid., 144.

63. Reuters, "China Says Soros' Criticism of Xi Is 'Meaningless,'" January 25, 2019, https://
www.reuters.com/article/us-davos-meeting-china-soros/china-says-soros-criticism-of
-xi-is-meaningless-idUSKCN1PJ0Z7; Steve Goldstein, "George Soros Says BlackRock Is on
Wrong Side of 'Life and Death' Conflict with China," MarketWatch, September 7, 2021,
https://www.marketwatch.com/story/george-soros-criticizes-blackrock-for-a-second
-time-on-china-11631006083.

64. John Solomon and Seamus Bruner, *Fallout: Nuclear Bribes, Russian Spies, and the Washington Lies That Enriched the Clinton and Biden Dynasties* (New York: Post Hill Press, 2020),
180–202.

65. Emily Feng, "Zelenskyy Has Consolidated Ukraine's TV Outlets and Dissolved Rival Political Parties," National Public Radio, July 8, 2022, https://www.npr.org/2022/07/08
/1110577439/zelenskyy-has-consolidated-ukraines-tv-outlets-and-dissolved-rival
-political-par; Julia Shapero, "Zelensky Announces Ban on 11 Ukrainian Political Parties with
Ties to Russia," *Axios*, March 20, 2022, https://www.axios.com/2022/03/20/ukraine-ban
-political-parties-russian-ties; Jonathan Tobin, "Zelensky: Defender of Democracy or Opponent of Religious Freedom?," *Newsweek*, December 12, 2022, https://www.newsweek.com
/zelensky-defender-democracy-opponent-religious-freedom-opinion-1766012.

66. "Our History," Open Society Foundations, accessed February 22, 2023, https://www
.opensocietyfoundations.org/who-we-are/our-history.

67. Zhou Xin, "How Beijing and Hong Kong Sent Billionaire George Soros Packing the Last
Time He Attacked Asian Markets," *South China Morning Post*, January 28, 2016, https://
www.scmp.com/news/china/economy/article/1906325/how-beijing-and-hong-kong
-sent-billionaire-george-soros-packing.

68. "Transcript: George Soros Interview," *Financial Times*, accessed December 12, 2022,
https://www.ft.com/content/6e2dfb82-c018-11de-aed2-00144feab49a.

69. Ibid.

70. *BlackRock 2023 Global Outlook: A New Investment Playbook*, BlackRock Investment Institute, 2022, accessed February 22, 2023, 11, https://www.blackrock.com/corporate/litera
ture/whitepaper/bii-global-outlook-2023.pdf; Anil Varma, "BlackRock Says Get Ready for
a Recession Unlike Any Other and 'What Worked in the Past Won't Work Now,'" *Business*

Insider, December 8, 2022, https://markets.businessinsider.com/news/stocks/blackrock
-recession-warning-stock-market-analysis-2023-economic-outlook-2022-12.

71. Nick Hanauer and David M. Rolf, "The Top 1% of Americans Have Taken $50 Trillion from
the Bottom 90%—and That's Made the US Less Secure," *Time*, September 14, 2020, https://
time.com/5888024/50-trillion-income-inequality-america.

72. "Yuval Noah Harari ve Daniel Kahneman Söyleşisi," posted by Kolektif Kitap, May 20,
2015, YouTube video, 29:54–31:16, https://www.youtube.com/watch?v=-3aPT8MuH_E.

73. "Russia Joins Centre for the Fourth Industrial Revolution Network," World Economic Forum, October 13, 2021, https://www.weforum.org/press/2021/10/russia-joins-centre-for
-the-fourth-industrial-revolution-network; "China Has Always Kept in Step with Davos
Spirit: *Global Times* Editorial," *Global Times*, January 16, 2023, https://www.globaltimes
.cn/page/202301/1283858.shtml.

74. Azeen Ghorayshi, "More Trans Teens Are Choosing 'Top Surgery,'" *New York Times*,
updated October 3, 2022, https://www.nytimes.com/2022/09/26/health/top-surgery
-transgender-teenagers.html; Rachel Wimpee and Teresa Iacobelli, "Funding a Sexual
Revolution: The Kinsey Reports," RE:Source, Rockefeller Archive Center, January 9, 2020,
https://resource.rockarch.org/story/funding-a-sexual-revolution-the-kinsey-reports.

75. Sarah L. Kaufman, "The Rockettes, Still Kicking after 85 Years. Here's Why We Love
Them," *Washington Post*, December 27, 2018, https://www.washingtonpost.com/enter
tainment/theater_danc/the-rockettes-still-kicking-after-85-years-heres-why-we-love
-them/2018/12/26/8f2cf174-0499-11e9-b6a9-0aa5c2fcc9e4_story.html.

76. Sarah Wallace, "Face Recognition Tech Gets Girl Scout Mom Booted from Rockettes
Show—Due to Where She Works," WNBC, updated December 20, 2022, https://www.nbc
newyork.com/investigations/face-recognition-tech-gets-girl-scout-mom-booted-from
-rockettes-show-due-to-her-employer/4004677.

77. Mariana Alfaro, "Pennsylvania Court Declares State's Mail-in Voting Law Unconstitutional, in Win for Republicans," *Washington Post*, updated January 31, 2022, https://www
.washingtonpost.com/politics/2022/01/28/pennsylvania-mail-voting-courts.

78. Alfaro, "Pennsylvania Court"; John Daniel Davidson, "The 2020 Election Wasn't Stolen, It
Was Vandalized by Democrats, Big Tech, and the Media," *Federalist*, October 14, 2021,
https://thefederalist.com/2021/10/14/the-2020-election-wasnt-stolen-it-was
-vandalized-by-democrats-big-tech-and-the-media.

79. Shannon Bond and Avie Schneider, "Trump Threatens to Shut Down Social Media After
Twitter Adds Warning to His Tweets," NPR, May 27, 2020, https://www.npr.org
/2020/05/27/863011399/trump-threatens-to-shut-down-social-media-after-twitter
-adds-warning-on-his-twee; Mary Papenfuss, "Mary Trump Calls Donald Trump a Mass
Murderer for His Handling of COVID Pandemic," *Yahoo! News*, October 24, 2022, https://
sg.news.yahoo.com/mary-trump-calls-donald-trump-060618133.html.

80. A. G. Schmitt, "Missouri and Louisiana Attorneys General Ask Court to Compel Department of Justice to Produce Communications between Top Officials and Media Companies," News, Eric Schmitt: Missouri Attorney General, September 1, 2022, https://ago
.mo.gov/home/news/2022/09/01/missouri-and-louisiana-attorneys-general-ask
-court-to-compel-department-of-justice-to-produce-communications-between-top
-officials-and-social-media-companies.

81. "Remarks by President Biden on the Continued Battle for the Soul of the Nation," The
White House.

82. Steven Nelson, "Heckler Chants 'F—k Joe Biden' throughout Primetime Speech," *New
York Post*, September 1, 2022, https://nypost.com/2022/09/01/heckler-chants-f-k-joe
-biden-throughout-primetime-speech; Gillian Brockell, "'A Republic, If You Can Keep It':
Did Ben Franklin Really Say Impeachment Day's Favorite Quote?," *Washington Post*, De-

cember 18, 2019, https://www.washingtonpost.com/history/2019/12/18/republic-if-you
-can-keep-it-did-ben-franklin-really-say-impeachment-days-favorite-quote.

83. Ronald Reagan, "First Inaugural Address," delivered on January 5, 1967, accessed December 12, 2022, The Governor's Gallery, California State Library, https://governors.li
brary.ca.gov/addresses/33-Reagan01.html.

Epilogue

1. George Orwell, *Nineteen Eighty-Four* (London: Secker & Warburg, 1949), 149.

Index